RAYMOND WILLIAMS
ON CULTURE & SOCIETY

SAGE has been part of the global academic community since 1965, supporting high quality research and learning that transforms society and our understanding of individuals, groups and cultures. SAGE is the independent, innovative, natural home for authors, editors and societies who share our commitment and passion for the social sciences.

Find out more at: **www.sagepublications.com**

RAYMOND WILLIAMS
ON CULTURE & SOCIETY
essential writings

EDITED BY
JIM MCGUIGAN

$SAGE

Los Angeles | London | New Delhi
Singapore | Washington DC

ⓈSAGE

Los Angeles | London | New Delhi
Singapore | Washington DC

SAGE Publications Ltd
1 Oliver's Yard
55 City Road
London EC1Y 1SP

SAGE Publications Inc.
2455 Teller Road
Thousand Oaks, California 91320

SAGE Publications India Pvt Ltd
B 1/I 1 Mohan Cooperative Industrial Area
Mathura Road
New Delhi 110 044

SAGE Publications Asia-Pacific Pte Ltd
3 Church Street
#10-04 Samsung Hub
Singapore 049483

Editor: Chris Rojek
Editorial assistant: Gemma Shields
Production editor: Katherine Haw
Copyeditor: Rose James
Proofreader: Mary Dalton
Indexer: Charmian Parkin
Marketing manager: Michael Ainsley
Cover design: Wendy Scott
Typeset by: C&M Digitals (P) Ltd, Chennai, India
Printed and bound by CPI Group (UK) Ltd,
  Croydon, CR0 4YY

MIX
Paper from responsible sources
FSC® C013604

© All editorial matters Jim McGuigan 2014

First published 2014

Apart from any fair dealing for the purposes of research or private study, or criticism or review, as permitted under the Copyright, Designs and Patents Act, 1988, this publication may be reproduced, stored or transmitted in any form, or by any means, only with the prior permission in writing of the publishers, or in the case of reprographic reproduction, in accordance with the terms of licences issued by the Copyright Licensing Agency. Enquiries concerning reproduction outside those terms should be sent to the publishers.

Library of Congress Control Number: 2013933583

British Library Cataloguing in Publication data

A catalogue record for this book is available from the British Library

ISBN 978-1-84920-770-6
ISBN 978-1-84920-771-3(pbk)

CONTENTS

About the Authors	vii
Acknowledgements	ix
Further Acknowledgements	xi
Introduction – Raymond Williams on Culture and Society	xv
1. Culture is Ordinary	1
2. Mass, Masses and Mass Communication	19
3. Structure of Feeling and Selective Tradition	27
4. Advertising – The Magic System	57
5. Communication Systems	85
6. The Idea of a Common Culture	93
7. Social Darwinism	101
8. Base and Superstructure in Marxist Cultural Theory	119
9. The Technology and the Society	139
10. Drama in a Dramatized Society	161
11. Communications as Cultural Science	173
12. Developments in the Sociology of Culture	185
13. Realism and Non-naturalism	199
14. A Lecture on Realism	207
15. Means of Communication as Means of Production	223
16. 'Industrial' and 'Post-Industrial' Society	237
17. The Culture of Nations	257
18. Resources for a Journey of Hope	279
19. State Culture and Beyond	305
20. The Future of Cultural Studies	313
Index	327

ABOUT THE AUTHORS

Raymond Williams (1921–1988) came from a working-class background in the Welsh Border Country and became a professor at the University of Cambridge. He was a tank commander during the Second World War. In the 1950s he worked in adult education, during which time he published his most celebrated book, *Culture and Society 1780–1950* (1958). He published many non-fiction books and wrote several novels, including *Border Country* (1960) and *Second Generation* (1964), and also plays. One of the leading socialist intellectuals in Britain from the late 1950s until his rather early death in the late 1980s, Williams was a master of thought comparable to great European continental theorists such as Pierre Bourdieu and Jurgen Habermas, with both of whom he had a great deal in common. During his career, Williams's work became increasingly interdisciplinary, branching out from the humanities and into the social sciences, especially sociology. He was also a major inspiration for the development of cultural studies and media studies. Especially notable among his later books are *Television – Technology and Cultural Form* (1974), *Keywords* (1976), *The Country and the City* (1975), *Marxism and Literature* (1977), *Culture* (1981) and *Towards 2000* (1983). Williams eventually named his distinctive perspective on modern culture and society, 'cultural materialism', of which there are a great many exponents around the world today.

Jim McGuigan is Professor of Cultural Analysis in the Department of Social Sciences at Loughborough University. He has written several book chapters and articles on Williams's work. In addition to editing *Raymond Williams on Culture and Society*, Jim has recently prepared a republication by Sage of Williams's book of the mid-1980s, *Towards 2000*, which had been written as a sequel to his earlier, *The Long Revolution* (1961). With the permission of the Williams Estate, the book has been re-entitled *A Short Counter-Revolution – Towards 2000 Revisited*. And, Jim has added a chapter that updates the original book with a survey of developments since 1983, particularly concerning the impact of neoliberalism, a phenomenon that was sighted early by Raymond Williams and named 'Plan X'. Jim's other books include *Cultural Populism* (1992), *Culture and the Public Sphere* (1996), *Modernity and Postmodern Culture* (1999, 2006), *Rethinking Cultural Policy* (2004), *Cool Capitalism* (2009) and *Cultural Analysis* (2010).

ACKNOWLEDGEMENTS

I first came across Raymond Williams as an undergraduate student when I read his great book *Culture and Society* on a literature course. It was only when I studied for a research degree in sociology at the University of Leeds in the mid 1970s, however, that I really became aware of his importance for sociological work. The inspiration in this respect came from two fellow postgraduates, Steve Ryan and Derek 'Mac' McKiernan. Unlike me, they had not actually studied literature at university yet they were both hugely enthusiastic about Williams. Around the same time, I met Tom Steele, who was working for the Workers' Educational Association and was also a Williams enthusiast. Tom hired Mac, Steve and myself to teach an evening class on communications and culture. I am still grateful to these old friends from Leeds for encouraging my early interest in Williams. Later in the 1970s, I had the honour of meeting Raymond Williams himself. In my experience, he was very approachable and an exceptionally interesting man with whom to talk.

Although I identify mostly with cultural studies, I have for several years taught sociology in a social sciences department where the study of culture has been somewhat marginalised, to my regret. In consequence, I have found it quite difficult to teach about Williams's work and its significance for sociology as well as cultural studies. I came to the conclusion that an edited collection of Williams's most 'sociological' writings that call on little in the way of a broader cultural learning might make him more teachable in this context as well as reminding the social sciences in general of Williams's enduring relevance to the study of culture and society. I must thank his daughter, Merryn, for aiding in this project and also Mac and Marie Moran for checking my selection of texts. And, I thank Chris Rojek yet again, in this case for believing in the value of the Williams project and backing it at Sage.

Jim McGuigan
Leamington
April 2013

FURTHER ACKNOWLEDGEMENTS

The Editor and the Publishers would like to express their thanks to the following for permission to reprint the works of Raymond Williams.

Culture is Ordinary – Originally published in McKenzie, N., ed., *Convictions*, MacGibbon & Kee, 1958. From Raymond Williams, *Resources of Hope*, Verso, 1989, pp. 3–18. Reprinted with kind permission of Verso.

Mass, Masses and Mass Communication – Originally published in 'Mass and Masses', 'Mass Communication', from Raymond Williams, *Culture and Society 1780–1950*, Chatto & Windus, 1958, Penguin, 1961, pp. 287–294. Reprinted by permission of The Random House Group Limited and printed with permission from *Culture and Society 1780–1950* by Raymond Williams. Copyright © 1983 Columbia University Press.

Structure of Feeling and Selective Tradition – Originally published in Raymond Williams, *The Long Revolution*, Chatto & Windus, 1961. Penguin, 1965, pp. 64–88. Reprinted with kind permission by The Random House Group Limited and Parthian Books/the Library of Wales.

Advertising – The Magic System – Originally published in *New Left Review/Listener*, 1960/1969. From Raymond Williams, *Problems in Materialism and Culture*, Verso, 1980, pp. 170–195. Reproduced by kind permission of Verso.

Communication Systems – Originally published in *Communications* (Third Edition), 1976, Penguin, pp. 129–137. Copyright © 1976 Raymond Williams. Reproduced by permission of Penguin Books Ltd.

The Idea of a Common Culture – Originally published in Eagleton, T. and B. Whicker, eds, *From Culture to Revolution – The Slant Symposium*,

1967. From Raymond Williams, *Resources of Hope*, Verso, 1989, pp. 32–38. Reprinted with kind permission of Verso.

Social Darwinism – Originally published in Benthal, J. ed., *The Limits of Human Nature*, Allen Lane, 1973. From Raymond Williams, *Problems in Materialism and Culture*, Verso, 1980, pp. 86–102. Reprinted with kind permission of the Estate of Raymond Williams and with kind permission of Verso.

Base and Superstructure in Marxist Cultural Theory – Originally published in *New Left Review* 82, 1973. From Raymond Williams, *Problems in Materialism and Culture*, Verso, 1980, pp. 31–49. Reprinted with kind permission of Verso.

The Technology and the Society – From Raymond Williams, *Television – Technology and Cultural Form*, Fontana, 1974, pp. 9–31. Reprinted with kind permission by the Estate of Raymond Williams and the Taylor & Francis Group.

Drama in a Dramatized Society – From Raymond Williams, *Writing in Society*, Verso, 1984, pp. 11–21. Reprinted with kind permission of Verso.

Communications as Cultural Science – Originally published in the *Journal of Communication* 24.3. September 1974, pp. 17–25. Copyright © 1974 Raymond Williams. Reprinted with kind permission of Blackwell Publishing Ltd.

Developments in the Sociology of Culture – From *Sociology* 10, 1976, pp. 497–504. Copyright SAGE Publications, reprinted by kind permission.

Realism and Non-naturalism – From *Edinburgh International Television Festival* 1977 Official Programme, *Broadcast*, 1977, pp. 30–32. Reprinted with kind permission of the Edinburgh International Television Festival.

A Lecture on Realism – From Raymond Williams, A Lecture on Realism (1977) *Screen* 18.1: 61–74. Copyright © 1977 Raymond Williams. Reprinted with kind permission of Oxford University Press.

Means of Communication as Means of Production – Originally published in Raymond Williams's *Problems in Materialism and Culture*, Verso, 1980, pp. 50–63. Reprinted with kind permission of Verso.

'Industrial' and 'Post-Industrial' Society – From Raymond Williams, *Towards 2000*, Chatto & Windus, 1983, Penguin, 1985, pp. 83–101. Reprinted with kind permission by The Random House Group Limited.

The Culture of Nations – From Raymond Williams, *Towards 2000*, Chatto & Windus, 1983, Penguin, 1985, pp. 177–199. Reprinted with kind permission by The Random House Group Limited.

Resources for a Journey of Hope – From Raymond Williams, *Towards 2000*, Chatto & Windus, 1983, Penguin, 1985, pp. 241–269. Reprinted with kind permission by The Random House Group Limited.

State Culture and Beyond – From Lisa Appignanesi, ed., *Culture and the State*, Institute of Contemporary Arts, 1984, pp. 3–5. Reprinted with kind permission of the Institute of Contemporary Arts (ICA).

The Future of Cultural Studies – From Raymond Williams, *The Politics of Modernism*, Verso, 1989, pp. 151–162. Reprinted with kind permission of Verso.

INTRODUCTION

Raymond Williams's Contributions to Cultural Studies and Sociology

Raymond Williams was the greatest cultural theorist of modern Britain. Meaningfully, however, he called himself a 'Welsh European', thereby signalling his national and continental sense of identity.[1] Born in 1921 in the Welsh Border Country, Williams came to prominence in the post-Second World War period, especially with the publication in 1958 of his much celebrated book, *Culture and Society 1780–1950*.[2] Williams's own education and official position in academia were literary; and his personal specialism was the history of dramatic form, the most social of the literary forms. He published *Drama from Ibsen to Eliot* in 1952, which was updated to *Drama from Ibsen to Brecht* in 1968. For Williams, the study of drama was not reducible to the written text but, rather, must be understood through its realisation in performance. His 1954 book, *Drama in Performance*, was also expanded in 1968 to include cinema and television alongside theatre. Williams's inaugural lecture as Professor of Drama at the University of Cambridge in the 1970s was entitled 'Drama in a Dramatized Society' (Chapter 10 of this selection), further indicating his emphasis on the relations between culture and society.

Williams's project was much broader than that of a literary scholar in the specialist academic sense. It was always a socially and politically informed project that eventually met up with the discipline of Sociology itself, as exemplified here in Williams's 1975 British Sociological Association keynote address, 'Developments in the Sociology of Culture' (Chapter 12) He also contributed to the formation of new fields of study, variously named Communication Studies, Cultural Studies and Media Studies. In effect, there was a social-scientific turn in Williams's work, which this book is dedicated to representing through its selection of his writings.

Since his death in 1988, the memory and enduring influence of Williams have been sustained very largely by literary scholars. For instance, in 1989, Oxford English Limited published a special issue of the journal *News From Nowhere*, mainly devoted to Williams's literary-critical work, edited by Tony Pinkney.[3] Interestingly, Pinkney's own contribution to that collection was 'Raymond Williams on Television'. Williams had been a columnist for *The Listener*, the broadcasting magazine.[4] Unusual among literary scholars in the 1960s and '70s, Williams treated television seriously and valued the best work produced for 'the box' (see, for instance, Chapter 14). He even wrote a book about it, *Television: Technology and Cultural Form* (1974), possibly the most 'social-scientific' of all Williams's writings. Pinkney also edited a collection of Williams's remaining unpublished essays that ranged around various current issues of culture and society, *The Politics of Modernism*, in the year after Williams's death.

The two extant biographies of Raymond Williams – Fred Inglis's *Raymond Williams* (1995)[5] and Dai Smith's *Raymond Williams – A Warrior's Tale* (2008)[6] – are both literary in their principal concerns, but Inglis's account of Williams has been controversial among scholars of his work. Smith's biography, which concludes with the publication of *The Long Revolution* in 1961, to be followed perhaps by a second volume, devotes a great many pages to summary of and commentary on Williams's fiction writing, much of it in unpublished manuscripts housed at the University of Swansea. Quite possibly, Williams himself would have preferred to be remembered more as a novelist (and playwright) than as a cultural theorist.[7] He did indeed publish several works of fiction that met with critical approval but, sadly, to no great acclaim. Since the present book is concerned with Williams's social as well as cultural theorising and also due to limitations of space, it would be inappropriate to comment further on his imaginative writing.

The Raymond Williams Society and the annual publication, *Keywords*, have carried out vital tasks in maintaining and promoting Williams's intellectual legacy. Again, however, this sterling work is sustained principally by literary scholarship, albeit linked to socialist politics, with relatively little social-scientific input.

So, this volume's particular selection of writings, dating from the 1950s to the late 1980s, aims to rebalance Williams's reputation by highlighting his recently neglected but continuing relevance for education and research in Cultural Studies and Sociology. Williams is, of course, widely acknowledged as a founding figure of Cultural Studies as a comparatively new and transdisciplinary field of enquiry that crosses over between the Humanities and the Social Sciences. His own distinctive perspective – which Williams came to name 'cultural materialism' – is usually noted as one of the 'paradigms' in the field. However, at the same time, the range and comprehensiveness of Williams's contribution tend to be taken for granted, in fact, so taken for granted that his approach is barely recognised as constitutive of basic procedures in cultural analysis today. Along with Richard Hoggart and Stuart Hall, Raymond Williams set the original parameters for Cultural Studies in Britain and had considerable international influence on developments in the field of study. Moreover, Williams himself formulated a set of innovative concepts – most notably, in my opinion, 'structure of feeling' and 'mobile privatisation' among several others – that remain valuable heuristic tools for making sense of a dauntingly complex culture/society nexus in the early decades of the twenty-first century.

Intellectual and Political Formation

Williams and his work are not easily pigeonholed. However, the intellectual and political formations through which he grew and matured are not at all obscure: the 'English' tradition of cultural criticism[8] and the 'New Left' that emerged towards the end of the 1950s.[9] In *Culture and Society* Williams questioned the reductionist Marxism that had characterised intellectual culture on the Left during the 1930s and which was connected to the triumph of Stalinism in the international communist movement. Revelations about the purges, the Gulag and eventually the Soviet repression of the Hungarian Revolution in 1956 all contributed to disillusionment with communism in its 'actually existing' mode (Williams had been a member of the Communist Party briefly as a teenager). Some moved to the Right, others became social democrats of one kind or another. A few, like Williams, had enthusiastically supported the establishment of a welfare state by the 1945–51 Attlee government but were dissatisfied with the British Labour Party's compromises and management of capitalism. They went on subsequently to seek further and far-reaching socialist reforms of economy, polity and culture, sometimes with and sometimes against Labour.

As a young literature student – before and after serving as a tank commander during the 1939–45 war – Williams came under the influence of an alternative to orthodox communist criticism of 'bourgeois' culture in the milieu of Cambridge English that was inspired by the maverick literary critic, F.R. Leavis. Leavis stressed the importance of close and appreciative reading of texts from 'the Great Tradition'[10] of English literature and sensitivity to the sociality and emotionality of experience. Close reading and experiential feeling became notable features of Williams's own critical activity, but he departed from Leavis's elitism and apolitical inclinations.[11] However, Terry Eagleton, a former student, was to criticise Williams for what he called 'Left Leavisism' in the 1970s,[12] though he later withdrew the criticism.[13]

On graduating from Cambridge in the late 1940s, Williams was employed in adult education, teaching Oxford University extension classes in the south of England and closely connected to the Workers Educational Association. It was in this context that Williams and others were to argue that Cultural Studies had actually originated as a form of popular and ideally working-class education.[14] Williams taught his literary specialisms and also addressed political issues concerning communications, out of which the book of that title was written (Chapter 5). Williams's critical populism is beautifully represented by one of his most famous pieces of the 1950s, 'Culture is Ordinary' (Chapter 1).

Culture and Society (1958), Williams's tracing of the English Romantic tradition and critique of mass-society thought, and *The Long Revolution* (1961), its immediate sequel, represent a transition in Williams's work from a predominantly literary orientation towards a much broader analysis of culture and society. The very notion of a 'long revolution', which Williams saw as a drawn-out process of democratic emancipation in post-Second World War Britain, captures the historical moment sharply. As well as setting out the terms of cultural analysis, including early formulations of 'selective tradition' and 'structure of feeling', Williams traced a series of historical developments in education, reading and writing, encompassing the growth of the press and trends in literature, and the use of English. He concluded *The Long Revolution* with a long essay, 'Britain in the Sixties', which was to be reprinted at the beginning of Williams's 1983 book, *Towards 2000*. Later, Williams was to acknowledge Juliet Mitchell's argument that the emancipation of women was 'the longest revolution'.[15]

After 13 years of Conservative government, Labour was re-elected in 1964. However, Williams and other New Leftists were soon disappointed by Harold Wilson's government. In collaboration with

Michael Barrett Brown, Terry Eagleton, Stuart Hall and Edward Thompson among several other activists, Williams issued a *May Day Manifesto* in 1967, which was reissued as a Penguin Special in 1968,[16] the year of revolutionary promise when, for instance, students on the Paris streets and blacks in Detroit rose up in spectacular protest.

The British New Left's *May Day Manifesto* presented a much more radical analysis of capitalist society and set out a revolutionary programme of reform that went well beyond anything envisaged by the leadership of the 1960s Labour governments. Williams himself would remain far to the Left of mainstream Labourism for the rest of his life. In this respect, his position was not at all unusual for a British socialist throughout the 1970s and '80s.

Around the same time there was a revival of Western-Marxist thought alongside various developments in cultural theory, including post-structuralism and postmodernism, that Williams engaged with in fashioning his own distinctively cultural-materialist position. His 1973 article, 'Base and Superstructure in Marxist Cultural Theory' (Chapter 8) is pivotal in this phase of Williams's work. As the article indicates, there was an evident affinity between Williams's holistic approach to culture and society and Antonio Gramsci's concept of hegemony, which was also adopted fruitfully in his work by Stuart Hall, one of the other major figures in developing British Cultural Studies.[17]

Cultural Materialism

Williams's objection to the base-superstructure model of orthodox Marxism was that its conceptualisation of society was insufficiently materialist. This may seem paradoxical since Marxists are often said to reduce everything to economic – that is, material – factors, the assumption being that the super-structural institutions of politics and law, ideology and culture are all determined by economic forces and interests. Seen from an early twenty-first-century vantage point, this is a very familiar refrain. However, it does not come from the Left but from the Right. It is the fundamental neoliberal orientation whereby social and cultural activity is submitted relentlessly to the discipline of the market and everything is understood in monetary terms.

However, materialist philosophy is not exclusively about economics, nor should it be confused with the common-sense notion of 'materialism' as an ethical failing in which money and the acquisition of commodities matter more than relationships with people. In philosophy, materialism is contrasted to idealism. Whereas idealism assumes that ideas alone are determining forces in the world, materialism objects that sensuous human activity is where the action really is. The point can be illustrated by comparing one of Williams's key concepts, *structure of feeling*, with the German idealist notion of the *Zeitgeist* (spirit of the time), which has a certain currency today in common-sense parlance. In this regard, 'the market' is the zeitgeist, but it is hardly spiritual, though it is ideological, masking over and obscuring the political-economic forces that use it as a kind of excuse or alibi.

In his famous discussion of postmodernism as 'the cultural logic of late capitalism', Fredric Jameson deployed Williams's conceptualisation of the prevailing structure of feeling to characterise it. From this point of view, postmodernism is not just a set of ideas but, instead, a framing of emotionality and practice that is dialectically related to transnational, high-tech capitalism, whereby the human subject is disoriented.[18]

Williams devoted a section of *Marxism and Literature* (1977, pp. 128–135) to conceptual clarification of structure of feeling. To give a concrete example, in the chapter on 'The Analysis of Culture' from *The Long Revolution* (Chapter 3 of this book), Williams had traced the emergence of a structure of feeling in 1840s English literature that is most profoundly represented by Emily Brontë's *Wuthering Heights*. Also in this chapter, Williams demonstrates how a process of selection actively constructs cultural tradition or 'heritage' in specific historical circumstances; it is socially produced and likely to be revised over time; and by no means indisputable. The selections are made according to prevalent attitudes and interests. For instance, *Wuthering Heights* was too advanced a book to be considered important in its own time. It was much later that *Wuthering Heights* entered the canon of the selective tradition when the structure of feeling it represented became more widespread.

Williams objected to the treatment of culture as epiphenomenal, as though it were not of material significance, merely ideational. For him, signifying practice – that is, culture in the making – is, in effect, material practice, embedded in institutionalised arrangements and relations of production through which the products of human creativity are actually made. A paper that he delivered in Zagreb during the 1970s spelt out this understanding of the materiality of cultural activity systematically, 'Means of Communication as Means of Production' (Chapter 15 of this book). The argument here can be related to Williams's own formal definition of cultural materialism: 'Cultural materialism is the analysis of all forms of signification, including quite centrally writing, within the actual means and conditions of their production.'[19] Considering his literary background and the provenance of this definition on the occasion of fierce public dispute over 'theory' in the Cambridge English Department, it is not surprising that Williams should have remarked, 'quite centrally writing'. And his remark certainly justified a strand of politicised literary history naming itself 'cultural materialism'.[20] However, stressing the centrality of writing in such a manner severely understated the scope of cultural materialism as a *sociological* methodology. It has had unfortunate consequences in artificially delimiting the potential applications of cultural materialism in the Social Sciences. This point may usefully be illustrated with reference to Williams's critique of technological determinism in the media and in society generally, which is germane to making sense of the dynamics of our 'digital age'.

Williams's cultural materialism has an affinity with Douglas Kellner's advocacy of multidimensional cultural analysis.[21] Such an approach seeks to articulate the interaction of conditions of production and consumption with textual meaning within specifiable socio-historical contexts. It resists one-dimensional and mono-causal explanation, which is actually the fundamental flaw of the technological determinism that, combined with neoliberal political economy, is the most prominent feature of ideological dominance around the world today.

The emergence and meaning-making properties of media are often said to be entirely reducible to direct technical innovation derived immediately from scientific discovery with inevitably beneficial results. Moreover, we are constantly encouraged to believe, in a quasi-spiritual manner, that 'technology' (usually meaning specifically information and communication technologies these days) is the main and perhaps sole driving force of significant social change and is the solution to all conceivable problems. Contrarily, Williams showed that the development of communication technologies and their applications result from a complex range of determinations, including cultural, economic and political factors; and that the historical outcomes of such development are never strictly inevitable (see Chapter 9). In Williams's cultural-materialist discourse, *determination* refers to the exertion of pressure and setting of limits on human activity rather than the simple and unilinear cause and effect relation of *determinism*. Human agency matters and, in the case of technological change, *intention* is always involved, which suggests the possibility of alternative purposes and different outcomes in any given circumstance.

Twenty-first Century Williams

At the beginning of the 1980s, Raymond Williams codified his ideas on cultural analysis in a textbook, simply entitled *Culture* (1981). He presented a framework of concepts and analytical procedures that remain especially fruitful for social-scientific research in addition to providing students new to transdisciplinary scholarship with an invaluable introduction to the methodology of cultural materialism.

His other major work of the 1980s was perhaps unfortunately entitled *Towards 2000* (1983), suggesting that it was merely a *fin-de-siècle* book rather than the critical conspectus for the early twenty-first century that, in fact, it really is. Parts of that book are included here in which Williams critiques the very notion of 'post-industrial' society decisively (Chapter 16), tackles persistent questions of nationhood and globalisation (Chapter 17) and focuses on the most salient issues concerning what we might today call 'neoliberalism' and the most promising sources of resistance to it, particularly urgent action for environmental protection and ecological politics in general as integral features of twenty-first-century socialism (Chapter 18).

Two of the most insightful and far-reaching concepts mentioned in this material are 'Plan X' and 'mobile privatisation'. *Plan X* refers to a ruthless politics of strategic and, it might be added, competitive advantage: particularly represented by the arms' race during Ronald Reagan's presidency of the United States in the 1980s but more generally manifested over the past 30 years in the capitalist response to crises of the 1970s that has resulted in the dismantlement of welfare states and erosion of the 'social wage'; deindustrialisation in the global north-west and the transfer of manufacturing and heavy industry to cheap labour markets in the east where the rate of exploitation is especially fierce; and increased scales of inequality throughout the world[22] in spite of disingenuous claims to the contrary; and much else besides.

Williams suggests in Chapter 17 that his first intimation of what he was later to call *mobile privatisation* was manifested in a passage from a novel of his as early as 1964 on the personal seclusion experienced while driving a motorcar through traffic that is circulating in more or less ordered coordination through public space.[23] Modern forms of transport had already greatly expanded the mobility of people, particularly in various waves of migration since the nineteenth century. In addition to his prophetic observations on innovation and corporate command over the development of new communication technologies in the *Television* book, Williams was later to identify mobile privatisation as virtually *the* representative mode of sociality in a highly mediated and increasingly capitalist world. Broadcasting – first radio then television – had brought enormous access to information and representations from around the country and subsequently the whole Earth into the small households of an urban-industrial labour force by the mid-twentieth century. Satellite communications pioneered from the 1960s made it possible for people sitting at home to witness events occurring on the other side of the globe in real time. Now, we have the personal computer, Internet, mobile phone and kindred devices.

From the Walkman of the 1980s to the 2g mobile phone of the 1990s to combined functions of the all-purpose mobile communication device of the 2000s, the mode of sociality that Williams named 'mobile privatisation' has become increasingly normalised. And the mobile young person in perpetual and commoditised communication with others at a distance while cocooned in a private shell out in public is now an ideal figure of the capitalist way of life.

The final pieces in this selection are from Williams's concluding observations on cultural policy and on Cultural Studies. In Chapter 19, Williams drew a distinction between what may be described as *cultural policy proper and as display*. Williams noted that nation-states aggrandise themselves through public displays of one kind or another and are inclined to reduce cultural policy to narrowly economic considerations, thereby losing sight of the specific value of culture as socially meaningful communication. He also recognised that the nation-state is both too big and too small for addressing vital issues of culture in their local/regional and international aspects. Finally, in Chapter 20, Williams affirmed the critical and democratic value of cultural education against the relentless pressures of instrumentalism and commodification that have actually become more intense since his own day.

Select Bibliography for Raymond Williams on Culture and Society[24]

Drama in Performance, London: Frederick Muller 1954 (revised and extended in 1968, London: C.A. Watts).
Culture and Society 1780–1950, London: Chatto & Windus 1958.
The Long Revolution, London: Chatto & Windus 1961.
Communications, Harmondsworth: Penguin 1962 (revised and updated in 1966 and 1976).
Drama from Ibsen to Brecht, London: Chatto & Windus 1968 (originally published as *Drama from Ibsen to Eliot* in 1952).
The Country and the City, London: Chatto & Windus 1973.
Television – Technology and Cultural Form, London: Fontana 1974.
Keywords – A Vocabulary of Culture and Society, London: Fontana 1976 (revised and expanded 1983).
Marxism and Literature, Oxford: Oxford University Press 1977.
Culture, London: Fontana 1981.
Towards 2000, London: Chatto & Windus, 1983.
The Politics of Modernism – Against the New Conformists, edited by Tony Pinkney, London & New York: Verso 1989.
Raymond Williams on Television – Selected Writings, edited by Alan O'Connor, London & New York: Routledge 1989.

Notes

1 See Raymond Williams, *Who Speaks for Wales? – Nation, Culture, Identity*, edited by Daniel Williams, Cardiff: University of Wales Press, 2003, a posthumous collection of Williams's ruminations on questions of 'identity', 'nationhood' and one of his favourite themes, 'community'.
2 Reference details for books by Williams cited here but not referenced in the footnotes are included in a select bibliography at the end of this Introduction.
3 'Raymond Williams – Third Generation', *News From Nowhere* No. 6, Oxford: Oxford English Limited, February 1989.
4 See Alan O'Connor, ed., *Raymond Williams an Television*, London and New York: Routledge 1989.
5 Fred Inglis, *Raymond Williams*, London and New York: Routledge 1995.
6 Dai Smith, *Raymond Williams – A Warrior's Tale*, Cardigan: Parthian 2008.

7 An extremely useful source on Williams's biography are the interviews conducted with him by editors of *New Left Review* in the late 1970s, Raymond Williams, *Politics and Letters – Interviews with New Left Review*, London: Verso 1979.
8 Francis Mulhern, *The Moment of 'Scrutiny'*, London: New Left Books 1979.
9 See Michael Kenny, *The First New Left – British Intellectuals After Stalin*, London: Lawrence & Wishart 1995.
10 F.R. Leavis, *The Great Tradition*, Harmondsworth: Penguin 1962 [1948].
11 Williams's *The English Novel from Dickens to Lawrence*, London: Chatto & Windus 1970, was a sociologically informed rebuttal to Leavis's readings in *The Great Tradition*. In a similar vein, Williams's *The Country and the City*, Chatto & Windus 1973 places a certain tradition of English writing in its place, socially and historically.
12 Terry Eagleton's *Criticism and Ideology – A Study in Marxist Literary Theory*, London: New Left Books 1976, represented a regrettable moment of distancing from Williams on grounds of theoretical 'correctness'.
13 The year after Williams's death, Eagleton edited a collection of appreciative essays on his mentor, *Raymond Williams – Critical Perspectives*, Cambridge: Polity, 1989.
14 Tom Steele, *The Emergence of Cultural Studies – Cultural Politics, Adult Education and the 'English' Question*, London: Lawrence & Wishart 1997.
15 See Juliet Mitchell's 'Women – The Longest Revolution', *New Left Review* 40, 1966, 11–37, and her later *Woman's Estate*, Harmondsworth: Penguin 1971.
16 Raymond Williams, ed., *May Day Manifesto 1968*, Harmondsworth: Penguin 1968.
17 See, for instance, Stuart Hall, *The Hard Road to Renewal – Thatcherism and the Crisis of the Left*, London: Verso 1988.
18 Fredric Jameson, *Postmodernism, or, the Cultural Logic of Late Capitalism*, London & New York: Verso 1991, p. xiv.
19 Raymond Williams, 'Marxism, Structuralism and Literary Analysis', *New Left Review* 129, September–October 1981, 64–65.
20 See Jonathan Dollimore and Alan Sinfield, eds, *Political Shakespeare – New Essays in Cultural Materialism*, Manchester: Manchester University Press 1985.
21 Douglas Kellner, 'Critical Theory and Cultural Studies – The Missed Articulation', in McGuigan, J., ed., *Cultural Methodologies*, London, Thousand Oaks and New Delhi: Sage 1997, pp. 12–41.

22 Richard Wilkinson and Kate Pickett's *The Spirit Level – Why More Equal Societies Almost Always Do Better*, London: Allen Lane 2009 resonates with Williams's deepest sociological concerns and anxieties about the future.
23 Raymond Williams, *Second Generation*, London: Chatto & Windus 1964, a companion work to his autobiographical novel, *Border Country*, Chatto & Windus 1960.
24 This selection of book titles – a baker's dozen – is meant to indicate Raymond Williams's most important contributions to the Social Sciences, especially Cultural Studies and Sociology. It is by no means an exhaustive list of William's many and varied writings.

1

CULTURE IS ORDINARY
(1958)

This early essay of Raymond Williams is clearly written against an exclusionary notion of culture as a body of works that is only meaningful to a highly educated minority. In one sense, it is making merely a banal and indeed well-established anthropological point about the sociality of culture, the very processes of communication between people in society. What is novel about Williams's essay, however, is that he puts this anthropological notion of culture into collision with the exclusionary concept and, also, calls into question elitist ideas concerning what counts as culture and its evaluation in education and learning.

The bus stop was outside the cathedral. I had been looking at the Mappa Mundi, with its rivers out of Paradise, and at the chained library, where a party of clergymen had got in easily, but where I had waited an hour and cajoled a verger before I even saw the chains. Now, across the street, a cinema advertised the *Six-Five Special* and a cartoon version of *Gulliver's Travels*. The bus arrived, with a driver and a conductress deeply absorbed in each other. We went out of the city, over the old bridge, and on through the orchards and the green meadows and the fields red under the plough. Ahead were the Black Mountains, and we climbed among them, watching the steep fields end at the grey walls, beyond which the bracken and heather and whin had not yet been driven back. To the east, along the ridge, stood, the line of grey Norman castles; to the west, the fortress wall of the mountains. Then, as we still climbed, the rock changed under us. Here, now, was limestone, and the line of the early iron workings along the scarp. The farming valleys, with their scattered white houses, fell away behind. Ahead of us were the narrower valleys: the steel-rolling mill, the gasworks, the grey terraces, the pitheads. The bus stopped, and the driver and conductress got out, still absorbed. They had done this journey so often, and seen all its stages. It is a journey, in fact, that in one form or another we have all made.

I was born and grew up halfway along that bus journey. Where I lived is still a farming valley, though the road through it is being widened and straightened, to carry the heavy lorries to the north. Not far away, my grandfather, and so back through the generations, worked as a farm labourer until he was turned out of his cottage and, in his fifties, became a roadman. His sons went at thirteen or fourteen on to the farms, his daughters into service. My father, his third son, left the farm at fifteen to be a boy porter on the railway, and later became a signalman, working in a box in this valley until he died. I went up the road to the village school, where a curtain divided the two classes – Second to eight or nine, First to fourteen. At eleven I went to the local grammar school, and later to Cambridge.

Culture is ordinary: that is where we must start. To grow up in that country was to see the shape of a culture, and its modes of change. I could stand on the mountains and look north to the farms and the cathedral, or south to the smoke and the flare of the blast furnace making a second sunset. To grow up in that family was to see the shaping of minds: the learning of new skills, the shifting of relationships, the emergence of different language and ideas. My grandfather, a big hard labourer, wept while he spoke, finely and excitedly, at the parish meeting, of being turned out of his cottage. My father, not long before he died, spoke quietly and happily of when he had started a trade-union branch and a Labour Party group in the village, and, without bitterness, of the 'kept men' of the new politics. I speak a different idiom, but I think of these same things.

Culture is ordinary: that is the first fact. Every human society has its own shape, its own purposes, its own meanings. Every human society expresses these, in institutions, and in arts and learning. The making of a society is the finding of common meanings and directions, and its growth is an active debate and amendment under the pressures of experience, contact, and discovery, writing themselves into the land. The growing society is there, yet it is also made and remade in every individual mind. The making of a mind is, first, the slow learning of shapes, purposes, and meanings, so that work, observation and communication are possible. Then, second, but equal in importance, is the testing of these in experience, the making of new observations, comparisons, and meanings. A culture has two aspects: the known meanings and directions, which its members are trained to; the new observations and meanings, which are offered and tested. These are the ordinary processes of human societies and human minds, and we see through them the nature of a culture: that it is always both traditional and creative; that it is both the most ordinary common meanings and the finest individual meanings. We use the word culture in these two senses: to mean a whole way of life – the common meanings; to mean the arts and learning – the special processes of discovery and creative effort. Some writers reserve the word for one or other of these senses; I insist on both, and on the significance of their conjunction. The questions I ask about our culture are questions about our general and common purposes, yet also questions about deep personal meanings. Culture is ordinary, in every society and in every mind.

Now there are two senses of culture – two colours attached to it – that I know about but refuse to learn. The first I discovered at Cambridge, in a teashop. I was not, by the way, oppressed by Cambridge. I was not cast down by old buildings, for I had come from a country with twenty centuries of history written visibly into the earth: I liked walking through a Tudor court, but it did not make me feel raw. I was not amazed by the existence of a place of learning; I had always known the cathedral, and the bookcases I now sit to work at in Oxford are of the same design as those in the chained library. Nor was learning, in my family, some strange eccentricity; I was not, on a scholarship in Cambridge, a new kind of animal up a brand-new ladder. Learning was ordinary; we learned where we could. Always, from those scattered white houses, it had made sense to go out and become a scholar or a poet or a teacher. Yet few of us could be spared from the immediate work; a price had been set on this kind of learning, and it was more, much more, than we could individually pay. Now, when we could pay in common, it was a good, ordinary life.

I was not oppressed by the university, but the teashop, acting as if it were one of the older and more respectable departments, was a different matter. Here was culture, not in any sense I knew, but in a special sense: the outward and emphatically visible sign of a special kind of people, cultivated people. They were not, the great majority of them, particularly learned; they practised few arts; but they had it, and they showed you they had it. They are still there, I suppose, still showing it, though even they must be hearing rude noises from outside, from a few scholars and writers they call – how comforting a label is! – angry young men. As a matter of fact there is no need to be rude. It is simply that if that is culture, we don't want it; we have seen other people living.

But of course it is not culture, and those of my colleagues who, hating the teashop, make culture, on its account, a dirty word, are mistaken. If the people in the teashop go on insisting that culture is their trivial differences of behaviour, their trivial variations of speech habit, we cannot stop them, but we can ignore them. They are not that important, to take culture from where it belongs.

Yet, probably also disliking the teashop, there were writers I read then, who went into the same category in my mind. When I now read a book such as Clive Bell's *Civilisation*, I experience not so much disagreement as stupor. What kind of life can it be, I wonder, to produce this extraordinary fussiness, this extraordinary decision to call certain things culture and then separate them, as with a park wall, from ordinary people and ordinary work? At home we met and made music, listened to it, recited and listened to poems, valued fine language. I have heard better music and better poems since; there is the world to draw on. But I know, from the most ordinary experience, that the interest is there, the capacity is there. Of course, farther along that bus journey, the old social organization in which these things had their place has been broken. People have been driven and concentrated into new kinds of work, new kinds of relationship; work, by the way, which built the park walls, and the houses inside them, and which is now at last bringing, to the unanimous disgust of the teashop, clean and decent and furnished living to the people themselves. Culture is ordinary: through every change let us hold fast to that.

The other sense, or colour, that I refuse to learn, is very different. Only two English words rhyme with culture, and these, as it happens, are sepulture and vulture. We don't yet call museums or galleries or even universities culture-sepultures, but I hear a lot, lately, about culture-vultures (man must rhyme), and I hear also, in the same North Atlantic argot, of do-gooders and highbrows and superior prigs. Now I don't like the teashop, but I don't like this drinking-hole either, I know there are people who are humourless about the arts and learning, and I know there is a difference between goodness and sanctimony. But the growing implications of this spreading argot – the true cant of a new kind of rogue – I reject absolutely.

For, honestly, how can anyone use a word like 'do-gooder' with this new, offbeat complacency? How can anyone wither himself to a state where he must use these new flip words for any attachment to learning or the arts? It is plain that what may have started as a feeling about hypocrisy, or about pretentiousness (in itself a two-edged word), is becoming a guilt-ridden tic at the mention of any serious standards whatever. And the word 'culture' has been heavily compromised by this conditioning: Goering reached for his gun; many reach for their chequebooks; a growing number, now, reach for the latest bit of argot.

'Good' has been drained of much of its meaning, in these circles, by the exclusion of its ethical content and emphasis on a purely technical standard; to do a good job is better than to be a do-gooder. But do we need reminding that any crook can, in his own terms, do a good job? The smooth reassurance of technical efficiency is no substitute for the whole positive human reference. Yet men who once made this reference, men who were or *wanted* to be writers or scholars, are now, with every appearance of satisfaction, advertising men, publicity boys, names in the strip newspapers. These men were given skills, given attachments, which are now in the service of the most brazen money-grabbing exploitation of the inexperience of ordinary people. And it is these men – this new, dangerous class – who have invented and disseminated the argot, in an attempt to influence ordinary people – who because they do real work have real standards in the fields they know – against real standards in the fields these men knew and have abandoned. The old cheapjack is still there in the market, with the country boys' half-crowns on his reputed packets of gold rings or watches. He thinks of his victims as a slow, ignorant crowd, but they live, and farm, while he coughs behind his portable stall. The new cheapjack is in offices with contemporary *décor*, using scraps of linguistics, psychology and sociology to influence what he thinks of as the mass mind. He too, however, will have to pick up and move on, and meanwhile we are not to be influenced by his argot; we can simply refuse to learn it. Culture is ordinary. An interest in learning or the arts is simple, pleasant and natural. A desire to know what is best, and to do what is good, is the whole positive nature of man. We are not to be scared from these things by noises. There are many versions of what is wrong with our culture. So far I have tried only to clear away the detritus which makes it difficult for us to think seriously about it at all. When I got to Cambridge I encountered two serious influences which have left a very deep impression on my mind. The first was Marxism, the second the teaching of Leavis. Through all subsequent disagreement I retain my respect for both.

The Marxists said many things, but those that mattered were three. First, they said that a culture must be finally interpreted in relation to its underlying system of production. I have argued this theoretically elsewhere – it is a more difficult idea than it looks – but I still accept its emphasis. Everything I had seen, growing up in that border country, had led me towards such an emphasis: a culture is a whole way of life, and the arts are part of a social organization which economic change clearly radically affects. I did not have to be taught dissatisfaction with the existing economic system, but the subsequent questions about our culture were, in these terms, vague. It was said that it was a class-dominated culture, deliberately restricting a common inheritance to a small class, while leaving the masses ignorant. The fact of restriction I accepted – it is still very obvious that only the *deserving* poor get much educational opportunity, and I was in no mood, as I walked about Cambridge, to feel glad that I had been thought deserving; I was no better and no worse than the people I came from. On the other hand, just because of this, I got angry at my friends' talk about the ignorant masses: one kind of Communist has always talked like this, and has got his answer, at Poznan and Budapest, as the imperialists, making the same assumption, were answered in India, in Indo-China, in Africa. There is an English bourgeois culture, with its powerful educational, literary and social institutions, in close contact with the actual centres of power. To say that most working people are excluded from these is self-evident, though the doors, under sustained pressure, are slowly opening. But to go on to say that working people are excluded from English culture is nonsense; they have their own growing institutions, and much of the strictly bourgeois culture they would in any case not want. A great part of the English way of life, and of its arts and learning, is not bourgeois in any discoverable sense. There are institutions, and common meanings, which are in no sense the sole product of the commercial middle class; and there are art and learning, a common English inheritance, produced by many kinds of men, including many who hated the very class and system which now take pride in consuming it. The bourgeoisie has given us much, including a narrow but real system of morality; that is at least better than its court predecessors. The leisure which the bourgeoisie attained has given us much of cultural value. But this is not to say that contemporary culture is bourgeois culture: a mistake that everyone, from Conservatives to Marxists, seems to make. There is a distinct working-class way of life, which I for one value – not only because I was bred in it, for I now, in certain respects, live differently. I think this way of life, with its emphases of neighbourhood, mutual obligation, and common betterment, as expressed in the great working-class political and industrial institutions, is in fact the best basis for any future English society. As for the arts and learning, they are in a real sense a national inheritance, which is, or should be, available to everyone. So when the Marxists say that we live in a dying culture, and that the masses are ignorant, I have to ask them, as I asked them then, where on earth they have lived. A dying culture, and ignorant masses, are not what I have known and see.

What I had got from the Marxists then, so far, was a relationship between culture and production, and the observation that education was restricted. The other things I rejected, as I rejected also their third point, that since culture and production are related, the advocacy of a different system of production is in some way a cultural directive, indicating not only a way of life but new arts and learning. I did some writing while I was, for eighteen months, a member of the Communist Party, and I found out in trivial ways what other writers, here and in Europe, have found out more gravely: the practical consequences of this kind of theoretical error. In this respect, I saw the future, and it didn't work. The Marxist interpretation of culture can never be accepted while it retains, as it need not retain, this directive element, this insistence that if you honestly want socialism you must write, think, learn in certain prescribed ways. A culture is common meanings, the product of a whole people, and offered individual meanings, the product of a man's whole committed personal and social experience. It is stupid and arrogant to suppose that any of these meanings can in any way be prescribed; they are made by living, made and remade, in ways we cannot know in advance. To try to jump the future, to pretend that in some way you *are* the future, is strictly insane. Prediction is another matter, an offered meaning, but the only thing we can say about culture in an England that has socialized its means of production is that all the channels of expression and communication should be cleared and open, so that the whole actual life, that we cannot know in advance, that we can know only in part even while it is being lived, may be brought to consciousness and meaning.

Leavis has never liked Marxists, which is in one way a pity, for they know more than he does about modern English society, and about its immediate history. He, on the other hand, knows more than any Marxist I have met about the real relations between art and experience. We have all learned from him in this, and we have also learned his version of what is wrong with English culture. The diagnosis is radical, and is rapidly becoming orthodox. There was an old, mainly agricultural England, with a traditional culture of great value. This has been replaced by a modern, organized, industrial state, whose characteristic institutions deliberately cheapen our natural human responses, making art and literature into desperate survivors and witnesses, while a new mechanized vulgarity sweeps into the centres of power. The only defence is in education, which will at least keep certain things alive, and which will also, at least in a minority, develop ways of thinking and feeling which are competent to understand what is happening and to maintain the finest individual values. I need not add how widespread this diagnosis has become, though little enough acknowledgement is still made to Leavis himself. For my own part, I was deeply impressed by it; deeply enough for my ultimate rejection of it to be a personal crisis lasting several years.

For, obviously, it seemed to fit a good deal of my experience. It did not tell me that my father and grandfather were ignorant wage-slaves; it did not tell me that the smart, busy, commercial culture (which I had come to as a stranger, so much so that for years I had violent headaches whenever I passed through London and saw underground advertisements and evening newspapers) was the thing I had to catch up with. I even made a fool of myself, or was made to think so, when after a lecture in which the usual point was made that 'neighbour' now does not mean what it did to Shakespeare, I said – imagine! – that to me it did. (When my father was dying, this year, one man came in and dug his garden; another loaded and delivered a lorry of sleepers for firewood; another came and chopped the sleepers into blocks; another – I don't know who, it was never said – left a sack of potatoes at the back door; a woman came in and took away a basket of washing.) But even this was explicable; I came from a bit of the old society, but my future was Surbiton (it took me years to find Surbiton, and have a good look at it, but it's served a good many as a symbol – without having lived there I couldn't say whether rightly). So there I was, and it all seemed to fit.

Yet not all. Once I got away, and thought about it, it didn't really fit properly. For one thing I knew this: at home we were glad of the Industrial Revolution, and of its consequent social and political changes. True, we lived in a very beautiful farming valley, and the valleys beyond the limestone we could all see were ugly. But there was one gift that was overriding, one gift which at any price we would take, the gift of power that is everything to men who have worked with their hands. It was slow in coming to us, in all its effects, but steam power, the petrol engine, electricity, these and their host of products in commodities and services, we took as quickly as we could get them, and were glad. I have seen all these things being used, and I have seen the things they replaced. I will not listen with patience to any acid listing of them – you know the sneer you can get into plumbing, baby Austins, aspirin, contraceptives, canned food. But I say to these Pharisees: dirty water, an earth bucket, a four-mile walk each way to work, headaches, broken women, hunger and monotony of diet. The working people, in town and country alike, will not listen (and I support them) to any account of our society which supposes that these things are not progress: not just mechanical, external progress either, but a real service of life. Moreover, in the new conditions, there was more real freedom to dispose of our lives, more real personal grasp where it mattered, more real say. Any account of our culture which explicitly or implicity denies the value of an industrial society is really irrelevant; not in a million years would you make us give up this power.

So then the social basis of the case was unacceptable, but could one, trying to be a writer, a scholar, a teacher, ignore the indictment of the new cultural vulgarity? For the plumbing and the tractors and the medicines could one ignore the strip newspapers, the multiplying cheapjacks, the raucous triviality? As a matter of priorities, yes, if necessary; but was the cheapening of response really a consequence of the cheapening of power? It looks like it, I know, but is this really as much as one can say? I believe the central problem of our society, in the coming half-century, is the use of our new resources to make a good common culture; the means to a good, abundant economy we already understand. I think the good common culture can be made, but before we can be serious about this, we must rid ourselves of a legacy from our most useful critics – a legacy of two false equations, one false analogy, and one false proposition.

The false proposition is easily disposed of. It is a fact that the new power brought ugliness: the coal brought dirt, the factory brought overcrowding, communications brought a mess of wires. But the proposition that ugliness is a price we pay, or refuse to pay, for economic power need no longer be true. New sources of power, new methods of production, improved systems of transport and communication can, quite practically, make England clean and pleasant again, and with much more power, not less. Any new ugliness is the product of stupidity, indifference, or simply incoordination; these things will be easier to deal with than when power was necessarily noisy, dirty, and disfiguring.

The false equations are more difficult. One is the equation between popular education and the new commercial culture: the latter proceeding inevitably from the former. Let the masses in, it is said, and this is what you inevitably get. Now the question is obviously difficult, but I can't accept this equation, for two reasons. The first is a matter of faith: I don't believe that the ordinary people in fact resemble the normal description of the masses, low and trivial in taste and habit. I put it another way: that there are in fact no masses, but only ways of seeing people as masses. With the coming of industrialism, much of the old social organization broke down and it became a matter of difficult personal experience that we were constantly seeing people we did not know, and it was tempting to mass them, as 'the others', in our minds. Again, people were physically massed, in the industrial towns, and a new class structure (the names of our social classes, and the word 'class' itself in this sense, date only from the Industrial Revolution) was practically imposed. The improvement in communications, in particular the development of new forms of multiple transmission of news and entertainment, created unbridgeable divisions between transmitter and audience, which again led to the audience being interpreted as an unknown mass. Masses became a new word for mob: the others, the unknown, the unwashed, the crowd beyond one. As a way of knowing other people, this formula is obviously ridiculous, but, in the new conditions, it seemed an effective formula – the only one possible. Certainly it was the formula that was used by those whose money gave them access to the new communication techniques; the lowness of taste and habit, which human beings assign very easily to other human beings, was assumed, as a bridge. The new culture was built on this formula, and if I reject the formula, if I insist that this lowness is not inherent in ordinary people, you can brush my insistence aside, but I shall go on holding to it. A different formula, I know from experience, gets a radically different response.

My second reason is historical: I deny, and can prove my denial, that popular education and commercial culture are cause and effect. I have shown elsewhere that the myth of 1870 – the Education Act which is said to have produced, as its children grew up, a new cheap and nasty press – is indeed myth. There was more than enough literacy, long before 1870, to support a cheap press, and in fact there were cheap and really bad newspapers selling in great quantities before the 1870 Act was heard of. The bad new commercial culture came out of the social chaos of industrialism, and out of the success, in this chaos, of the 'masses' formula, not out of popular education. Northcliffe did few worse things than start this myth, for while the connection between bad culture and the social chaos of industrialism is significant, the connection between it and popular education is vicious. The Northcliffe Revolution, by the way, was a radical change in the financial structure of the press, basing it on a new kind of revenue – the new mass advertising of the 1890s – rather than the making of a cheap popular press, in which he had been widely and successfully preceded. But I tire of making these points. Everyone prefers to believe Northcliffe. Yet does nobody, even a Royal Commission, read the most ordinarily accessible newspaper history? When people do read the history, the false equation between popular education and commercial culture will disappear for ever. Popular education came out of the other camp, and has had quite opposite effects.

The second false equation is this: that the observable badness of so much widely distributed popular culture is a true guide to the state of mind and feeling, the essential quality of living of its consumers. Too many good men have said this for me to treat it lightly, but I still, on evidence, can't accept it. It is easy to assemble, from print and cinema and television, a terrifying and fantastic congress of cheap feelings and moronic arguments. It is easy to go on from this and assume this deeply degrading version of the actual lives of our contemporaries. Yet do we find this confirmed, when we meet people? This is where 'masses' comes in again, of course: the people *we* meet aren't vulgar, but God, think of Bootle and Surbiton and Aston! I haven't lived in any of those places; have you? But a few weeks ago I was in a house with a commercial traveller, a lorry driver, a bricklayer, a shopgirl, a fitter, a signalman, a nylon operative, a domestic help (perhaps, dear, she is your very own treasure). I hate describing people like this, for in fact they were my family and family friends. Now they read, they watch, this work we are talking about; some of them quite critically, others with a good deal of pleasure. Very well, I read different things, watch different entertainments, and I am quite sure why they are better. But could I sit down in that house and make this equation we are offered? Not, you understand, that shame was stopping me; I've learned, thank you, how to behave. But talking to my family, to my friends, talking, as we were, about our own lives, about people, about feelings, could I in fact find this lack of quality we are discussing? I'll be honest – I looked; my training has done that for me. I can only say that I found as much natural fineness of feeling, as much quick discrimination, as much clear grasp of ideas within the range of experience as I have found anywhere. I don't altogether understand this, though I am not really surprised. Clearly there is something in the psychology of print and image that none of us has yet quite grasped. For the equation looks sensible, yet when you test it, in experience – and there's nowhere else you can test it – it's wrong. I can understand the protection of critical and intelligent reading: my father, for instance, a satisfied reader of the *Daily Herald*, got simply from reading the company reports a clear idea, based on names, of the rapid development of combine and interlocking ownership in British industry, which I had had made easy for me in two or three academic essays; and he had gone on to set these facts against the opinions in a number of articles in the paper on industrial ownership. That I understand; that is simply intelligence, however partly trained. But there is still this other surprising fact: that people whose quality of personal living is high are apparently satisfied by a low quality of printed feeling and opinion. Many of them still live, it is true, in a surprisingly enclosed personal world, much more so than mine, and some of their personal observations are the finer for it. Perhaps this is enough to explain it, but in any case, I submit, we need a new equation, to fit the observable facts.

Now the false analogy, that we must also reject. This is known, in discussions of culture, as a 'kind of Gresham's Law'. Just as bad money will drive out good, so bad culture will drive out good, and this, it is said, has in fact been happening. If you can't see, straight away, the defect of the analogy, your answer, equally effective, will have to be historical. For in fact, of course, it has not been happening. There is more, much more bad culture about; it is easier, now, to distribute it, and there is more leisure to receive it. But test this in any field you like, and see if this has been accompanied by a shrinking consumption of things we can all agree to be good. The editions of good literature are very much larger than they were; the listeners to good music are much more numerous than they were; the number of people who look at good visual art is larger than it has ever been. If bad newspapers drive out good newspapers, by a kind of Gresham's Law, why is it that, allowing for the rise in population, *The Times* sells nearly three times as many copies as in the days of its virtual monopoly of the press, in 1850? It is the law I am questioning, not the seriousness of the facts as a whole. Instead of a kind of Gresham's Law, keeping people awake at nights with the now orthodox putropian nightmare, let us put it another way, to fit the actual facts: we live in an expanding culture, and all the elements in this culture are themselves expanding. If we start from this, we can then ask real questions: about relative rates of expansion; about the social and economic problems raised by these; about the social and economic answers. I am working now on a book to follow my *Culture and Society*, trying to interpret, historically and theoretically, the nature and conditions of an expanding culture of our kind. I could not have begun this work if I had not learned from the Marxists and from Leavis; I cannot complete it unless I radically amend some of the ideas which they and others have left us.

I give myself three wishes, one for each of the swans I have just been watching on the lake. I ask for things that are part of the ethos of our working-class movement. I ask that we may be strong and human enough to realize them. And I ask, naturally, in my own fields of interest.

I wish, first, that we should recognize that education is ordinary: that it is, before everything else, the process of giving to the ordinary members of society its full common meanings, and the skills that will enable them to amend these meanings, in the light of their personal and common experience. If we start from that, we can get rid of the remaining restrictions, and make the necessary changes. I do not mean only money restrictions, though these, of course, are ridiculous and must go. I mean also restrictions in the mind: the insistence, for example, that there is a hard maximum number – a fraction of the population as a whole – capable of really profiting by a university education, or a grammar school education, or by any full course of liberal studies. We are told that this is not a question of what we might personally prefer, but of the hard cold facts of human intelligence, as shown by biology and psychology. But let us be frank about this: are biology and psychology different in the USA and USSR (each committed to expansion, and not to any class rigidities), where much larger numbers, much larger fractions, pass through comparable stages of education? Or were the English merely behind in the queue for intelligence? I believe, myself, that our educational system, with its golden fractions, is too like our social system – a top layer of leaders, a middle layer of supervisors, a large bottom layer of operatives – to be coincidence. I cannot accept that education is a training for jobs, or for making useful citizens (that is, fitting into this system). It is a society's confirmation of its common meanings, and of the human skills for their amendment. Jobs follow from this confirmation: the purpose, and then the working skill. We are moving into an economy where we shall need many more highly trained specialists. For this precise reason. I ask for a common education that will give our society its cohesion, and prevent it disintegrating into a series of specialist departments, the nation become a firm.

But I do not mean only the reorganization of entry into particular kinds of education, though I welcome and watch the experiments in this. I mean also the rethinking of content, which is even more important. I have the honour to work for an organization through which, quite practically, working men amended the English university curriculum. It is now as it was then: the defect is not what is in, but what is out. It will be a test of our cultural seriousness whether we can, in the coming generation, redesign our syllabuses to a point of full human relevance and control. I should like to see a group working on this, and offering its conclusions. For we need not fear change; oldness may or may not be relevant. I come from an old place; if a man tells me that his family came over with the Normans, I say 'Yes, how interesting; and are you liking it here?' Oldness is relative, and many immemorial English traditions were invented, just like that, in the nineteenth century. What that vital century did for its own needs, we can do for ours; we can make, in our turn, a true twentieth-century syllabus. And by this I do not mean simply more technology; I mean a full liberal education for everyone in our society, and then full specialist training to earn our living in terms of what we want to make of our lives. Our specialisms will be finer if they have grown from a common culture, rather than being a distinction from it. And we must at all costs avoid the polarization of our culture, of which there are growing signs. High literacy is expanding, in direct relation to exceptional educational opportunities, and the gap between this and common literacy may widen, to the great damage of both, and with great consequent tension. We must emphasize not the ladder but the common highway, for every man's ignorance diminishes me, and every man's skill is a common gain of breath.

My second wish is complementary: for more and more active public provision for the arts and for adult learning. We now spend £20,000,000 annually on all our libraries, museums, galleries, orchestras, on the Arts Council, and on all forms of adult education. At the same time we spend £365,000,000 annually on advertising. When these figures are reversed, we can claim some sense of proportion and value. And until they are reversed, let there be no sermons from the Establishment about materialism: this is their way of life, let them look at it. (But there is no shame in them: for years, with their own children away at school, they have lectured working-class mothers on the virtues of family life; this is a similar case.)

I ask for increased provision on three conditions. It is not to be a disguised way of keeping up consumption, but a thing done for its own sake. A minister in the last Labour government said that we didn't want any geniuses in the film industry; he wanted, presumably, just to keep the turnstiles clicking. The short answer to this is that we don't want any Wardour Street thinkers in the leadership of the Labour Party. We want leaders of a society, not repair-workers on this kind of cultural economy.

The second condition is that while we must obviously preserve and extend the great national institutions, we must do something to reverse the concentration of this part of our culture. We should welcome, encourage and foster the tendencies to regional recreation that are showing themselves; for culture is ordinary, you should not have to go to London to find it.

The third condition is controversial. We should not seek to extend a ready-made culture to the benighted masses. We should accept, frankly, that if we extend our culture we shall change it: some that is offered will be rejected, other parts will be radically criticized. And this is as it should be, for our arts, now, are in no condition to go down to eternity unchallenged. There is much fine work; there is also shoddy work, and work based on values that will find no acceptance if they ever come out into the full light of England. To take our arts to new audiences is to be quite certain that in many respects those arts will be changed. I, for one, do not fear this. I would not expect the working people of England to support works which, after proper and patient preparation, they could not accept. The real growth will be slow and uneven, but state provision, frankly, should be a growth in this direction, and not a means of diverting public money to the preservation of a fixed and finished partial culture. At the same time, if we understand cultural growth, we shall know that it is a continual offering for common acceptance; that we should not, therefore, try to determine in advance what should be offered, but clear the channels and let all the offerings be made, taking care to give the difficult full space, the original full time, so that it is a real growth, and not just a wider confirmation of old rules.

Now, of course, we shall hear the old cry that things shouldn't be supported at a loss. Once again, this is a nation, not a firm. Parliament itself runs at a loss, because we need it, and if it would be better at a greater loss, I and others would willingly pay. But why, says Sir George Mammon, should *I* support a lot of doubtful artists? Why, says Mrs. Mink, should I pay good money to educate, at *my* expense, a lot of irresponsible and ungrateful state scholars? The answer, dear sir, dear madam, is that *you* don't. On your own – learn your size – you could do practically nothing. We are talking about a method of common payment, for common services; we too shall be paying.

My third wish is in a related field: the field now dominated by the institutions of 'mass culture'. Often, it is the people at the head of these institutions who complain of running things at a loss. But the great popular newspapers, as newspapers, run at a loss. The independent television companies are planned to run at a loss. I don't mean temporary subsidies, but the whole basis of financing such institutions. The newspapers run at a heavy loss, which they make up with money from advertising – that is to say a particular use of part of the product of our common industry. To run at a loss, and then cover yourself with this kind of income, is of the essence of this kind of cultural institution, and this is entirely characteristic of our kind of capitalist society. The whole powerful array of mass cultural institutions has one keystone: money from advertising. Let them stop being complacent about other cultural institutions which run at a smaller loss, and meet it out of another part of the common product.

But what is it then that I wish? To pull out this keystone? No, not just like that. I point out merely that the organization of our present mass culture is so closely involved with the organization of capitalist society that the future of one cannot be considered except in terms of the future of the other. I think much of contemporary advertising is necessary only in terms of the kind of economy we now have: a stimulation of consumption in the direction of particular products and firms, often by irrelevant devices, rather than real advertising, which is an ordinary form of public notice. In a socialist economy, which I and others want, the whole of this pseudo-advertising would be irrelevant. But then what? My wish is that we may solve the problems that would then arise, where necessary things like newspapers would be running at something like their real loss, without either pricing them out of ordinary means, or exposing them to the dangers of control and standardization (for we want a more free and more varied press, not one less so). It is going to be very difficult, but I do not believe we are so uninventive as to be left showing each other a pair of grim alternatives: either the continuance of this crazy peddling, in which news and opinion are inextricably involved with the shouts of the market, bringing in their train the new slavery and prostitution of the selling of personalities: or else a dull, monolithic, controlled system, in which news and opinion are in the gift of a ruling party. We should be thinking, now, about ways of paying for our common services which will guarantee proper freedom to those who actually provide the service, while protecting them and us against a domineering minority whether political or financial. I think there are ways, if we really believe in democracy.

But that is the final question: how many of us really believe in it? The capitalists don't; they are consolidating a power which can survive parliamentary changes. Many Labour planners don't; they interpret it as a society run by experts for an abstraction called the public interest. The people in the teashop don't; they are quite sure it is not going to be nice. And the others, the new dissenters? Nothing has done more to sour the democratic idea, among its natural supporters, and to drive them back into an angry self-exile, than the plain, overwhelming cultural issues: the apparent division of our culture into, on the one hand, a remote and self-gracious sophistication, on the other hand, a doped mass. So who then believes in democracy? The answer is really quite simple: the millions in England who still haven't got it, where they work and feel. There, as always, is the transforming energy, and the business of the socialist intellectual is what it always was: to attack the clamps on that energy – in industrial relations, public administration, education, for a start; and to work in his own field on ways in which that energy, as released, can be concentrated and fertile. The technical means are difficult enough, but the biggest difficulty is in accepting, deep in our minds, the values on which they depend: that the ordinary people should govern; that culture and education are ordinary; that there are no masses to save, to capture, or to direct, but rather this crowded people in the course of an extraordinarily rapid and confusing expansion of their lives. A writer's job is with individual meanings, and with making these meanings common. I find these meanings in the expansion, there along the journey where the necessary changes are writing themselves into the land, and where the language changes but the voice is the same.

Reference

McKenzie, N., ed., *Convictions*, MacGibbon & Gee, 1958. From Raymond Williams, *Resources of Hope*, Verso, 1989, pp. 3–18. Reprinted with kind permission of Verso.

2

MASS, MASSES AND MASS COMMUNICATION (1958)

In these passages from his celebrated and most famous book, Culture and Society, *Raymond Williams points to an early meaning of the term 'mass' with reference to people as, in effect, a 'mob', that is, a dangerous and subversive crowd with the potential of disrupting and perhaps overthrowing the newly established bourgeois order of society in the nineteenth century. He contends that the negative connotation of 'mass' and 'masses' remains in the naming of modern media as 'mass communication'. This illustrates two important features of Williams's work: first, his emphasis on the historicity of words and the accumulated meanings that they acquire over time, exemplified more fully in his book,* Keywords *(1976/1983), which developed out of Williams's research on the culture and society tradition in English letters; and, second, his critique of the naming of a new field of study as 'mass communications' research. These arguments had a huge influence, resulting in (re)naming the field in a more neutral manner, such as 'communication studies', 'cultural studies' and 'media studies'.*

Mass and Masses

We now regularly use both the idea of the 'masses', and the consequent ideas of 'mass-civilization', 'mass-democracy', 'mass-communication' and others. Here, I think, lies a central and very difficult issue which more than any other needs revision.

Masses was a new word for mob, and it is a very significant word. It seems probable that three social tendencies joined to confirm its meaning. First, there was the concentration of population in the industrial towns, a physical massing of persons which the great increase in total population accentuated, and which has continued with continuing urbanization. Second, there was the concentration of workers into factories: again, a physical massing, made necessary by machine production; also, a social massing, in the work-relations made necessary by the development of large-scale collective production. Third, there was the consequent development of an organized and self-organizing working class: a social and political massing. The masses, in practice, have been any of these particular aggregates, and because the tendencies have been interrelated, it has been possible to use the term with a certain unity. And then, on the basis of each tendency, the derived ideas have arisen: from urbanization, the mass meeting; from the factory, in part in relation to the workers, but mainly in relation to the things made, mass-production; from the working class, mass-action. Yet, masses was a new word for mob, and the traditional characteristics of the mob were retained in its significance: gullibility, fickleness, herd-prejudice, lowness of taste and habit. The masses, on this evidence, formed the perpetual threat to culture. Mass-thinking, mass-suggestion, mass-prejudice would threaten to swamp considered individual thinking and feeling. Even democracy, which had both a classical and a liberal reputation, would lose its savour in becoming mass-democracy.

Now mass-democracy, to take the latest example, can be either an observation or a prejudice; sometimes, indeed, it is both. As an observation, the term draws attention to certain problems of a modern democratic society which could not have been foreseen by its early partisans. The existence of immensely powerful media of mass-communication is at the heart of these problems, for through these public opinion has been observably moulded and directed, often by questionable means, often for questionable ends. I shall discuss this issue separately, in relation to the new means of communication.

But the term mass-democracy is also, evidently, a prejudice. Democracy, as in England we have interpreted it, is majority rule. The means to this, in representation and freedom of expression, are generally approved. But, with universal suffrage, majority rule will, if we believe in the existence of the masses, be mass-rule. Further, if the masses are, essentially, the mob, democracy will be mob-rule. This will hardly be good government, or a good society; it will, rather, be the rule of lowness or mediocrity. At this point, which it is evidently very satisfying to some thinkers to reach, it is necessary to ask again: who are the masses? In practice, in our society and in this context, they can hardly be other than the working people. But if this is so, it is clear that what is in question is not only gullibility, fickleness, herd-prejudice, or lowness of taste and habit. It is also, from the open record, the declared intention of the working people to alter society, in many of its aspects, in ways which those to whom the franchise was formerly restricted deeply disapprove. It seems to me, when this is considered, that what is being questioned is not mass-democracy, but democracy. If a majority can be achieved in favour of these changes, the democratic criterion is satisfied. But if you disapprove of the changes you can, it seems, avoid open opposition to democracy as such by inventing a new category, mass-democracy, which is not such a good thing at all. The submerged opposite is class-democracy, where democracy will merely describe the processes by which a ruling class conducts its business of ruling. Yet democracy, as interpreted in England in this century, does not mean this. So, if change reaches the point where it deeply hurts and cannot be accepted, either democracy must be denied or refuge taken in a new term of opprobrium. It is clear that this confusion of the issue cannot be tolerated. Masses = majority cannot be glibly equated with masses = mob.

A difficulty arises here with the whole concept of masses. Here, most urgently, we have to return the meanings to experience. Our normal public conception of an individual person, for example, is 'the man in the street'. But nobody feels himself to be only the man in the street; we all know much more about ourselves than that. The man in the street is a collective image, but we know, all the time, our own difference from him. It is the same with 'the public', which includes us, but yet is not us. 'Masses' is a little more complicated, yet similar. I do not think of my relatives, friends, neighbours, colleagues, acquaintances, as masses; we none of us can or do. The masses are always the others, whom we don't know, and can't know. Yet now, in our kind of society, we see these others regularly, in their myriad variations; stand, physically, beside them. They are here, and we are here with them. And that we are with them is of course the whole point. To other people, we also are masses. Masses are other people.

There are in fact no masses; there are only ways of seeing people as masses. In an urban industrial society there are many opportunities for such ways of seeing. The point is not to reiterate the objective conditions but to consider, personally and collectively, what these have done to our thinking. The fact is, surely, that a way of seeing other people which has become characteristic of our kind of society, has been capitalized for the purposes of political or cultural exploitation. What we see, neutrally, is other people, many others, people unknown to us. In practice, we mass them, and interpret them, according to some convenient formula. Within its terms, the formula will hold. Yet it is the formula, not the mass, which it is our real business to examine. It may help us to do this if we remember that we ourselves are all the time being massed by others. To the degree that we find the formula inadequate for ourselves, we can wish to extend to others the courtesy of acknowledging the unknown.

I have mentioned the political formula by means of which it seems possible to convert the majority of one's fellow human beings into masses, and thence into something to be hated or feared. I wish now to examine another formula, which underlies the idea of mass-communication.

Mass-communication

The new means of communication represent a major technical advance. The oldest, and still the most important, is printing, which has itself passed through major technical changes, in particular the corning of the steam-driven machine press in 1811, and the development of ever faster cylinder and rotary presses from 1815. The major advances in transport, by road, rail, sea, and air, themselves greatly affected printing: at once in the collection of news and in the wide and quick distribution of the printed product. The development of the cable, telegraph, and telephone services even more remarkably facilitated the collection of news. Then, as new media, came sound broadcasting, the cinema, and television.

We need to look again at these familiar factual elements if we are to be able adequately to review the idea of 'mass-communication' which is their product. In sum, these changes have given us more and normally cheaper books, magazines, and newspapers; more bills and posters; broadcasting and television programmes; various kinds of film. It would be difficult, I think, to express a simple and definite judgement of value about all these very varied products, yet they are all things that need to be valued. My question is whether the idea of 'mass-communication' is a useful formula for this.

Two preliminary points are evident: first, that there is a general tendency to confuse the techniques themselves with the uses to which, in a given society, they have been put; second, that, in considering these uses, our argument is commonly selective, at times to an extreme degree.

The techniques, in my view, are at worst neutral. The only substantial objection that is made to them is that they are relatively impersonal, by comparison with older techniques serving the same ends. Where the theatre presented actors, the cinema presents the photographs of actors. Where the meeting presented a man speaking, the wireless presents a voice, or television a voice and a photograph. Points of this kind are relevant, but need to be carefully made. It is not relevant to contrast an evening spent watching television with an evening spent in conversation, although this is often done. There is, I believe, no form of social activity which the use of these techniques has replaced. At most by adding alternatives, they have allowed altered emphases in the time given to given to particular activities. But these alterations are obviously conditioned, not only by the techniques, but mainly by the whole circumstances of the common life. The point about impersonality often carries a ludicrous rider. It is supposed, for instance, that it is an objection to listening to wireless talks or discussions that the listener cannot answer the speakers back. But the situation is that of almost any reader; printing, after all, was the first great impersonal medium. It is as easy to send an answer to a broadcast speaker or a newspaper editor as to send one to a contemporary author; both are very much easier than to try to answer Aristotle, Burke, or Marx. We fail to realize, in this matter, that much of what we call communication is, necessarily, no more in itself than transmission: that is to say, a one-way sending. Reception and response, which complete communication, depend on other factors than the techniques.

What can be observed as a fact about the development of these techniques is steady growth of what I propose to call *multiple transmission*. The printed book is the first great model of this, and the other techniques have followed. The new factor, in our society, is an expansion of the potential audience for such transmissions, so great as to present new kinds of problem. Yet it is clear that it is not to this expansion that we can properly object, at least without committing ourselves to some rather extraordinary politics. The expansion of the audience is due to two factors: first, the growth of general education, which has accompanied the growth of democracy; second, the technical improvements themselves. It is interesting, in the light of the earlier discussion of 'masses', that this expansion should have been interpreted by the phrase 'mass-communication'.

A speaker or writer, addressing a limited audience, is often able to get to know this audience well enough to feel a directly personal relationship with them which can affect his mode of address. Once this audience has been expanded, as with everything from books to televised parlour-games it has been expanded, this is clearly impossible. It would be rash, however, to assume that this is necessarily to his and the audience's disadvantage. Certain types of address, notably serious art, argument, and exposition, seem indeed to be distinguished by a quality of impersonality which enables them frequently to survive their immediate occasion. How far this ultimate impersonality may be dependent on a close immediate relationship is in fact very difficult to assess. But it is always unlikely that any such speaker or writer will use, as a model for communication, any concept so crude as 'masses'. The idea of mass-communication, it would seem, depends very much more on the intention of the speaker or writer, than on the particular technique employed.

A speaker or writer who knows, at the time of his address, that it will reach almost immediately several million persons, is faced with an obviously difficult problem of interpretation. Yet, whatever the difficulty, a good speaker or writer will be conscious of his immediate responsibility to the matter being communicated. He cannot, indeed, feel otherwise, if he is conscious of himself as the source of a particular transmission. His task is the adequate expression of this source, whether it be of feeling, opinion, or information. He will use for this expression the common language, to the limit of his particular skill. That this expression is then given multiple transmission is a next stage, of which he may well be conscious, but which cannot, of its nature, affect the source. The difficulties of expressing this source – difficulties of common experience, convention, and language – are certainly always his concern. But the source cannot in any event be denied, or he denies himself.

Now if on this perennial problem of communication, we impose the idea of masses, we radically alter the position. The conception of persons as masses springs, not from an inability to know them, but from an interpretation of them according to a formula. Here the question of the intention of the transmission makes its decisive return. Our formula can be that of the rational being speaking our language. It can be that of the interested being sharing our common experience. Or – and it is here that 'masses' will operate – it can be that of the mob: gullible, fickle, herd-like, low in taste and habit. The formula, in fact, will proceed from our intention. If our purpose is art, education, the giving of information or opinion, our interpretation will be in terms of the rational and interested being. If, on the other hand, our purpose is manipulation – the persuasion of a large number of people to act, feel, think, know, in certain ways – the convenient formula will be that of the masses.

There is an important distinction to be drawn here between source and agent. A man offering an opinion, a proposal, a feeling, of course normally desires that other persons will accept this, and act or feel in the ways that he defines. Yet such a man may be properly described as a source, in distinction from an agent, whose characteristic is that his expression is subordinated to an undeclared intention. He is an agent, and not a source, because the intention lies elsewhere. In social terms, the agent will normally in fact be a subordinate – of a government, a commercial firm, a newspaper proprietor. Agency, in the simple sense, is necessary in any complex administration. But it is always dangerous unless its function and intention are not only openly declared but commonly approved and controlled. If this is so, the agent becomes a collective source, and he will observe the standards of such expression if what he is required to transmit is such that he can wholly acknowledge and accept it – re-create it in his own person. Where he cannot thus accept it for himself, but allows himself to be persuaded that it is in a fit form for others – presumably inferiors – and that it is his business merely to see that it reaches them effectively, then he is in the bad sense an agent, and what he is doing is inferior to that done by the poorest kind of source. Any practical denial of the relation between conviction and communication, between experience and expression, is morally damaging alike to the individual and to the common language.

Yet it is certainly true, in our society, that many men, many of them intelligent, accept, whether in good or bad faith, so dubious a role and activity. The acceptance in bad faith is a matter for the law, although we have not yet gone very far in working out this necessary common control. The acceptance in good faith, on the other hand, is a matter of culture. It would clearly not be possible unless it appeared to be ratified by a conception of society which relegates the majority of its members to mob-status. The idea of the masses is an expression of this conception, and the idea of mass-communication a comment on its functioning. This is the real danger to democracy, not the existence of effective and powerful means of multiple transmission. It is less a product of democracy than its denial, springing from that half-world of feeling in which we are invited to have our being. Where the principle of democracy is accepted, and yet its full and active practice feared, the mind is lulled into an acquiescence, which is yet not so complete that a fitful conscience, a defensive irony, cannot visit it. 'Democracy would be all right,' we can come to say, 'it is indeed what we personally would prefer, if it were not for the actual people. So, in a good cause if we can find it, in some other if we can not, we will try to get by at a level of communication which our experience and training tell us is inferior. Since the people are as they are, the thing will do.' But it is as well to face the fact that what we are really doing, in such a case, is to cheapen our own experience and to adulterate the common language.

Reference

'Mass and Masses', 'Mass Communication', from Raymond Williams, *Culture and Society 1780–1950*, Chatto & Windus, 1958, Penguin, 1961, pp. 287–294. Reprinted by permission of The Random House Group Limited and printed with permission from *Culture and Society 1780–1950* by Raymond Williams. Copyright © 1983 Columbia University Press.

3

STRUCTURE OF FEELING AND SELECTIVE TRADITION
(1961)

In 'The Analysis of Culture' chapter from his second most celebrated book, The Long Revolution, *Raymond Williams distinguishes three meanings of* culture: *first, the* ideal; *second, the* documentary; *and, third, the* social *– all of which are of value, though the idealisation of universal culture is now very much out of fashion. The documents – writings, pictures, buildings and so on – remaining from the past are the means through which we construct a sense of history interpretatively. The social definition refers to ways of life. Williams is interested in a holistic analysis of culture, that is 'the relation between elements in a whole way of life', which is understood here largely though not entirely as the way of life of a nation.*

Williams also introduces two extremely useful concepts: structure of feeling *and* selective tradition *into his repertoire of cultural analysis. 'Structure of feeling' is Williams's alternative to the idealist notion of the zeitgeist, the spirit of the times. He says 'it is as firm and definite as "structure" suggests, yet it operates in the most delicate and less tangible parts of our activity'.*

'Selective tradition' refers here to how the canon of culture is constructed over time, that educational curricula, most notably, include selections from cultures past and present and, by definition, involve exclusions, work that is no longer thought valuable, if ever it was. This can be related further to feminist and black cultural projects in education and research to question selected traditions and create new ones in which

the selection is from work that was marginalised in its own time and perhaps forgotten, in effect, cultural history 'from below'.

The Analysis of Culture

I

There are three general categories in the definition of culture. There is, first, the 'ideal', in which culture is a state or process of human perfection, in terms of certain absolute or universal values. The analysis of culture, if such a definition is accepted, is essentially the discovery and description, in lives and works, of those values which can be seen to compose a timeless order, or to have permanent reference to the universal human condition. Then, second, there is the 'documentary', in which culture is the body of intellectual and imaginative work, in which, in a detailed way, human thought and experience are variously recorded. The analysis of culture, from such a definition, is the activity of criticism, by which the nature of the thought and experience, the details of the language, form and convention in which these are active, are described and valued. Such criticism can range from a process very similar to the 'ideal' analysis, the discovery of 'the best that has been thought and written in the world', through a process which, while interested in tradition, takes as its primary emphasis the particular work being studied (its clarification and valuation being the principal end in view) to a kind of historical criticism which, after analysis of particular works, seeks to relate them to the particular traditions and societies in which they appeared. Finally, third, there is the 'social' definition of culture, in which culture is a description of a particular way of life, which expresses certain meanings and values not only in art and learning but also in institutions and ordinary behaviour. The analysis of culture, from such a definition, is the clarification of the meanings and values implicit and explicit in a particular way of life, a particular culture. Such analysis will include the historical criticism already referred to, in which intellectual and imaginative works are analysed in relation to particular traditions and societies, but will also include analysis of elements in the way of life that to followers of the other definitions are not 'culture' at all: the organization of production, the structure of the family, the structure of institutions which express or govern social relationships, the characteristic forms through which members of the society communicate. Again, such analysis ranges from an 'ideal' emphasis, the discovery of certain absolute or universal, or at least higher and lower, meanings and values, through the 'documentary' emphasis, in which clarification of a particular way of life is the main end in view, to an emphasis which, from studying particular meanings and values, seeks not so much to compare these, as a way of establishing a scale, but by studying their modes of change to discover certain general 'laws' or 'trends', by which social and cultural development as a whole can be better understood.

It seems to me that there is value in each of these kinds of definition. For it certainly seems necessary to look for meanings and values, the record of creative human activity, not only in art and intellectual work, but also in institutions and forms of behaviour. At the same time, the degree to which we depend, in our knowledge of many past societies and past stages of our own, on the body of intellectual and imaginative work which has retained its major communicative power, makes the description of culture in these terms, if not complete, at least reasonable. It can indeed be argued that since we have 'society' for the broader description, we can properly restrict 'culture' to this more limited reference. Yet there are elements in the 'ideal' definition which also seem to me valuable, and which encourage the retention of the broad reference. I find it very difficult, after the many comparative studies now on record, to identify the process of human perfection with the discovery of 'absolute' values, as these have been ordinarily defined. I accept the criticism that these are normally an extension of the values of a particular tradition or society. Yet, if we call the process, not human perfection, which implies a known ideal towards which we can move, but human evolution, to mean a process of general growth of man as a kind, we are able to recognize areas of fact which the other definitions might exclude. For it seems to me to be true that meanings and values, discovered in particular societies and by particular individuals, and kept alive by social inheritance and by embodiment in particular kinds of work, have proved to be universal in the sense that when they are learned, in any particular situation, they can contribute radically to the growth of man's powers to enrich his life, to regulate his society, and to control his environment. We are most aware of these elements in the form of particular techniques, in medicine, production, and communications, but it is clear not only that these depend on more purely intellectual disciplines, which had to be wrought out in the creative handling of experience, but also that these disciplines in themselves, together with certain basic ethical assumptions and certain major art forms, have proved similarly capable of being gathered into a general tradition which seems to represent, through many variations and conflicts, a line of common growth. It seems reasonable to speak of this tradition as a general human culture, while adding that it can only become active within particular societies, being shaped, as it does so, by more local and temporary systems.

The variations of meaning and reference, in the use of culture as a term, must be seen, I am arguing, not simply as a disadvantage, which prevents any kind of neat and exclusive definition, but as a genuine complexity, corresponding to real elements in experience. There is a significant reference in each of the three main kinds of definition, and, if this is so, it is the relations between them that should claim our attention. It seems to me that any adequate theory of culture must include the three areas of fact to which the definitions point, and conversely that any particular definition, within any of the categories, which would exclude reference to the others, is inadequate. Thus an 'ideal' definition which attempts to abstract the process it describes from its detailed embodiment and shaping by particular societies – regarding man's ideal development as something separate from and even opposed to his 'animal nature' or the satisfaction of material needs – seems to me unacceptable. A 'documentary' definition which sees value only in the written and painted records, and marks this area off from the rest of man's life in society, is equally unacceptable. Again, a 'social' definition, which treats either the general process or the body of art and learning as a mere by-product, a passive reflection of the real interests of the society, seems to me equally wrong. However difficult it may be in practice, we have to try to see the process as a whole, and to relate our particular studies, if not explicitly at least by ultimate reference, to the actual and complex organization.

We can take one example, from analytic method, to illustrate this. If we take a particular work of art, say the *Antigone* of Sophocles, we can analyse it in ideal terms – the discovery of certain absolute values, or in documentary terms – the communication of certain values by certain artistic means. Much will be gained from either analysis, for the first will point to the absolute value of reverence for the dead; the second will point to the expression of certain basic human tensions through the particular dramatic form of chorus and double *kommos*, and the specific intensity of the verse. Yet it is clear that neither analysis is complete. The reverence, as an absolute value, is limited in the play by the terms of a particular kinship system and its conventional obligations – Antigone would do this for a brother but not for a husband. Similarly, the dramatic form, the metres of the verse, not only have an artistic tradition behind them, the work of many men, but can be seen to have been shaped, not only by the demands of the experience, but by the particular social forms through which the dramatic tradition developed. We can accept such extensions of our original analysis, but we cannot go on to accept that, because of the extensions, the value of reverence, or the dramatic form and the specific verse, have meaning only in the contexts to which we have assigned them. The learning of reverence, through such intense examples, passes beyond its context into the general growth of human consciousness. The dramatic form passes beyond its context, and becomes an element in a major and general dramatic tradition, in quite different societies. The play itself, a specific communication, survives the society and the religion which helped to shape it, and can be re-created to speak directly to unimagined audiences. Thus, while we could not abstract the ideal value or the specific document, neither could we reduce these to explanation within the local terms of a particular culture. If we study real relations, in any actual analysis, we reach the point where we see that we are studying a general organization in a particular example, and in this general organization there is no element that we can abstract and separate from the rest. It was certainly an error to suppose that values or art-works could be adequately studied without reference to the particular society within which they were expressed, but it is equally an error to suppose that the social explanation is determining, or that the values and works are mere by-products. We have got into the habit, since we realized how deeply works or values could be determined by the whole situation in which they are expressed, of asking about these relationships in a standard form: 'what is the relation of this art to this society?' But 'society', in this question, is a specious whole. If the art is part of the society, there is no solid whole, outside it, to which, by the form of our question, we concede priority. The art is there, as an activity, with the production, the trading, the politics, the raising of families. To study the relations adequately we must study them actively, seeing all the activities as particular and contemporary forms of human energy. If we take any one of these activities, we can see how many of the others are reflected in it, in various ways according to the nature of the whole organization. It seems likely, also, that the very fact that we can distinguish any particular activity, as serving certain specific ends, suggests that without this activity the whole of the human organization at that place and time could not have been realized. Thus art, while clearly related to the other activities, can be seen as expressing certain elements in the organization which, within that organization's terms, could only have been expressed in this way. It is then not a question of relating the art to the society, but of studying all the activities and their interrelations, without any concession of priority to any one of them we may choose to abstract. If we find, as often, that a particular activity came radically to change the whole organization, we can still not say that it is to this activity that all the others must be related; we can only study the varying ways in which, within the changing organization, the particular activities and their interrelations were affected. Further, since the particular activities will be serving varying and sometimes conflicting ends, the sort of change we must look for will rarely be of a simple kind: elements of persistence, adjustment, unconscious assimilation, active resistance, alternative effort, will all normally be present, in particular activities and in the whole organization.

The analysis of culture, in the documentary sense, is of great importance because it can yield specific evidence about the whole organization within which it was expressed. We cannot say that we know a particular form or period of society, and that we will see how its art and theory relate to it, for until we know these, we cannot really claim to know the society. This is a problem of method, and is mentioned here because a good deal of history has in fact been written on the assumption that the bases of the society, its political, economic, and 'social' arrangements, form the central core of facts, after which the art and theory can be adduced, for marginal illustration or 'correlation'. There has been a neat reversal of this procedure in the histories of literature, art, science, and philosophy, when these are described as developing by their own laws, and then something called the 'background' (what in general history was the central core) is sketched in. Obviously it is necessary, in exposition, to select certain activities for emphasis, and it is entirely reasonable to trace particular lines of development in temporary isolation. But the history of a culture, slowly built up from such particular work, can only be written when the active relations are restored, and the activities seen in a genuine parity. Cultural history must be more than the sum of the particular histories, for it is with the relations between them, the particular forms of the whole organization, that it is especially concerned. I would then define the theory of culture as the study of relationships between elements in a whole way of life. The analysis of culture is the attempt to discover the nature of the organization which is the complex of these relationships. Analysis of particular works or institutions is, in this context, analysis of their essential kind of organization, the relationships which works or institutions embody as parts of the organization as a whole. A key-word, in such analysis, is pattern: it is with the discovery of patterns of a characteristic kind that any useful cultural analysis begins, and it is with the relationships between these patterns, which sometimes reveal unexpected identities and correspondences in hitherto separately considered activities, sometimes again reveal discontinuities of an unexpected kind, that general cultural analysis is concerned.

It is only in our own time and place that we can expect to know, in any substantial way, the general organization. We can learn a great deal of the life of other places and times, but certain elements, it seems to me, will always be irrecoverable. Even those that can be recovered are recovered in abstraction, and this is of crucial importance. We learn each element as a precipitate, but in the living experience of the time every element was in solution, an inseparable part of a complex whole. The most difficult thing to get hold of, in studying any past period, is this felt sense of the quality of life at a particular place and time: a sense of the ways in which the particular activities combined into a way of thinking and living. We can go some way in restoring the outlines of a particular organization of life; we can even recover what Fromm calls the 'social character' or Benedict the 'pattern of culture'. The social character – a valued system of behaviour and attitudes – is taught formally and informally; it is both an ideal and a mode. The 'pattern of culture' is a selection and configuration of interests and activities, and a particular valuation of them, producing a distinct organization, a 'way of life'. Yet even these, as we recover them, are usually abstract. Possibly, however, we can gain the sense of a further common element, which is neither the character nor the pattern, but as it were the actual experience through which these were lived. This is potentially of very great importance, and I think the fact is that we are most conscious of such contact in the arts of a period. It can happen that when we have measured these against the external characteristics of the period, and then allowed for individual variations, there is still some important common element that we cannot easily place. I think we can best understand this if we think of any similar analysis of a way of life that we ourselves share. For we find here a particular sense of life, a particular community of experience hardly needing expression, through which the characteristics of our way of life that an external analyst could describe are in some way passed, giving them a particular and characteristic colour. We are usually most aware of this when we notice the contrasts between generations, who never talk quite 'the same language', or when we read an account of our lives by someone from outside the community, or watch the small differences in style, of speech or behaviour, in someone who has learned our ways yet was not bred in them. Almost any formal description would be too crude to express this nevertheless quite distinct sense of a particular and native style. And if this is so, in a way of life we know intimately, it will surely be so when we ourselves are in the position of the visitor, the learner, the guest from a different generation: the position, in fact, that we are all in, when we study any past period. Though it can be turned to trivial account, the fact of such a characteristic is neither trivial nor marginal; it feels quite central.

The term I would suggest to describe it is *structure of feeling*: it is as firm and definite as 'structure' suggests, yet it operates in the most delicate and least tangible parts of our activity. In one sense, this structure of feeling is the culture of a period: it is the particular living result of all the elements in the general organization. And it is in this respect that the arts of a period, taking these to include characteristic approaches and tones in argument, are of major importance. For here, if anywhere, this characteristic is likely to be expressed; often not consciously, but by the fact that here, in the only example we have of recorded communication that outlives its bearers, the actual living sense, the deep community that makes the communication possible, is naturally drawn upon. I do not mean that the structure of feeling, any more than the social character, is possessed in the same way by the many individuals in the community. But I think it is a very deep and very wide possession, in all actual communities, precisely because it is on it that communication depends.

And what is particularly interesting is that it does not seem to be, in any formal sense, learned. One generation may train its successor, with reasonable success, in the social character or the general cultural pattern, but the new generation will have its own structure of feeling, which will not appear to have come 'from' anywhere. For here, most distinctly, the changing organization is enacted in the organism: the new generation responds in its own ways to the unique world it is inheriting, taking up many continuities, that can be traced, and reproducing many aspects of the organization, which can be separately described, yet feeling its whole life in certain ways differently, and shaping its creative response into a new structure of feeling.

Once the carriers of such a structure die, the nearest we can get to this vital element is in the documentary culture, from poems to buildings and dress-fashions, and it is this relation that gives significance to the definition of culture in documentary terms. This in no way means that the documents are autonomous. It is simply that, as previously argued, the significance of an activity must be sought in terms of the whole organization, which is more than the sum of its separable parts. What we are looking for, always, is the actual life that the whole organization is there to express. The significance of documentary culture is that, more clearly than anything else, it expresses that life to us in direct terms, when the living witnesses are silent. At the same time, if we reflect on the nature of a structure of feeling, and see how it can fail to be fully understood even by living people in close contact with it, with ample material at their disposal, including the contemporary arts, we shall not suppose that we can ever do more than make an approach, an approximation, using any channels.

We need to distinguish three levels of culture, even in its most general definition. There is the lived culture of a particular time and place, only fully accessible to those living in that time and place. There is the recorded culture, of every kind, from art to the most everyday facts: the culture of a period. There is also, as the factor connecting lived culture and period cultures, the culture of the selective tradition.

When it is no longer being lived, but in a narrower way survives in its records, the culture of a period can be very carefully studied, until we feel that we have reasonably clear ideas of its cultural work, its social character, its general patterns of activity and value, and in part of its structure of feeling. Yet the survival is governed, not by the period itself, but by new periods, which gradually compose a tradition. Even most specialists in a period know only a part of even its records. One can say with confidence, for example, that nobody really knows the nineteenth-century novel; nobody has read, or could have read, all its examples, over the whole range from printed volumes to penny serials. The real specialist may know some hundreds; the ordinary specialist somewhat less; educated readers a decreasing number; though all will have clear ideas on the subject. A selective process, of a quite drastic kind, is at once evident, and this is true of every field of activity. Equally, of course, no nineteenth-century reader would have read all the novels; no individual in the society would have known more than a selection of its facts. But everyone living in the period would have had something which, I have argued, no later individual can wholly recover: that sense of the life within which the novels were written, and which we now approach through our selection. Theoretically, a period is recorded; in practice, this record is absorbed into a selective tradition; and both are different from the culture as lived.

It is very important to try to understand the operation of a selective tradition. To some extent, the selection begins within the period itself; from the whole body of activities, certain things are selected for value and emphasis. In general this selection will reflect the organization of the period as a whole, though this does not mean that the values and emphases will later be confirmed. We see this clearly enough in the case of past periods, but we never really believe it about our own. We can take an example from the novels of the last decade. Nobody has read all the English novels of the nineteen-fifties; the fastest reader, giving twenty hours a day to this activity alone, could not do it. Yet it is clear, in print and in education, not only that certain general characteristics of the novel in this period have been set down, but also that a reasonably agreed short list has been made, of what seem to be the best and most relevant works. If we take the list as containing perhaps thirty titles (already a very drastic selection indeed) we may suppose that in fifty years the specialist in the novel of the 1950s will know these thirty, and the general reader will know perhaps five or six. Yet we can surely be quite certain that, once the 1950s have passed, another selective process will be begun. As well as reducing the number of works, this new process will also alter, in some cases drastically, the expressed valuations. It is true that when fifty years have passed it is likely that reasonably permanent valuations will have been arrived at, though these may continue to fluctuate. Yet to any of us who had lived this long process through, it would remain true that elements important to us had been neglected. We would say, in a vulnerable elderly way, 'I don't understand why these young people don't read X any more', but also, more firmly, 'No, that isn't really what it was like; it is your version'. Since any period includes at least three generations, we are always seeing examples of this, and one complicating factor is that none of us stay still, even in our most significant period: many of the adjustments we should not protest against, many of the omissions, distortions and reinterpretations we should accept or not even notice, because we had been part of the change which brought them about. But then, when living witnesses had gone, a further change would occur. The lived culture would not only have been fined down to selected documents; it would be used, in its reduced form, partly as a contribution (inevitably quite small) to the general line of human growth; partly for historical reconstruction; partly, again, as a way of having done with us, of naming and placing a particular stage of the past. The selective tradition thus creates, at one level, a general human culture; at another level, the historical record of a particular society; at a third level, most difficult to accept and assess, a rejection of considerable areas of what was once a living culture.

Within a given society, selection will be governed by many kinds of special interest, including class interests. Just as the actual social situation will largely govern contemporary selection, so the development of the society, the process of historical change, will largely determine the selective tradition. The traditional culture of a society will always tend to correspond to its *contemporary* system of interests and values, for it is not an absolute body of work but a continual selection and interpretation. In theory, and to a limited extent in practice, those institutions which are formally concerned with keeping the tradition alive (in particular the institutions of education and scholarship) are committed to the tradition as a whole, and not to some selection from it according to contemporary interests. The importance of this commitment is very great, because we see again and again, in the workings of a selective tradition, reversals and re-discoveries, returns to work apparently abandoned as dead, and clearly this is only possible if there are institutions whose business it is to keep large areas of past culture, if not alive, at least available. It is natural and inevitable that the selective tradition should follow the lines of growth of a society, but because such growth is complex and continuous, the relevance of past work, in any future situation, is unforeseeable. There is a natural pressure on academic institutions to follow the lines of growth of a society, but a wise society, while ensuring this kind of relevance, will encourage the institutions to give sufficient resources to the ordinary work of preservation, and to resist the criticism, which any particular period may make with great confidence, that much of this activity is irrelevant and useless. It is often an obstacle to the growth of a society that so many academic institutions are, to an important extent, self-perpetuating and resistant to change. The changes have to be made, in new institutions if necessary, but if we properly understand the process of the selective tradition, and look at it over a sufficiently long period to get a real sense of historical change and fluctuation, the corresponding value of such perpetuation will be appreciated.

In a society as a whole, and in all its particular activities, the cultural tradition can be seen as a continual selection and re-selection of ancestors. Particular lines will be drawn, often for as long as a century, and then suddenly with some new stage in growth these will be cancelled or weakened, and new lines drawn. In the analysis of contemporary culture, the existing state of the selective tradition is of vital importance, for it is often true that some change in this tradition – establishing new lines with the past, breaking or re-drawing existing lines – is a radical kind of *contemporary* change. We tend to underestimate the extent to which the cultural tradition is not only a selection but also an interpretation. We see most past work through our own experience, without even making the effort to see it in something like its original terms. What analysis can do is not so much to reverse this, returning a work to its period, as to make the interpretation conscious, by showing historical alternatives; to relate the interpretation to the particular contemporary values on which it rests; and, by exploring the real patterns of the work, confront us with the real nature of the choices we are making. We shall find, in some cases, that we are keeping the work alive because it is a genuine contribution to cultural growth. We shall find, in other cases, that we are using the work in a particular way for our own reasons, and it is better to know this than to surrender to the mysticism of the 'great valuer, Time'. To put on to Time, the abstraction, the responsibility for our own active choices is to suppress a central part of our experience. The more actively all cultural work can be related, either to the whole organization within which it was expressed, or to the contemporary organization within which it is used, the more clearly shall we see its true values. Thus 'documentary' analysis will lead out to 'social' analysis, whether in a lived culture, a past period, or in the selective tradition which is itself a social organization. And the discovery of permanent contributions will lead to the same kind of general analysis, if we accept the process at this level, not as human perfection (a movement towards determined values), but as a part of man's general evolution, to which many individuals and groups contribute. Every element that we analyse will be in this sense active: that it will be seen in certain real relations, at many different levels. In describing these relations, the real cultural process will emerge.

II

Any theoretical account of the analysis of culture must submit to be tested in the course of actual analysis. I propose to take one period, the 1840s in England, and to examine, in the context of its culture, the theoretical methods and concepts I have been discussing.

The first and most striking fact, as we begin to study the 1840s in a direct way, is the degree to which the selective tradition has worked on it. A simple example is in the field of newspapers, for it is customary to think of *The Times* as the characteristic paper of the period, and to draw our ideas of early Victorian journalism from its practice. Certainly *The Times* was the leading daily paper, but the most widely read newspapers in this decade were the Sunday papers, *Dispatch, Chronicle, Lloyd's Weekly* and *News of the World*. These had what we can now recognize as a distinctly 'Sunday paper' selection of news: *Bell's Penny Dispatch* (1842) is sub-titled *Sporting and Police Gazette, and Newspaper of Romance*, and a characteristic headline is 'Daring Conspiracy and Attempted Violation', illustrated by a large woodcut and backed by a detailed story. The total circulation of newspapers of this kind, at the end of the decade, was about 275,000, as compared with a total of 60,000 for the daily papers. If we are examining the actual culture of the period, we must begin from this fact, rather than from the isolation of *The Times* which its continuing importance in a tradition of high politics has brought about.

In the case of literature, the working of the selective tradition is similarly obvious. We think of the period as that of Dickens, Thackeray, Charlotte and Emily Brontë, at the upper levels of the novel, and of Elizabeth Gaskell, Kingsley, Disraeli, in a subsidiary range. We know also, as 'period' authors, Lytton, Marryat, Reade. Dickens, of course, was very widely read at the time. *Pickwick*, to take one example, had sold 40,000 copies a number in periodical publication, and later examples climbed to 70,000 and above. Yet if we look at the other most widely read writers of the period, we find the following list, in order of popularity, given by W. H. Smith's bookstalls, opened in 1848: Lytton, Marryat, G. P. R. James, James Grant, Miss Sinclair, Haliburton, Mrs Trollope, Lever, Mrs Gaskell, Jane Austen. The two most popular series of cheap novels, the Parlour and Railway Libraries (1847 and 1849), included as their leading authors G. P. R. James (47 titles), Lytton (19), Mrs Marsh (16), Marryat (15), Ainsworth (14), Mrs Gore (10), Grant (8), Grattan (8), Maxwell (7), Mrs Trollope (7), Emma Robinson (6), Mayne Reid (6), W. Carleton (6), Jane Austen (6), Mrs Grey (6). A list of titles from these authors gives an idea of the range: *Agincourt, Last Days of Pompeii, Midshipman Easy, Tower of London, Romance of War, Heiress of Bruges, Stories from Waterloo, Refugee in America, Scalp Hunters, Rody the Rover, Pride and Prejudice, The Little Wife*. In 1851 *The Times* commented:

> Every addition to the stock was positively made on the assumption that persons of the better class who constitute the larger portion of railway readers lose their accustomed taste the moment they enter the station.

However this may be, it is clear that the fiction mentioned was not merely the reading of the degraded poor, but that, at least for railway journeys, this was the taste of 'persons of the better class'. If we take the whole range of readers, we must include an author not yet mentioned, G. W. M. Reynolds, of whom *The Bookseller* at his death said that he was 'the most popular writer of our time', having previously said that he had written more and sold in far greater numbers than Dickens. Reynolds was at his height in the new popular periodicals of the 1840s, the *London Journal* and his own *Reynolds' Miscellany*, in which appeared such typical works as *Mysteries of the Inquisition* and *Mysteries of the Court of London*. We must add to this list of the reading of the period what has been described as a 'huge trade' in pornographic books, illegally produced and distributed from the 'filthy cellars of Holywell Street'. We must also add the works of Carlyle, Ruskin, Macaulay, Mill, Thomas Arnold, Pugin, and of Tennyson, Browning, Clough, Matthew Arnold and Rossetti, as selections from a great body of philosophical, historical, religious and poetic writing. The operation of the selective tradition, to compose what we now think of as the characteristic work of the period, hardly needs stressing.

Already, from looking at the documents, we are necessarily led out to the social history of the period. We come to see certain crucial changes in cultural institutions: the effective establishment of a popular Sunday press as the most successful element in journalism; the growth of new kinds of periodical, combining sensational and romantic fiction with recipes, household hints, and advice to correspondents, as opposed to the more sober 'popular education' journals of the previous decade (the *Penny Magazine* ceased publication in 1845, the year in which the new-type *London Journal* began); the coming of cheap fiction, at one level with the 'penny dreadful', from 1841, at another with half-crown and shilling Parlour and Railway Libraries; important changes in the theatre, with the ending of the monopoly of the Patent Theatres in 1843, the development of minor theatres and, from 1849, the rise of the music-halls. Moreover, these changes at the institutional level, in distribution, relate to a variety of causes that take us far out into the whole history of the period. Thus, technical changes (in newspapers, developed steam-printing and rotary presses; in books, ink-blocking on cloth) provided part of the basis of the printed expansion. The railway boom led to new reading needs and, more centrally, to new points of distribution. Yet the kind of people who made use of these technical opportunities must equally attract our attention. There is an important increase, in this decade, in the entry of pure speculators into these profitable businesses: Lloyd and Bell, in newspapers and periodicals, combining (as did Reynolds more seriously) a generalized radicalism with a sharp commercial instinct; or, in the theatre, the essential beginning of the ownership of theatres by men not directly concerned with the drama, but finding commercial opportunity in building and letting to actor-managers and companies, a method that has had a profound effect on English theatrical development. Again, a large part of the impetus to cheap periodical publishing was the desire to control the development of working-class opinion, and in this the observable shift from popular educational journals to family magazines (the latter the immediate ancestors of the women's magazines of our own time) is significant. Respectable schemes of moral and domestic improvement became deeply entangled with the teaching and implication of particular social values, in the interests of the existing class society. These changes, in a wide field, are necessary parts of the real cultural process that we must examine.

As we move into this wider field, we see, of course, that the selective tradition operates here as in the documents. The institutional developments just noted, representing a critical phase in the commercial organization of popular culture, interest us primarily because they relate to a subsequent major trend. So also do developments of a different kind, in the same field; the beginnings of public museums (a limited Bill in 1845), public libraries (limited provisions in 1850), and public parks (allowed from the rates in 1847). The fierce controversy surrounding these innovations (from the charges of extravagance to the anxious pleas that the working people must be 'civilized') tends to drop away, in our minds, according to subsequent interpretations. The complexity we have to grasp, in the field of cultural institutions, is that this decade brought crucial developments in the commercial exploitation of culture, in its valuable popular expansion, and in enlightened public provision. This is the reality that various strands of the selective tradition tend to reduce, seeking always a single line of development.

This is true also of the general political and social history of the period. As I see it, it is dominated by seven features. There is the crucial Free Trade victory in the Repeal of the Corn Laws, in 1846. There is the virtual re-creation of a new-style Tory Party, under Disraeli, with some influence from the ideas of Young England. There is the Chartist movement, among other things a major stage in the development of working-class political consciousness. There is the factory legislation, culminating in the Ten Hours Bill of 1847. There is the complicated story of the punitive Poor Law and the attempts to amend its operation in 1844 and 1847, and, linked with this by Chadwick, the fight for the Public Health Act of 1848. There is the important re-involvement of the churches, in different ways, in social conflict. There is the major expansion in heavy industries and in capital investment, notably in the railways. Other factors might easily be added, but already from these we can observe two points in analysis. First, that these 'factors' compose a single story, though one of great complexity and conflict: several of them are obviously linked, and none of them, in the real life of the period, can be considered in isolation. Second, that each is subject to highly selective interpretation, according to subsequent directions and commitments. The case of Chartism is the most obvious example. Few would now regard it as dangerous and wicked, as it was widely regarded at the time: too many of its principles have been subsequently built into the 'British way of life' for it to be easy openly to agree with Macaulay, for example, that universal suffrage is 'incompatible with the very existence of civilization'. Yet other selective images of the movement remain powerful: that, like the General Strike of 1926, it was a tragic example of 'the wrong way to get change', the right way being the actually succeeding phase; or, again, that it was muddled and even ridiculous, with its oddly mixed supporters and its monster petitions which were simply disregarded. But the fact is that we have no adequate history of Chartism; we have substitutes for such a history, on one or other of the partial versions thrown up by the selective tradition. We see from this, also, the importance of our theoretical observation on one aspect of the working of the selective tradition: that it is not only affected, even governed, by subsequent main lines of growth, but also changes, as it were retrospectively, in terms of subsequent change. The attention now given to the growth of working-class movements in the nineteenth century would have seemed absurd in 1880, and is governed, now, less by the material itself than by the knowledge of the fruition of these movements, or commitment to them. The stress on economic history has a similar basis of retrospective change.

In the case of literature, the working of the selective tradition needs separate examination. To a considerable extent it is true that the work we now know from the 1840s is the best work of the period: that repeated reading, in a variety of situations, has sifted the good from the less good and bad. Yet there are other factors. Mrs Gaskell and probably Disraeli survive by this criterion, but in both their cases there are other affecting elements: in Mrs Gaskell the documentary interest that is useful to a social history preoccupied by this period; in Disraeli, the fact of his subsequent fame in politics. Kingsley's novels, in my view, would not have survived on literary merit at all, but again they have some documentary interest, and his contribution to intellectual history, in Christian Socialism, has been thought important. Thackeray, Dickens, and Charlotte

Brontë survive on strict literary merit, but we see that their best works have carried inferior works that in other authors would have vanished. Emily Brontë would now be said by many critics to be the finest novelist of the decade, but *Wuthering Heights*, for a long time, was carried by the fame of Charlotte, and its major importance, now, is related to changes in twentieth-century literature, moving towards the theme and language of *Wuthering Heights* and away from the main fictional tradition of the decade in which it was written. In verse, we read Tennyson and Browning for their intrinsic interest, though their reputations have violently fluctuated, but I do not think we should read many of Matthew Arnold's 1849 poems if he had not subsequently acquired a reputation of a different kind. We read Carlyle, Ruskin, and Mill because, in spite of obvious faults, they are major writers and additionally belong to living intellectual traditions. But, where we read Thomas Arnold, it is because of his educational importance; where we read Pugin, we have had to remake his significance, with our own emphasis on the relations between art and society; where we read Macaulay, we read perhaps with less interest, not because his ability seems less, but because his way of thinking seems increasingly irrelevant. Thus the selective tradition, which we can be certain will continue to change, is in part the emphasis of works of general value, in part the use of past work in terms of our own growth. The selective tradition which relates to this period is different from the period itself, just as the period culture, consciously studied, is necessarily different from the culture as lived.

The work of conscious reconstruction, and of the selective tradition, tends to specialization of different classes of activity, and we must look now at the area of relations between these, to see if our theoretical description of such relations is valid. We have already seen one important class of relationships, in the field of cultural institutions. Such factors in the society as the class situation (particularly the range of middle-class attitudes to the dissident working class), the technical expansion which followed from the growth of an industrial economy, and the kinds of ownership and distribution natural to such an economy, can be seen to have affected such institutions as the press, book publishing, and the theatre, and the form of these institutions, with the purposes they expressed, had observable effects on some cultural work; new styles in journalism, changes in the novel because of serial publication, some adaptation of material in terms of the new publics being reached. With this kind of interrelation we are reasonably familiar, but it is not the only kind.

A second kind, in which, knowing the society, we look for its direct reflection in cultural work, is, in this period, quite clear. Of the seven general features listed, from the political and social history of the 1840s, all are extensively reflected in contemporary literature, particularly in the novel. If we read only *Mary Barton, Sybil, Coningsby, Dombey and Son, Yeast, Alton Locke, Past and Present*, we move directly into the world of Chartism, factory legislation, the Poor Law, the railways, the involvement of the churches (the decade produced several novels of the crisis of religious belief and affiliation), and the politics of Free Trade and Young England. The interrelation is important, but again it is not the only kind, and indeed, if we limit relationships to this direct description and discussion, we shall find it difficult to estimate even these.

The further area of relations, that we must now examine, is that described and interpreted by such concepts as the social character and the structure of feeling. The dominant social character of the period can be briefly outlined. There is the belief in the value of work, and this is seen in relation to individual effort, with a strong attachment to success gained in these terms. A class society is assumed, but social position is increasingly defined by actual status rather than by birth. The poor are seen as the victims of their own failings, and it is strongly held that the best among them will climb out of their class. A punitive Poor Law is necessary in order to stimulate effort; if a man could fall back on relief, without grave hardship in the form of separation from his family, minimum sustenance, and such work as stone-breaking or oakum-picking, he would not make the necessary effort to provide for himself. In this and a wider field, suffering is in one sense ennobling, in that it teaches humility and courage, and leads to the hard dedication to duty. Thrift, sobriety, and piety are the principal virtues, and the family is their central institution. The sanctity of marriage is absolute, and adultery and fornication are unpardonable. Duty includes helping the weak provided that the help is not of such a kind as to confirm the weakness: condoning sexual error, and comforting the poor, are weaknesses by this definition. Training to the prevailing virtues must be necessarily severe, but there is an obligation to see that the institutions for such training are strengthened.

This can be fairly called the dominant social character of the period, if we look at its characteristic legislation, the terms in which this was argued, the majority content of public writing and speaking, and the characters of the men most admired. Yet, of course, as a social character, it varied considerably in success of transmission, and was subject to many personal variations. The more serious difficulty arises as we look more closely at the period and realize that alternative social characters were in fact active, and that these affected, in important ways, the whole life of the time. A social character is the abstract of a dominant group, and there can be no doubt that the character described – a developed form of the morality of the industrial and commercial middle class – was at this time the most powerful. At the same time, there were other social characters with substantial bases in the society. The aristocratic character was visibly weakening, but its variations – that birth mattered more than money; that work was not the sole social value and that civilization involved play; that sobriety and chastity, at least in young men, were not cardinal virtues but might even be a sign of meanness or dullness – are still alive in the period, all in practice, some in theory. In attitudes to the poor, this character is ambiguous: it includes a stress on charity, as part of one's station, very different from punitive rehabilitation, but also a brutality, a willingness to cut down troublemakers, a natural habit of repression, which again differ from the middle-class attitude. The 1840s are very interesting in this respect, for they show the interaction of different social characters: Tory charity against Whig rehabilitation; brutality and repression against positive civilization through institution. Some of the best criticism of the Whig Poor Law came from Tories with a conscious aristocratic ideal, as most notably in Young England. Brutality and repression are ready, in crisis, but as compared with the twenties and thirties, are being steadily abandoned in favour of positive legislation. Play may be frowned on by the social character, but the decade shows a large increase in light entertainment, from cheap novels to the music-halls. Not only is the dominant social character different, in many ways, from the life lived in its shadow, but alternative social characters lead to the real conflicts of the time. This is a central difficulty of the social character concept, for in stressing a dominant abstraction it seriously underestimates the historical process of change and conflict, which are found even when, as in the 1840s, such a social character is very strong. For we must add another alternative, of major importance: the developing social character of the working class, different in important respects from its competitors. As the victims of repression and punitive rehabilitation, of the gospel of success and the pride of birth, of the real nature of work and the exposure to suffering, working-class people were beginning to formulate alternative ideals. They had important allies from the interaction of the other systems, and could be a major force either in the Corn Laws repeal or in the Factory legislation, when these were sponsored by different sections of the ruling class. But the 1840s show an important development of independent aims, though these are to be realized, mainly, through alliance with other groups. Thus Chartism is an ideal beyond the terms of any dominant group in the society, and is more than an expression of democratic aspirations; is also an assertion of an individual dignity transcending class. The Ten Hours Bill, in working-class minds, was more than a good piece of paternal legislation on work: it was also the claim to leisure, and hence again to a wider life. At the same time, in their own developing organizations, the most radical criticism of all was being made: the refusal of a society based either on birth or on individual success, the conception of a society based on mutual aid and co-operation.

We can then distinguish three social characters operative in the period, and it is with the study of relations between them that we enter the reality of the whole life. All contribute to the growth of the society: the aristocratic ideals tempering the harshness of middle-class ideals at their worst; working-class ideals entering into a fruitful and decisive combination with middle-class ideals at their best. The middle-class social character remains dominant, and both aristocrats and working people, in many respects, come to terms with it. But equally, the middle-class social character as it entered the forties is in many respects modified as the forties end. The values of work and self-help, of social position by status rather than birth, of the sanctity of marriage and the emphasis on thrift, sobriety and charity, are still dominant. But punitive rehabilitation, and the attitudes to weakness and suffering on which it rests, have been, while not rejected, joined by a major ideal of public service, in which the effort towards civilization is actively promoted by a genuine altruism and the making of positive institutions.

This is one level of change, and such analysis is necessary if we are to explore the reality of the social character. In some respects, the structure of feeling corresponds to the dominant social character, but it is also an expression of the interaction described. Again, however, the structure of feeling is not uniform throughout the society; it is primarily evident in the dominant productive group. At this level, however, it is different from any of the distinguishable social characters, for it has to deal not only with the public ideals but with their omissions and consequences, as lived. If we look at the fiction of the forties, we shall see this clearly.

The popular fiction of the periodicals, so carefully studied by Dalziel, is very interesting in this context. At first sight we find what we expect: the unshakeable assumptions of a class society, but with the stress on wealth rather than birth (aristocrats, indeed, being often personally vicious); the conviction that the poor are so by their own faults – their stupidity and depravity stressed, their mutual help ignored; the absolute sanctity of marriage, the manipulation of plot to bring sexual offenders to actual suffering; the fight against weakness, however terrible, as one of the main creators of humble virtue. All this, often consciously didactic, is the direct expression of the dominant social character, and the assumptions tend to be shared by the pious 'improving' fiction (cf. Mrs Tonna's *Helen Fleetwood*) and by the sensational fiction which the improvers condemned. But then we are reminded of the extent to which popular fiction retains older systems of value, often through stereotyped conventions of character. The 'fashionable novel' of high life only became unfashionable late in the decade. The typical hero is sometimes the successful exponent of self-help, but often he is an older type, the cultivated gentleman, the soldier governed by a code of honour, even the man who finds pleasure a blessing and work a curse. To the earlier hero, loss of income and the need to work were misfortunes to be endured; to have a safe fortune was undoubtedly best. The new attitude to work came in only slowly, for understandable reasons. (Ordinary middle-class life was still thought too plain and dull for a really interesting novel.) Further, heroes of either kind are capable of strong overt emotion; they can burst into public tears, or even swoon, as strong men used to do but were soon to do no more. Heroines have more continuity: they are weak, dependent, and shown as glad to be so, and of course they are beautiful and chaste. One interesting factor, obviously related to a continuing general attitude in the period, is that schools, almost without exception, are shown as terrible: not only are they places of temptation and wickedness, mean, cruel and educationally ridiculous, but also they are inferior to the home and family, as a way of bringing up children. This is perhaps the last period in which a majority of English public opinion believed that home education was the ideal. From the sixteenth century, this belief had been gaining ground, and its complete reversal, with the new public-school ethos after Arnold, is of considerable general importance. But the new attitude does not appear in fiction until *Tom Brown's Schooldays* in 1857.

In the popular fiction of the forties, then, we find many marks of older ways of feeling, as well as faithful reproduction of certain standard feelings of the approved social character. We find also, in an interesting way, the interaction between these and actual experience. The crucial point, in this period, is in the field of success and money. The confident assertions of the social character, that success followed effort, and that wealth was the mark of respect, had to contend, if only unconsciously, with a practical world in which things were not so simple. The confidence of this fiction is often only superficial. What comes through with great force is a pervasive atmosphere of instability and debt. A normal element, in these stories, is the loss of fortune, and this is hardly ever presented in terms consistent with the social character: that success or failure correspond to personal quality. Debt and ruin haunt this apparently confident world, and in a majority of cases simply happen to the characters, as a result of a process outside them. At one level, the assumptions of the social character are maintained: if you lose your fortune, you get out of the way – you cannot embarrass yourself or your friends by staying. But this ruthless code is ordinarily confined to subsidiary characters: the parents of hero or heroine. For the people who matter, some other expedient is necessary. It is found, over the whole range of fiction, by two devices: the unexpected legacy, and the Empire. These devices are extremely interesting, both at the level of magic and at the level of developing attitudes necessary to the society.

Magic is indeed necessary, to postpone the conflict between the ethic and the experience. It is widely used in sexual situations, where hero or heroine is tied to an unloved wife or husband, while the true lover waits in the wings. Solutions involving infidelity or breaking the marriage are normally unthinkable, and so a formula is evolved, for standard use: the unsuitable partner is not merely unloved, but alcoholic or insane; at a given point, and after the required amount of resigned suffering, there is a convenient, often spectacular death, in which the unloving partner shows great qualities of care, duty, and piety; and then, of course, the real love can be consummated. In money, the process is similar: legacies, at the crucial moment, turn up from almost anywhere, and fortunes are restored. Nobody has to go against the principle that money is central to success, but equally very few have to be bound by the ethic preached to the poor: that the deserving prosper by effort. This element of cheating marks one crucial point of difference between the social character and the actual structure of feeling.

The use of the Empire is similar but more complex. Of course there were actual legacies, and these eventually changed the self-help ethic, in its simplest form: the magic, at this stage, lay in their timing. But the Empire was a more universally available escape-route: black sheep could be lost in it; ruined or misunderstood heroes could go out and return with fortunes; the weak of every kind could be transferred to it, to make a new life. Often indeed, the Empire is the source of the unexpected legacy, and the two devices are joined. It is clear that the use of the Empire relates to real factors in the society. At a simple level, going out to the new lands could be seen as self-help and enterprise of the purest kinds. Also, in the new lands, there was a great need for labourers, and emigration as a solution to working-class problems was being widely urged, often by the most humane critics of the existing system. In 1840, 90,000 people a year were emigrating, and in 1850 three times as many. In a different way, in terms of capital and trade, the Empire had been one of the levers of industrialization, and was to prove one major way of keeping the capitalist system viable. These factors are reflected in fiction, though not to the same extent as later in the century, when Imperialism had become a conscious policy. Meanwhile, alongside this reflection of real factors, there was the use as magic: characters whose destinies could not be worked out within the system as given were simply put on the boat, a simpler way of resolving the conflict between ethic and experience than any radical questioning of the ethic. This method had the additional advantage that it was consonant with another main element of the structure of feeling: that there could be no general solution to the social problems of the time; there could be only individual solutions, the rescue by legacy or emigration, the resolution by some timely change of heart.

Now the fascinating thing about the structure of feeling as described is that it is present in almost all the novels we now read as literature, as well as in the now disregarded popular fiction. This is true of the reflections and of the magic. Disraeli seems daring in dramatizing the two-nation problem in the love of an aristocrat and a Chartist girl, but Sybil, following the pattern of almost all poor heroines in such situations in the periodicals, is discovered in the end to be 'really' a dispossessed aristocrat. (The uniting of the two nations is in fact, in Disraeli, the combination of agricultural and industrial property, a very sanguine political forecast, and the same pattern is followed in *Coningsby*, where the young aristocrat marries the Lancashire manufacturer's daughter, and is elected for an industrial constituency.) Mrs Gaskell, though refusing the popular fiction that the poor suffered by their own faults, succeeds in *Mary Barton* in compromising working-class organization with murder, and steers all her loved characters to Canada. Kingsley, in *Alton Locke*, sends his Chartist hero to America. And these are the humane critics, in many ways dissenting from the social character, but remaining bound by the structure of feeling.

The same correspondence is evident in novels less concerned with the problems of the society. The novels of Charlotte and Anne Brontë are, in terms of plot and structure of feeling, virtually identical with many stories in the periodicals: the governess-heroine, the insane wife or alcoholic husband, the resolution through resignation, duty, and magic. Dickens, similarly, uses the situations, the feelings, and the magic of periodical fiction again and again.

This connexion between the popular structure of feeling and that used in the literature of the time is of major importance in the analysis of culture. It is here, at a level even more important than that of institutions, that the real relations within the whole culture are made clear: relations that can easily be neglected when only the best writing survives, or when this is studied outside its social context. Yet the connexion must be carefully defined. Often it is simply that in the good novel the ordinary situations and feelings are worked through to their maximum intensity. In other cases, though the framework is retained, one element of the experience floods through the work, in such a way as to make it relevant in its own right, outside the conventional terms. This is true of Elizabeth Gaskell, in the early parts of *Mary Barton*; of Charlotte Brontë, taking lonely personal desire to an intensity that really questions the conventions by which it is opposed; of Dickens, certainly, in that the conventional figure of the orphan, or the child exposed by loss of fortune, comes to transcend the system to which he refers, and to embody many of the deepest feelings in the real experience of the time. These are the creative elements, though the connexion with the ordinary structure of feeling is still clear. The orphan, the exposed child, the lonely governess, the girl from a poor family: these are the figures which express the deepest response to the reality of the way of life. In the ordinary fiction, they were conventional figures; in the literature they emerge carrying an irresistible authenticity, not merely as exemplars of the accidents of the social system, but as expressions of a *general* judgement of the human quality of the whole way of life. Here, in the 1840s, is the first body of fiction (apart from occasional earlier examples, in Godwin and perhaps Richardson) expressing, even through the conventional forms, a radical human dissent. At the level of social character, the society might be confident of its assumptions and its future, but these lonely exposed figures seem to us, at least, the personal and social reality of the system which in part the social character rationalized. Man alone, afraid, a victim: this is the enduring experience. The magic solutions will be grasped at, in many cases, in the end, but the intensity of the central experience is on record and survives them. And it is at this point that we find the link with a novel like *Wuthering Heights*, which rejects so much more of the conventional structure. Here, at a peak of intensity, the complicated barriers of a system of relationships are broken through, finally, by an absolute human commitment. The commitment is realized through death, and the essential tragedy, embodied elsewhere in individual figures who may, by magic, be rescued from it, becomes the form of the whole work. The creative elements in the other fiction are raised to a wholeness which takes the work right outside the ordinary structure of feeling, and teaches a new feeling.

 Art reflects its society and works a social character through to its reality in experience. But also art creates, by new perceptions and responses, elements which the society, as such, is not able to realize. If we compare art with its society, we find a series of real relationships showing its deep and central connexions with the rest of the general life. We find description, discussion, exposition through plot, and experience of the social character. We find also, in certain characteristic forms and devices, evidence of the deadlocks and unsolved problems of the society: often admitted to consciousness for the first time in this way. Part of this evidence will show a false consciousness, designed to prevent any substantial recognition; part again a deep desire, as yet uncharted, to move beyond this. As George Eliot wrote, recording this latter feeling, in 1848:

> The day will come when there will be a temple of white marble, where sweet incense and anthems shall rise to the memory of every man and woman who has had a deep *Ahnung*, a presentiment, a yearning, or a clear vision of the time when this miserable reign of Mammon shall end – when men shall be no longer 'like the fishes of the sea' – society no more like a face one half of which – the side of profession, of lip-faith – is fair and God-like, the other half – the side of deeds and institutions – with a hard old wrinkled skin puckered into the sneer of a Mephistopheles.

Much of the art, much of the magic, of the 1840s, expressed this desire. And at this point we find ourselves moving into a process which cannot be the simple comparison of art and society, but which must start from the recognition that all the acts of men compose a general reality within which both art and what we ordinarily call society are comprised. We do not now compare the art with the society; we compare both with the whole complex of human actions and feelings. We find some art expressing feelings which the society, in its general character, could not express. These may be the creative responses which bring new feelings to light. They may be also the simple record of omissions: the nourishment or attempted nourishment of human needs unsatisfied. An element in the 1840s that we have not yet noted shows this kind of evidence clearly. The characteristic verse of Tennyson and Arnold in the decade, from *Morte d'Arthur* and *Ulysses* to *The Forsaken Merman*, is a late phase of that part of the Romantic movement which sought to express, through other places and other times, a richness not evident in ordinary contemporary life. That this poetry is weaker than that of Coleridge and Keats, which it formally resembles, seems to mark a further and perhaps disastrous moving away from the energies of the actual life; yet the impulse is characteristic, and in strength and weakness indicates experience that study of the society alone could not adduce. Then again we can link with this the general romanticizing of the past, at a serious level in Carlyle, at a popular level in the form of the historical novel, again a Romantic creation and at a high level of production and popularity in the early 1840s, beginning to fade in the later years. Linking the weak romanticism of exotic colour and richness with the strong romanticism of the vision of a fuller human life is the sense of omission, from the bleak reality and dominant ideals of the period, of certain basic human needs. The magic and tinsel of illegitimate theatre and music-hall, the ornate furnishing, the Gothicism in architecture, belong in the same category. And 1848, the last year of the Chartists, is also the first year of the Pre-Raphaelite Brotherhood. It is not that we cannot relate this art to the rest of the general life, but that we see it, by its very contrast with the main features of the society, as an element of the general human organization which found expression in this specific way, and which must be set in parity with the other elements, if we are to analyse the culture as a whole.

Finally, as we look at the whole period, we recognize that its creative activities are to be found, not only in art but, following the main lines of the society, in industry and engineering, and, questioning the society, in new hinds of social institution. We cannot understand any period of the Industrial Revolution if we fail to recognize the real miracle that was being worked, by human skill and effort. Again and again, even by critics of the society, the excitement of this extraordinary release of man's powers was acknowledged and shared. The society could not have been acceptable to anybody, without that. 'These are our poems', Carlyle said in 1842, looking at one of the new locomotives, and this element, now so easily overlooked, is central to the whole culture.

In a quite different way, in new institutions, the slow creation of different images of community, different forms of relationship, by the newly-organizing workers and by middle-class reformers, marks a reaching-out of the mind of comparable importance. We cannot understand even the creative part of a culture without reference to activities of this kind, in industry and institutions, which are as strong and as valuable an expression of direct human feeling as the major art and thought.

To make a complete analysis of the culture of the 1840s would go far beyond the scope and intention of this chapter. I have simply looked at this fascinating decade as a way of considering what any such analysis involves. I have only indicated the ways in which it might begin, but I think it is clear that analysis of the kind described is feasible, and that the exploration of relations between apparently separate elements of the way of life can be illuminating. In any event, as we follow the analysis through, and as we see the ways in which it could be continued, we can decide for ourselves the extent to which the main theoretical approach, and the theoretical distinctions which follow from it, are valid.

Reference

From Raymond Williams, *The Long Revolution*, Chatto & Windus, 1961. Penguin, 1965, pp. 64–88. Reprinted with kind permission by The Random House Group Limited and Parthian Books/the Library of Wales.

4

ADVERTISING – THE MAGIC SYSTEM (1960/1969)

'Advertising – The Magic System' was originally written as a chapter for inclusion in The Long Revolution *but, instead, it was published in the journal that Williams was closely associated with,* New Left Review. *The text printed here includes an addendum written for the now defunct broadcasting magazine,* The Listener, *in 1969. Although Williams argues controversially perhaps that advertising is the official art of the twentieth century, more importantly still, he notes how advertising discourse invades other discourses and obliterates a proper distinction between editorial content and commercial speech.*

1. History

It is customary to begin even the shortest account of the history of advertising by recalling the three thousand year old papyrus from Thebes, offering a reward for a runaway slave, and to go on to such recollections as the crier in the streets of Athens, the paintings of gladiators, with sentences urging attendance at their combats, in ruined Pompeii, and the fly-bills on the pillars of the Forum in Rome. This pleasant little ritual can be quickly performed, and as quickly forgotten: it is, of course, altogether too modest. If by advertising we mean what was meant by Shakespeare and the translators of the Authorized Version—the processes of taking or giving notice of something—it is as old as human society, and some pleasant recollections from the Stone Age could be quite easily devised.

The real business of the historian of advertising is more difficult: to trace the development from processes of specific attention and information to an institutionalized system of commercial information and persuasion; to relate this to changes in society and in the economy: and to trace changes in method in the context of changing organizations and intentions.

The spreading of information, by the crier or by handwritten and printed broadsheets, is known from all periods of English society. The first signs of anything more organized come in the seventeenth century, with the development of news books, mercuries and newspapers. Already certain places, such as St Paul's in London, were recognized as centres for the posting of specific bills, and the extension of such posting to the new printed publications was a natural development. The material of such advertisements ranged from offers and wants in personal service, notices of the publication of books, and details of runaway servants, apprentices, horses and dogs, to announcements of new commodities available at particular shops, enthusiastic announcements of remedies and specifics, and notices of the public showing of monsters, prodigies and freaks. While the majority were the simple, basically factual and specific notices we now call 'classified', there were also direct recommendations, as here, from 1658:

> That Excellent, and by all Physicians, approved China drink, called by the Chineans Tcha, by other nations *Tay* alias *Tee*, is sold at the Sultaness Head Cophee-House in Sweeting's Rents, by the Royal Exchange, London.

Mention of the physicians begins that process of extension from the conventional recommendations of books as 'excellent' or 'admirable' and the conventional adjectives which soon become part of the noun, in a given context (as in my native village, every dance is a Grand Dance). The most extravagant early extensions were in the field of medicines, and it was noted in 1652, of the writers of copy in news-books:

> There is never a mountebank who, either by professing of chymistry or any other art drains money from the people of the nation but these arch-cheats have a share in the booty—because the fellow cannot lye sufficiently himself he gets one of these to do't for him.

Looking up, in the 1950s, from the British Dental Association's complaints of misleading television advertising of toothpastes, we can recognize the advertisement, in 1660, of a 'most Excellent and Approved DENTIFRICE', which not only makes the teeth 'white as Ivory', but

> being constantly used, the Parties using it are never troubled with the Tooth-ache. It fastens the Teeth, sweetens the Breath, and preserves the Gums and Mouth from Cankers and Imposthumes.

Moreover

> the right are only to be had at: Thomas Rookes, Stationer, at the Holy Lamb at the east end of St Paul's Church, near the School, in sealed papers at 12d the paper.

In the year of the Plague, London was full of

> SOVEREIGN Cordials against the Corruption of the Air.

These did not exactly succeed, but a long and profitable trade, and certain means of promoting it, were now firmly established.

With the major growth of newspapers, from the 1690s, the volume of advertisements notably increased. The great majority of them were still of the specific 'classified' kind, and were grouped in regular sections of the paper or magazine. Ordinary household goods were rarely advertised; people knew where to get these. But, apart from the wants and the runaways, new things, from the latest book or play to new kinds of luxury or 'cosmatick' made their way through these columns. By and large, it was still only in the pseudo-medical and toilet advertisements that persuasion methods were evident. The announcements were conventionally printed, and there was hardly any illustration. Devices of emphasis—the hand, the asterisk, the NB—can be found, and sailing announcements had small woodcuts of a ship, runaway notices similar cuts of a man looking back over his shoulder. But, in the early eighteenth century, these conventional figures became too numerous, and most newspapers banned them. The manufacturer of a 'Spring Truss' who illustrated his device, had few early imitators.

A more general tendency was noted by Johnson in 1758:

> Advertisements are now so numerous that they are very negligently perused, and it is therefore become necessary to gain attention by magnificence of promises and by eloquence sometimes sublime and sometimes pathetick. Promise, large promise, is the soul of an advertisement. I remember a washball that had a quality truly wonderful—it gave *an exquisite edge to the razor!* The trade of advertising is now so near to perfection that it is not easy to propose any improvement.

This is one of the earliest of 'gone about as far as they can go' conclusions on advertisers, but Johnson, after all, was sane. Within the situation he knew, of newspapers directed to a small public largely centred on the coffee-houses, the natural range was from private notices (of service wanted and offered, of things lost, found, offered and needed) through shopkeepers' information (of actual goods in their establishments) to puffs for occasional and marginal products. In this last kind, and within the techniques open to them, the puffmen had indeed used, intensively, all the traditional forms of persuasion, and of cheating and lying. The mountebank and the huckster had got into print, and, while the majority of advertisements remained straightforward, the influence of this particular group was on its way to giving 'advertising' a more specialized meaning.

2. Development

There is no doubt that the Industrial Revolution, and the associated revolution in communications, fundamentally changed the nature of advertising. But the change was not simple, and must be understood in specific relation to particular developments. It is not true, for example, that with the coming of factory production large-scale advertising became economically necessary. By the 1850s, a century after Johnson's comment, and with Britain already an industrial nation, the advertising pages of the newspapers, whether *The Times* or the *News of the World*, were still basically similar to those in eighteenth-century journals, except that there were more of them, that they were more closely printed, and that there were certain exclusions (lists of whores, for example, were no longer advertised in the *Morning Post*).

The general increase was mainly due to the general growth in trade, but was aided by the reduction and then abolition of a long-standing Advertisement Tax. First imposed in 1712, at one shilling an announcement, this had been a means, with the Stamp Duty, of hampering the growth of newspapers, which successive Governments had good reason to fear. By the time of the worst repression, after the Napoleonic Wars, Stamp Duty was at 4d a sheet, and Advertisement Tax at 3s 6d. In 1833, Stamp Duty was reduced to 1d, and Advertisement Tax to 1s 6d. A comparison of figures for 1830 and 1838 shows the effect of this reduction: the number of advertisements in papers on the British mainland in the former year was 877,972; by the later date is stood at 1,491,991. Then in 1853 the Advertisement Tax was abolished, and in 1855 the Stamp Duty. The rise in the circulation of newspapers, and in the number of advertisements, was then rapid.

Yet still in the 1850s advertising was mainly of a classified kind, in specified parts of the publication. It was still widely felt, in many lands of trade, that (as a local newspaper summarized the argument in 1859)

> it is not *respectable*. Advertising is resorted to for the purposes of introducing inferior articles into the market.

Rejecting this argument, the newspaper (*The Eastbourne Gazette and Fashionable Intelligencer*) continued:

> Competition is the soul of business, and what fairer or more legitimate means of competition can be adopted than the availing oneself of a channel to recommend goods to public notice which is open to all? Advertising is an open, fair, legitimate and respectable means of competition; bearing upon its face the impress of free-trade, and of as much advantage to the consumer as the producer.

The interesting thing is not so much the nature of this argument, but that, in 1859, it still had to be put in quite this way. Of course the article concluded by drawing attention to the paper's own advertising rates, but even then, to get the feel of the whole situation, we have to look at the actual advertisements flanking the article. Not only are they all from local tradesmen, but their tone is still eighteenth-century, as for example:

> To all who pay cash and can appreciate
>
> GOOD AND FINE TEAS
>
> CHARLES LEA
>
> Begs most respectfully to solicit a trial of his present stock which has been selected with the greatest care, and paid for before being cleared from the Bonded warehouses in London
>
> ...

In all papers, this was still the usual tone, but, as in the eighteenth century, one class of product attracted different methods. Probably the first nationally advertised product was Warren's Shoe Blacking, closely followed by Rowland's Macassar Oil (which produced the counter-offensive of the antimacassar), Spencer's Chinese Liquid Hair Dye, and Morison's Universal Pill. In this familiar field, as in the eighteenth century, the new advertising was effectively shaped, while for selling cheap books the practice of including puffs in announcements was widely extended. Warren's Shoe Blacking had a drawing of a cat spitting at its own reflection, and back verses were widely used:

> The goose that on our Ock's green shore
>
> Thrives to the size of Albatross
>
> Is twice the goose it was before
>
> When washed with Neighbour Goodman's sauce.

Commercial purple was another writing style, especially for pills:

> The spring and fall of the leaf has been always remarked as the periods when disease, if it be lurking in the system, is sure to show itself. (Parr's Life Pills, 1843).

The manner runs back to that of the eighteenth-century hucksters and mountebanks, but what is new is its scale. The crowned heads of Europe were being signed up for testimonials (the Tsar of all the Russias took and recommended Revalenta Arabica, while the

Balm of Syriacum, a 'sovereign remedy for both bodily and mental decay', was advertised as used in Queen Victoria's household). Holloway, of course a 'Professor', spent £5,000 a year, in the 1840s, spreading his Universal Ointment, and in 1855 exceeded £30,000.

Moreover, with the newspaper public still limited, the puffmen were going on the streets. Fly-posting, on every available space, was now a large and organized trade, though made hazardous by rival gangs (paste for your own, blacking for the others). It was necessary in 1837 to pass a London act prohibiting posting without the owner's consent (it proved extremely difficult to enforce). In 1862 came the United Kingdom Billposters Association, with an organized system of special hoardings, which had become steadily more necessary as the flood of paste swelled. Handbills ('throwaways') were distributed in the streets of Victorian London with extraordinary intensity of coverage; in some areas a walk down one street would collect as many as two hundred different leaflets. Advertising vans and vehicles of all sorts, such as the seven-foot lath-and-plaster Hat in the Strand, on which Carlyle commented, crowded the streets until 1853, when they were forbidden. Hundreds of casual labourers were sent out with placards and sandwich boards, and again in 1853 had to be officially removed from pavement to gutter. Thus the streets of Victorian London bore increasingly upon their face 'the impress of free trade', yet still, with such methods largely reserved to the sellers of pills, adornments and sensational literature, the basic relation between advertising and production had only partly changed. Carlyle said of the hatter, whose 'whole industry is turned to *persuade* us that he has made' better hats, that 'the quack has become God'. But as yet, on the whole, it was only the quack.

The period between the 1850s and the end of the century saw a further expansion in advertising, but still mainly along the lines already established. After the 1855 abolition of Stamp Duty, the circulation of newspapers rapidly increased, and many new ones were successfully founded. But the attitude of the Press to advertising, throughout the second half of the century, remained cautious. In particular, editors were extremely resistant to any break-up in the column layout of their pages, and hence to any increase in size of display type. Advertisers tried in many ways to get round this, but with little success.

As for products mainly advertised, the way was still led by the makers of pills, soaps and similar articles. Beecham's and Pears are important by reason of their introduction of the catch-phrase on a really large scale; 'Worth a Guinea a Box' and 'Good morning! Have you used Pears' Soap?' passed into everyday language. Behind this familiar vanguard came two heavily advertised classes: the patent food, which belongs technically to this period, and which by the end of the century had made Bovril, Hovis, Nestlé, Cadbury, Fry and Kellogg into 'household names'; and new inventions of a more serious kind, such as the sewing-machine, the camera, the bicycle and the typewriter. If we add the new department-stores, towards the end of the century, we have the effective range of general advertising in the period, and need only note that in method the patent foods followed the patent medicines, while the new appliances varied between genuine information and the now familiar technique of slogan and association.

The pressure on newspapers to adapt to techniques drawn from the poster began to be successful from the 1880s. The change came first in the illustrated magazines, with a crop of purity nudes and similar figures; the Borax nude, for example, dispelling Disease and Decay; girls delighted by cigarettes or soap or shampoos. The poster industry, with its organized hoardings, was able from 1867 to use large lithographs, and Pears introduced the 'Bubbles' poster in 1887. A mail-order catalogue used the first colour advertisement, of a rug. Slowly, a familiar world was forming, and in the first years of the new century came the coloured electric sign. The newspapers, with Northcliffe's *Daily Mail* in the lead, dropped their columns rule, and allowed large type and illustrations. It was noted in 1897 that '*The Times* itself' was permitting 'advertisements in type which three years ago would have been considered fit only for the street hoardings', while the front page of the *Daily Mail* already held rows of drawings of rather bashful women in combinations. Courtesy, Service and Integrity, as part of the same process, acquired the dignity of large-type abstractions. The draper, the grocer and their suppliers had followed the quack.

To many people, yet again, it seemed that the advertisers had 'gone about as far as they can go'. For many people, also, it was much too far. A society for Checking the Abuses of Public Advertising (SCAPA) had been formed in 1898, and of course had been described by the United Bill Posters Association as 'super-sensitive faddists'. SCAPA had local successes, in removing or checking some outdoor signs, and the 1890s saw other legislation: prohibiting uniform for sandwich-men (casual labourers, dressed as the Royal Marine Light Infantry or some other regiment, had been advertising soaps and pills); regulating skyline and balloon advertisements; restricting flashing electric signs, which had been blamed for street accidents. It is a familiar situation, this running fight between traditional standards (whether the familiar layout of newspapers or respect for building and landscape) and the vigorous inventiveness of advertisers (whether turning hoardings into the 'art-galleries of the people', or putting an eight-ton patent food sign halfway up the cliffs of Dover). Indeed ordinary public argument about advertising has stuck at this point, first clarified in the 1890s with 'taste' and 'the needs of commerce' as adversaries. In fact, however, even as this battle was raging, the whole situation was being transformed, by deep changes in the economy.

3. Transformation

The strange fact is, looking back, that the great bulk of products of the early stages of the factory system had been sold without extensive advertising, which had grown up mainly in relation to fringe products and novelties. Such advertising as there was, of basic articles, was mainly by shopkeepers, drawing attention to the quality and competitive pricing of the goods they stocked. In this comparatively simple phase of competition, large-scale advertising and the brand-naming of goods were necessary only at the margin, or in genuinely new things. The real signs of change began to appear in the 1880s and 1890s, though they can only be correctly interpreted when seen in the light of the fully developed 'new' advertising of the period between the wars.

The formation of modern advertising has to be traced, essentially, to certain characteristics of the new 'monopoly' (corporate) capitalism, first clearly evident in this same period of the end and turn of the nineteenth century. The Great Depression which in general dominated the period from 1875 to the middle 1890s (though broken by occasional recoveries and local strengths) marked the turning point between two modes of industrial organization and two basically different approaches to distribution. After the Depression, and its big falls in prices, there was a more general and growing fear of productive capacity, a marked tendency to reorganize industrial ownership into larger units and combines, and a growing desire, by different methods, to organize and where possible control the market. Among the means of achieving the latter purposes, advertising on a new scale, and applied to an increasing range of products, took an important place.

Modern advertising, that is to say, belongs to the system of market-control which, at its full development, includes the growth of tariffs and privileged areas, cartel-quotas, trade campaigns, price-fixing by manufacturers, and that form of economic imperialism which assured certain markets overseas by political control of their territories. There was a concerted expansion of export advertising, and at home the biggest advertising campaign yet seen accompanied the merger of several tobacco firms into the Imperial Tobacco Company, to resist American competition. In 1901, a 'fabulous sum' was offered for the entire eight pages of *The Star*, by a British tobacco advertiser, and when this was refused four pages were taken, a 'world's record', to print 'the most costly, colossal and convincing advertisement ever used in an evening newspaper the wide world o'er'. Since the American firms retaliated, with larger advertisements of their own, the campaign was both heavy and prolonged. This can be taken as the first major example of a new advertising situation.

That this period of fundamental change in the economy is the key to the emergence of full-scale modern advertising is shown also by radical changes within the organization of advertising itself. From the eighteenth century, certain shops had been recognized as collecting agencies for advertisements, on behalf of newspapers. In the nineteenth century, this system (which still holds today for some classified advertisements) was extended to the buying of space by individual agents, who then sold it to advertisers. With the growth in the volume of advertising, this kind of space-selling, and then a more developed system of space-brokerage, led to a growth of importance in the agencies, which still, however, were virtually agents of the Press, or at most intermediaries. Gradually, and with increasing emphasis from the 1880s, the agencies began to change their functions, offering advice and service to manufacturers, though still having space to sell for the newspapers. By the turn of the century, the modern system had emerged: newspapers had their own advertising managers, who advanced quite rapidly in status from junior employees to important executives, while the agencies stopped selling space, and went over to serving and advising manufacturers, and booking space after a campaign had been agreed. In 1900 the Advertisers Protection Society, later the Incorporated Society of British Advertisers, was formed: partly to defend advertising against such attacks as those of SCAPA, partly to bring pressure on newspapers to publish their sales figures, so that campaigns might be properly planned. Northcliffe, after initial hesitations about advertising (he had wanted to run *Answers* without it), came to realize its possibilities as a new basis for financing newspapers. He published his sales figures, challenged his rivals to do the same, and in effect created the modern structure of the Press as an industry, in close relation to the new advertising. In 1917 the Association of British Advertising Agents was founded, and in 1931, with the founding of the Audit Bureau of Circulations, publishing audited net sales, the basic structure was complete.

It is in this same period that we hear first, with any emphasis, of advertising as a profession, a public service, and a necessary part of the economy. A further aspect of the reorganization was a more conscious and more serious attention to the 'psychology of advertising'. As it neared the centre of the economy, it began staking its claims to be not only a profession, but an art and a science.

The half-century between 1880 and 1930, then, saw the full development of an organized system of commercial information and persuasion, as part of the modern distributive system in conditions of large-scale capitalism. Although extended to new kinds of product, advertising drew, in its methods, on its own history and experience. There is an obvious continuity between the methods used to sell pills and washballs in the eighteenth century ('promise, large promise, a quality truly wonderful') and the methods used in the twentieth century to sell anything from a drink to a political party. In this sense, it is true to say that all commerce has followed the quack. But if we look at advertising before, say, 1914, its comparative crudeness is immediately evident. The 'most costly, colossal and convincing advertisement' of 1901 shows two badly-drawn men in tails, clinking port-glasses between announcements that the cigarettes are five a penny, and the slogan ('The Englishman's Toast—Don't be gulled by Yankee bluff, support John Bull with every puff') is in minute type by comparison with 'Most Costly' and 'Advertisement'. Play on fear of illness was of course normal, as it had been throughout quack advertising, and there were simple promises of attractiveness and reputation if particular products were used. But true 'psychological' advertising is very little in evidence before the First War, and where it is its techniques both in appeal and in draughtsmanship and layout, are crude. Appropriately enough, perhaps, it was in the war itself, when now not a market but a nation had to be controlled and organized, yet in democratic conditions and without some of the older compulsions, that new kinds of persuasion were developed and applied. Where the badly-drawn men with their port and gaspers belong to an old world, such a poster as 'Daddy, what did YOU do in the Great War' belongs to the new. The drawing is careful and detailed: the curtains, the armchair, the grim numb face of the father, the little girl on his knee pointing to her open picture-book, the boy at his feet intent on his toy-soldiers. Alongside the traditional appeals to patriotism lay this kind of entry into basic personal relationships and anxieties. Another poster managed to suggest that a man who would let down his country would also let down his sweetheart or his wife.

The pressures, of course, were immense: the needs of the war, the needs of the economic system. We shall not understand advertising if we keep the argument at the level of appeals to taste and decency, which advertisers should respect. The need to control nominally free men, like the need to control nominally free customers, lay very deep in the new kind of society. Kitchener, demanding an Army, was as startled by the new methods as many a traditional manufacturer by the whole idea of advertising, which he associated with dubious products. In both cases, the needs of the system dictated the methods, and traditional standards and reticences were steadily abandoned when ruin seemed the only alternative.

Slowly, after the war, advertising turned from the simple proclamation and reiteration, with simple associations, of the earlier respectable trade, and prepared to develop, for all kinds of product, the old methods of the quack and the new methods of psychological warfare. The turn was not even yet complete, but the tendencies, from the twenties, were evident. Another method of organizing the market, through consumer credit, had to be popularized, and in the process changed from the 'never-never', which was not at all respectable, to the primly respectable 'hire-purchase' and the positively respectable 'consumer credit'. By 1933, a husband had lost his wife because he had failed to take this 'easy way' of providing a home for her. Meanwhile Body Odour, Iron Starvation, Night Starvation, Listlessness and similar disabilities menaced not only personal health, but jobs, marriages and social success.

These developments, of course, produced a renewed wave of criticism of advertising, and, in particular, ridicule of its confident absurdities. In part this was met by a now standard formula: 'one still hears criticism of advertising, but it is not realized how much has been done, within the profession, to improve it' (for example, a code of ethics, in 1924, pledging the industry, *inter alia* 'to tell the advertising story simply and without exaggeration and to avoid even a tendency to mislead'. If advertisers write such pledges, who then writes the advertisements?). The 'super-sensitive faddists' were rediscovered, and the 'enemies of free enterprise'. Proposals by Huxley, Russell, Leavis, Thompson and others, that children should be trained to study advertisements critically, were described, in a book called *The Ethics of Advertising*, as amounting to 'cynical manipulation of the infant mind'.

But the most significant reply to the mood of critical scepticism was in the advertisements themselves: the development of a knowing, sophisticated, humorous advertising, which acknowledged the scepticism and made claims either casual and offhand or so ludicrously exaggerated as to include the critical response (for example, the Guinness advertisements, written by Dorothy Sayers, later a critic of advertising). Thus it became possible to 'know all the arguments' against advertising, and yet accept or write pieces of charming or amusing copy.

One sustained special attack, on an obviously vulnerable point, was in the field of patent medicines. A vast amount of misleading and dangerous advertising of this kind had been repeatedly exposed, and eventually, by Acts of 1939 and 1941, and by a Code of Standards in 1950, the advertisement of cures for certain specified diseases, and a range of misleading devices, was banned. This was a considerable step forward, in a limited field, and the Advertising Association was among its sponsors. If we remember the history of advertising, and how the sellers of ordinary products learned from the quack methods that are still used in less obviously dangerous fields, the change is significant. It is like nothing so much as the newly-crowned Henry the Fifth dismissing Falstaff with contempt. Advertising had come to power, at the centre of the economy, and it had to get rid of the disreputable friends of its youth: it now both wanted and needed to be respectable.

4. Advertising in Power

Of the coming to power there was now no question. Estimates of expenditure in the inter-war years vary considerably, but the lowest figure, for direct advertising in a single year, is £85,000,000 and the highest £200,000,000. Newspapers derived half their income from advertising, and almost every industry and service, outside the old professions, advertised extensively. With this kind of weight behind it, advertising was and knew itself to be a solid sector of the establishment.

Some figures from 1935 are interesting, showing advertising expenditure as a proportion of sales:

Table 4.1

Proprietary medicines	29.4%
Toilet goods	21.3%
Soaps, polishes etc	14.1%
Tobacco	9.3%
Petrol and oil	8.2%
Cereals, jams, biscuits	5.9%
Sweets	3.2%
Beer	1.8%
Boots and Shoes	1.0%
Flour	0.5%

The industry's connections with its origins are evident: the three leading categories are those which pioneered advertising of the modern kind. But more significant, perhaps, is that such ordinary things as boots, shoes and flour should be in the table at all. This, indeed, is the new economy, deriving not so much from the factory system and the growth of communications, as from an advanced system of capitalist production, distribution and market control.

Alongside the development of new kinds of appeal came new media. Apart from such frills as sky-writing, there was commercial radio, not yet established in Britain (though the pressure was there) but begun elsewhere in the 1920s and beamed to Britain from the 1930s. Commercial television, in the 1950s, got through fairly easily. Among new methods, in this growth, are the product jingle, begun in commercial radio and now reaching classic status, and the open alliance between advertisers and apparently independent journalists and broadcasters. To build a reputation as an honest reporter, and then use it either openly to recommend a product or to write or speak about it alongside an advertisement for it, as in the evening-paper 'special supplements', became commonplace. And what was wrong? After all, the crowned heads of Europe, and many of our own Ladies, had been selling pills and soaps for years. The extension to political advertising, either direct or by pressure-groups also belongs, in its extensive phase, to this period of establishment; in the 1950s it has been running at a very high rate indeed.

The only check, in fact, to this rapidly expanding industry was during the last war, though this was only partial and temporary, and the years since the war, and especially the 1950s, have brought a further spectacular extension. It is ironic to look back at a book published in wartime, by one of the best writers on advertising, Denys Thompson, and read this:

> A second reason for these extensive extracts is that advertising as we know it may be dispensed with, after the war. We are getting on very well with a greatly diminished volume of commercial advertising in wartime, and it is difficult to envisage a return to the 1919–1939 conditions in which publicity proliferated.

Mr Thompson, like Dr Johnson two centuries earlier, is a sane man, but it is never safe to conclude that puffing has reached its maximum distension. The history, rightly read, points to a further major growth, and to more new methods. The highly organized field of market study, motivation research, and retained sociologists and psychologists, is extremely formidable, and no doubt has many surprises in store for us. Talent of quite new kinds is hired with increasing ease. And there is one significant development which must be noted in conclusion: the extension of organized publicity.

'Public Relations'

Advertising was developed to sell goods, in a particular kind of economy. Publicity has been developed to sell persons, in a particular kind of cultures. The methods are often basically similar: the arranged incident, the 'mention', the advice on branding, packaging and a good 'selling line'. I remember being told by a man I knew at university (he had previously explained how useful, to his profession as an advertiser, had been his training in the practical criticism of advertisements) that advertisements you booked and paid for were really old stuff; the real thing was what got through as ordinary news. This seems to happen now with goods: 'product centenaries', for example. But with persons it is even more extensive. It began in entertainment, particularly with film actors, and it is still in this field that it does most of its work. It is very difficult to pin down, because the borderline between the item or photograph picked up in the ordinary course of journalism and broadcasting, and the similar item or photograph that has been arranged and paid for, either directly or through special hospitality by a publicity agent, is obviously difficult to draw. Enough stories get through, and are even boasted about, to indicate that the paid practice is extensive, though payment, except to the agent, is usually in hospitality (if that word can be used) or in kind. Certainly, readers of newspapers should be aware that the 'personality' items, presented as ordinary news stories or gossip, will often have been paid for, in one way or another, in a system that makes straightforward advertising, by comparison, look respectable. Nor is this confined to what is called 'show business'; it has certainly entered literature, and it has probably entered politics.

The extension is natural, in a society where selling, by any effective means, has become a primary ethic. The spectacular growth of advertising, and then its extension to apparently independent reporting, has behind it not a mere pressure-group, as in the days of the quacks, but the whole impetus of a society. It can then be agreed that we have come a long way from the papyrus of the runaway slave and the shouts of the town-crier: that what we have to look at is an organized and extending system, at the centre of our national life.

5. The System

In the last hundred years, then, advertising has developed from the simple announcements of shopkeepers and the persuasive arts of a few marginal dealers into a major part of capitalist business organization. This is important enough, but the place of advertising in society goes far beyond this commercial context. It is increasingly the source of finance for a whole range of general communication, to the extent that in 1960 our majority television service and almost all our newspapers and periodicals could not exist without it. Further, in the last forty years and now at an increasing rate, it has passed the frontier of the selling of goods and services and has become involved with the teaching of social and personal values; it is also rapidly entering the world of politics. Advertising is also, in a sense, the official art of modern capitalist society: it is what 'we' put up in 'our' streets and use to fill up to half of 'our' newspapers and magazines: and it commands the services of perhaps the largest organized body of writers and artists, with their attendant managers and advisers, in the whole society. Since this is the actual social status of advertising, we shall only understand it with any adequacy if we can develop a kind of total analysis in which the economic, social and cultural facts are visibly related. We may then also find, taking advertising as a major form of modern social communication, that we can understand our society itself in new ways.

It is often said that our society is too materialist, and that advertising reflects this. We are in the phase of a relatively rapid distribution of what are called 'consumer goods', and advertising, with its emphasis on 'bringing the good things of life', is taken as central for this reason. But it seems to me that in this respect our society is quite evidently not materialist enough, and that this, paradoxically, is the result of a failure in social meanings, values and ideals.

It is impossible to look at modern advertising without realising that the material object being sold is never enough: this indeed is the crucial cultural quality of its modern forms. If we were sensibly materialist, in that part of our living in which we use things, we should find most advertising to be of an insane irrelevance. Beer would be enough for us, without the additional promise that in drinking it we show ourselves to be manly, young in heart, or neighbourly. A washing-machine would be a useful machine to wash clothes, rather than an indication that we are forward-looking or an object of envy to our neighbours. But if these associations sell beer and washing-machines, as some of the evidence suggests, it is clear that we have a cultural pattern in which the objects are not enough but must be validated, if only in fantasy, by association with social and personal meanings which in a different cultural pattern might be more directly available. The short description of the pattern we have is *magic*: a highly organized and professional system of magical inducements and satisfactions, functionally very similar to magical systems in simpler societies, but rather strangely coexistent with a highly developed scientific technology.

This contradiction is of the greatest importance in any analysis of modern capitalist society. The coming of large-scale industrial production necessarily raised critical problems of social organization, which in many fields we are still only struggling to solve. In the production of goods for personal use, the critical problem posed by the factory of advanced machines was that of the organization of the market. The modern factory requires not only smooth and steady distributive channels (without which it would suffocate under its own product) but also definite indications of demand without which the expensive processes of capitalization and equipment would be too great a risk. The historical choice posed by the development of industrial production is between different forms of organization and planning in the society to which it is central. In our own century, the choice has been and remains between some form of socialism and a new form of capitalism. In Britain, since the 1890s and with rapidly continuing emphasis, we have had the new capitalism, based on a series of devices for organizing and ensuring the market. Modern advertising, taking on its distinctive features in just this economic phase, is one of the most important of these devices, and it is perfectly true to say that modern capitalism could not function without it.

Yet the essence of capitalism is that the basic means of production are not socially but privately owned, and that decisions about production are therefore in the hands of a group occupying a minority position in the society and in no direct way responsible to it. Obviously, since the capitalist wishes to be successful, he is influenced in his decisions about production by what other members of the society need. But he is influenced also by considerations of industrial convenience and likely profit, and his decisions tend to be a balance of these varying factors. The challenge of socialism, still very powerful elsewhere but in Britain deeply confused by political immaturities and errors, is essentially that decisions about production should be in the hands of the society as a whole, in the sense that control of the means of production is made part of the general system of decision which the society as a whole creates. The conflict between capitalism and socialism is now commonly seen in terms of a competition in productive efficiency, and we need not doubt that much of our future history, on a world scale, will be determined by the results of this competition. Yet the conflict is really much deeper than this, and is also a conflict between different approaches to and forms of socialism. The fundamental choice that emerges, in the problems set to us by modern industrial production, is between man as consumer and man as user. The system of organized magic which is modern advertising is primarily important as a functional obscuring of this choice.

'Consumers'

The popularity of 'consumer', as a way of describing the ordinary member of modern capitalist society in a main part of his economic capacity, is very significant. The description is spreading very rapidly, and is now habitually used by people to whom it ought, logically, to be repugnant. It is not only that, at a simple level, 'consumption' is a very strange description of our ordinary use of goods and services. This metaphor drawn from the stomach or the furnace is only partially relevant even to our use of things. Yet we say 'consumer', rather than 'user', because in the form of society we now have, and in the forms of thinking which it almost imperceptibly fosters, it is as consumers that the majority of people are seen. We are the market, which the system of industrial production has organized. We are the channels along which the product flows and disappears. In every aspect of social communication, and in every version of what we are as a community, the pressure of a system of industrial production is towards these impersonal forms.

Yet it is by no means necessary that these versions should prevail, just because we use advanced productive techniques. It is simply that once these have entered a society, new questions of structure and purpose in social organization are inevitably posed. One set of answers is the development of genuine democracy, in which the human needs of all the people in the society are taken as the central purpose of all social activity, so that politics is not a system of government but of self-government, and the systems of production and communication are rooted in the satisfaction of human needs and the development of human capacities. Another set of answers, of which we have had more experience, retains, often in very subtle forms, a more limited social purpose. In the first phase, loyal subjects, as they were previously seen, became the labour market of industrial 'hands'. Later, as the 'hands' reject this version of themselves, and claim a higher human status, the emphasis is changed. Any real concession of higher status would mean the end of class-society and the coming of socialist democracy. But intermediate concessions are possible, including material concessions. The 'subjects' become the 'electorate', and 'the mob' becomes 'public opinion'.

Decision is still a function of the minority, but a new system of decision, in which the majority can be organized to this end, has to be devised. The majority are seen as 'the masses', whose opinion, *as masses* but not as real individuals or groups, is a factor in the business of governing. In practical terms, this version can succeed for a long time, but it then becomes increasingly difficult to state the nature of the society, since there is a real gap between profession and fact. Moreover, as the governing minority changes in character, and increasingly rests for real power on a modern economic system, older social purposes become vestigial, and whether expressed or implied, the maintenance of the economic system becomes the main factual purpose of all social activity. Politics and culture become deeply affected by this dominant pattern, and ways of thinking derived from the economic market—political parties considering how to sell themselves to the electorate, to create a favourable brand image; education being primarily organized in terms of a graded supply of labour; culture being organized and even evaluated in terms of commercial profit—become increasingly evident.

Still, however, the purposes of the society have to be declared in terms that will command the effort of a majority of its people. It is here that the idea of the 'consumer' has proved so useful. Since consumption is within its limits a satisfactory activity, it can be plausibly offered as a commanding social purpose. At the same time, its ambiguity is such that it ratifies the subjection of society to the operations of the existing economic system. An irresponsible economic system can supply the 'consumption' market, whereas it could only meet the criterion of human use by becoming genuinely responsible: that is to say, shaped in its use of human labour and resources by general social decisions. The consumer asks for an adequate supply of personal 'consumer goods' at a tolerable price: over the last ten years, this has been the primary aim of British government. But users ask for more than this, necessarily. They ask for the satisfaction of human needs which consumption, as such, can never really supply. Since many of these needs are social—roads, hospitals, schools, quiet—they are not only not covered by the consumer ideal: they are even denied by it, because consumption tends always to materialize as an individual activity. And to satisfy this range of needs would involve questioning the autonomy of the economic system, in its actual setting of priorities. This is where the consumption ideal is not only misleading, as a form of defence of the system, but ultimately destructive to the broad general purposes of the society.

Advertising, in its modern forms, then operates to preserve the consumption ideal from the criticism inexorably made of it by experience. If the consumption of individual goods leaves that whole area of human need unsatisfied, the attempt is made, by magic, to associate this consumption with human desires to which it has no real reference. You do not only buy an object: you buy social respect, discrimination, health, beauty, success, power to control your environment. The magic obscures the real sources of general satisfaction because their discovery would involve radical change in the whole common way of life.

Of course, when a magical pattern has become established in a society, it is capable of some real if limited success. Many people will indeed look twice at you, upgrade you, upmarket you, respond to your displayed signals, if you have made the right purchases within a system of meanings to which you are all trained. Thus the fantasy seems to be validated, at a personal level, but only at the cost of preserving the general unreality which it obscures: the real failures of the society which however are not easily traced to this pattern.

It must not be assumed that magicians—in this case, advertising-agents—disbelieve their own magic. They may have a limited professional cynicism about it, from knowing how some of the tricks are done. But fundamentally they are involved, with the rest of the society, in the confusion to which the magical gestures are a response. Magic is always an unsuccessful attempt to provide meanings and values, but it is often very difficult to distinguish magic from genuine knowledge and from art. The belief that high consumption is a high standard of living is a general belief of the society. The conversion of numerous objects into sources of sexual or pre-sexual satisfaction is evidently not only a process in the minds of advertisers, but also a deep and general confusion in which much energy is locked.

At one level, the advertisers are people using certain skills and knowledge, created by real art and science, against the public for commercial advantage. This hostile stance is rarely confessed in general propaganda for advertising, where the normal emphasis is the blind consumption ethic ('Advertising brings you the good things of life'), but it is common in advertisers' propaganda to their clients. 'Hunt with the mind of the hunter', one recent announcement begins, and another, under the heading 'Getting any honey from the hive industry?', is rich in the language of attack:

> One of the most important weapons used in successful marketing is advertising.
>
> Commando Sales Limited, steeped to the nerve ends in the skills of unarmed combat, are ready to move into battle on any sales front at the crack of an accepted estimate. These are the front line troops to call in when your own sales force is hopelessly outnumbered by the forces of sales resistance...

This is the structure of feeling in which 'impact' has become the normal description of the effect of successful communication, and 'impact' like 'consumer' is now habitually used by people to whom it ought to be repugnant. What sort of person really wants to 'make an impact' or create a 'smash hit', and what state is a society in when this can be its normal cultural language?

It is indeed monstrous that human advances in psychology, sociology and communication should be used or thought of as powerful techniques *against* people, just as it is rotten to try to reduce the faculty of human choice to 'sales resistance'. In these respects, the claim of advertising to be a service is not particularly plausible. But equally, much of this talk of weapons and impact is the jejune bravado of deeply confused men. It is in the end the language of frustration rather than of power. Most advertising is not the cool creation of skilled professionals, but the confused creation of bad thinkers and artists. If we look at the petrol with the huge clenched fist, the cigarette against loneliness in the deserted street, the puppet facing death with a life-insurance policy (the modern protection, unlike the magical symbols painstakingly listed from earlier societies), or the man in the cradle which is an aeroplane, we are looking at attempts to express and resolve real human tensions which may be crude but which also involve deep feelings of a personal and social kind.

The structural similarity between much advertising and much modern art is not simply copying by the advertisers. It is the result of comparable responses to the contemporary human condition, and the only distinction that matters is between the clarification achieved by some art and the displacement normal in bad art and most advertising. The skilled magicians, the masters of the masses, must be seen as ultimately involved in the general weakness which they not only exploit but are exploited by. If the meanings and values generally operative in the society give no answers to, no means of negotiating, problems of death, loneliness, frustration, the need for identity and respect, then the magical system must come, mixing its charms and expedients with reality in easily available forms, and binding the weakness to the condition which has created it. Advertising is then no longer merely a way of selling goods, it is a true part of the culture of a confused society.

Afterword (1969): Advertising and Communications

A main characteristic of our society is a willed coexistence of very new technology and very old social forms. Advertising is the most visible expression of just this combination. In its main contemporary forms it is the result of a failure to find means of social decision, in matters of production and distribution, relevant to a large-scale and increasingly integrated economy. Classical liberalism ceased to have anything to say about these problems from the period of depression and consequent reorganization of the market in the late nineteenth century. What we now know as advertising takes its origins from that period, in direct relation to the new capitalist corporations. That the same liberalism had produced the idea of a free press, and of a general social policy of public education and enlightenment, is a continuing irony. Before the corporate reorganization, the social ideas of liberalism had been to an important extent compatible with its commercial ideas. Widespread ownership of the means of communication had been sustained by comparable kinds of ownership in the economy as a whole. When the standing enemy of free expression was the state, this diverse commercial world found certain important means to freedom, notably in the newspapers.

What was then called advertising was directly comparable in method and scale. It was mainly specific and local, and though it was often absurd—and had long been recognized as such in its description as puff—it remained a secondary and subordinate activity at the critical point where commercial pressure interacted with free public communication. That early phase is now more than half a century in the past. From the 1890s advertising began to be a major factor in newspaper publishing, and from the same period control began to pass from families and small firms to the new corporations. Ever since that time, and with mounting pressure in each decade, the old institutions of commercial liberalism have been beaten back by the corporations. These sought not so much to supply the market as to organize it.

The consequent crisis has been most visible in newspapers, which have been very sharply reduced in number and variety through a period of expanding readership and the increasing importance of public opinion. But while some of the other liberal ideas seemed to hold, and were even protected as such, as in broadcasting, by the state, it was always possible to believe that the general situation could be held too. Commercial priorities were extending in scale and range, but an entire set of liberal ideas, which in practice the priorities were steadily contradicting, seemed to stay firm in the mind: indeed, so firm that it was often difficult to describe reality, because the evidence of practice was met so regularly by the complacent response of the ideas.

What is now happening, I believe, is that just enough people, at just enough of the points of decision, are with a certain sadness and bewilderment, and with many backward looks, giving that kind of liberalism up. What used to be an uneasy compromise between commercial pressures and public policy is now seen as at worst a bargain, at best a division of labour. The coexistence of commercial and public-service television, which was planned by nobody but was the result of intense pressure to let in the commercial interest, is now rationalized, after the fact, as a kind of conscious policy of pluralism. The new name for compromise is 'mixed economy', or there is an even grander name: a 'planned diversity of structures'.

What has really happened is that a majority of those formerly dedicated to public policy have decided that the opposing forces are simply too strong. They will fight some delaying actions, they will make reservations, but a political situation, long prepared and anticipated, is coming through with such a force that these are mainly gestures. Public money raised in public ways and subject to public control has been made desperately (but deliberately) short. Public money raised in the margin of other transactions and consequently subject to no public control is at the same time continually on offer. Practical men, puzzling over the accounts in committees, think they have at last glimpsed reality. Either they must join the commercial interests, or they must behave like them as a condition of their temporary survival. And so a mood is created in which all decisions seem inevitable and in which people speaking of different solutions seem remote and impractical. It is a mood of submission, under the pressures of an effectively occupying power.

What must then, of course, be most desperately denied is that anything so crude as submission is in fact occurring. Some people are always ready with talk of a new forward-looking order. But the central sign of this sort of submission is a reluctance, in public, to call the enemy by its real name. I see the form of the enemy as advertising, but what I mean by advertising is rather different from some other versions. Plenty of people still criticize advertising in secondary ways: that it is vulgar or superficial, that it is unreliable, that it is intrusive. Much of this is true, but it is the kind of criticism advertising can learn to take in its stride. Does it not now employ many talented people, does it not set up rules and bodies to control and improve standards, is it not limited to natural breaks? While criticism is discrete in these ways, it has only marginal effects.

So I repeat my own central criticism. Advertising is the consequence of a social failure to find means of public information and decision over a wide range of everyday economic life. This failure, of course, is not abstract. It is the result of allowing control of the means of production and distribution to remain in minority hands, and one might add, for it is of increasing importance in the British economy, into foreign hands, so that some of the minority decisions are not even taken inside the society which they affect.

The most evident contradiction of late capitalism is between this controlling minority and a widely expectant majority. What will eventually happen, if we are very lucky, is that majority expectations will surpass the minority controls. In a number of areas this is beginning to happen, in small and temporary ways, and it is called, stupidly, indiscipline or greed or perversity or disruption. But the more evident fact, in the years we are living through, is the emergence and elaboration of a social and cultural form—advertising—which responds to the gap between expectation and control by a kind of organized fantasy.

In economic terms this fantasy operates to project the production decisions of the major corporations as 'your' choice, the 'consumer's' selection of priorities, methods and style. Professional and amateur actors, locally directed by people who in a different culture might be writing and producing plays or films, are hired to mime the forms of the only available choices, to display satisfaction and the achievement of their expectations, or to pretend to a linkage of values between quite mundane products and the now generally unattached values of love, respect, significance or fulfilment. What was once the local absurdity of puffing is now a system of mimed celebration of other people's decisions. As such, of course, advertising is very closely related to a whole system of styles in official politics. Indeed some of its adepts have a direct hand in propaganda, in the competition of the parties and in the formation of public opinion.

Seen from any distance—of time, space or intelligence—the system is so obvious, in its fundamental procedures, that one might reasonably expect to be able to break it by describing it. But this is now very doubtful. If advertising is the consequence of a failure to achieve new forms of social information and decision, this failure has been compounded by the development of the Labour government, which in submitting to the organized market of the corporations has paved the way to a more open and more total submission in the seventies. Historically, this may be seen as the last attempt to solve our crisis in liberal terms, but the consequences of the failure go beyond simple political history. For it has led to habits of resignation and deference to the new power: not only among decision-makers but much more widely, I think, among people who now need the system of fantasy to confirm the forms of their immediate satisfaction or to cover the illusion that they are shaping their own lives.

It is in this atmosphere that the crucial decisions about communications are now being taken. Some of them could have been worse. Pressure on the BBC to take advertising money has been held off, though there is still a lobby, of an elitist kind, prepared to admit it to Radio 1, where all things vulgar may lie down together. On the contrary, this is just where it must not be admitted, for the pressure to tie the cultural preferences of a young generation to the open exploitation of a 'young market' is the most intense and destructive of them all. Again, the emphasis on the licence, as means of revenue, is welcome, as a way of preserving the principle of open public money. The fee is still comparatively low in Britain, and could easily be graduated for pensioners and in some cases abolished. In the BBC and in the government, some local stands are being made.

But it is not only that other people are already adjusting to the altered political climate of the seventies, in which the commercial interests expect to take full control. It is also that the decisions possible to this sort of government, or to a public corporation, are marginal to the continuing trend of economic concentration. A newspaper with two and a half million readers is now likely to shut down: not because such a readership is in a general way uneconomic, but because within a structure determined by competitive advertising revenue it is a relative loser. That process of cutting down choices will continue unless met by the most vigorous public intervention. Commercial radio would rapidly accelerate it.

And what then happens, apart from the long-term hedges and options, is that new figures for viability are accepted for almost all communications services. It is absurd that a sale of a million should be too low for a newspaper. But think of other figures. What is called a vast throng—a hundred thousand people—in Wembley Stadium or Hyde Park is called a tiny minority, a negligible percentage, in a radio programme. Content is then increasingly determined, even in a public service, by the law of quick numbers, which advertising revenue has forced on the communications system.

Submission is not always overt. One of its most popular forms is to change as the conqueror appears on the horizon, so that by the time he arrives you are so like him that you may hope to get by. I don't believe we have yet lost but the position is very critical. What was originally a manageable support cost, in the necessary freedom of communications, has been allowed to turn the world upside down, until all other services are dependent, or likely to be dependent, on its quite local, narrow and temporary needs. An outdated and inefficient kind of information about goods and services has been surpassed by the competitive needs of the corporations, and these increasingly demand not a sector but a world, not a reservation but a whole society, not a break or a column but whole newspapers and broadcasting services in which to operate. Unless they are driven back now, there will be no easy second chance.

Reference

Originally published in *New Left Review/Listener*, 1960/1969. From Raymond Williams, *Problems in Materialism and Culture*, Verso, 1980, pp. 170–195. Reprinted with kind permission of Verso.

5

COMMUNICATION SYSTEMS
(1976 [1962])

Raymond Williams's Penguin Special Communications, *which became a widely used handbook for the nascent subject of Communication Studies, was first published in 1962. It was revised and updated for subsequent editions in 1966 and 1976. The extract here on the topic of 'controversy' is from the third edition of 1976, Penguin, pp. 129–137.*

In the chapter entitled 'Controversy', Williams ranges across a number of issues of public debate concerning communications. And, in order to clarify what is at stake, analytically and politically, he offers a four-part typology of communication systems: first, the authoritarian; *second, the* paternal; *third, the* commercial; *and, fourth, the* democratic. *The British system had developed historically from authoritarianism towards a mixed system of commercialism (particularly in the press) and paternalism (exemplified by the Reithian BBC). Williams proposed an alternative to both, a democratic system that had never yet been tried in which the state provided the facilities for a range of different constituencies and views to be represented. Since then, Williams's hopes for a more democratic system of communications have been frustrated while paternalism has been undermined and commercialism has come to dominate comprehensively, not only in Britain but throughout most of the world.*

The Systems

Perhaps it comes down to this: either the communication system is controlled or it is free. In a democracy there can be no argument on this point: the system must be free or there is no democracy. In a free system many of the things produced may be bad or offensive, or may seem bad and offensive to some people. But the only alternative is a controlled system, or monopoly, in which some people are imposing their tastes on others. 'In fact,' said Sir Robert Fraser, Head of the Independent Television Authority, defending the introduction of commercial television, 'the old system of monopoly in Britain was carried away by a wave of democratic thought and feeling.'

It would be easy to score debating points against Sir Robert Fraser: to ask, for example, what 'a wave of democratic thought and feeling' has in common with the actual process of pressure-group lobbying, much of it by persons with a direct financial interest, which got commercial television through. But this is not the main issue, since behind all the detail of contemporary controversy lies an evident conflict of principles, which has to be faced and understood.

In one way, the basic choice is between control and freedom, but in actual terms it is more often a choice between a measure of control and a measure of freedom, and the substantial argument is about how these can be combined. Further, the bare words 'controlled' and 'free' do not seem sufficiently precise, in themselves, to describe the kinds of communication system which we have had or known about or wanted. I believe that we can distinguish four main kinds, and that to describe and compare these will make our thinking about control and freedom more realistic. The four kinds are: authoritarian, paternal, commercial, and democratic.

Authoritarian

In this system, communications are seen as part of the total machine through which a minority governs a society. The first purpose of communication is to transmit the instructions, ideas, and attitudes of the ruling group. As a matter of policy, alternative instructions, ideas, and attitudes are excluded. Monopoly of the means of communication is a necessary part of the whole political system: only certain printers, publishing houses, newspapers, theatres, broadcasting stations will be allowed. Sometimes these will be directly controlled by the ruling group, who will then directly decide what is transmitted. At other times, a more indirect control will be completed by a system of censorship, and often by a system of political and administrative action against sources unfavourable to those in power.

Such a system can operate with varying degrees of severity, and in the interest of several different kinds of society. We can see it in past periods in Britain as clearly as in modern totalitarian states. The distinguishing characteristic of such a system is that the purpose of communication is to protect, maintain, or advance a social order based on minority power.

Paternal

A paternal system is an authoritarian system with a conscience: that is to say, with values and purposes beyond the maintenance of its own power. Authoritarians, on various grounds, claim the right to rule. In a paternal system, what is asserted is the duty to protect and guide. This involves the exercise of control, but it is a control directed towards the development of the majority in ways thought desirable by the minority. If monopoly of the means of communication is used, it is argued that this is to prevent the means being abused by groups which are destructive or evil. Censorship is widely used, in such a system, both directly and indirectly, but it is defended on the grounds that certain groups and individuals need, in their own interest and in the public interest, protection against certain kinds of art or ideas which would be harmful to them. Where the authoritarian system transmits orders, and the ideas and attitudes which will promote their acceptance, the paternal system transmits values, habits, and tastes, which are its own justification as a ruling minority, and which it wishes to extend to the people as a whole. Criticism of such values, habits, and tastes will be seen as at best a kind of rawness and inexperience, at worst a moral insurrection against a tried and trusted way of life. The controllers of a paternal system see themselves as guardians. Though patient, they must be uncompromising in defence of their central values. At the same time, the proper discharge of their duty requires a high sense of responsibility and seriousness. At different times, and serving different social orders, the paternal system can vary in the degree to which it explicitly announces its role or explains its methods. The actual methods can also vary widely: sometimes putting the blanket over everything; sometimes allowing a measure of controlled dissent or tolerance as a safety-valve. But the general purpose and atmosphere of the system remain unmistakable.

Commercial

The commercial attitude to communications is powerfully opposed to both authoritarianism and paternalism. Instead of communication being for government or for guidance, it is argued that men have the right to offer for sale any kind of work, and that all men have the right to buy any kind that is offered. In this way, it is claimed, the freedom of communication is assured. You do not have to ask anybody's leave to publish or to read. Works are openly offered for sale and openly bought, as people actually choose.

In its early stages, and in some of its later stages, such a system is certainly a means to freedom by comparison with either of the former systems. But since this freedom depends on the market it can run into difficulties. Can a work be offered for sale if there is no certainty that people will in fact buy it? When production is cheap, this risk will often be taken. When production is expensive, it may not be. In a modern system of communications many kinds of production are inevitably expensive. What, then, happens to the simple original principle? First: works whose sale is uncertain, or likely to be very small in relation to cost, may not be offered at all. Second: speed of sale becomes an important factor – it is not easy to wait for years for a return on a very large investment if the act of buying and selling is the most important consideration. Investment elsewhere might bring much quicker returns. Third: if the amount of capital needed to finance a work is large, there can be no free offering for sale, as in the original principle. Individual artists will almost certainly not possess the necessary capital. They have then to be financed by individuals or groups with such capital, and it is probable that considerations of extent or speed of sale, and so of return or profit on the investment, will be decisive as to whether such an offer of financing is made. But then practical control of the means of communications, over large areas and particularly in the more expensive kinds, can pass to individuals or groups whose main, if not only, qualification will be that they possess or can raise the necessary capital. Such groups, by the fact of this qualification, will often be quite unrepresentative of the society as a whole; they will be, in fact, a minority within it. Thus the control claimed as a matter of power by authoritarians, and as a matter of principle by paternalists, is often achieved as a matter of practice in the operation of the commercial system. Anything can be said, provided that you can afford to say it and that you can say it profitably.

Democratic

We have experienced the other three systems, but the democratic system, in any full sense, we can only discuss and imagine. It shares with the early commercial system a definition of communication which insists that all men have the right to offer what they choose and to receive what they choose. It is firmly against authoritarian control of what can be said, and against paternal control of what ought to be said. But also it is against commercial control of what can profitably be said, because this also can be a tyranny.

All proposals for new systems appear abstract, and at times unconvincing, because it is only when they are put into practice that they can be felt to be real. The working out of any democratic system will obviously be long and difficult, but what matters first is to define the general nature of a cultural system compatible with democracy, since there is only any chance of success in building it if enough of us can agree that this is the kind of thing we want.

There are two related considerations: the right to transmit and the right to receive. It must be the basis of any democratic culture, first, that these are basic rights; second, that they can never be tampered with by minorities; third, that if they are ever in any way limited, by some majority decision of the society, this can happen only after open and adequate public discussion, to which all are free to contribute and which will remain open to challenge and review.

On the right to transmit, the basic principle of democracy is that since all are full members of the society, all have the right to speak as they wish or find. This is not only an individual right, but a social need, since democracy depends on the active participation and the free contribution of all its members. The right to receive is complementary to this: it is the means of participation and of common discussion.

The institutions necessary to guarantee these freedoms must clearly be of a public-service kind, but it is very important that the idea of public service should not be used as a cover for a paternal or even authoritarian system. The idea of public service must be detached from the idea of public monopoly, yet remain public service in the true sense. The only way of achieving this is to create new kinds of institution.

The principle should be that the active contributors have control of their own means of expression. In the case of contributors not immediately dependent on institutions, this means guaranteeing them, if they want, certain facilities which will be their means of living and working. In cases where the work can only be done through institutions, it means creating the opportunity for the setting up, by various working groups, of their own companies, which will then be guaranteed the facilities they need. Some of these guarantees can be given by various intermediate institutions, themselves not dependent or directly dependent on the organs of government. But probably the greater part of the necessary resources will have to come directly from public funds. It is then necessary to create intermediate bodies, including representatives of the public and of the companies, to hold these public resources in trust for the society as a whole and for the needs of the various companies.

There should be no direct control by government over contributors. The creation of intermediate bodies, and of a contractual system by which individuals and companies are guaranteed certain resources for the work they want to do, can in practice make governmental control impossible, so long as the general life of the society remains democratic. In any system, if general democracy goes, cultural democracy will go too. But while there is general democracy (in defence of which an active cultural democracy is continually necessary) what matters most is a clear acceptance of the principle that the resources exist for the contributors to use for the work they themselves want to do, and that all decisions about the actual allocation of resources should be publicly argued and open to challenge and review.

There are two difficulties in this principle, certain also to be difficult in practice. The case for control by the contributors is that the society cannot by any means be better served than by giving the contributors their freedom and the necessary resources to work with. Control by functionless financial groups, or by political or administrative factions, is certain to be damaging. But will there, can there be no control at all: either by the allocation of resources to this work rather than that, or by any measures thought generally necessary to protect the public interest?

A democratic culture would need to allot considerable resources, to keep the first danger small. It would need in any case to resist any tendency to restrict work to its own channels, however adequate. If, even in the most enlightened system, an individual or a group cannot get support, it must be quite clear that there is nothing to stop them working in any way they can, and offering their work in any way they can: a situation in which they would be much as now. The more difficult aspect of this question is that a healthy culture depends on growth, yet at any given moment new kinds of work may command little interest, and there might be considerable public pressure to give them little or no support. How can this be overcome, in any democratic way? There is no simple answer, and the only possible answer is that if it is of the nature of democratic culture that it keeps the channels of growth clear, it is a public duty to see that individuals or groups offering new kinds of work are given at least a fair chance. The problem is really one of holding the ring, to give new work the time (it will often be a long time) to prove itself. The more varied the organization, the more independent companies there are, the more this chance is likely to be given.

The second difficulty is severe. We have seen how in certain cases it can be deeply held that there are certain things which ought not to be offered, because they are likely, on the available evidence, to harm people. Will not such restrictions have to be made? Even if they are publicly argued, publicly decided, and continually open to review, are they not still restrictions? Is not paternalism in some form necessary after all? In fact, of course, if it is a majority decision it is not paternalism. But it will still feel like it, to those affected. Again, there is no simple answer to this. The general issues, and all particular cases, need continual discussion. I believe that with the pressure of profit lifted there would be less work of this difficult kind. Yet there would always be some, and you might get a majority decision against serious work. The only way to prevent this is to promote the most open discussion, including the contributor's own reasoning, or reasoning on his behalf. I do not believe that, when this is done, people usually choose wrongly. In any event, one case lost is often the next case won, for in arguing the cases there is a real growth of understanding.

It seems to be best to let the contribution be made, and let the contributor take responsibility for it. The curious situation now, in a commercial culture, is that the contributor is often neither free nor responsible: neither doing what he would independently have done, nor answerable to public criticism for what he has actually done. The balance inherent in democracy requires the creation of both these new conditions: freedom to do and freedom to answer, as an active process between many individuals.

Summary

The four systems described, authoritarian, paternal, commercial, and democratic, are all to some extent active, in practice or in local experiment, in contemporary Britain. The vestiges of authoritarianism are there, in certain kinds of censorship; the first experiments in democracy are also there, in local ways. But the main struggle, over the last generation, has been between the paternal and commercial systems, and it looks as if the commercial has been steadily winning. It is most important, in this situation, that we should not confine the debate to the limited contrast of 'controlled' and 'free' systems, but instead should look over the whole range, and into detailed comparisons and possibilities.

Reference

Originally published in *Communications* (Third Edition), 1976, Penguin, pp. 129–137. Copyright © 1976 Raymond Williams. Reproduced by permission of Penguin Books Ltd.

6

THE IDEA OF A COMMON CULTURE
(1967)

Here, Williams reviews T.S. Eliot's and F.R. Leavis's arguments about culture in the post-Second World War period. Eliot had insisted that culture was not confined to an educated minority but existed in a hierarchy of levels down to the everyday tastes and practices of the masses. Leavis was more concerned with preserving and protecting 'minority' (that is, 'high') culture from the incursions of mass-commercial culture and believed that education should lead the way, particularly through the discipline of English and the teaching of fine literature.

In Culture and Society, *Williams had already taken up R.H. Tawney's social-democratic notion of a 'common culture', by which Tawney meant the dissemination of high culture to the masses through education and cultural policy. Williams challenged this version of common culture and argued that with increased access to education, including higher education, the common culture would inevitably change and come to represent the popular culture of ordinary people, not just a 'Great Tradition' handed down from the past that had previously been confined to an educated elite.*

In a political vein, Williams called for the creation of an 'educated and participatory democracy', a more dynamic and processual conception of common culture than Tawney had proposed.

We begin to think where we live, and it is really not surprising that, in this time and place, I should have been trying to think about culture, as a particular experience which I share with many others, and which is in that sense the preoccupation of a generation. Culture was the way in which the process of education, the experience of literature, and – for someone moving out of a working-class family to a higher education – inequality, came through. What other people, in different situations, might experience more directly as economic or political inequality, was naturally experienced, from my own route, as primarily an inequality of culture; an inequality which was also, in an obvious sense, an uncommunity. This is, I think, still the most important way to follow the argument about culture, because everywhere, but very specifically in England, culture is one way in which class, the fact of major divisions between men, shows itself.

I think, however, that it took me a long time (looking back, it seems an absurdly long time) to understand that there were different meanings within the idea of culture itself, to which one was responding simultaneously but which clearly had to be distinguished. For a long time it seemed to me that the problem of culture was primarily a problem of the relationship between writer and audience – the problem of connecting in writing – and I find that the first way in which I tried to discuss culture was within this context, determined by ideas of the relation of writer and audience which would now seem to me to be limited. The terms I used, then, were 'community of sensibility', 'community of process': the idea of a connection between a writer and his audience which in a sense preceded the act of writing itself, out of which the act of writing grew, and within which the response to that act continued. These terms do not seem to me, now, a particularly satisfactory way of speaking about culture; they had to be developed, inevitably, into thinking about a whole particular society, and into thinking about culture as the most immediately available way of thinking about society itself.

The personal aspect of this development should not be overemphasized; but it is, nevertheless, a fact that the movement between classes, between life situations and life styles, which has characterized what little extension of higher education has gone on, has focused attention on questions which seem centred in the idea of culture, and are in themselves a way of fusing all those other aspects of living which one believes to be the general experience. It is true that one would probably have thought much more directly about social, political and economic barriers and failures, if it had not happened that a particular English tradition of social thinking contained a vital strand which was really a debate about the nature of culture itself. What was involved in that debate was complicated, including people, and attitudes from many different social and political traditions; but the idea of culture had been, from the early nineteenth century – from the generation after the Industrial Revolution – an attempt to focus questions about the quality of life available in a particular community, as a way of putting questions to the simple material progress, or the simple social confidence, of the dominant kind of society. In the debate about the bearings of the idea of culture on the nature of general community, much of an essentially English kind of social thinking had been done; to any student of literature, this was going to be, inevitably, his first major contact with the process of thinking about contemporary society and its problems – this tradition would be nearest to hand.

Among immediate contemporaries, one was very aware of three writers who represented emphases in this debate about culture: Eliot, Leavis and (one shouldn't call him a contemporary, although he felt like one) Marx. One saw Eliot taking a conservative position, fearing that the extension of a different kind of society and education, perhaps also of urban and industrial living, certainly, too, of democracy, would inevitably dilute and destroy the meaning of culture. One saw Leavis, committing himself to no such systematic case, but undeniably laying the same kind of emphasis on the values of a received minority culture, which it was the business of the student of literature to defend, before there was any question of extension. There was not, here, the same settled opposition to the idea of extending a cultural tradition that one had found in Eliot; but there was a radical scepticism about its possibility, and a certainty that something else came first. And then there was Marx, actually at first the Marxists, insisting that culture is inseparable from the nature of our general living, that in a society divided into classes culture would have an inevitable class content and class bearing, and that, in the historical development of a society, a culture will necessarily change as relations between men and classes change.

This complex of ideas was available for a whole range of questions, which could be concentrated into what is now called the debate about culture. It seemed to me, looking at these questions, that one had to put a certain emphasis which really was different from any of these three approaches. It was impossible for me to accept Eliot's position, both because it seemed essentially to ratify a society which was overridingly objectionable on other grounds, in its intolerable social and economic inequalities, and also because the attempt to preserve a class society in the control of traditional institutions was in any case unrealistic, in a world in which a transformation of that traditional culture by advanced capitalism was going on. What Eliot was demanding was, at a simple level, inconceivable. Leavis's approach was more immediately attractive, in that it offered an emphasis on the primacy of literature which one was very ready to put; it called on one to do a certain job (incidentally of reading, not of writing), and it had a radical tinge which supported a critical interest and engagement in the problems of contemporary civilization. But it seemed to me, ultimately, that when this case was generalized, its emphasis on a minority culture was subject to the same objections as that of Eliot. Indeed, if one found Eliot sourer, it was really only because he had been, in the final analysis, more consistent: because he had faced, and accepted, the implications of what he was saying. The Leavis position seemed to me to lead directly to such a social position, but there was a certain understandable hesitancy about taking the last step: it was said that such a social position was not necessary, and a virtue was made about it not being necessary, but it seemed to me that the cultural position inevitably implied it, and this has been confirmed, as we have watched, as the years have gone by. As for Marx, one accepted the emphases on history, on change, on the inevitably close relationships between class and culture, but the way this came through was, at another level, unacceptable. There was, in this position, a polarization and abstraction of economic life on the one hand and culture on the other, which did not seem to me to correspond to the social experience of culture as others had lived it, and as one was trying to live it oneself.

It was, then, as a way of exploring an alternative emphasis, of discovering a standpoint within this complex territory, that one tried to speak of a common culture, or (the phrase now seems to me different) of a culture in common. Related to this stress was the assertion that culture is ordinary: that there is not a special class, or group of men, who are involved in the creation of meanings and values, either in a general sense or in specific art and belief. Such creation could not be reserved to a minority, however gifted, and was not, even in practice, so reserved: the meanings of a particular form of life of a people, at a particular time, seemed to come from the whole of their common experience, and from its complicated general articulation. And if this is indeed so, that meanings and values are widely, not sectionally, created (and the example that one used in the first instance was that of language, which is no individual's creation, although certain individuals extend and deepen its possibilities), then one had to talk about the general fact of a community of culture, and to assert the need for a common culture as a critique of what was imposed, what was done to that general condition in the structure of particular societies. In talking of a common culture, then, one was saying first that culture was the way of life of a people, as well as the vital and indispensable contributions of specially gifted and identifiable persons, and one was using the idea of the *common* element of the culture – its community – as a way of criticizing that divided and fragmented culture we actually have.

If it is at all true that the creation of meanings is an activity which engages all men, then one is bound to be shocked by any society which, in its most explicit culture, either suppresses the meanings and values of whole groups, or which fails to extend to these groups the possibility of articulating and communicating those meanings. This, precisely, was what one wanted to assert about contemporary Britain, even at a point where we were being assured, in the usual kind of happy retrospect, that most of the social problems had been resolved. It was, on the contrary, perfectly clear that the majority of people, while living *as* people, creating their own values, were both shut out by the nature of the educational system from access to the full range of meanings of their predecessors in that place, and excluded by the whole structure of communications – the character of its material ownership, its limiting social assumptions – from any adequate participation in the process of changing and developing meanings which was in any case going on. One was therefore both affirming a general truth, which I would hold to be independent of any particular historical stage, that there is, in that sense, community of culture; and criticizing a particular society because it limited, and in many ways actively prevented, that community's self-realization.

It is here that a critique which began as cultural extends itself to what is properly social and political criticism. It is as well to make this clear, because I do not think that there is any possibility of a common culture as I mean it, coming about simply by an act of extension of the minority values of a specific group – probably, in any such case, a ruling group – to other people. It would not be a common culture (though it might be possible to call it a culture in common) if some existing segment of experience, articulated in a particular way, were simply extended – taught – to others, so that they then had it as a common possession. For it follows, from the original emphasis, that the culture of a people can only be what all its members are engaged in creating in the act of living: that a common culture is not the general extension of what a minority mean and believe, but the creation of a condition in which the people as a whole participate in the articulation of meanings and values, and in the consequent decisions between this meaning and that, this value and that. This would involve, in any real world, the removal of all the material obstacles to just this form of participation: this was the ground for the later interest in the institutions of communication, which, dominated by capital or state power, set up the idea of the few communicating to the many, disregarding the contributions of those who are seen not as communicators but merely as communicable to. In the same way, it would mean changing the educational system from its dominant pattern of sorting people, from so early an age, into 'educated' people and others, or in other words transmitters and receivers, to a view of the interlocking processes of determining meanings and values as involving contribution and reception by everyone.

When one had criticized the institutions of communication and the methods of divisive education, one saw, quite clearly, that these rested on what was indeed a solid social structure of private property in just these means of exchange; one saw, too, that this kind of private property, which prevents the full access of the people as a whole to its governing institutions, rules also in the direction of the energy of the community, principally in the forms of control over work. Private property in the means of labour had resulted in a situation in which the energies of a majority of men were being directed, under severe and normally irresistible pressure, to ends decided by a minority; if this were so, in so central a part of our lives, it was bound to affect the processes by which meanings and values could be created and exchanged.

In speaking of a common culture, then, one was speaking critically of what could be summarized as a class society; but one was also speaking positively of an idea of society which seemed at least to sound different from some contemporary definitions of socialism. I had no doubt, at any stage, that the means of changing this kind of society would be socialist means, or that the institutions which would lead into a different society would be socialist institutions. But because of what one was meaning, in the first place, about the nature of society and community in general, the first question which one put to the idea of a different society was in terms of its capacity for participation in just this central process of a people living together. I defined this in a phrase which has since been widely used, in some places I don't much like, but which still seems to me important; the idea of an *educated and participating democracy*. Participating, for the reasons which we have said; educated, because it must be the case that the whole tradition of what has been thought and valued, a tradition which has been abstracted as a minority possession, is in fact a common human inheritance without which any man's participation would be crippled and disadvantaged. In this meaning of education, a man would not see himself simply as continuing a particular tradition, educated into a particular way of thought, as so much of education is viewed at present; the point, simply, is that one would not be fully qualified to participate in this active process unless the education which provides its immediate means – developed speaking, writing, and reading – and which allows access to the terms of the argument so far, were made commonly available. So a common culture is an educated and participating democracy, and the idea of a socialist democracy is based, very firmly, on those values. The argument about culture can never pass in a simple way to an argument about politics; but when a political case is made, in these terms, it tries always to base itself on the originating values.

It is this emphasis, on a mutual determination of values and meanings, that I think one has to remember in considering one possible meaning of a common culture. There is some danger in conceiving of a common culture as a situation in which all people mean the same thing, value the same thing, or, in that usual abstraction of culture, have an equal possession of so much cultural property. It is possible to understand the demand for a common culture in any of these ways, but not, I think, seriously, if one has followed the course of the argument. That kind of view of a common culture is perhaps better described by the phrase 'a culture in common', but the argument is in any case unreal. In any society towards which we are likely to move, there will, first of all, be such considerable complexity that nobody will in that sense 'possess cultural property' in the same way; people, inevitably, will have different aspects of the culture, will choose that rather than this, concentrate on this and neglect that. When this is an act of choice, it is completely desirable; when it is an act of someone else's choice as to what is made available and what is neglected, then of course one objects. But it is not only that the society will be complex: that people will not and cannot share it in an even and uniform way. It is also that the idea of a common culture is in no sense the idea of a simply consenting, and certainly not of a merely conforming, society. One returns, once more, to the original emphasis of a common determination of meanings by all the people, acting sometimes as individuals, sometimes as groups, in a process which has no particular end, and which can never be supposed at any time to have finally realized itself, to have become complete. In this common process, the only absolute will be the keeping of the channels and institutions of communication clear, so that all may contribute, and be helped to contribute. If that is so, then the fantasy that some critics have had, that a common culture would be a uniform and conformist culture, or the fear that some friends have expressed, that a common culture would be notoriously difficult to attain because it is impossible to find any large number of people in general agreement, do not seem to hold. In speaking of a common culture, one is asking, precisely, for that free, contributive and common *process* of participation in the creation of meanings and values, as I have tried to define it.

Reference

Originally published in Eagleton, T. and B. Whicker, eds, *From Culture to Revolution – The Slant Symposium*, 1967. From Raymond Williams, *Resources of Hope*, Verso, 1989, pp. 32–38. Reprinted with kind permission of Verso.

7

SOCIAL DARWINISM
(1973)

This is Raymond Williams's most important essay on an ideology; and it is probably even more apposite now in the early decades of the twenty-first century than it was when originally written in the early-1970s. Social Darwinism is the British sociologist Herbert Spencer's distorted application of Charles Darwin's theory of evolution to the development of society and social relations. The oft-repeated phrase and indeed slogan of 'the survival of the fittest' is typically mistaken as Darwin's whereas, in fact, it was Spencer's. Social Darwinism is an ideology of competitive individualism that, in effect, justifies brutal supremacism. Although it was originally formulated in the service of British imperialism by a near forgotten pioneer of sociology in Britain, it has been articulated most insistently by American capitalism ever since. In the essay, Williams traces the pernicious influence of Social Darwinism in the work of an extraordinary catalogue of intellectuals during the early twentieth century on the Left as well as the Right of politics.

Social Darwinism is the conventional term for a variant of social theory which emerged in the 1870s, mainly in Britain and the United States, and which I'm sorry to say has not entirely died out; indeed, under other names, is being widely revived. I want to describe its ideas in the context of an analysis of various applications of evolutionary theory to social theory, and of its use in creative literature. And so I shall be describing, first, the Social Darwinism which is conventionally known by that name, and which has been so well studied by Richard

Hofstadter in *Social Darwinism in American Thought*; and then looking at some of the variations.

In a sense, we can provide a very adequate analysis of Social Darwinism in terms of the errors of emphasis it makes in extending the theory of natural selection to social and political theory. We can say: this is a false extension or a false application of biology. But while that is true, I think it simplifies the matter a little too much, in that the biology itself has from the beginning a strong social component, as Robert Young has shown in detail.[1] Indeed, my own position is that theories of evolution and natural selection in biology had a social component before there was any question of reapplying them to social and political theory. We have to think of this dialectical movement between the two areas of study as a fact from the beginning. For example, in the case of Darwin himself, we have the impressive note on his reading of Malthus, whom he picked up to read for amusement: it's not the most likely motive for reading Malthus but there we are. He writes:

> Being well-prepared to appreciate the struggle for existence which everywhere goes on from long-continued observation of plants and animals, it at once struck me that under these circumstances favourable variations would tend to be preserved and unfavourable ones to be destroyed; the result of this would be the formation of new species.

And Darwin's co-discoverer of natural selection, Wallace, says that Malthus gave him the long-sought clue to the effective agent in the evolution of organic species. This has been disputed: many historians of science have argued that the Malthus clue was a very minor element. But to me it is significant that a theory about the relation between population and resources—an explicit social theory which had great influence on nineteenth-century social thought—was at any rate one of the organizing elements in the emergence of the great generalization about natural selection.

But then one must make clear that Social Darwinism, the popular application of the biological idea to social thought, comes not so much from Darwin as from the whole tradition of evolutionary theory, which is much older than Charles Darwin, which indeed goes back at least to his grandfather, Erasmus, at the end of the eighteenth century, and which, in the first half of the nineteenth century, is already a well-founded system of thought. The explanation of the means of evolution might have to wait on further discoveries, but the idea of evolution was there. It was in many cases built into systems, and—above all for the purpose of understanding Social Darwinism in the narrow sense—it was built into a system by Herbert Spencer. Indeed, it was Spencer, as a social philosopher, who first, in 1864, coined the phrase which was to have such a history in the debate, 'the survival of the fittest'.

Spencer's view of progress, which, he said, was not an accident but a necessity, a visible evolution in human history, carried some consequences which are the real origins of the narrow kind of Social Darwinism. He believed, for example, that there was a principle of social selection operative in human history, and that because this was so it was extremely important that men didn't interfere with it, and in particular that governments didn't interfere with it. He opposed state aid to the poor on the grounds that this would preserve the weaker and less successful members of the race.

Whatever we may now think of the social ethics of this position, it was seen as a logically deducible consequence of the theory of progressive evolution by social selection. The weaker or less able members of society should not be artificially preserved, because the process of social selection which was creating the most vigorous and self-reliant types was something that ought not to be interfered with: its ultimate achievement would be human happiness of a general kind. So he was specifically against what he called artificial preservation of those least able to take care of themselves: a Spencerian theory which has, I suppose, survived to our own decade in the concept of the lame duck and beyond that quaint metaphor for a failing enterprise into the more virulent versions of a market economy and its consequent social order which are now again being put into practice. If you really believe this, if you really believe that there is a system of progressive social selection going on, it can seem wild infamy to interfere with it. And it is the confidence that evolution is leading to this development that forms the ethical or quasi-ethical component of what becomes Social Darwinism. Otherwise it seems the merest random cruelty and rationalization.

The idea of competition as a fundamental social principle is, of course, not new. It was most powerfully prefigured in English thought by Hobbes, who believed that life is the war of all against all, until some sovereign power intervenes and takes control of what would otherwise be a self-destroying horde. Until the intervention of the power to control men and to prevent them destroying one another, that is the natural condition of man. A critical constituent of the full Social Darwinist theory was the growing nineteenth-century belief that character was in a simple sense determined by environment: the doctrine of Robert Owen, for example, that you could wholly reform the moral character of the entire population in a short period of time by altering their environment. If you put the two things together you still don't have Social Darwinism in its full sense, but you have competition, inherent competition, as a natural state; and the idea of character being influenced by circumstances can very easily modulate into its being selected by favourable circumstances. Add to that the theory of historical progressive development and you have Social Darwinism in its developed form.

Darwin himself did not take a consistent position on any of these applications. In a letter he observed ironically that he had just received 'a squib', printed in a newspaper, showing that 'I have proved might is right and therefore that Napoleon is right and every cheating tradesman also right'—obviously a reaction to one of the first and crudest kinds of Social Darwinism. He was against anything which smacked to him of selfish and contentious policies. However he did, from his long early experience of the breeding of domestic creatures, the famous pigeons, take the view that a society was in some peril which didn't in a conscious way select and discard. He did say: 'We civilized men do our utmost to check the process of elimination. This must be highly injurious to the race of man.' In other words, if the weak or the unfavourable variations are, as Spencer would have put it, artificially preserved, the general condition of the race is likely to deteriorate. On the other hand, Darwin was much too humane a man to think in terms which were later to become possible—of the elimination of unfavourable variations, or of social policy in this conscious sense, to which he never fully applied himself.

Almost at once, however, the extensions began to be made: moving out from the social ideas of Spencer and gaining a lot of support from the general climate of harsh competitive individualism as a social ideology at that stage of industrial capitalism and general industrial development. And we can trace the process, in part in the work of particular thinkers, but as much in the ground-swell of a certain kind of public opinion. Look, for example, at Bagehot's *Physics and Politics*, published in 1876. Bagehot was a country banker, editor of the *Economist*, literary essayist, author of *The English Constitution*. In *Physics and Politics* he wrote a work which he subtitled 'Thoughts on the Application of the Principles of Natural Selection and Inheritance to Political Society'. It is one of the first conscious attempts to do just this. And in a sense it comes surprisingly from Bagehot, who was always a moderating man. His famous analysis of the English Constitution was in its way a superb piece of demystification, but of a rather special kind: demystification in order to remystify. He analysed the English Constitution in terms of its theatrical show—he wrote quite sharply about the Widow of Windsor—and he saw and approved the whole panoply of the British State as a means of creating deference in its subjects. He then argued with a quite new tone in Victorian social argument that this was necessary to any well-ordered state. In a way, the conclusions of *Physics and Politics*, after what seem some rather bolder speculations, are essentially similar. He takes from Spencer the idea of the progress of human society by certain well-ordered stages. Primitive or preliminary: the military stage in which human relations are basically those of armed conflict. But then a stage of civilization which he thought he was living in, a stage of order in which conflict is resolved by discussion. He did believe that in human societies there was intrinsic competition: not so much of all against all, individual against individual, but rather an intrinsic competition for the best shape of the society. This or that notion of how the society might be had to engage in competition with all other notions, and in a sense what emerged as the constituting notion of any particular state was the superior notion. This could be so, however, only in a period of ordered discussion, as distinct from a period of military conflict in which a better idea might be destroyed by a physically stronger enemy. Europe, having been the central area of conflict between states founded on different notions, different ideas of the social polity, different ideas of religion, was also the centre of progress. The conflict and the progress were directly correlated.

This was soon overtaken by something which has a more sinister ring, although many of the ideas of the next stage can already be found in Spencer. Sumner in the 1880s offers what becomes, if you read in the period, a very familiar definition: that civilization is the survival of the fittest, that the survival of the unfittest is anti-civilization. Socialism is an absurd notion because it proposes both the development of civilization and the survival of the unfittest, which are manifestly contradictory, he argues. Competition is a law of nature and to interfere with the results of competition is radically to undermine civilization. So let no one pretend to believe in civilization if on some other grounds he argues for intervention. Millionaires, Sumner said, are a product of natural selection. So we can see that within twenty years of the formulation of the biological idea of natural selection we have got a quite new phrase—not that earlier phrases had been lacking to rationalize rich men—to describe the internal logic and necessity of the social process.

Not surprisingly, Sumner was almost at once echoed by John D. Rockefeller, who said that the growth of a large business is merely the survival of the fittest and made a rather pretty analogy with a prize rose bloom which has to be debudded of its subsidiary minor blooms before it can come to its perfection. The processes of industrial monopoly which were occurring at this time could be rationalized as the production either of the most beautiful blooms or of the next stage in the social species.

Of course, this was an ideology: it was consciously in opposition to liberal egalitarian tendencies, to measures of social welfare and reform, and classically to ideas of socialism. Because it was an ideology, not all the implications of this rather stark and powerful theory were always welcome even to some of its exponents. It is very significant that along this line—through Spencer to Bagehot, Sumner and others—the main inheritance function which is assumed biologically is still that of Lamarck rather than Darwin: in other words, the physical inheritance of acquired characteristics rather than the kind of variation in adaptation to environment which Darwin relied on. Spencer continued to believe in Lamarck long after Darwin, and the concept of physical inheritance in this sense gave the ideologists of Social Darwinism a particularly fortunate opportunity to modify competition of an absolutely open kind when it came to the preservation of family property. After all, if you take their argument quite seriously, the war of all against all should never stop, because to interfere with it would prevent the emergence of the strongest types: so that inherited family property, which means that somebody who may not have strong individual talents which are going to evolve the higher kind of man starts with an advantage, is a kind of interference with competition. But if you have a Lamarckian notion of physical inheritance, then you can rationalize the family and family property as precisely the continuation of what you can now see to be the strongest and best species.

So, too, with the inheritance of capital: nobody could look at the nineteenth century and suppose that it was a society in which one day somebody fired a pistol and said: 'Go on, compete economically, and the strongest will come out at the top of the heap.' Quite evidently, huge fortunes were there at the start of the play, and the great majority of the players came to the table bearing nothing but their hands. If there is really to be competition in the full ruthless sense, then you must all come to the table with empty hands. But financial inheritance is defended with the ideology because the possession of capital provides a measure of continuity. It is really very painful to follow these convolutions of men who had committed themselves to a rhetorically powerful theory which rationalized competition as a principle of society, dismissing as sentimental all apparently ethical and moral objections to it, and then find them having to turn to defend things which were quite evidently qualifications of the competitive principle as such.

Nevertheless, the survival of the fittest, the struggle for existence—nobody had to invent these as descriptions of nineteenth-century society, they were most people's everyday experience. Millions of men in this country went out each day knowing they had to be stronger or more cunning than their fellows if they were to survive or take anything home to their family. The idea is in a way as popular among the victims of that kind of competitive process as it is among its promoters, because it corresponds very directly to their daily experience of life. Whether or not anybody can conceive a better social order, the idea does seem to fit the experience of life as it is ordinarily lived. The popularity of phrases like 'the rat race' to describe our own society is a direct continuation of these earlier descriptions among the victims. And, of course, anyone who has succeeded, whether or not he has had advantages, has been very willing to invoke the principle of 'the survival of the fittest'.

There are two particular applications of this principle which ought to be noted before we go on to some of the other variants. First is the development of eugenics as a movement. It's a natural consequence of this theory that you should breed only from the most perfectly endowed types. The whole future of man was thought to depend upon this kind of selective physical inheritance. Although there are signs of it throughout the second half of the nineteenth century, it is in the nineties, and especially up to the period of the First World War, which did a little selection of its own, that eugenics gets put forward by a whole range of people otherwise sharing different views. Eugenics as a positive policy is one thing: it amounts to very little more than the argument that every encouragement to breed should be given to the most physically and intellectually favoured. The negative side of eugenics is a more serious matter. There is a direct link back to Malthus and to the thought that the unfit should be prevented from breeding.

Everything then depends on the concept of fitness. It is one thing to hear the eugenic argument about the breeding of children from the physically malformed or those carrying some hereditary disease: it is quite another to hear the eugenic argument against breeding from the disfavoured, the unsuccessful, the socially and economically weak. And yet it gets entangled with this, because very quickly it combines with theories of race, which again don't have a specific origin in the biological argument. Gobineau's argument about the inequality of races had appeared in 1853, well before this phase, but it is readily applicable to race because Darwin had at times used 'race' as a biological term for species—a continuing confusion—and so the idea of a particular human race—the Anglo-Saxon was a particular favourite—as the vigorous stock, the survivor in the competitive battle, inheriting a certain natural right to mastery, became a very powerful component of the ideology of imperialism. In the case for imperialism it was perfectly possible to argue, and many did, that the strongest, the best survivors, the Anglo-Saxon race, had a duty to humanity to continue to assert itself, not to limit its competition with weaker peoples out of some false ethical consideration for them or out of some legalistic notion of their rights. If the competitive struggle produces the strongest human types, then clearly the strongest race must in no way be limited.

You get an interesting variant of this in the North American theory that an even more vigorous hybrid of the Anglo-Saxon race happens to have established itself in the United States, and its turn will come. The general idea of the Aryans as a race with these attributes becomes intensely popular, and in a natural fit of self-defence somebody reinvents the Celts. For if you follow the logic of the crude argument of strength through competition, then you do arrive at imperialism, you do arrive at racist theories, although there may be different choices as to the most favoured race, according to where you happen to live. You also arrive at the rationalization of war. Von Moltke argued that war is the supreme example in human history of the Darwinian struggle for existence, because here, under the most intense conditions, men are set against one another, and the strongest survive, and it is right that it should be so, because only if the strongest survive can the future of humanity be assured.

Social Darwinism in this sense was not the only product of the application of these theories. It is very interesting to see that Marx in 1860, looking into *The Origin of Species*, wrote to Engels saying: 'Darwin's book is very important and serves me as a basis in natural science for the class struggle in history.' And immediately you turn it that way round you see that you can provide a basis for a theory of class struggle on the same analogy. Once again, human history is a struggle—but now between classes rather than races or individuals. On the other hand Engels was among the first to see the faults of the analogy. Arguing, if too simply, that

> the whole Darwinian theory of the struggle for existence is simply the transference from society to organic nature of Hobbes's theory of *bellum omnium contra omnes*, and of the bourgeois theory of competition, as well as the Malthusian theory of population

he went on, in the The Dialectics of Nature, to show that

> it is very easy to transfer these theories back again from natural history to the history of society, and altogether too naive to maintain that thereby these assertions have been proved as eternal natural laws of society.

The distinguishing feature of human society was production, and when

> the means of development are socially produced the categories taken from the animal kingdom are already totally inapplicable.

However, the concept of the struggle for existence must be retained. It expresses the struggle of the producers against the capitalists who have appropriated their means of production and reduced them to poverty. Thus

> the conception of history as a series of class struggles is already much richer in content and deeper than merely reducing it to weakly distinguished phases of the struggle for existence.

This is complex. The analogy is criticized and rejected but then in a way reinstated. Engels had earlier recognized that there was a different kind of analogy from nature, its harmonious cooperative working; which many thinkers had emphasized. But

> hardly was Darwin recognized before these same people saw everywhere nothing but struggle. Both views are justified within narrow limits, but both are equally one-sided and prejudiced.

This is right, but it can hardly be doubted that for his own version of history Engels drew on the rhetorical strength—now differently applied and directed—of the analogized 'struggle for existence'.

One of the results of Spencerian ideas of political development had been the belief that although progress is going to happen by a natural evolutionary mechanism, it can't be hurried. There's nothing you can do about it. In the natural processes of social selection higher types eventually emerge: this is the whole process, but you can't hurry it along. Therefore evolution becomes a way of describing an attitude to social change. If somebody says to you, 'Here is a wicked condition, a case of poverty or corruption or exploitation,' you say: 'Yes, it is very bad, but there is nothing we can do about it. The evolutionary process will eventually take us beyond it and if we interfere now we shall merely prevent that happening.' Then this led to a popular contrast between evolution and revolution, and the rhyme helped. You could not bring about change in society by intervention, let alone by violent intervention. 'We believe,' many thousands of people then started to say, 'in evolution, not revolution.' Yet given the bizarre nature of the analogies from biology, it is not surprising that when De Vries established the evolution of species from mutations, socialist writers who were engaged in the argument against the theorists of social evolution quickly seized on the mutation as the justification precisely for the sharp revolutionary break. 'There you are, you see,' they said: 'nature does not work by the inevitability of gradualism,' which had been the ordinary assumption and which was built into the ideology of the Fabians. 'It works by the sharp mutation which establishes a new...' And then you say 'species' or 'order of society' according to which argument you're involved in. The argument between evolution and revolution, which ought to have been a social and political argument because it is really an argument about particular societies and about means of changing them, thus attracted very early a strong biological or pseudo-biological component.

Now let us look at some of the reactions from within the same tradition to some of these applications. Veblen, for example, in 1899, in *The Theory of the Leisure Class*, said, 'It is quite true that our social system selects certain men,' granting the point that Sumner had made, that millionaires are the product of 'natural selection': the point is, Veblen argued, does it select the right human traits? May not our social system be selecting altogether the wrong human qualities—for example, shrewd practice, chicanery or low cunning? Granted all your arguments about the mechanism of selection as inevitable, may not the social system be producing precisely the wrong emphases, and giving success and power to the wrong human types? This argument was very much developed around the turn of the century.

Benjamin Kidd in his *Social Evolution* said in 1894: 'We must above all take social action to preserve real competition.' At the moment the majority of men are shut out from effectively competing. They don't have the means to compete in society, they're not educated, they don't have money. He therefore uses a social democratic or liberal kind of argument about extending education, giving opportunity, but its purpose is to promote competition, to make the competitive struggle more active and more general. W.H. Mallock, on the other hand, taking a conservative view in his *Aristocracy and Evolution*, argued against democracy and the extension of education on the grounds—more in line with conventional Social Darwinism— that the one desirable product of the competitive process was the great man, the leader, and the one condition of a leader was that he should have enough power, that he should be instantly obeyed, that he should have the means of control to put his great visions into operation, because if the great man cannot put his visions into operation, dragged back by the mediocrity of the mass, human society will never solve its problems. This theory, with its biological component, became, in the twentieth century, first a theory of élites and then a theory of Fascism.

Meanwhile, however, there had been a response of a rather surprising kind. For Kropotkin, in *Mutual Aid* in 1902, said in effect: 'Yes, let us indeed learn from the order of nature. If we look at nature we find it full of examples of mutual aid. Look at the herds of deer, or of cattle. Look at the ants, look at the bees, look at all the social insects. We will find that everywhere there are examples of mutual aid.' Of course, this was co-operation within species. Most of the competitive theories had been based on struggle *between* species, and then covertly applied to competition within one species—man. Kropotkin reversed this: the order of nature, he argued, teaches us mutual aid, collectivism, a quite different sort of social order.

It was Thomas Huxley who made the decisive point, in his *Evolution and Ethics* in 1893. He said: 'The whole confusion has arisen from identifying fittest with best.' 'Fittest', after all, in the Darwinian sense, although not in the Spencerian sense, had meant those best adapted to their environment. If 'fittest' had meant strongest, most powerful, then presumably the dinosaurs would still be here and masters of the earth. 'Fittest' meaning 'adapted to the environment' didn't necessarily mean any of the things which it meant in the social analogy—the strongest, the fiercest, the most cunning, the most enduring. It meant that which in its situation was best adapted to survive. If this is so, Huxley argued, we realize that we can derive no ethical principle from a process of largely random survivals. If we look at the real process of the origins and survivals of species, we learn that fitness to environment cannot be based on any abstract principle and, therefore, that ethics cannot be founded on biological evidence.

Advanced societies, Huxley argued, develop ethical systems whose precise purpose is to modify natural law. Huxley assumes, which I take leave to doubt, that natural law, the order of nature, is a process of unrestrained struggle, and that ethics is then a qualifying mechanism to what, unrestrained, would be a cosmic law. Huxley is, surprisingly, as firm as many of the others that there is such a cosmic law, but he proposes social ethics, cultural development, as a way of modifying it. This position has been repeated by his grandson Julian, who argues that cultural evolution is now the main process, cultural evolution within man.

Meanwhile, this climate of ideas had been pervading imaginative literature in ways that went very deep, but in many different directions. You can pick it up, for example, in Strindberg, especially in the preface to *Miss Julie*, that remarkably powerful play about a single destructive relationship which he wrote in 1888. Strindberg in the preface describes the servant, Jean, as the rising type, the man who is sexually on the upgrade. Risen from a poor family, he is vigorous, adaptable and will survive in his struggle with Lady Julie, the weak aristocrat belonging to a fixed and therefore rather decadent strain. A powerfully-observed sexual relationship of a direct kind is thus interpreted in terms derived from the context of the Darwinist or pseudo-Darwinist argument.

I cannot reckon how many successors there have been to that proposition: the idea of a vigorous, rising working-class male, or a male from a submerged racial group, who enters into a relationship of sex and conflict with the representative of a comparatively weak, comparatively declining or fixed social stratum. A resolution which might be seen as destructive, as in the kind of imposed suicide of Julie which is Jean's culmination, can be ethically rationalized as the emergence of the most vigorous stock. The metaphors for such a process are everywhere apparent in subsequent imaginative literature.

There were more direct applications of the idea in, for example, Jack London, a socialist, a man deeply influenced by Spencer and Darwin, with experience of struggle under very primitive conditions and also with experience of the social jungle that, within the same order of analogy, was an increasingly popular way of describing the late-nineteenth-century city. London develops a characteristic imaginative structure in which struggle is a virtue. The survival of the most vigorous type is seen at once in terms of a kind of individual primitivism and also in terms of the rising class, the class which had hitherto been submerged. In some of his work—for example, *White Fang*—it is the emergence of the powerful individual who has competed under wilderness conditions; in *The Iron Heel* it is the emergence of the class that has been long suppressed but is historically due to rise.

H.G. Wells's ideas on the subject derive most directly from Thomas Huxley's, but imaginatively he reaches well beyond them. Think, for example, of *The Time Machine*, which is the imaginative projection of a particular phase of evolution operating at several different levels. It is in one sense a projection of the division between the rich and the labouring poor in nineteenth-century industrial society. When the time traveller goes far into the future, he discovers two races of creatures sharing the earth. The race that he first finds is pretty, doll-like;

it plays games with flowers, has charming manners, has a playful but weak kind of life in the sunshine, like children. Unnoticed at first, but eventually emerging from below the ground, there appears the other race, the Morlocks, who are dark and bestial.

You can see in all this the evolutionary protection of an idle playful rich and a working population submerged in the darkness and reduced to animal conditions. But the whole situation is imaginatively reversed because the Morlocks keep the Eloi as food: the pretty playmates on the surface of the earth are not the dominant race, for the Morlocks are waiting their time, in evolutionary terms, to come back to the surface again, and meanwhile they feed on the playful ones as cattle.

This idea of the struggle for existence, projected from deep social stratifications, resulting in a branching of the race of man into these two extremes, is one of Wells's most powerful ideas, unforgettably expressed, with the kind of horror with which so many of these ideas of the inevitable struggle for existence were imaginatively received. Wells uses everywhere in his imaginative fiction (and a whole tradition of Science Fiction and scientific romance has followed him) the idea of evolution into new physical types of man, the idea of differently evolving intelligent species on other planets and the idea of competition between them.

When alternative species meet they make war: this idea is deeply established in Science Fiction. *The War of the Worlds* and the whole vast tradition of intergalactic war that we've had ever since in books and films represent to some degree a reaction to twentieth-century experience of war. But the tradition began before the epoch of major wars, and represents also a reaction to the idea of the fundamental struggle for existence: if one species meets another, it will inevitably compete with it and try to destroy it. The extraordinary physical beings that we have been regaled with in Science Fiction are a product of this idea of evolution playing on situations of great tension, great fear.

Utopias have been quite differently projected. Instead of the static Utopias of pre-nineteenth-century writing, when men would find an ideal condition, an island or some point in the future, where their social problems would have been solved, Utopias now, as Wells observed, must be dynamic: they will not stand still. That is what we learn from Darwin, he said: there has to be progression through higher stages. Moreover, they are fraught with great threat: there is inherent danger and conflict in them. Wells's Utopias characteristically are arrived at only after a period of exceptionally destructive conflict.

Some other writers may be mentioned. Shaw, for example, takes a version of creative evolution which is, one might say, more naïve even than Spencer's. The evolution of the final ideal type in *Back to Methuselah* we might be happy to read as a caricature of Spencer. But it is clear from the preface that we are asked to take seriously the emergence of those He-Ancients and She-Ancients (and I think it isn't only the pronouns which remind us of goats) who have pressed on to human perfection, which is, guess what, the goal of redemption from the flesh: pure intelligence has emancipated itself from the body. This is the sort of thing that Wells imagined in his extraordinary race of Selenites on the Moon, with the enormous brain case and the tiny legs: but with Shaw it really was a kind of evolutionary idea that man should get rid of this flesh stuff.

In Ibsen and Hardy there is a very interesting preoccupation with heredity, directly influenced by Darwin and the evolutionary debate, but in each case the critical imaginative difference is this: survival is not unproblematically taken as a criterion of value. Ibsen and Hardy were perfectly prepared to accept that there is intense struggle and competition, that people do get defeated, often the most aspiring being the most deeply defeated. Nearly all Ibsen's heroes aspire, climb (spiritually in most cases) and are defeated in the very act of climbing, overwhelmed because they aspire.

In Hardy it is very often the aspiring or the exceptionally pure character, the Jude the Obscure or Tess, who is the most absolutely destroyed. You cannot read Ibsen or Hardy without realizing that survival is not the demonstration of value: struggle is a necessary process, but in a different sense from the rationalized struggle of the Social Darwinists. It is the constant self-urging towards the light, towards a different, higher kind of human life, which is repeatedly imagined in Hardy and in Ibsen. The attempt is defeated, but the manner of the defeat is such that what is confirmed is the impulse to the light, with a very sober, very sombre look at the possibility or probability that the darkness will win. It is not a teaching of darkness, nor is it any kind of rationalization of the results of crude struggle.

The final example I can give—and it is a surprising one in this context because he used to say he didn't believe in evolution and didn't believe in science much at all—is D.H. Lawrence. Like Strindberg, he uses the idea of the vital rising type and a rather decadent or fixed or imprisoned alternative social type: generally the vigorous rising man and the sexually imprisoned, socially imprisoned or socially declining woman.

He makes of the encounter a cosmic process: it is precisely the cosmic character of the Lawrence sexual relationships of this kind that gives them their place in this tradition. For these are not simple personal relationships; they have something to do with the future of the race, and the physically rising vigorous type is strongly emphasized. But beyond that, at the end of *Women in Love*, having reached a kind of deadlock in human relationships, having seen the failure of one cold, willed relationship between Gerald and Gudrun, having recognized that the relative warmth and friendliness of the relationship between Birkin and Ursula had its limits, that it was more decent but not necessarily complete, Lawrence suddenly in a very surprising version repeats the imaginative conclusion of so much of this tradition, that perhaps we shall have to evolve beyond being human. The merely human is the merely disappointing. He puts it in direct evolutionary terms: just as the horse, he writes, has taken the place of the mastodon, so the eternal creative mystery would dispose of man:

> Races came and went, species passed away, but ever new species arose, more lovely, or equally lovely, always surpassing wonder. The fountain-head was incorruptible and unsearchable. It had no limits. It could bring forth miracles, create utterly new races and new species in its own hour, new forms of consciousness, new forms of body, new units of being.

It is a positive transforming idea, that the creative mystery could evolve beyond man, if man in his present condition failed to attain an adequate consciousness. It is in that sense at the very opposite pole from the pessimistic rationalizations of struggle. But all these matters—issues of societies, of social, economic and political relationships, issues of human relationships between individuals—have been affected, both fundamentally and at the level of their persuasive content, by ideas of what is held to be a scientific process—which, as we have seen, can be applied in many different directions according to the main bearing of the argument or the work.

We then come back (or I at least come back, particularly remembering the social component in the biological theories themselves) to saying that man cannot derive lessons and laws from the processes of what he sees as a separated nature, lessons and laws supposed to be conditions of himself, conditions to which he must in some way conform. The nineteenth-century and early-twentieth-century examples have, at this distance, a certain faded air. Some of them, indeed, can be too easily introduced for mild astonishment or amusement. Yet in our own time, of course with a show of more up-to-date science, the crudest ideas of Social Darwinism, and the crudest analogical interpretations of human relationships in quasi-scientific terms, have been remarkably revived and given extraordinary publicity. Theories of unrestrained and in effect unrestrainable natural aggression have again been launched, with an extraordinary imaginative commitment to the jaws of the great predators. Advertising, typically, has used the tiger as an image for a brand of petrol, in effect animalizing—indeed making predatory—the car. The territoriality of some species has been rationalized as the natural basis of the nation-state and its means of armed defence. The actual complexities of territoriality in different animals and in different periods of human society are overridden by what are finally crude images of property and its defence. Again the highly differentiated internal relations between members of species have been selected and narrowed to crude images of necessary hierarchy—the 'pecking order'—which are used to ideologize and ratify contemporary class and status relationships.

In a familiar confusion and overlap between certain animal species and human prehistory, there has been a rhetorical projection of 'man the hunter', which typically overrides the varied evidence we have of the character of hunting societies, in their internal relations and in their often finely modulated attitudes to the animals they kill and eat. This is important because complex evidence is overriden by an image which is not really that of the hunter but of the aggressive hunter-killer, where not the food but the killing is taken as determining. And this in its turn is used to interpret violence in twentieth-century societies, as a 'more profound' alternative—the burden of the 'beast brain'—to political, economic and historical investigations. In the commercial culture of our own period—a culture which includes works passed off as scientific and theoretical—this new wave of Social Darwinism, now extended beyond its original matrix, is very pervasive and must be supposed to be influential.

It may then be necessary to do more than keep saying that most of the images are demonstrably false, in their characteristic selectivity and uncritical transference. That is a quiet point; quiet and perhaps insufficient, while these brutal images range. There is then another way of putting it, which this tradition seems to invite. If we must have an analogy, these theories and analogies are like one kind of scavenger: darting opportunists around the body of actual science. But then it is not the science that is dead. It is the social theory of that system which had promised order and progress and yet produced the twentieth century. Instead of facing that fact, in all its immense complexity, the rationalizers and the natural rhetoricians have now moved in to snap at and discourage us: not now to ratify an imperialist and capitalist order, but to universalize its breakdown and to persuade us that it has no alternatives, since all 'nature' is like that. In this respect they are worse than their predecessors and must be even more resolutely driven off.

Note

1. Robert M. Young, 'The Human Limits of Nature' in *The Limits of Human Nature*, J. Benthall, London 1973.

Reference

Expanded from a talk at the Institute of Contemporary Arts in 1972 and originally published in Benthal, J. ed., *The Limits of Human Nature*, Allen Lane, 1973. From Raymond Williams, *Problems in Materialism and Culture*, Verso, 1980, pp. 86–102. Reprinted with kind permission of Verso and the Estate of Raymond Williams.

8

BASE AND SUPERSTRUCTURE IN MARXIST CULTURAL THEORY
(1973)

Raymond Williams's 1973 article reproduced here signalled a more explicit engagement with Marxist theory than hitherto in his work. Williams, however, makes it clear that he objects to the economic reductionism of an unexamined base–superstructure model of society that had deformed aspects of the Marxist tradition in theory and politics. For Williams, culture is never a simple reflex or reflection of economic structure and process. He is also critical of the kind of determinism that is derived from idealist philosophy and favours, instead, a notion of determination whereby limits and pressures are set on the scope for action and the potential and possibility of change. Williams preferred a rather more holistic model of interacting elements in a totality of relations than the base–superstructure model typically allows. The holistic model is characteristic of his earlier work but it is also represented in humanistic strands of the Marxist tradition.

Here, Williams draws on the Italian Marxist Antonio Gramsci's concept of hegemony to inform cultural analysis. And, he himself makes an original contribution in the conceptual distinctions between residual and emergent cultures and between alternative practice – seeking coexistence with prevailing hegemonic arrangements – and oppositional practice that aims to go beyond the prevailing hegemony.

Any modern approach to a Marxist theory of culture must begin by considering the proposition of a determining base and a determined superstructure. From a strictly theoretical point of view this is not, in fact, where we might choose to begin. It would be in many ways preferable if we could begin from a proposition which originally was equally central, equally authentic: namely the proposition that social being determines consciousness. It is not that the two propositions necessarily deny each other or are in contradiction. But the proposition of base and superstructure, with its figurative element, with its suggestion of a fixed and definite spatial relationship, constitutes, at least in certain hands, a very specialized and at times unacceptable version of the other proposition. Yet in the transition from Marx to Marxism, and in the development of mainstream Marxism itself, the proposition of the determining base and the determined superstructure has been commonly held to be the key to Marxist cultural analysis.

It is important, as we try to analyse this proposition, to be aware that the term of relationship which is involved, that is to say 'determines', is of great linguistic and theoretical complexity. The language of determination and even more of determinism was inherited from idealist and especially theological accounts of the world and man. It is significant that it is in one of his familiar inversions, his contradictions of received propositions, that Marx uses the word which becomes, in English translation, 'determines' (the usual but not invariable German word is *bestimmen*). He is opposing an ideology that had been insistent on the power of certain forces outside man, or, in its secular version, on an abstract determining consciousness. Marx's own proposition explicitly denies this, and puts the origin of determination in men's own activities. Nevertheless, the particular history and continuity of the term serves to remind us that there are, within ordinary use—and this is true of most of the major European languages—quite different possible meanings and implications of the word 'determine'. There is, on the one hand, from its theological inheritance, the notion of an external cause which totally predicts or prefigures, indeed totally controls a subsequent activity. But there is also, from the experience of social practice, a notion of determination as setting limits, exerting pressures.*

Now there is clearly a difference between a process of setting limits and exerting pressures, whether by some external force or by the internal laws of a particular development, and that other process in which a subsequent content is essentially prefigured, predicted and controlled by a pre-existing external force. Yet it is fair to say, looking at many applications of Marxist cultural analysis, that it is the second sense, the notion of prefiguration, prediction or control, which has often explicitly or implicitly been used.

Superstructure: Qualifications and Amendments

The term of relationship is then the first thing that we have to examine in this proposition, but we have to do this by going on to look at the related terms themselves. 'Superstructure' (*Überbau*) has had most attention. In common usage, after Marx, it acquired a main sense of a unitary 'area' within which all cultural and ideological activities could be placed. But already in Marx himself, in the later correspondence of Engels, and at many points in the subsequent Marxist tradition, qualifications were made about the determined character of certain superstructural activities. The first kind of qualification had to do with delays in time, with complications, and with certain indirect or relatively distant relationships. The simplest notion of a superstructure, which is still by no means entirely abandoned, had been the reflection, the imitation or the reproduction of the reality of the base in the superstructure in a more or less direct way. Positivist notions of reflection and reproduction of course directly supported this. But since in many real cultural activities this relationship cannot be found, or cannot be found without effort or even violence to the material or practice being studied, the notion was introduced of delays in time, the famous lags; of various technical complications; and of indirectness, in which certain kinds of activity in the cultural sphere—philosophy, for example—were situated at a greater distance from the primary economic activities. That was the first stage of qualification of the notion of superstructure: in effect, an operational qualification. The second stage was related but more fundamental, in that the process of the relationship itself was more substantially looked at. This was the kind of reconsideration which gave rise to the modern notion of 'mediation', in which something more than simple reflection or reproduction—indeed something radically different from either reflection or reproduction—actively occurs. In the later twentieth century there is the notion of 'homologous structures', where there may be no direct or easily apparent similarity, and certainly nothing like reflection or reproduction, between the superstructural process and the reality of the base, but in which there is an essential homology or correspondence of structures, which can be discovered by analysis. This is not the same notion as 'mediation', but it is the same kind of amendment in that the relationship between the base and the superstructure is not supposed to be direct, nor simply operationally subject to lags and complications and indirectnesses, but that of its nature it is not direct reproduction.

These qualifications and amendments are important. But it seems to me that what has not been looked at with equal care is the received notion of the 'base' (*Basis, Grundlage*). And indeed I would argue that the base is the more important concept to look at if we are to understand the realities of cultural process. In many uses of the proposition of base and superstructure, as a matter of verbal habit, 'the base' has come to be considered virtually as an object, or in less crude cases, it has been considered in essentially uniform and usually static ways. 'The base' is the real social existence of man. 'The base' is the real relations of production corresponding to a stage of development of the material productive forces. 'The base' is a mode of production at a particular stage of its development. We make and repeat propositions of this kind, but the usage is then very different from Marx's emphasis on productive activities, in particular structural relations, constituting the foundation of all other activities. For while a particular stage of the development of production can be discovered and made precise by analysis, it is never in practice either uniform or static. It is indeed one of the central propositions of Marx's sense of history that there are deep contradictions in the relationships of production and in the consequent social relationships. There is therefore the continual possibility of the dynamic variation of these forces. Moreover, when these forces are considered, as Marx always considers them, as the specific activities and relationships of real men, they mean something very much more active, more complicated and more contradictory than the developed metaphorical notion of 'the base' could possibly allow us to realize.

The Base and the Productive Forces

So we have to say that when we talk of 'the base', we are talking of a process and not a state. And we cannot ascribe to that process certain fixed properties for subsequent translation to the variable processes of the superstructure. Most people who have wanted to make the ordinary proposition more reasonable have concentrated on refining the notion of superstructure. But I would say that each term of the proposition has to be revalued in a particular direction. We have to revalue 'determination' towards the setting of limits and the exertion of pressure, and away from a predicted, prefigured and controlled content. We have to revalue 'superstructure' towards a related range of cultural practices, and away from a reflected, reproduced or specifically dependent content. And, crucially, we have to revalue 'the base' away from the notion of a fixed economic or technological abstraction, and towards the specific activities of men in real social and economic relationships, containing fundamental contradictions and variations and therefore always in a state of dynamic process.

It is worth observing one further implication behind the customary definitions. 'The base' has come to include, especially in certain twentieth-century developments, a strong and limiting sense of basic industry. The emphasis on heavy industry, even, has played a certain cultural role. And this raises a more general problem, for we find ourselves forced to look again at the ordinary notion of 'productive forces'. Clearly what we are examining in the base is primary productive forces. Yet some very crucial distinctions have to be made here. It is true that in his analysis of capitalist production Marx considered 'productive work' in a very particular and specialized sense corresponding to that mode of production. There is a difficult passage in the *Grundrisse* in which he argues that while the man who makes a piano is a productive worker, there is a real question whether the man who distributes the piano is also a productive worker; but he probably is, since he contributes to the realization of surplus value. Yet when it comes to the man who plays the piano, whether to himself or to others, there is no question: he is not a productive worker at all. So piano-maker is base, but pianist superstructure. As a way of considering cultural activity, and incidentally the economics of modern cultural activity, this is very clearly a dead-end. But for any theoretical clarification it is crucial to recognize that Marx was there engaged in an analysis of a particular kind of production, that is capitalist commodity production. Within his analysis of this mode, he had to give to the notion of 'productive labour' and 'productive forces' a specialized sense of primary work on materials in a form which produced commodities.

But this has narrowed remarkably, and in a cultural context very damagingly, from his more central notion of *productive forces*, in which, to give just brief reminders, the most important thing a worker ever produces is himself, himself in the fact of that kind of labour, or the broader historical emphasis of men producing themselves, themselves and their history. Now when we talk of the base, and of primary productive forces, it matters very much whether we are referring, as in one degenerate form of this proposition became habitual, to primary production within the terms of capitalist economic relationships, or to the primary production of society itself, and of men themselves, the material production and reproduction of real life. If we have the broad sense of productive forces, we look at the whole question of the base differently, and we are then less tempted to dismiss as superstructural, and in that sense as merely secondary, certain vital productive social forces, which are in the broad sense, from the beginning, basic.

Uses of Totality

Yet, because of the difficulties of the ordinary proposition of base and superstructure, there was an alternative and very important development, an emphasis primarily associated with Lukács, on a social 'totality'. The totality of social practices was opposed to this layered notion of base and a consequent superstructure. This concept of a totality of practices is compatible with the notion of social being determining consciousness, but it does not necessarily interpret this process in terms of a base and a superstructure. Now the language of totality has become common, and it is indeed in many ways more acceptable than the notion of base and superstructure. But with one very important reservation. It is very easy for the notion of totality to empty of its essential content the original Marxist proposition. For if we come to say that society is composed of a large number of social practices which form a concrete social whole, and if we give to each practice a certain specific recognition, adding only that they interact, relate and combine in very complicated ways, we are at one level much more obviously talking about reality, but we are at another level withdrawing from the claim that there is any process of determination. And this I, for one, would be very unwilling to do. Indeed, the key question to ask about any notion of totality in cultural theory is this: whether the notion of totality includes the notion of intention.

If totality is simply concrete, if it is simply the recognition of a large variety of miscellaneous and contemporaneous practices, then it is essentially empty of any content that could be called Marxist. Intention, the notion of intention, restores the key question, or rather the key emphasis. For while it is true that any society is a complex whole of such practices, it is also true that any society has a specific organization, a specific structure, and that the principles of this organization and structure can be seen as directly related to certain social intentions, intentions by which we define the society, intentions which in all our experience have been the rule of a particular class. One of the unexpected consequences of the crudeness of the base/superstructure model has been the too easy acceptance of models which appear less crude—models of totality or of a complex whole—but which exclude the facts of social intention, the class character of a particular society and so on. And this reminds us of how much we lose if we abandon the superstructural emphasis altogether. Thus I have great difficulty in seeing processes of art and thought as superstructural in the sense of the formula as it is commonly used. But in many areas of social and political thought—certain kinds of ratifying theory, certain kinds of law, certain kinds of institution, which after all in Marx's original formulations were very much part of the superstructure—in all that kind of social apparatus, and in a decisive area of political and ideological activity and construction, if we fail to see a superstructural element we fail to recognize reality at all. These laws, constitutions, theories, ideologies, which are so often claimed as natural, or as having universal validity or significance, simply have to be seen as expressing and ratifying the domination of a particular class. Indeed the difficulty of revising the formula of base and superstructure has had much to do with the perception of many militants—who have to fight such institutions and notions as well as fighting economic battles—that if these institutions and their ideologies are not perceived as having that kind of dependent and ratifying relationship, if their claims to universal validity or legitimacy are not denied and fought, then the class character of the society can no longer be seen. And this has been the effect of some versions of totality as the description of cultural process. Indeed I think we can properly use the notion of totality only when we combine it with that other crucial Marxist concept of 'hegemony'.

The Complexity of Hegemony

It is Gramsci's great contribution to have emphasized hegemony, and also to have understood it at a depth which is, I think, rare. For hegemony supposes the existence of something which is truly total, which is not merely secondary or superstructural, like the weak sense of ideology, but which is lived at such a depth, which saturates the society to such an extent, and which, as Gramsci put it, even constitutes the substance and limit of common sense for most people under its sway, that it corresponds to the reality of social experience very much more clearly than any notions derived from the formula of base and superstructure. For if ideology were merely some abstract, imposed set of notions, if our social and political and cultural ideas and assumptions and habits were merely the result of specific manipulation, of a kind of overt training which might be simply ended or withdrawn, then the society would be very much easier to move and to change than in practice it has ever been or is. This notion of hegemony as deeply saturating the consciousness of a society seems to me to be fundamental. And hegemony has the advantage over general notions of totality, that it at the same time emphasizes the facts of domination.

Yet there are times when I hear discussions of hegemony and feel that it too, as a concept, is being dragged back to the relatively simple, uniform and static notion which 'superstructure' in ordinary use had become. Indeed I think that we have to give a very complex account of hegemony if we are talking about any real social formation. Above all we have to give an account which allows for its elements of real and constant change. We have to emphasize that hegemony is not singular; indeed that its own internal structures are highly complex, and have continually to be renewed, recreated and defended; and by the same token, that they can be continually challenged and in certain respects modified. That is why instead of speaking simply of 'the hegemony', 'a hegemony', I would propose a model which allows for this kind of variation and contradiction, its sets of alternatives and its processes of change.

For one thing that is evident in some of the best Marxist cultural analysis is that it is very much more at home in what one might call *epochal* questions than in what one has to call *historical* questions. That is to say, it is usually very much better at distinguishing the large features of different epochs of society, as commonly between feudal and bourgeois, than at distinguishing between different phases of bourgeois society, and different moments within these phases: that true historical process which demands a much greater precision and delicacy of analysis than the always striking epochal analysis which is concerned with main lineaments and features.

The theoretical model which I have been trying to work with is this. I would say first that in any society, in any particular period, there is a central system of practices, meanings and values, which we can properly call dominant and effective. This implies no presumption about its value. All I am saying is that it is central. Indeed I would call it a corporate system, but this might be confusing, since Gramsci uses 'corporate' to mean the subordinate as opposed to the general and dominant elements of hegemony. In any case what I have in mind is the central, effective and dominant system of meanings and values, which are not merely abstract but which are organized and lived. That is why hegemony is not to be understood at the level of mere opinion or mere manipulation. It is a whole body of practices and expectations; our assignments of energy, our ordinary understanding of the nature of man and of his world. It is a set of meanings and values which as they are experienced as practices appear as reciprocally confirming. It thus constitutes a sense of reality for most people in the society, a sense of absolute because experienced reality beyond which it is very difficult for most members of the society to move, in most areas of their lives. But this is not, except in the operation of a moment of abstract analysis, in any sense a static system. On the contrary we can only understand an effective and dominant culture if we understand the real social process on which it depends: I mean the process of incorporation. The modes of incorporation are of great social significance. The educational institutions are usually the main agencies of the transmission of an effective dominant culture, and this is now a major economic as well as a cultural activity; indeed it is both in the same moment. Moreover, at a philosophical level, at the true level of theory and at the level of the history of various practices, there is a process which I call the *selective tradition*: that which, within the terms of an effective dominant culture, is always passed off as '*the* tradition', '*the* significant past'. But always the selectivity is the point; the way in which from a whole possible area of past and present, certain meanings and practices are chosen for emphasis, certain other meanings and practices are neglected and excluded. Even more crucially, some of these meanings and practices are reinterpreted, diluted, or put into forms which support or at least do not contradict other elements within the effective dominant culture. The processes of education; the processes of a much wider social training within institutions like the family; the practical definitions and organization of work; the selective tradition at an intellectual and theoretical level: all these forces are involved in a continual making and remaking of an effective dominant culture, and on them, as experienced, as built into our living, its reality depends. If what we learn there were merely an imposed ideology, or if it were only the isolable meanings and practices of the ruling class, or of a section of the ruling class, which gets imposed on others, occupying merely the top of our minds, it would be—and one would be glad—a very much easier thing to overthrow.

It is not only the depths to which this process reaches, selecting and organizing and interpreting our experience. It is also that it is continually active and adjusting; it isn't just the past, the dry husks of ideology which we can more easily discard. And this can only be so, in a complex society, if it is something more substantial and more flexible than any abstract imposed ideology. Thus we have to recognize the alternative meanings and values, the alternative opinions and attitudes, even some alternative senses of the world, which can be accommodated and tolerated within a particular effective and dominant culture. This has been much under-emphasized in our notions of a superstructure, and even in some notions of hegemony. And the under-emphasis opens the way for retreat to an indifferent complexity. In the practice of politics, for example, there are certain truly incorporated modes of what are nevertheless, within those terms, real oppositions, that are felt and fought out. Their existence within the incorporation is recognizable by the fact that, whatever the degree of internal conflict or internal variation, they do not in practice go beyond the limits of the central effective and dominant definitions. This is true, for example, of the practice of parliamentary politics, though its internal oppositions are real. It is true about a whole range of practices and arguments, in any real society, which can by no means be reduced to an ideological cover, but which can nevertheless be properly analysed as in my sense corporate, if we find that, whatever the degree of internal controversy and variation, they do not in the end exceed the limits of the central corporate definitions. But if we are to say this, we have to think again about the sources of that which is not corporate; of those practices, experiences, meanings, values which are not part of the effective dominant culture. We can express this in two ways. There is clearly something that we can call alternative to the effective dominant culture, and there is something else that we can call oppositional, in a true sense. The degree of existence of these alternative and oppositional forms is itself a matter of constant historical variation in real circumstances. In certain societies it is possible to find areas of social life in which quite real alternatives are at least left alone. (If they are made available, of course, they are part of the corporate organization.) The existence of the possibility of opposition, and of its articulation, its degree of openness, and so on, again depends on very precise social and political forces. The facts of alternative and oppositional forms of social life and culture, in relation to the effective and dominant culture, have then to be recognized as subject to historical variation, and as having sources which are very significant as a fact about the dominant culture itself.

Residual and Emergent Cultures

I have next to introduce a further distinction, between *residual* and *emergent* forms, both of alternative and of oppositional culture. By 'residual' I mean that some experiences, meanings and values, which cannot be verified or cannot be expressed in terms of the dominant culture, are nevertheless lived and practised on the basis of the residue—cultural as well as social—of some previous social formation. There is a real case of this in certain religious values, by contrast with the very evident incorporation of most religious meanings and values into the dominant system. The same is true, in a culture like Britain, of certain notions derived from a rural past, which have a very significant popularity. A residual culture is usually at some distance from the effective dominant culture, but one has to recognize that, in real cultural activities, it may get incorporated into it. This is because some part of it, some version of it—and especially if the residue is from some major area of the past—will in many cases have had to be incorporated if the effective dominant culture is to make sense in those areas. It is also because at certain points a dominant culture cannot allow too much of this kind of practice and experience outside itself, at least without risk. Thus the pressures are real, but certain genuinely residual meanings and practices in some important cases survive.

By 'emergent' I mean, first, that new meanings and values, new practices, new significances and experiences, are continually being created. But there is then a much earlier attempt to incorporate them, just because they are part—and yet not a defined part—of effective contemporary practice. Indeed it is significant in our own period how very early this attempt is, how alert the dominant culture now is to anything that can be seen as emergent. We have then to see, first, as it were a temporal relation between a dominant culture and on the one hand a residual and on the other hand an emergent culture. But we can only understand this if we can make distinctions, that usually require very precise analysis, between residual-incorporated and residual not incorporated, and between emergent-incorporated and emergent not incorporated. It is an important fact about any particular society, how far it reaches into the whole range of human practices and experiences in an attempt at incorporation. It may be true of some earlier phases of bourgeois society, for example, that there were some areas of experience which it was willing to dispense with, which it was prepared to assign as the sphere of private or artistic life, and as being no particular business of society or the state. This went along with certain kinds of political tolerance, even if the reality of that tolerance was malign neglect. But I am sure it is true of the society that has come into existence since the last war, that progressively, because of developments in the social character of labour, in the social character of communications, and in the social character of decision, it extends much further than ever before in capitalist society into certain hitherto resigned areas of experience and practice and meaning. Thus the effective decision, as to whether a practice is alternative or oppositional, is often now made within a very much narrower scope. There is a simple theoretical distinction between alternative and oppositional, that is to say between someone who simply finds a different way to live and wishes to be left alone with it, and someone who finds a different way to live and wants to change the society in its light. This is usually the difference between individual and small-group solutions to social crisis and those solutions which properly belong to political and ultimately revolutionary practice. But it is often a very narrow line, in reality, between alternative and oppositional. A meaning or a practice may be tolerated as a deviation, and yet still be seen only as another particular way to live. But as the necessary area of effective dominance extends, the same meanings and practices can be seen by the dominant culture, not merely as disregarding or despising it, but as challenging it.

Now it is crucial to any Marxist theory of culture that it can give an adequate explanation of the sources of these practices and meanings. We can understand, from an ordinary historical approach, at least some of the sources of residual meanings and practices. These are the results of earlier social formations, in which certain real meanings and values were generated. In the subsequent default of a particular phase of a dominant culture, there is then a reaching back to those meanings and values which were created in real societies in the past, and which still seem to have some significance because they represent areas of human experience, aspiration and achievement, which the dominant culture under-values or opposes, or even cannot recognize. But our hardest task, theoretically, is to find a non-metaphysical and non-subjectivist explanation of emergent cultural practice. Moreover, part of our answer to this question bears on the process of persistence of residual practices.

Class and Human Practice

We have indeed one source to hand from the central body of Marxist theory. We have the formation of a new class, the coming to consciousness of a new class. This remains, without doubt, quite centrally important. Of course, in itself, this process of formation complicates any simple model of base and superstructure. It also complicates some of the ordinary versions of hegemony, although it was Gramsci's whole purpose to see and to create by organization that hegemony of a proletarian kind which would be capable of challenging the bourgeois hegemony. We have then one central source of new practice, in the emergence of a new class. But we have also to recognize certain other kinds of source, and in cultural practice some of these are very important. I would say that we can recognize them on the basis of this proposition: that no mode of production, and therefore no dominant society or order of society, and therefore no dominant culture, in reality exhausts the full range of human practice, human energy, human intention (this range is not the inventory of some original 'human nature' but, on the contrary, is that extraordinary range of variations, both practised and imagined, of which human beings are and have shown themselves to be capable). Indeed it seems to me that this emphasis is not merely a negative proposition, allowing us to account for certain things which happen outside the dominant mode. On the contrary, it is a fact about the modes of domination that they select from and consequently exclude the full range of actual and possible human practice. The difficulties of human practice outside or against the dominant mode are, of course, real. It depends very much whether it is in an area in which the dominant class and the dominant culture have an interest and a stake. If the interest and the stake are explicit, many new practices will be reached for, and if possible incorporated, or else extirpated with extraordinary vigour. But in certain areas, there will be in certain periods practices and meanings which are not reached for. There will be areas of practice and meaning which, almost by definition from its own limited character, or in its profound deformation, the dominant culture is unable in any real terms to recognize. This gives us a bearing on the observable difference between, for example, the practices of a capitalist state and a state like the contemporary Soviet Union in relation to writers. Since from the whole Marxist tradition literature was seen as an important activity, indeed a crucial activity, the Soviet state is very much sharper in investigating areas where different versions of practice, different meanings and values, are being attempted and expressed. In capitalist practice, if the thing is not making a profit, or if it is not being widely circulated, then it can for some time be overlooked, at least while it remains alternative. When it becomes oppositional in an explicit way, it does, of course, get approached or attacked.

I am saying then that in relation to the full range of human practice at any one time, the dominant mode is a conscious selection and organization. At least in its fully formed state it is conscious. But there are always sources of actual human practice which it neglects or excludes. And these can be different in quality from the developing and articulate interests of a rising class. They can include, for example, alternative perceptions of others, in immediate personal relationships, or new perceptions of material and media, in art and science, and within certain limits these new perceptions can be practised. The relations between the two kinds of source—the emerging class and either the dominatively excluded or the more generally new practices—are by no means necessarily contradictory. At times they can be very close, and on the relations between them much in political practice depends. But culturally and as a matter of theory the areas can be seen as distinct.

Now if we go back to the cultural question in its most usual form—what are the relations between art and society, or literature and society?—in the light of the preceding discussion, we have to say first that there are no relations between literature and society in that abstracted way. The literature is there from the beginning as a practice in the society. Indeed until it and all other practices are present, the society cannot be seen as fully formed. A society is not fully available for analysis until each of its practices is included. But if we make that emphasis we must make a corresponding emphasis: that we cannot separate literature and art from other kinds of social practice, in such a way as to make them subject to quite special and distinct laws. They may have quite specific features as practices, but they cannot be separated from the general social process. Indeed one way of emphasizing this is to say, to insist, that literature is not restricted to operating in any one of the sectors I have been seeking to describe in this model. It would be easy to say, it is a familiar rhetoric, that literature operates in the emergent cultural sector, that it represents the new feelings, the new meanings, the new values. We might persuade ourselves of this theoretically, by abstract argument, but when we read much literature, over the whole range, without the sleight-of-hand of calling Literature only that which we have already selected as embodying certain meanings and values at a certain scale of intensity, we are bound to recognize that the act of writing, the practices of discourse in writing and speech, the making of novels and poems and plays and theories, all this activity takes place in all areas of the culture.

Literature appears by no means only in the emergent sector, which is always, in fact, quite rare. A great deal of writing is of a residual kind, and this has been deeply true of much English literature in the last half-century. Some of its fundamental meanings and values have belonged to the cultural achievements of long-past stages of society. So widespread is this fact, and the habits of mind it supports, that in many minds 'literature' and 'the past' acquire a certain identity, and it is then said that there is now no literature: all that glory is over. Yet most writing, in any period, including our own, is a form of contribution to the effective dominant culture. Indeed many of the specific qualities of literature—its capacity to embody and enact and perform certain meanings and values, or to create in single particular ways what would be otherwise merely general truths—enable it to fulfil this effective function with great power. To literature, of course, we must add the visual arts and music, and in our own society the powerful arts of film and of broadcasting. But the general theoretical point should be clear. If we are looking for the relations between literature and society, we cannot either separate out this one practice from a formed body of other practices, nor when we have identified a particular practice can we give it a uniform, static and ahistorical relation to some abstract social formation. The arts of writing and the arts of creation and performance, over their whole range, are parts of the cultural process in all the different ways, the different sectors, that I have been seeking to describe. They contribute to the effective dominant culture and are a central articulation of it. They embody residual meanings and values, not all of which are incorporated, though many are. They express also and significantly some emergent practices and meanings, yet some of these may eventually be incorporated, as they reach people and begin to move them. Thus it was very evident in the sixties, in some of the emergent arts of performance, that the dominant culture reached out to transform, or seek to transform, them. In this process, of course, the dominant culture itself changes, not in its central formation, but in many of its articulated features. But then in a modern society it must always change in this way, if it is to remain dominant, if it is still to be felt as in real ways central in all our many activities and interests.

Critical Theory as Consumption

What then are the implications of this general analysis for the analysis of particular works of art? This is the question towards which most discussion of cultural theory seems to be directed: the discovery of a method, perhaps even a methodology, through which particular works of art can be understood and described. I would not myself agree that this is the central use of cultural theory, but let us for a moment consider it. What seems to me very striking is that nearly all forms of contemporary critical theory are theories of *consumption*. That is to say, they are concerned with understanding an object in such a way that it can profitably or correctly be consumed. The earliest stage of consumption theory was the theory of 'taste', where the link between the practice and the theory was direct in the metaphor. From taste there came the more elevated notion of 'sensibility', in which it was the consumption by sensibility of elevated or insightful works that was held to be the essential practice of reading, and critical activity was then a function of this sensibility. There were then more developed theories, in the 1920s with I.A. Richards, and later in New Criticism, in which the effects of consumption were studied directly. The language of the work of art as object then became more overt. 'What effect does this work ("the poem" as it was ordinarily described) have on me?' Or, 'what impact does it have on me?', as it was later to be put in a much wider area of communication studies. Naturally enough, the notion of the work of art as *object*, as text, as an isolated artefact, became central in all these later consumption theories. It was not only that the practices of *production* were then overlooked, though this fused with the notion that most important literature anyway was from the past. The real social conditions of production were in any case neglected because they were believed to be at best secondary. The true relationship was seen always as between the taste, the sensibility or the training of the reader and this isolated work, this object 'as in itself it really is', as most people came to put it. But the notion of the work of art as object had a further large theoretical effect. If you ask questions about the work of art seen as object, they may include questions about the components of its production. Now, as it happened, there was a use of the formula of base and superstructure which was precisely in line with this. The components of a work of art were the real activities of the base, and you could study the object to discover these components. Sometimes you even studied the components and then projected the object. But in any case the relationship that was looked for was one between an object and its components. But this was not only true of Marxist suppositions of a base and a superstructure. It was true also of various kinds of psychological theory, whether in the form of archetypes, or the images of the collective unconscious, or the myths and symbols which were seen as the *components* of particular works of art. Or again there was biography, or psycho-biography and its like, where the components were in the man's life and the work of art was an object in which components of this kind were discovered. Even in some of the more rigorous forms of New Criticism and of structuralist criticism, this essential procedure of regarding the work as an object which has to be reduced to its components, even if later it may be reconstituted, came to persist.

Objects and Practices

Now I think the true crisis in cultural theory, in our own time, is between this view of the work of art as object and the alternative view of art as a practice. Of course it is at once argued that the work of art *is* an object: that various works have survived from the past, particular sculptures, particular paintings, particular buildings, and these are objects. This is of course true, but the same way of thinking is applied to works which have no such singular existence. There is no *Hamlet*, no *Brothers Karamazov*, no *Wuthering Heights*, in the sense that there is a particular great painting. There is no *Fifth Symphony*, there is no work in the whole area of music and dance and performance, which is an object in any way comparable to those works in the visual arts which have survived. And yet the habit of treating all such works as objects has persisted because this is a basic theoretical and practical presupposition. But in literature (especially in drama), in music and in a very wide area of the performing arts, what we permanently have are not objects but *notations*. These notations have then to be interpreted in an active way, according to the particular conventions. But indeed this is true over an even wider field. The relationship between the making of a work of art and its reception is always active, and subject to conventions, which in themselves are forms of (changing) social organization and relationship, and this is radically different from the production and consumption of an object. It is indeed an activity and a practice, and in its accessible forms, although it may in some arts have the character of a singular object, it is still only accessible through active perception and interpretation. This makes the case of notation, in arts like drama and literature and music, only a special case of a much wider truth. What this can show us here about the practice of analysis is that we have to break from the common procedure of isolating the object and then discovering its components. On the contrary we have to discover the nature of a practice and then its conditions.

Often these two procedures may in part resemble each other, but in many other cases they are of radically different kinds, and I would conclude with an observation on the way this distinction bears on the Marxist tradition of the relation between primary economic and social practices, and cultural practices. If we suppose that what is produced in cultural practice is a series of objects, we shall, as in most current forms of sociological-critical procedure, set about discovering their components. Within a Marxist emphasis these components will be from what we have been in the habit of calling the base. We then isolate certain features which we can so to say recognize *in component form*, or we ask what processes of transformation or mediation these components have gone through before they arrived in this accessible state.

But I am saying that we should look not for the components of a product but for the conditions of a practice. When we find ourselves looking at a particular work, or group of works, often realizing, as we do so, their essential community as well as their irreducible individuality, we should find ourselves attending first to the reality of their practice and the conditions of the practice as it was then executed. And from this I think we ask essentially different questions. Take for example the way in which an object—'a text'—is related to a genre, in orthodox criticism. We identify it by certain leading features, we then assign it to a larger category, the genre, and then we may find the components of the genre in a particular social history (although in some variants of criticism not even that is done, and the genre is supposed to be some permanent category of the mind).

It is not that way of proceeding that is now required. The recognition of the relation of a collective mode and an individual project—and these are the only categories that we can initially presume—is a recognition of related practices. That is to say, the irreducibly individual projects that particular works are, may come in experience and in analysis to show resemblances which allow us to group them into collective modes. These are by no means always genres. They may exist as resemblances within and across genres. They may be the practice of a group in a period, rather than the practice of a phase in a genre. But as we discover the nature of a particular practice, and the nature of the relation between an individual project and a collective mode, we find that we are analysing, as two forms of the same process, both its active composition and its conditions of composition, and in either direction this is a complex of extending active relationships. This means, of course, that we have no built-in procedure of the kind which is indicated by the fixed character of an object. We have the principles of the relations of practices, within a discoverably intentional organization, and we have the available hypotheses of dominant, residual and emergent. But what we are actively seeking is the true practice which has been alienated to an object, and the true conditions of practice—whether as literary conventions or as social relationships—which have been alienated to components or to mere background.

As a general proposition this is only an emphasis, but it seems to me to suggest at once the point of break and the point of departure, in practical and theoretical work, within an active and self-renewing Marxist cultural tradition.

Note

*For a further discussion of the range of meanings in 'determine' see *Keywords*, London 1976, pp. 87–91.

Reference

Originally published in *New Left Review* 82, 1973. From Raymond Williams, *Problems in Materialism and Culture*, Verso, 1980, pp. 3.1–49. Reprinted with kind permission of Verso.

9

THE TECHNOLOGY AND THE SOCIETY

(1974)

An outstanding, indeed hegemonic and ideological example of the kind of determinism that Williams rejects in the previous chapter is technological determinism. *The present extract comes from Williams's pioneering book on television in which he itemises the criticisms of technological determinism with regard to the development of television and its impact on society. Often missed by commentators, Williams also questions the alternative notion that technology is merely symptomatic of broader historical change. Against both positions, Williams traces the emergence of different technologies that combined together in the development of television (not unlike the convergence of technologies in digital media today). And, he stresses how technologies are developed deliberately to fulfil social purposes, thus bringing out the importance of* intention *in technological innovation.*

It is often said that television has altered our world. In the same way, people often speak of a new world, a new society, a new phase of history, being created – 'brought about' – by this or that new technology: the steam-engine, the automobile, the atomic bomb. Most of us know what is generally implied when such things are said. But this may be the central difficulty: that we have got so used to statements of this general kind, in our most ordinary discussions, that we can fail to realise their specific meanings.

For behind all such statements lie some of the most difficult and most unresolved historical and philosophical questions. Yet the questions are not posed by the statements; indeed they are ordinarily masked by them. Thus we often discuss, with animation, this or that 'effect' of television, or the kinds of social behaviour, the cultural and psychological conditions, which television has 'led to', without feeling ourselves obliged to ask whether it is reasonable to describe any technology as a cause, or, if we think of it as a cause, as what kind of cause, and in what relations with other kinds of causes. The most precise and discriminating local study of 'effects' can remain superficial if we have not looked into the notions of cause and effect, as between a technology and a society, a technology and a culture, a technology and a psychology, which underlie our questions and may often determine our answers.

It can of course be said that these fundamental questions are very much too difficult; and that they are indeed difficult is very soon obvious to anyone who tries to follow them through. We could spend our lives trying to answer them, whereas here and now, in a society in which television is important, there is immediate and practical work to be done: surveys to be made, research undertaken; surveys and research, moreover, which we know how to do. It is an appealing position, and it has the advantage, in our kind of society, that it is understood as practical, so that it can then be supported and funded. By contrast, other kinds of question seem merely theoretical and abstract.

Yet all questions about cause and effect, as between a technology and a society, are intensely practical. Until we have begun to answer them, we really do not know, in any particular case, whether, for example, we are talking about a technology or about the uses of a technology; about necessary institutions or particular and changeable institutions; about a content or about a form. And this is not only a matter of intellectual uncertainty; it is a matter of social practice. If the technology is a cause, we can at best modify or seek to control its effects. Or if the technology, as used, is an effect, to what other kinds of cause, and other kinds of action, should we refer and relate our experience of its uses? These are not abstract questions. They form an increasingly important part of our social and cultural arguments, and they are being decided all the time in real practice, by real and effective decisions.

It is with these problems in mind that I want to try to analyse television as a particular cultural technology, and to look at its development, its institutions, its forms and its effects, in this critical dimension. In the present chapter, I shall begin the analysis under three headings: (a) versions of cause and effect in technology and society; (b) the social history of television as a technology; (c) the social history of the uses of television technology.

A. Versions of Cause and Effect in Technology and Society

We can begin by looking again at the general statement that television has altered our world. It is worth setting down some of the different things this kind of statement has been taken to mean. For example:

(i) Television was invented as a result of scientific and technical research. Its power as a medium of news and entertainment was then so great that it altered all preceding media of news and entertainment.

(ii) Television was invented as a result of scientific and technical research. Its power as a medium of social communication was then so great that it altered many of our institutions and forms of social relationships.

(iii) Television was invented as a result of scientific and technical research. Its inherent properties as an electronic medium altered our basic perceptions of reality, and thence our relations with each other and with the world.

(iv) Television was invented as a result of scientific and technical research. As a powerful medium of communication and entertainment it took its place with other factors – such as greatly increased physical mobility, itself the result of other newly invented technologies – in altering the scale and form of our societies.

(v) Television was invented as a result of scientific and technical research, and developed as a medium of entertainment and news. It then had unforeseen consequences, not only on other entertainment and news media, which it reduced in viability and importance, but on some of the central processes of family, cultural and social life.

(vi) Television, discovered as a possibility by scientific and technical research, was selected for investment and development to meet the needs of a new kind of society, especially in the provision of centralised entertainment and in the centralised formation of opinions and styles of behaviour.

(vii) Television, discovered as a possibility by scientific and technical research, was selected for investment and promotion as a new and profitable phase of a domestic consumer economy; it is then one of the characteristic 'machines for the home'.

(viii) Television became available as a result of scientific and technical research, and in its character and uses exploited and emphasised elements of a passivity, a cultural and psychological inadequacy, which had always been latent in people, but which television now organised and came to represent.

(ix) Television became available as a result of scientific and technical research, and in its character and uses both served and exploited the needs of a new kind of large-scale and complex but atomised society.

These are only some of the possible glosses on the ordinary bald statement that television has altered our world. Many people hold mixed versions of what are really alternative opinions, and in some cases there is some inevitable overlapping. But we can distinguish between two broad classes of opinion.

In the first – (i) to (v) – the technology is in effect accidental. Beyond the strictly internal development of the technology there is no reason why any particular invention should have come about. Similarly it then has consequences which are also in the true sense accidental, since they follow directly from the technology itself. If television had not been invented, this argument would run, certain definite social and cultural events would not have occurred.

In the second – (vi) to (ix) – television is again, in effect, a technological accident, but its significance lies in its uses, which are held to be symptomatic of some order of society or some qualities of human nature which are otherwise determined. If television had not been invented, this argument runs, we would still be manipulated or mindlessly entertained, but in some other way and perhaps less powerfully.

For all the variations of local interpretation and emphasis, these two classes of opinion underlie the overwhelming majority of both professional and amateur views of the effects of television. What they have in common is the fundamental form of the statement: 'television has altered our world'.

It is then necessary to make a further theoretical distinction. The first class of opinion, described above, is that usually known, at least to its opponents, as *technological determinism*. It is an immensely powerful and now largely orthodox view of the nature of social change. New technologies are discovered, by an essentially internal process of research and development, which then sets the conditions for social change and progress. Progress, in particular, is the history of these inventions, which 'created the modern world'. The effects of the technologies, whether direct or indirect, foreseen or unforeseen, are as it were the rest of history. The steam-engine, the automobile, television, the atomic bomb, have *made* modern man and the modern condition.

The second class opinion appears less determinist. Television like any other technology becomes available as an element or a medium in a process of change that is in any case occurring or about to occur. By contrast with pure technological determinism, this view emphasises other causal factors in social change. It then considers particular technologies, or a complex of technologies, as *symptoms* of change of some other kind. Any particular technology is then as it were a by-product of a social process that is otherwise determined. It only acquires effective status when it is used for purposes which are already contained in this known social process.

The debate between these two general positions occupies the greater part of our thinking about technology and society. It is a real debate, and each side makes important points. But it is in the end sterile, because each position, though in different ways, has abstracted technology from society. In *technological determinism*, research and development have been assumed as self-generating. The new technologies are invented as it were in an independent sphere, and then create new societies or new human conditions. The view of *symptomatic technology*, similarly, assumes that research and development are self-generating, but in a more marginal way. What is discovered in the margin is then taken up and used.

Each view can then be seen to depend on the isolation of technology. It is either a self-acting force which creates new ways of life, or it is a self-acting force which provides materials for new ways of life. These positions are so deeply established, in modern social thought, that it is very difficult to think beyond them. Most histories of technology, like most histories of scientific discovery, are written from their assumptions. An appeal to 'the facts', against this or that interpretation, is made very difficult simply because the histories are usually written, consciously or unconsciously, to illustrate the assumptions. This is either explicit, with the consequential interpretation attached, or more often implicit, in that the history of technology or of scientific development is offered as a history on its own. This can be seen as a device of specialisation or of emphasis, but it then necessarily implies merely internal intentions and criteria.

To change these emphases would require prolonged and cooperative intellectual effort. But in the particular case of television it may be possible to outline a different kind of interpretation, which would allow us to see not only its history but also its uses in a more radical way. Such an interpretation would differ from technological determinism in that it would restore *intention* to the process of research and development. The technology would be seen, that is to say, as being looked for and developed with certain purposes and practices already in mind. At the same time the interpretation would differ from symptomatic technology in that these purposes and practices would be seen as *direct*: as known social needs, purposes and practices to which the technology is not marginal but central.

B. The Social History of Television as a Technology

The invention of television was no single event or series of events. It depended on a complex of inventions and developments in electricity, telegraphy, photography and motion pictures, and radio. It can be said to have separated out as a specific technological objective in the period 1875–1890, and then, after a lag, to have developed as a specific technological enterprise from 1920 through to the first public television systems of the 1930s. Yet in each of these stages it depended for parts of its realisation on inventions made with other ends primarily in view.

Until the early nineteenth century, investigations of electricity, which had long been known as a phenomenon, were primarily philosophical: investigations of a puzzling natural effect. The technology associated with these investigations was mainly directed towards isolation and concentration of the effect, for its clearer study. Towards the end of the eighteenth century there began to be applications, characteristically in relation to other known natural effects (lightning conductors). But there is then a key transitional period in a cluster of inventions between 1800 and 1831, ranging from Volta's battery to Faraday's demonstration of electro-magnetic induction, leading quickly to the production of generators. This can be properly traced as a scientific history, but it is significant that the key period of advance coincides with an important stage of the development of industrial production. The advantages of electric power were closely related to new industrial needs: for mobility and transfer in the location of power sources, and for flexible and rapid controllable conversion. The steam engine had been well suited to textiles, and its industries had been based on local siting. A more extensive development, both physically and in the complexity of multiple-part processes, such as engineering, could be attempted with other power sources but could only be fully realised with electricity. There was a very complex interaction between new needs and new inventions, at the level of primary production, of new applied industries (plating) and of new social needs which were themselves related to industrial development (city and house lighting). From 1830 to large-scale generation in the 1880s there was this continuing complex of need and invention and application.

In telegraphy the development was simpler. The transmission of messages by beacons and similar primary devices had been long established. In the development of navigation and naval warfare the flag-system had been standardised in the course of the sixteenth and seventeenth centuries. During the Napoleonic wars there was a marked development of land telegraphy, by semaphore stations, and some of this survived into peacetime. Electrical telegraphy had been suggested as a technical system as early as 1753, and was actually demonstrated in several places in the early nineteenth century. An English inventor in 1816 was told that the Admiralty was not interested. It is interesting that it was the development of the railways, themselves a response to the development of an industrial system and the related growth of cities, which clarified the need for improved telegraphy. A complex of technical possibilities was brought to a working system from 1837 onwards. The development of international trade and transport brought rapid extensions of the system, including the transatlantic cable in the 1850s and the l860s. A general system of electric telegraphy had been established by the 1870s, and in the same decade the telephone system began to be developed, in this case as a new and intended invention.

In photography, the idea of light-writing had been suggested by (among others) Wedgwood and Davy in 1802, and the *camera obscura* had already been developed. It was not the projection but the fixing of images which at first awaited technical solution, and from 1816 (Niepce) and through to 1839 (Daguerre) this was worked on, together with the improvement of camera devices. Professional and then amateur photography spread rapidly, and reproduction and then transmission, in the developing newspaper press, were achieved. By the 1880s the idea of a 'photographed reality' – still more for record than for observation – was familiar.

The idea of moving pictures had been similarly developing. The magic lantern (slide projection) had been known from the seventeenth century, and had acquired simple motion (one slide over another) by 1736. From at latest 1826 there was a development of mechanical motion-picture devices, such as the wheel-of-life, and these came to be linked with the magic lantern. The effect of persistence in human vision – that is to say, our capacity to hold the 'memory' of an image through an interval to the next image, thus allowing the possibility of a sequence built from rapidly succeeding units – had been known since classical times. Series of cameras photographing stages of a sequence were followed (Marey, 1882) by multiple-shot cameras. Friese-Greene and Edison worked on techniques of filming and protection, and celluloid was substituted for paper reels. By the 1890s the first public motion-picture shows were being given in France, America and England.

Television, as an idea, was involved with many of these developments. It is difficult to separate it, in its earliest stages, from photo-telegraphy. Bain proposed a device for transmitting pictures by electric wires in 1842; Bakewell in 1847 showed the copying telegraph; Caselli in 1862 transmitted pictures by wire over a considerable distance. In 1873, while working at a terminal of the Atlantic telegraph cable, May observed the light-sensitive properties of selenium (which had been isolated by Berzelius in 1817 and was in use for resistors). In a host of ways, following an already defined need, the means of transmitting still pictures and moving pictures were actively sought and to a considerable extent discovered. The list is long even when selective: Carey's electric eye in 1875; Nipkow's scanning system in 1884; Elster and Geitel's photo-electric cells in 1890; Braun's cathode-ray rube in 1897; Rosing's cathode-ray receiver in 1907; Campbell Swinton's electronic camera proposal in 1911. Through this whole period two facts are evident: that a system of television was foreseen, and its means were being actively sought; but also that, by comparison with electrical generation and electrical telegraphy and telephony, there was very little social investment to bring the scattered work together. It is true that there were technical blocks before 1914 – the thermionic valve and the multi-stage amplifier can be seen to have been needed and were not yet invented. But the critical difference between the various spheres of applied technology can be stated in terms of a social dimension: the new systems of production and of business or transport communication were already organised, at an economic level; the new systems of social communication were not. Thus when motion pictures were developed, their application was characteristically in the margin of established social forms – the sideshows – until their success was capitalised in a version of an established form, the motion-picture *theatre.*

The development of radio, in its significant scientific and technical stages between 1885 and 1911, was at first conceived, within already effective social systems, as an advanced form of telegraphy. Its application as a significantly new social form belongs to the immediate post-war period, in a changed social situation. It is significant that the hiatus in technical television development then also ended. In 1923 Zworykin introduced the electronic television camera tube. Through the early 1920s Baird and Jenkins, separately and competitively, were working on systems using mechanical scanning. From 1925 the rate of progress was qualitatively changed, through important technical advances but also with the example of sound broadcasting systems as a model. The Bell System in 1927 demonstrated wire transmission through a radio link, and the pre-history of the form can be seen to be ending. There was great rivalry between systems – especially those of mechanical and electronic scanning – and there is still great controversy about contributions and priorities. But this is characteristic of the phase in which the development of a technology moves into the stage of a new social form.

What is interesting throughout is that in a number of complex and related fields, these systems of mobility and transfer in production and communication, whether in mechanical and electric transport, or in telegraphy, photography, motion pictures, radio and television, were at once incentives and responses within a phase of general social transformation. Though some of the crucial scientific and technical discoveries were made by isolated and unsupported individuals, there was a crucial community of selected emphasis and intention, in a society characterised at its most general levels by a mobility and extension of the scale of organisations: forms of growth which brought with them immediate and longer-term problems of operative communication. In many different countries, and in apparently unconnected ways, such needs were at once isolated and technically defined. It is especially a characteristic of the communications systems that *all were foreseen – not in utopian but in technical ways – before the crucial components of the developed systems had been discovered and refined*. In no way is this a history of communications systems creating a new society or new social conditions. The decisive and earlier transformation of industrial production, and its new social forms, which had grown out of a long history of capital accumulation and working technical improvements, created new needs but also new possibilities, and the communications systems, down to television, were their intrinsic outcome.

C. The Social History of the Uses of Television Technology

It is never quite true to say that in modern societies, when a social need has been demonstrated, its appropriate technology will be found. This is partly because some real needs, in any particular period, are beyond the scope of existing or foreseeable scientific and technical knowledge. It is even more because the key question, about technological response to a need, is less a question about the need itself than about its place in an existing social formation. A need which corresponds with the priorities of the real decision-making groups will, obviously, more quickly attract the investment of resources and the official permission, approval or encouragement on which a working technology, as distinct from available technical devices, depends. We can see this clearly in the major developments of industrial production and, significantly, in military technology. The social history of communications technology is interestingly different from either of these, and it is important to try to discover what are the real factors of this variation.

The problem must be seen at several different levels. In the very broadest perspective, there is an operative relationship between a new kind of expanded, mobile and complex society and the development of a modern communications technology. At one level this relationship can be reasonably seen as causal, in a direct way. The principal incentives to first-stage improvements in communications technology came from problems of communication and control in expanded military and commercial operations. This was both direct, arising from factors of greatly extending distance and scale, and indirect, as a factor within the development of transport technology, which was for obvious reasons the major direct response. Thus telegraphy and telephony, and in its early stages radio, were secondary factors within a primary communications system which was directly serving the needs of an established and developing military and commercial system. Through the nineteenth and into the twentieth century this was the decisive pattern.

But there were other social and political relationships and needs emerging from this complex of change. Indeed it is a consequence of the particular and dominant interpretation of these changes that the complex was at first seen as one requiring improvement in *operational* communication. The direct priorities of the expanding commercial system, and in certain periods of the military system, led to a definition of needs within the terms of these systems. The objectives and the consequent technologies were operational within the structures of these systems: passing necessary specific information, or maintaining contact and control. Modern electric technology, in this phase, was thus oriented to uses of person to person, operator and operative to operator and operative, within established specific structures. This quality can best be emphasised by contrast with the electric technology of the second phase, which was properly and significantly called *broadcasting*. A technology of specific messages to specific persons was complemented, but only relatively late, by a technology of varied messages to a general public.

Yet to understand this development we have to look at a wider communications system. The true basis of this system had preceded the developments in technology. Then as now there was a major, indeed dominant, area of social communication, by word of mouth, within every kind of social group. In addition, then as now, there were specific institutions of that kind of communication which involves or is predicated on social teaching and control: churches, schools, assemblies and proclamations, direction in places of work. All these interacted with forms of communication within the family.

What then were the new needs which led to the development of a new technology of social communication? The development of the press gives us the evidence for our first major instance. It was at once a response to the development of an extended social, economic and political system and a response to crisis within that system. The centralisation of political power led to a need for messages from that centre along other than official lines. Early newspapers were a combination of that kind of message – political and social information – and the specific messages – classified advertising and general commercial news – of an expanding system of trade. In Britain the development of the press went through its major formative stages in periods of crisis: the Civil War and Commonwealth, when the newspaper form was defined; the Industrial Revolution, when new forms of popular journalism were successively established; the major wars of the twentieth century, when the newspaper became a universal social form. For the transmission of simple orders, a communications system already existed. For the transmission of an ideology, there were specific traditional institutions. But for the transmission of news and background – the whole orienting, predictive and updating process which the fully developed press represented – there was an evident need for a new form, which the largely traditional institutions of church and school could not meet. And to the large extent that the crises of general change provoked both anxiety and controversy, this flexible and competitive form met social needs of a new kind. As the struggle for a share in decision and control became sharper, in campaigns for the vote and then in competition for the vote, the press became not only a new communications system but, centrally, a new social institution.

This can be interpreted as response to a political need and a political crisis, and it was certainly this. But a wider social need and social crisis can also be recognised. In a changing society, and especially after the Industrial Revolution, problems of social perspective and social orientation became more acute. New relations between men, and between men and things, were being intensely experienced, and in this area, especially, the traditional institutions of church and school, or of settled community and persisting family, had very little to say. A great deal was of course said, but from positions defined within an older kind of society. In a number of ways, and drawing on a range of impulses from curiosity to anxiety, new information and new kinds of orientation were deeply required: more deeply, indeed, than any specialisation to political military or commercial information can account for. An increased awareness of mobility and change, not just as abstractions but as lived experiences, led to a major redefinition, in practice and then in theory, of the function and process of social communication.

What can be seen most evidently in the press can be seen also in the development of photography and the motion picture. The photograph is in one sense a popular extension of the portrait, for recognition and for record. But in a period of great mobility, with new separations of families and with internal and external migrations, it became more centrally necessary as a form of maintaining, over distance and through time, certain personal connections. Moreover, in altering relations to the physical world, the photograph as an object became a form of the photography of objects: moments of isolation and stasis within an experienced rush of change; and then, in its technical extension to motion, a means of observing and analysing motion itself, in new ways – a dynamic form in which new kinds of recognition were not only possible but necessary.

Now it is significant that until the period after the First World War, and in some ways until the period after the Second World War, these varying needs of a new kind of society and a new way of life were met by what were seen as specialised means; the press for political and economic information; the photograph for community, family and personal life; the motion picture for curiosity and entertainment; telegraphy and telephony for business information and some important personal messages. It was within this complex of specialised forms that broadcasting arrived.

The consequent difficulty of defining its social uses, and the intense kind of controversy which has ever since surrounded it, can then be more broadly understood. Moreover, the first definitions of broadcasting were made for sound radio. It is significant and perhaps puzzling that the definitions and institutions then created were those within which television developed.

We have now become used to a situation in which broadcasting is a major social institution, about which there is always controversy but which, in its familiar form, seems to have been predestined by the technology. This predestination, however, when closely examined, proves to be no more than a set of particular social decisions, in particular circumstances, which were then so widely if imperfectly ratified that it is now difficult to see them as decisions rather than as (retrospectively) inevitable results.

Thus, if seen only in hindsight, broadcasting can be diagnosed as a new and powerful form of social integration and control, many of its main uses can be seen as socially, commercially and at times politically manipulative. Moreover, this viewpoint is rationalised by its description as 'mass communication', a phrase used by almost all its agents and advisers as well, curiously, as by most of its radical critics. 'Masses' had been the new nineteenth-century term of contempt for what was formerly described as 'the mob'. The physical 'massing' of the urban and industrial revolution underwrote this. A new radical class-consciousness adopted the term to express the material of new social formations: 'mass organisations'. The 'mass meeting' was an observable physical effect. So pervasive was this description that in the twentieth century multiple serial production was called, falsely but significantly, 'mass production': mass now meant large numbers (but within certain assumed social relationships) rather than any physical or social aggregate. Sound radio and television, for reasons we shall look at, were developed for transmission to *individual* homes, though there was nothing in the technology to make this inevitable. But then this new form of social communication – broadcasting – was obscured by its definition as 'mass communication': an abstraction to its most general characteristic, that it went to many people, 'the masses', which obscured the fact that the means chosen was the offer of individual sets, a method much better described by the earlier word 'broadcasting'. It is interesting that the only developed 'mass' use of radio was in Nazi Germany, where under Goebbels' orders the Party organised compulsory public listening groups and the receivers were in the streets. There has been some imitation of this by similar regimes, and Goebbels was deeply interested in television for the same kind of use. What was developed within most capitalist societies, though called 'mass communication' was significantly different.

There was early official intervention in the development of broadcasting, but in form this was only at a technical level. In the earlier struggle against the development of the press, the State had licensed and taxed newspapers, but for a century before the coming of broadcasting the alternative idea of an independent press had been realised both in practice and in theory. State intervention in broadcasting had some real and some plausible technical grounds: the distribution of wavelengths. But to these were added, though always controversially, more general social directions or attempts at direction. This social history of broadcasting can be discussed on its own, at the levels of practice and principle. Yet it is unrealistic to extract it from another and perhaps more decisive process, through which, in particular economic situations, a set of scattered technical devices became an applied technology and then a social technology.

A Fascist regime might quickly see the use of broadcasting for direct political and social control. But that, in any case, was when the technology had already been developed elsewhere. In capitalist democracies, the thrust for conversion from scattered techniques to a technology was not political but economic. The characteristically isolated inventors, from Nipkow and Rosing to Baird and Jenkins and Zwyorkin, found their point of development, if at all, in the manufacturers and prospective manufacturers of the technical apparatus. The history at one level is of these isolated names, but at another level it is of EMI, RCA and a score of similar companies and corporations. In the history of motion pictures, capitalist development was primarily in production; large-scale capitalist distribution came, much later, as a way of controlling and organising a market for given production. In broadcasting, both in sound radio and later in television, the major investment was in the means of distribution, and was devoted to production only so far as to make the distribution technically possible and then attractive. Unlike previous communications technologies, radio and television were *systems primarily devised for transmission and reception as abstract processes, with little or no definition of preceding content.* When the question of content was raised, it was resolved, in the main, parasitically. There were state occasions, public sporting events, theatres and so on, which would be communicatively distributed by these new technical means. *It is not only that the supply of broadcasting facilities preceded the demand; it is that the means of communication preceded their content.*

The period of decisive development in sound broadcasting was the 1920s. After the technical advances in sound telegraphy which had been made for military purposes during the war, there was at once an economic opportunity and the need for a new social definition. No nation or manufacturing group held a monopoly of the technical means of broadcasting, and there was a period of intensive litigation followed by cross-licensing of the scattered basic components of successful transmission and reception (the vacuum tube or valve, developed from 1904 to 1913; the feedback circuit, developed from 1912; the neutrodyne and heterodyne circuits, from 1923). Crucially, in the mid-1920s, there was a series of investment-guided technical solutions to the problem of building a small and simple domestic receiver, on which the whole qualitative transformation from wireless telegraphy to broadcasting depended. By the mid-1920s – 1923 and 1924 are especially decisive years – this breakthrough had happened in the leading industrial societies: the United States, Britain, Germany and France. By the end of the 1920s the radio industry had become a major sector of industrial production, within a rapid general expansion of the new kinds of machines which were eventually to be called 'consumer durables'. This complex of developments included the motorcycle and motorcar, the box camera and its successors, home electrical appliances, and radio sets. Socially, this complex is characterised by the two apparently paradoxical yet deeply connected tendencies of modern urban industrial living: on the one hand mobility, on the other hand the more apparently self-sufficient family home. The earlier period of public technology, best exemplified by the railways and city lighting, was being replaced by a kind of technology for which no satisfactory name has yet been found: that which served an at once mobile and home-centred way of living: a form of *mobile privatisation*. Broadcasting in its applied form was a social product of this distinctive tendency.

The contradictory pressures of this phase of industrial capitalist society were indeed resolved, at a certain level, by the institution of broadcasting. For mobility was only in part the impulse of an independent curiosity: the wish to go out and see new places. It was essentially an impulse formed in the breakdown and dissolution of older and smaller kinds of settlement and productive labour. The new and larger settlements and industrial organisations required major internal mobility, at a primary level, and this was joined by secondary consequences in the dispersal of extended families and in the needs of new kinds of social organisation. Social processes long implicit in the revolution of industrial capitalism were then greatly intensified: especially an increasing distance between immediate living areas and the directed places of work and government. No effective kinds of social control over these transformed industrial and political processes had come anywhere near being achieved or even foreseen. Most people were living in the fall-out area of processes determined beyond them. What had been gained, nevertheless, in intense social struggle, had been the improvement of immediate conditions, within the limits and pressures of these decisive large-scale processes. There was some relative improvement in wages and working conditions, and there was a qualitative change in the distribution of the day, the week and the year between work and off-work periods. These two effects combined in a major emphasis on improvement of the small family home. Yet this privatisation, which was at once an effective achievement and a defensive response, carried, as a consequence, an imperative need for new kinds of contact. The new homes might appear private and 'self-sufficient' but could be maintained only by regular funding and supply from external sources, and these, over a range from employment and prices to depressions and wars, had a decisive and often a disrupting influence on what was nevertheless seen as a separable 'family' project. This relationship created both the need and the form of a new kind of 'communication': news from 'outside', from otherwise inaccessible sources. Already in the drama of the 1880s and 1890s (Ibsen, Chekhov) this structure had appeared: the centre of dramatic interest was now for the first time the family home but men and women stared from its windows, or waited anxiously for messages, to learn about forces, 'out there', which would determine the conditions of their lives. The new 'consumer' technology which reached its first decisive stage in the 1920s served this complex of needs within just these limits and pressures. There were immediate improvements of the condition and efficiency of the privatised home; there were new facilities, in private transport, for expeditions from the home; and then, in radio, there was a facility for a new kind of social input – news and entertainment brought into the home. Some people spoke of the new machines as gadgets, but they were always much more than this. They were the applied technology of a set of emphases and responses within the determining limits and pressures of industrial capitalist society.

The cheap radio receiver is then a significant index of a general condition and response. It was especially welcomed by all those who had least social opportunities of other kinds; who lacked independent mobility or access to the previously diverse places of entertainment and information. Broadcasting could also come to serve, or seem to serve, as a form of *unified* social intake, at the most general levels. What had been intensively promoted by the radio manufacturing companies thus interlocked with this kind of social need, itself defined within general limits and pressures. In the early stages of radio manufacturing, transmission was conceived before content. By the end of the 1920s the network was there, but still at a low level of content-definition. It was in the 1930s, in the second phase of radio, that most of the significant advances in content were made. The transmission and reception networks created, *as a by-product*, the facilities of primary broadcasting production. But the general social definition of 'content' was already there.

This theoretical model of the general development of broadcasting is necessary to an understanding of the particular development of television. For there were, in the abstract, several different ways in which television as a technical means might have been developed. After a generation of universal domestic television it is not easy to realise this. But it remains true that, after a great deal of intensive research and development, the domestic television set is in a number of ways an inefficient medium of visual broadcasting. Its visual inefficiency by comparison with the cinema is especially striking, whereas in the case of radio there was by the 1930s a highly efficient sound broadcasting receiver, without any real competitors in its own line. Within the limits of the television home-set emphasis it has so far not been possible to make more than minor qualitative improvements. Higher-definition systems, and colour, have still only brought the domestic television set, as a machine, to the standard of a very inferior kind of cinema. Yet most people have adapted to this inferior visual medium, in an unusual kind of preference for an inferior immediate technology, because of the social complex and especially that of the privatised home – within which broadcasting, as a system, is operative. The cinema had remained at an earlier level of social definition; it was and remains a special kind of theatre, offering specific and discrete works of one general kind. Broadcasting, by contrast, offered a whole social intake: music, news, entertainment, sport. The advantages of this general intake, within the home, much more than outweighed the technical advantages of visual transmission and reception in the cinema, confined as this was to specific and discrete works. While broadcasting was confined to sound, the powerful visual medium of cinema was an immensely popular alternative. But when broadcasting became visual, the option for its social advantages outweighed the immediate technical deficits.

The transition to television broadcasting would have occurred quite generally in the late 1930s and early 1940s, if the war had not intervened. Public television services had begun in Britain in 1936 and in the United States in 1939, but with still very expensive receivers. The full investment in transmission and reception facilities did not occur until the late 1940s and early 1950s, but the growth was thereafter very rapid. The key social tendencies which had led to the definition of broadcasting were by then even more pronounced. There was significantly higher investment in the privatised home, and the social and physical distances between these homes and the decisive political and productive centres of the society had become much greater. Broadcasting, as it had developed in radio, seemed an inevitable model: the central transmitters and the domestic sets.

Television then went through some of the same phases as radio. Essentially, again, the technology of transmission and reception developed before the content, and important parts of the content were and have remained by-products of the technology rather than independent enterprises. As late as the introduction of colour, 'colourful' programmes were being devised to persuade people to buy colour sets. In the earliest stages there was the familiar parasitism on existing events: a coronation, a major sporting event, theatres. A comparable parasitism on the cinema was slower to show itself, until the decline of the cinema altered the terms of trade; it is now very widespread, most evidently in the United States. But again, as in radio, the end of the first general decade brought significant independent television production. By the middle and late 1950s, as in radio in the middle and late 1930s, new kinds of programme were being made for television and there were very important advances in the productive use of the medium, including, as again at a comparable stage in radio, some kinds of original work.

Yet the complex social and technical definition of broadcasting led to inevitable difficulties, especially in the productive field. What television could do relatively cheaply was to transmit something that was in any case happening or had happened. In news, sport, and some similar areas it could provide a service of transmission at comparatively low cost. But in every kind of new work, which it had to produce, it became a very expensive medium, within the broadcasting model. It was never as expensive as film, but the cinema, as a distributive medium, could directly control its revenues. It was, on the other hand, implicit in broadcasting that given the tunable receiver, all programmes could be received without immediate charge. There could have been and can still be a socially financed system of production and distribution within which local and specific charges would be unnecessary; the BBC, based on the licence system for domestic receivers, came nearest to this. But short of monopoly, which still exists in some state-controlled systems, the problems of investment for production, in any broadcasting system, are severe.

Thus within the broadcasting model there was this deep contradiction, of centralised transmission and privatised reception. One economic response was licensing. Another, less direct, was commercial sponsorship and then supportive advertising. But the crisis of production control and financing has been endemic in broadcasting precisely because of the social and technical model that was adopted and that has become so deeply established. The problem is masked, rather than solved, by the fact that as a transmitting technology – its functions largely limited to relay and commentary on other events – some balance could be struck; a limited revenue could finance this limited service. But many of the creative possibilities of television have been frustrated precisely by this apparent solution, and this has far more than local effects on producers and on the balance of programmes. When there has been such heavy investment in a particular model of social communications, there is a restraining complex of financial institutions, of cultural expectations and of specific technical developments, which though it can be seen, superficially, as the effect of a technology is in fact a social complex of a new and central kind.

It is against this background that we have to look at the development of broadcasting institutions, at their uses of the media, and at the social problems of the new technical phase which we are about to enter.

Reference

From Raymond Williams, *Television – Technology and Cultural Form*, Fontana, 1974, pp. 9–31. Reprinted with kind permission by the Estate of Raymond Williams and the Taylor & Francis Group.

10

DRAMA IN A DRAMATIZED SOCIETY
(1974)

In his inaugural lecture as Professor of Drama at the University of Cambridge, Raymond Williams notes the pervasiveness of the dramatic in modern society and its ubiquity in the modern media, especially television. Again, we see here Williams's wealth of historical knowledge and the meticulousness with which he traces the historical formation of present-day cultural and social phenomena.

The problems of drama, in any of its many perspectives, are now serious enough to be genuinely interesting and indeed to provoke quite new kinds of question. Real and nominal continuities can of course be traced, but my own emphasis is on a transformed situation: one that I have tried to indicate in my title. Drama is no longer, for example, coextensive with theatre; many dramatic performances are now in film and television studios. In the theatre itself—national theatre or street theatre—there is an exceptional variety of intention and method. New kinds of text, new kinds of notation, new media and new conventions press actively alongside the texts and conventions that we think we know, but that I find problematic just because these others are there. Dramatic time and sequence in a play of Shakespeare, the intricate rhythms and relationships of chorus and three actors in a Greek tragedy: these, I believe, become active in new ways as we look at a cutting bench or an editing machine, in a film or television studio, or as we see new relations between actor and audience in the improvised theatre of the streets and the basements.

Again, we have never as a society acted so much or watched so many others acting. Watching, of course, carries its own problems. Watching itself has become problematic. For drama was originally occasional, in a literal sense: at the Festival of Dionysus in Athens or in medieval England on the day of Corpus Christi when the waggons were pulled through the streets. The innovating commercial theatres of Elizabethan London moved beyond occasion but still in fixed localities: a capital city, then a tour of provincial cities. There was to be both expansion and contraction. In Restoration London two patent theatres—the monopoly centres of legitimate drama—could hardly be filled. The provincial theatre-building of the eighteenth century, the development of variety theatres and music-halls, the expansion of London's West End theatres in the second half of the nineteenth century: all these qualified occasion but in the light of what was to come were mainly quantitative changes. It is in our own century, in cinema, in radio and in television, that the audience for drama has gone through a qualitative change. I mean not only that *Battleship Potemkin* and *Stagecoach* have been seen by hundreds of millions of people, in many places and over a continuing period, nor only that a play by Ibsen or O'Neill is now seen simultaneously by ten to twenty million people on television. This, though the figures are enormous, is still an understandable extension. It means that for the first time a majority of the population has regular and constant access to drama, beyond occasion or season. But what is really new—so new I think that it is difficult to see its significance—is that it is not just a matter of audiences for particular plays. It is that drama, in quite new ways, is built into the rhythms of everyday life. On television alone it is normal for viewers—the substantial majority of the population—to see anything up to three hours of drama, of course drama of several different kinds, a day. And not just one day; almost every day. This is part of what I mean by a dramatized society. In earlier periods drama was important at a festival, in a season, or as a conscious journey to a theatre; from honouring Dionysus or Christ to taking in a show. What we now have is drama as habitual experience: more in a week, in many cases, than most human beings would previously have seen in a lifetime.

Can this be merely extension: a thing like eating more beef muscle or wearing out more shirts than any ancestor could have conceived as a widespread human habit? It certainly doesn't look like a straight-line extension. To watch simulated action, of several recurrent kinds, not just occasionally but regularly, for longer than eating and for up to half as long as work or sleep; this, in our kind of society, as majority behaviour, is indeed a new form and pressure. It would of course be easy to excise or exorcise this remarkable fact if we could agree, as some propose, that what millions of people are so steadily watching is all or for the most part rubbish. That would be no exorcism: if it were true it would make the fact even more extraordinary. And it is in any case not true. Only dead cultures have scales that are reliable. There are discernible, important and varying proportions of significant and trivial work, but for all that, today, you can find kitsch in a national theatre and an intensely original play in a police series. The critical discriminations are at once important and unassumable in advance. But in one perspective they pale before the generality of the habit itself. What is it, we have to ask, in us and in our contemporaries, that draws us repeatedly to these hundreds and thousands of simulated actions; these plays, these representations, these dramatizations?

It depends where you ask that question from. I ask it from watching and from contributing to the extraordinary process itself. But I can hear—who can not?—some familiar voices: the grave merchants whose apprentices and shopboys slipped away to Bankside; the heads of households whose wives, and the heads of colleges whose students, admitted to read English, would read novels and comedies in the morning. These sober men would know what to say about contemporary California, where you can watch your first movie at six-thirty in the morning and if you really try can see seven or eight more before you watch the late movie in the next recurrent small hours. Fiction; acting; idle dreaming and vicarious spectacle; the simultaneous satisfaction of sloth and appetite; distraction from distraction by distraction. It is a heavy, even a gross catalogue of our errors, but now millions of people are sending the catalogue back, unopened. Till the eyes tire, millions of us watch the shadows of shadows and find them substance; watch scenes, situations, actions, exchanges, crises. The slice of life, once a project of naturalist drama, is now a voluntary, habitual, internal rhythm; the flow of action and acting, of representation and performance, raised to a new convention, that of a basic need.

We cannot know what would have happened if there had been, for example, outside broadcasting facilities at the Globe. In some measure, at least, we must retain the hypothesis of simple extension of access. Yet I would argue that what has happened is much more than this. There are indeed discoverable factors of a probably causal kind. We are all used to saying—and it still means something—that we live in a society which is at once more mobile and more complex, and therefore, in some crucial respects, relatively more unknowable, relatively more opaque than most societies of the past, and yet which is also more insistently pressing, penetrating and even determining. What we try to resolve from the opaque and the unknowable, in one mode by statistics—which give us summaries and breakdowns, moderately accurate summaries and even more accurate breakdowns, of how we live and what we think—is offered to be resolved in another mode by one kind of dramatization. Miner and power worker, minister and general, burglar and terrorist, schizophrenic and genius; a back-to-back home and a country house; metropolitan apartment and suburban villa; bed-sitter and hill-farm: images, types, representations: a relationship beginning, a marriage breaking down; a crisis of illness or money or dislocation or disturbance. It is not only that all these are represented. It is that much drama now sees its function in this experimental, investigative way; finding a subject, a setting, a situation; and with some emphasis on novelty, on bringing some of that kind of life into drama.

Of course all societies have had their dark and unknowable areas, some of them by agreement, some by default. But the clear public order of much traditional drama has not, for many generations, been really available to us. It was for this reason that the great naturalist dramatists, from Ibsen, left the palaces, the forums and the streets of earlier actions. They created, above all, rooms; enclosed rooms on enclosed stages; rooms in which life was centred but inside which people waited for the knock on the door, the letter or the message, the shout from the street, to know what would happen to them; what would come to intersect and to decide their own still intense and immediate lives. There is a direct cultural continuity, it seems to me, from those enclosed rooms, enclosed and lighted framed rooms, to the rooms in which we watch the framed images of television: at home, in our own lives, but needing to watch what is happening, as we say, 'out there': not out there in a particular street or a specific community but in a complex and otherwise unfocused and unfocusable national and international life, where our area of concern and apparent concern is unprecedentedly wide, and where what happens on another continent can work through to our own lives in a matter of days and weeks—in the worst image, in hours and minutes. Yet our lives are still here, still substantially here, with the people we know, in our own rooms, in the similar rooms of our friends and neighbours, and they too are watching: not only for public events, or for distraction, but from a need for images, for representations, of what living is now like, for this kind of person and that, in this situation and place and that. It is perhaps the full development of what Wordsworth saw at an early stage, when the crowd in the street (the new kind of urban crowd, who are physically very close but still absolute strangers) had lost any common and settled idea of man and so needed representations—the images on hoardings, the new kinds of sign—to simulate if not affirm a human identity: what life is and looks like beyond this intense and anxious, but also this pushed and jostled, private world of the head.

That is one way of putting it; the new need, the new exposure—the need and exposure in the same movement—to a flow of images, of constant representations, as distinct from less complex and less mobile cultures in which a representation of meaning, a spectacle of order, is clearly, solidly, rigidly present, at certain fixed points, and is then more actively affirmed on a special occasion, a high day or a festival, the day of the play or the procession. But there is never only need and exposure: each is both made and used. In the simplest sense our society has been dramatized by the inclusion of constant dramatic representation as a daily habit and need. But the real process is more active than that.

Drama is a special kind of use of quite general processes of presentation, representation, signification. The raised place of power—the eminence of the royal platform—was built historically before the raised place of the stage. The presentation of power, in hierarchical groupings, in the moving emphases of procession, preceded the now comparable modes of a represented dramatic state. Gods were made present or made accessible by precise movements, precise words, in a known conventional form. Drama is now so often associated with what are called myth and ritual that the general point is easily made. But the relation cannot be reduced to the usual loose association. Drama is a precise separation of certain common modes for new and specific ends. It is neither ritual which discloses the God, nor myth which requires and sustains repetition. It is specific, active, interactive composition: an action not an act; an open practice that has been deliberately abstracted from temporary practical or magical ends; a complex opening of ritual to public and variable action; a moving beyond myth to dramatic *versions* of myth and history. It was this active variable experimental drama—not the closed world of known signs and meanings—that came through in its own right and in its own power; significantly often in periods of crisis and change, when an order was known and still formally present but when experience was pressing it, testing it, conceiving breaks and alternatives; the dramatic possibility of what might be done within what was known to have been done, and each could be present, and mutually, contradictorily potent, in specific acted forms. We need to see this especially now, when myth and ritual, in their ordinary senses, have been broken up by historical development, when they are little more, in fact, than the nostalgia or the rhetoric of one kind of scholar and thinker, and yet when the basic social processes, of presentation, representation, signification have never been more important. Drama broke from fixed signs, established its permanent distance from myth and ritual and from the hierarchical figures and processions of state; broke for precise historical and cultural reasons into a more complex, more active and more questioning world. There are relativities within its subsequent history, and the break has been made many more times than once. Any system of signs, presenting and representing, can become incorporated into a passive order, and new strange images, of repressed experience, repressed people, have again to break beyond this. The drama of any period, including our own, is an intricate set of practices of which some are incorporated—the known rhythms and movements of a residual but still active system—and some are exploratory—the difficult rhythms and. movements of an emergent representation, rearrangement, new identification. Under real pressures these distinct kinds are often intricately and powerfully fused; it is rarely a simple case of the old drama and the new.

But drama, which separated out, did not separate out altogether. Congruous and comparable practices exist in other parts of the society as in the drama, and these are often interactive: the more interactive as the world of fixed signs is less formal. Indeed what we often have now is a new convention of deliberate overlap. Let me give the simplest example. Actors now often move from a part in a play, which we can all specify as dramatic art, to deploy the same or similar skills in the hired but rapturous discovery of a cigar or a facecream. They may be uneasy about it but, as they say, it's better than resting. It's still acting after all; they are no more personally committed to that cigar than to the character of that bluff inspector, for which they were also hired. Somebody wrote it, somebody's directing it: you're still in the profession. Commercials in Britain have conventional signs to tell you they're coming, but the overlap of method, of skill and of actual individuals is a small and less easily read sign of a more general process, in which the breaks are much harder to discern.

Our present society, in ways it is merely painful to reiterate, is sufficiently dramatic in one obvious sense. Actions of a kind and scale that attract dramatic comparisons are being played out in ways that leave us continually uncertain whether we are spectators or participants. The specific vocabulary of the dramatic mode—drama itself, and then tragedy, scenario, situation, actors, performances, roles, images—is continually and conventionally appropriated for these immense actions. It would moreover be easier, one can now often feel, if only actors acted, and only dramatists wrote scenarios. But we are far past that. On what is called the public stage, or in the public eye, improbable but plausible figures continually appear to represent us. Specific men are magnified to temporary universality, and so active and complex is this process that we are often invited to see them rehearsing their roles, or discussing their scenarios. Walter Bagehot once distinguished between a real ruling class and a theatrical ruling show: the widow of Windsor, he argued, in his innovating style of approving and elegant cynicism, is needed to be shown, to be paraded, before a people who could never comprehend the more complex realities of power. I watched this morning the televised State opening of Parliament. It is one thing to say that it was pure theatre; it is harder to see, and to say, that beyond its residual pageantry was another more naturalized process which is also in part a cousin of theatre. Monarchs, of course, have always done something like this, or had it done for them. Those who lasted were conscious of their images even if they called them their majesties. Moreover, like many actors, people find roles growing on them: they come to fit the part, as he who would play the King. What is new, really, is not in them but in us.

It is often genuinely difficult to believe in any part of this pervasive dramatization. If we see it in another period or in or from another place, it visibly struts and frets, its machinery starts audibly creaking. In moments of crisis, we sometimes leave this social theatre or, as easily, fall asleep in it. But these are not only roles and scenarios;

they are conventions. When you can see a convention, become really conscious of it, it is probably already breaking down. Beyond what many people can see as the theatricality of our image-conscious public world, there is a more serious, more effective, more deeply rooted drama: the dramatization of consciousness itself. 'I speak for Britain' runs the written line of that miming public figure, though since we were let in on the auditions, and saw other actors trying for the part, we may have our reservations; we may even say 'Well I'm here and you don't speak for me'. 'Exactly,' the figure replies, with an unruffled confidence in his role, for now a different consciousness, a more profound dramatization, begins to take effect; 'you speak for yourself, but I speak for Britain.' 'Where is that?', you may think to ask, looking wonderingly around. On a good day from a high place you can see about fifty miles. But you know some places, you remember others; you have memories, definitions and a history.

Yet at some point along that continuum, usually in fact very early, you have—what? Representations; typifications; active images; active parts to play that people are playing, or sometimes refusing to play. The specific conventions of this particular dramatization—a country, a society, a period of history, a crisis of civilization; these conventions are not abstract. They are profoundly worked and reworked in our actual living relationships. They are our ways of seeing and knowing, which every day we put into practice, and while the conventions hold, while the relationships hold, most practice confirms them. One kind of specific autonomy—thisness, hereness—is in part free of them; but this is usually an autonomy of privacy, and the private figure—the character of the self—is already widely offered to be appropriated in one or other of these dramatized forms: producer or consumer, married or single, member or exile or vagrant. Beyond all these there is what we call the irreducible: the still unaccommodated man. But the process has reached in so far that there are now, in practice, conventions of isolation itself. The lonely individual is now a common type: that is an example of what I mean by a dramatic convention, extending from play to consciousness. Within a generation of that naturalist drama which created the closed room—the room in which people lived but had to wait for news from outside—another movement had created another centre: the isolated figure, the stranger, who in Strindberg's *Road to Damascus* was still actively looking for himself and his world, testing and discarding this role and that image, this affirming memory and that confirming situation, with each in turn breaking down until he came back, each time, to the same place. Half a century later two ultimately isolated figures, their world not gone but never created, sat down on the road waiting for what?—call it Godot—to come. Let's go, they said, but they didn't move. A decade later other more radically isolated figures were seen as buried to their neck, and all that was finally audible, within that partial and persuasive convention, was a cry, a breath. Privacy; deprivation. A lost public world; an uncreatable public world.

These images challenge and engage us, for to begin with, at least, they were images of dissent, of conscious dissent from fixed forms. But that other miming, the public dramatization, is so continuous, so insistent, that dissent, alone, has proved quite powerless against it. Dissent, that is, like any modern tragic hero, can die but no more. And critical dissent, a public form you can carry around to lectures or even examinations: it too comes back to the place where it started, and may or may not know it for the first time. A man I knew from France, a man who had learned, none better, the modes of perception that are critical dissent, said to me once, rather happily: 'France, you know, is a bad bourgeois novel.' I could see how far he was right: the modes of dramatization, of fictionalization, which are active as social and cultural conventions, as ways not only of seeing but of organizing reality, are as he said: a bourgeois novel, its human types still fixed but losing some of their conviction; its human actions, its struggles for property and position, for careers and careering relationships, still as limited as ever but still bitterly holding the field, in an interactive public reality and public consciousness. 'Well, yes,' I said politely, 'England's a bad bourgeois novel too. And New York is a bad metropolitan novel. But there's one difficulty, at least I find it a difficulty. You can't send them back to the library. You're stuck with them. You have to read them over and over.' 'But critically', he said, with an engaging alertness. 'Still reading them'. I said.

I think that is where we now are. People have often asked me why, trained in literature and expressly in drama, making an ordinary career in writing and teaching dramatic history and analysis, I turned—*turned*—to what they would call sociology if they were quite sure I wouldn't be offended (some were sure the other way and I'm obliquely grateful to them). I could have said, debating the point, that Ruskin didn't turn from architecture to society; he saw society in architecture—in its styles, its shaping intentions, its structures of power and of feeling, its façades and its interiors and the relations between them; he could then learn to read both architecture and society in new ways. But I would prefer to speak for myself. I learned something from analysing drama which seemed to me effective not only as a way of seeing certain aspects of society but as a way of getting through to some of the fundamental conventions which we group as society itself. These, in their turn, make some of the problems of drama quite newly active. It was by looking both ways, at a stage and a text, and at a society active, enacted, in them, that I thought I saw the significance of the enclosed room—the room on the stage, with its new metaphor of the fourth wall lifted—as at once a dramatic and a social fact.

For the room is there, not as one scenic convention among all the possible others, but because it is an actively shaping environment—the particular structure within which we live—and also, in continuity, in inheritance, in crisis—the solid form, the conventional declaration, of how we are living and what we value. This room on the stage, this enclosed living room, where important things happen and where quite another order of importance arrives as news from a shut-off outside world; this room is a convention, now a habit, of theatre; but it is also, subtly and persistently, a personage, an actor: a set that defines us and can trap us: the alienated object that now represents us in the world. I have watched, fascinated, as that room has broken up; the furniture got rid of, a space cleared; people facing each other across an emptiness, with only the body, the body as object or the body as rhythm, to discover, to play with, to exhaust itself. But more important than this has been a dynamic process when the room is dissolved, for scene is no longer external and yet is still active, and what we see is a projection of observed, remembered and desired images. While Strindberg at the turn of the century was writing a new drama of moving images—a wall papered with faces; aspects of character and appearance dissolving, fragmenting, fusing, haunting; objects changing literally as you look at them; while Strindberg was writing this, beyond the capacity of the theatre of his time, other men, in quite different ways, were discovering means of making images move; finding the technical basis for the motion picture: the new mobility and with it the fade, the dissolve, the cut, the flashback, the voice over, the montage, that are technical forms but also, in new ways, modes of perceiving, of relating, of composing and of finding our way.

Again I heard, as if for the first time, what was still, by habit, called dramatic speech, even dialogue; heard it in Chekhov and noticed a now habitual strangeness: that the voices were no longer speaking to or at each other; were speaking with each other perhaps, with themselves in the presence of others. But there was a new composition, in which a group was speaking, yet a strange negative group; no individual ever quite finishing what he had begun to say, but intersecting, being intersected by the words of others, casual and distracted, words in their turn unfinished: a weaving of voices in which, though still negatively, the group was speaking and yet no single person was ever finally articulate. It is by now so normal a process, in writing dramatic speech, that it can be heard, any night, in a television serial, and this is not just imitation. It is a way of speaking and of listening, a specific rhythm of a particular consciousness; in the end a form of unfinished, transient, anxious relationship, which is there on the stage or in the text but which is also, pervasively, a structure of feeling in a precise contemporary world, in a period of history which has that familiar and complex transience. I don't think I could have understood these dramatic procedures as *methods*—that is to say, as significant general modes—if I had not been looking both ways. I could have seen them, perhaps, as techniques: a professional viewpoint but in my experience not professional enough, for it is where technique and method have either an identity or, as now commonly, a significant fracture, that all the hard questions of this difficult discipline begin.

Reference

From Raymond Williams, *Writing in Society*, Verso, 1984, pp. 11–21. Reprinted with kind permission of Verso.

11

COMMUNICATIONS AS CULTURAL SCIENCE (1974)

Williams's own disciplinary background was in drama and literature but his most significant educational contribution was to the formation of a new field of university study, variously known as 'Communication', 'Cultural' or 'Media Studies'. This particular essay makes it clear that his own personal preference was, in effect, for 'Cultural Studies'. He questions the positivistic legacy of largely American journalism and communications curricula and research while recommending the European continental tradition of 'cultural science', which gave rise to an interpretative style of sociology and is consistent with the kind of interdisciplinary cultural analysis that Williams himself favoured.

Human communication has been seriously and intensively studied as far back as we have records of organized thought. In western civilization the sciences of grammar and rhetoric were for two millennia at the center of education, and though the names have changed, studies of language and its practical skills have remained central. The study of communications—that significant plural—is by contrast, at least at first sight, a modern phenomenon.

There are two obvious reasons for this altered definition. First, the institutions of communications in modern societies are of a size and importance which give them, inevitably, social and political significance and, increasingly, economic significance as well. Second, there has been the well-known series of technical developments in communication, involving radical changes in the possibilities of transmission and reception and, as significantly, in reproducibility and reproduction. Because of these changes our kinds of attention and study have altered.

Necessarily, then, the communication scientist materializes in many specialized forms. He is a sociologist, concerned with these institutions and their effects. He is an engineer, concerned with these technologies and with the systems which are essential to design, understand and control. He is a cultural analyst, concerned with the meanings and values of particular artifacts and classes of artifact, from poems and paintings to films and newspapers, from buildings to fashions in dress. He is a psychologist, concerned with the basic units and patterns of communicative interaction, face to face (though if we always spoke face to face, in each other's presence, the problem would be very much simpler) or in the differential use of machines. Or he is a linguist or linguistic philosopher, concerned with the basic forms and structures of the acts of expression and communication.

The problems are so great—and not only great but extraordinarily subtle and intricate—that we ought first, in a general way, to welcome this diversity of emphasis and discipline. But this is rarely how it goes. That communication scientists cannot communicate with each other is by now one of those old jokes which with repetition becomes melancholy.

The situation reminds me of that perhaps apocryphal story of a conference on Latin studies, to be attended by Latin scholars from all over the world. Someone had the plausible notion that they should conduct their proceedings in Latin, but it didn't work. What they had in common as their subject was in practice less than the linguistic history that divided them. Some, I am sure, felt a kind of despair that there should have been this drifting apart. Others, I am also sure, went home and mocked those extraordinary others who said 'veer' or 'wire' or similar incomprehensible jargon for *vir*. But some at least, I would hope, came to reflect on their situation with some sense of the history which simultaneously united and divided them: the common interest and the divergent habits, and the need, as in all communication, to listen as well as to state and assert.

That is as much as can be done, in the short term. In Britain especially the waters of higher education are just now unusually brackish. You can go on doing, in effect without challenge, virtually anything that has ever been done, but if you propose anything new you are lucky if your integrity escapes whipping; your intelligence and sensibility will have been long given up as dead. For suppose you said, 'There are these different kinds of communication studies; shall we try, in some form—in a department, in a colloquium, in an interdisciplinary programme, to put them physically if in no other way in contact for say the next five years, and see if we learn anything?'—not only would you have committed an error of taste and judgement but you would find, rising from the ground like armed men or armed ghosts, tame literary scholars insisting on the paramount importance of keeping out sociology, tame sociologists saying the same thing the other way round—and to hear the curled sneer that can be got into 'sociology' or 'literary' is one of the communication experiences of our times. Fortunately, however, not all men, not even all scholars, are tame. Under whatever difficulties, the work will have to be done and is in some places being attempted.

The approach I want to describe is that of cultural studies, which is English for 'cultural science.' Here, centrally, communication is a practice. Communication study is open to whatever can be learned of the basis of this practice: the detailed processes of language and of gesture, in expression and interaction, and of course any general features of underlying human structures and conventions. It is open, also, to the effects on these processes and features of particular technologies which, since it is a modern study, it necessarily considers over a range from the printed book and the photograph to broadcasting and motion pictures and beyond these to the specialized electronic media.

Within a living culture, so many of these processes will have been naturalized, and those which have not will have been identified as conscious and isolable modernisms, that without this dimension of openness to the fundamental processes much of the working analysis will be naive, or will at best be limited to the unexamined conventions of its culture. Nevertheless, cultural study is concerned with practice. It draws to it a proportion—now markedly increasing—of those students whose received discipline is the understanding of cultural artifacts.

Over many centuries, ways have been found of talking to the point, though in varying and usually controversial ways, about poems, paintings, buildings, songs, novels, films, symphonies, newspapers, advertisements, political speeches, styles of dress; a whole range of cultural practice which may be separated as artifacts for more specific study, but which have also to be seen as the practical communication—or, more strictly, that special part of it which has survived because it is in some way recorded—of a particular people or class of a people at a particular place and time.

Many of the disciplines which deal with these artifacts are remarkably developed in their own terms, and in an academic context can separate out from each other and from that more central perception that they were made by real men in real places in real and significant social relationships. More crucially, in their concentration on artifacts, the disciplines, especially as they develop in scholarly and historical ways, can convert all practices to artifacts, and in the shadow of this delusion suppose themselves absolved, in the name of the excellence and achievement of the past, from the comparable practices of their own time.

It is then not only, to take an example, that in the study of literature at Oxford there was for many years a classical time-stop at 1830, since the practice of our great-great-grandfathers and their embarrassingly pressing descendants was altogether too turbulent and uncertain; or that in the study of the history of the English language at Cambridge there is in effect a time-stop at the point in the late middle ages when the language became that which we now write and speak and keep changing. It is also that a practice has to become an artifact, and moreover an artifact of the kind that is conventionally found in libraries and museums, to deserve much attention. A seventeenth-century political pamphlet deserves disciplined attention; a current party political broadcast does not.

There is, then, a resistance, in the name of standards, to a very wide area of contemporary cultural practice; but moreover, from the habits of mind thus induced (the conversion of practices into artifacts, of real expressive and communicative process into isolable objects) several modes of analysis which depend on the recognition of practice—the reconstruction of composition, the study of social relations within which the practice occurred, the study of related practices which lead to distinguishable artifacts but which are still related—all these and other modes become attenuated or unattempted and the discipline narrows, losing its touch with life.

We say cultural studies because we are concerned with practice and with the relations between practices. Culture itself was originally a practice: the growth and tending of wheat or the growth and tending of minds. The significance of the emergence of the modern meaning of culture—that meaning which took it beyond specific cultural practices to a general process or state—is that the individual practices were seen as related parts of a general development or achievement. Culture became, in the eighteenth century, an idea which expressed a secular sense of general human development, and its advance, in this respect, over metaphysical notions of a providential or aberrant civilization is remarkable.

But almost at once it encountered the central problem of all subsequent cultural theory: that of the relations between different practices, within what was nevertheless seen as a general development. The first form of this difficulty was the use of culture to indicate all general human development—in the popular form of the universal histories, which recounted the growth of civilization—and the alternative and almost contemporary use of the same term, 'culture,' to indicate the specific development of a particular people, a national culture.

This difficulty has persisted, and is still of radical theoretical importance in anthropology and in history. But the next phase of difficulty was even harder. In idealist thought it had been assumed that the guiding element in this general cultural process was spirit or consciousness (although in its later forms this was a human and not a divine spirit). Marx challenged that by naming the guiding element—even, in language he inherited, the determining element—as material production and the social relations it embodies. That theoretical conflict is also, still, of profound importance. In our own immediate terms, it underlies all questions about the relations between practices, and unless these questions are faced, no studies of communications can get very far.

Out of this argument, about the relation between practices, came the new concept of cultural science and with it a significant part of modern sociology. Dilthey, for example, was concerned to distinguish between the natural and cultural sciences, in respect of their fields of research, their forms of experience, and the role of the attitudes of the investigator. His distinctions, I believe, are still fundamental, though they leave many problems unsolved.

Weber, even more extensively, was persistently concerned with the relations between fundamental social and cultural practices, and his hypothesis of elective affinities—at times in the more modern guise of 'correspondences' and 'homologous structures'—has proved an attractive halfway house in cultural analysis; halfway, or so it seems, between simple idealist theories and the simpler kinds of materialist determinism.

Now the spirit of this whole inquiry—to which literally thousands of people have contributed—is profoundly open, alert, and general. It has had its bitter and even its squalid controversies, and this is understandable; but in temper and approach it is in a wholly different dimension from what seems our own world of small cultivators, heads down to their own fields; or if they have their heads down, good luck to them, for some at least are much busier at the walls and fences, erecting improbable signs that trespassers will be prosecuted, or exploiting the natural desire of young men and women to be qualified and certificated by a self-interested definition of the discipline and its boundaries.

I recall the spirit of cultural science because I am interested in its heirs—who will change its methods but will still inherit its vigorous and general humanity. If I speak with some feeling it is because until quite recently opportunities were missed here in Britain—in a country which has a very rich tradition of just this kind—for the effective reconstitution of cultural studies, within which, as I am arguing, a central kind of communications study should be pursued.

The opportunities were missed, largely, because of a demarcation dispute. People coming to communications analysis from the tradition of cultural studies were looked up and down and eventually identified as literary types. Some part of this error was explicable. Literary study itself, for the reasons I gave earlier, had been in some places reduced to the specialized analysis of isolated artifacts. Indeed there has been a critical culmination of a long process of narrowing-down. Literature itself, as a concept, was a Renaissance specialization from the more general area of discourse in writing and speech: a specialization directly related to the printed book. In the late eighteenth and early nineteenth centuries there was a further specialization: literature, which had till then included all forms of writing, came to be specialized, though with some exceptions and overlaps, to imaginative literature. (The theoretical complications of that limitation are only just beginning to be grasped.) As modern literary study entered the universities there was a further specialization; literature was the 'good' or 'serious' part of such work.

So the natural area of interest of this kind of person—an interest in all discourse in writing or speech—had been specialized and even restricted to printed imaginative compositions of a certain quality. Of course, when people looked around, most of these had been written in the past. Today—it was said—there was only television and all that rubbish, so that literature, in some places, came to resemble that proverbial bird which flew in ever-decreasing circles until it finally and fundamentally disappeared.

Now this definition of a discipline had undoubtedly made some of its disciples strange. It was no wonder they got looked at. But who was doing the looking? I remember a friend of mine being rebuked for having attempted some cultural analysis on the grounds that this was wanton and ignorant trespass into sociology, by the practitioners of a discipline which in this country at that time had produced not a single piece of cultural analysis of its own and indeed showed no signs of wanting to try.

There was a central area of overlap—more or less adequately recognized and negotiated—between these varying cultural studies and the specifically aesthetic or specifically social studies which lay in either direction. What the practice of aesthetic analysis contributed was a capacity for sustained and detailed analysis of actual cultural works. What was much more open to question was the extension of this kind of analysis and insight to matters of cultural and social generalization where, quite properly, there were other real disciplines to act as a check, or, better, as an incentive. The study of cultural institutions or of cultural effects could not properly be pursued by projected aesthetic analysis.

Yet for a generation this problem was masked by a notion which, as it happened, was widely shared by those who had approached modern communications from what was called 'high culture' and by orthodox social and political scientists. This notion—an ideology if ever there was one—was that of a 'mass society,' based on deep social, cultural and political assumptions and experiences.

And so it came about that the study of communications was deeply and almost disastrously deformed by being confidently named as the study of 'mass-communications'. 'Mass-communications' is a term which seems to have got into every language and into the most diverse schools, which describes and too often predicts departments and research programs and conferences, and which it is time to bury. Not only is it disastrous in its limitation of communication studies to a few specialized areas like broadcasting and the cinema and what it miscalls popular literature, when there is the whole common area of discourse in speech and writing that always needs to be considered. It is also disastrous in its consequent definition of the 'mass media'. The 'mass' metaphor overtook us in its weakest meaning, of the large ultimate audience, and then positively prevented the analysis of most specific modern communication situations and of most specific modern communication conventions and forms.

But it had one lingering effect. If most people are masses, they are inherently stupid, unstable, easily influenced. Sex and violence not only rear but propagate their ugly heads. The only question worth asking, it seemed, about jazz or television or cinema or even football (for a while they left out politics) was first how, then whether, it corrupted people. The residual result is that it is still easier to get resources for impact-studies—perhaps we should call them corruption-studies—in television and the like than for any other single kind of work. Much of what is then called the sociology of communications is this kind of impact-study, and indeed some of it is valuable, though it is always necessary to add, as everyone trained in really precise observation of behaviour will confirm, that the scientific discovery and demonstration of effects is one of the toughest areas you can enter.

For, again, there is corruption and corruption. I would like to see a system of parallel grants: for every inquiry into the consumption of television or the like, equal resources for an inquiry into production. The great or at least large institutions of modern communications need intensive and continuous study. This has so far been done only in part-time and occasional ways. And I should add while I am saying this that it seems to me very significant that the most detailed information that exists in Britain about reading habits, and some associated behavior, is in the regular and highly specific surveys and reports of the Institute of Practitioners in Advertising: a highly intentional form of research, to say the least, but one which puts any comparable scholarly work in this country to shame.

Studies of institutions, in the full sense—of the productive institutions, of their audiences, and of the forms of relationship between them—will have to be carried out by procedures of social science from which, in result and by example, all cultural analysts will learn a great deal. Indeed in this respect the orthodox suspicion of cultural studies can be seen as justified, and it can only be overcome, from both sides, by practical work. But, of course, this kind of study does not exhaust cultural analysis, or leave it merely to describe, to analyze, and to generalize particular works. Detailed aesthetic analysis tends to be continued and extended. But the real questions arise when we come to forms. Questions about forms in communications are also questions about institutions and about the organization of social relationships. Let me give an example.

When I first started reading social and political science, at about the time when I was getting interested in communications, I came across a formula which I was told was standard for communication sciences: 'Who says what how to whom with what effect?' I was reasonably impressed, after some of my literary studies. That there was a 'who' and a 'whom' as well as a 'what' seemed encouraging, and 'effect,' of course, we were all talking about anyway. But as I went on, I noticed what might be called a diminution of the 'what'; a problem that arises, incidentally, in many communication studies, where the relationship—the 'who' and the 'whom' that communication postulates—can come to override the full substance of the communication, though the relationship and the substance must be seen as in fact inseparable.

To anyone with literary experience, the 'what' is irreducible, as well as active, and needs precise attention as a way of understanding the 'who' and the 'whom' in their most significant senses, and certainly as a way of understanding 'effect'. And I suppose it was this that led me to noticing the formula's most extraordinary omission: 'Who says what how to whom with what effect'—but 'with what purpose?' Nobody seemed to be mentioning or inquiring into that. I know now that this exclusion of *intention* was characteristic of a whole phase of functionalist social theory, in communications as in much else. But I noticed the exclusion first because I knew nobody could answer questions about the 'what' or give reality and specificity to the variables abstracted as 'who' and 'whom', or speak in other than unconsciously manipulative ways about 'effect', unless intention—not necessarily conscious intention, but the intention informed in the 'what', the shaping intention, the active composition of what is always more than an object—the practice of communication—was seriously and continuously investigated. So I amended the formula, in a paper in a social-scientific journal; but the amendment would have happened anyway, for new people were coming and new frontiers were being crossed.

There is a sense that we are only beginning. It is in this spirit that I offer my example of what communication study involves. It occurred to me recently that the television discussion—the sort of thing we see in Britain on *Panorama* or *Midweek* or *Nationwide*—is now the principal medium of formal social and political argument for the majority of our people. Now I know, as I say that, that the old high-cultural reflex is waiting—I wonder how many of you experienced it; something along the lines of—'Then God help us!'

But I don't feel it like that, if only because I'm glad that so many people now have at least that minimal access to general discussion. I don't, that is to say, write it off as beneath investigation; on the contrary, even when I agree about its limits and its faults, I see the case for investigation. And how this investigation would be done seems to be to set the task, by example, for communication studies.

First, there is a necessary approach through social and political science. Even highly educated people know comparatively little about the precise social structures within which such discussions are arranged—I mean the formal research, editing, and production relationships; the departmental relationships within the broadcasting institutions; the structures of those institutions and their relations with others. There is this factual description and analysis and social questions arising from it: the critical comparison of models of institutions, models of audiences, and models of representative viewpoints, to take only these obvious examples.

And with these we begin to enter an area where conscious and unconscious models would have to be analyzed and distinguished. Take the model of an active chairman, for example, and the wealth of questions around his role in this precise situation: questions that could be approached, among other ways, by analyzing the notions of presentation and introduction, of chairing and interviewing, or the older notions of mediator and moderator.

Some of these could be tackled with known tools of social analysis; others would require a different dimension of analysis. Someone trained in the analysis of language would in any case have much to contribute: descriptively, as with someone noting and analyzing the conscious politics; critically, to attend to the forms of the discourse—the diction and imagery but also the basic strategies of address, the encounters and evasions, the mode of question and answer and rhetorical question and non-answer: for all of which, if we would use them, we have very serviceable tools.

We would need someone sensitized to dramatic analysis; to the significance of physical groupings, to take only one example, and to the modulation of these by the specific television environment both internally, within the studio, and in quite different ways in the transmitted version (whether edited or live); a recognition of the significance of viewpoint, close-up, variation of angle, cutting—a technical yet central kind of analysis of the precise communication situation.

We would need an understanding of the positive requirements of the technology and the overlapping but not identical version of those requirements adopted by the professionals now using it. For very close work we would need the techniques developed by experimental psychologists for precise analysis of verbal and nonverbal interaction; indeed, their combination with dramatic and cinematic analysis would be extraordinarily instructive. And we would have to go on to include the other part of the communication situation— the viewers; not only studying persistent effects and influences but recording and discussing them in more precise ways while the process is still alive.

We can describe all these methods serially, but most of the really interesting questions would only arise when we came to put the findings together or, more likely, to push each other's findings around: around the proposition, for example, that the television discussion is not only a political event but also a cultural form, and that the form indicates many overt and covert relationships.

The work will be done because I think there are now enough of us who want to work in these ways to survive the defenses of vested interests, the general drizzle of discouragement, and even the more deeply-rooted inertia of contemporary orthodox culture; to announce in effect an open conspiracy: that in new ways, by trial and error but always openly and publicly, we shall do this work because it needs to be done.

Reference

Originally published in the *Journal of Communication* 24.3. September 1974, pp. 17–25. Copyright © 1974 Raymond Williams. Reprinted with kind permission of Blackwell Publishing Ltd.

12

DEVELOPMENTS IN THE SOCIOLOGY OF CULTURE (1975)

Raymond Williams was primarily a cultural historian and critic yet, in 1975, he was invited to address the British Sociological Association (BSA) on the topic of the sociology of culture. The paper he gave was a prelude to another invitation, to write a textbook on the sociology of culture for a series on the various branches of sociology, which was published in 1981 and entitled simply, Culture. *In his BSA paper, Williams surveyed the comparative underdevelopment of the sociology of culture within the discipline of Sociology in comparison with, say, the sociology of religion. He identified the positivistic limitations of sociological work on culture, particularly the obsession with 'effects' that it shared with psychology. Williams thus sought to draw the sociology of culture closer to the humanities – and indeed his own preoccupations – particularly concerning the study of cultural forms and cultural formations. This involved greater appreciation of the materiality of signs and for social scientists to take textual analysis, a practice more typical of the Humanities, seriously as well as research into institutional processes.*

Abstract

This paper reviews general aspects of the theory and practice of the sociology of culture. It considers the contributions of mainline sociology, in the analysis of effects, institutions and formations, and relates the emphasis on effects, the selectively smaller emphasis on institutions and the relative neglect of formations to theoretical and methodological assumptions in orthodox sociology. It then considers contributions to the sociology of culture from other disciplines, in the study of traditions and of forms, and in attempts (Lukács, Goldman, the Frankfurt School) to relate forms to formations. In this connection it reviews selections between orthodox cultural sociology and the theories and practices of formalism and structuralism. Finally, the paper proposes an approach based on recognition of the materiality of signs' and the consequent recognition of cultural technologies—'sign-systems'—as forms of historical and social relationship and practice.

1. Introduction

The sociology of culture is often now seen as a relatively specialized and marginal area. It is also evidently underdeveloped. In the full historical context of social thought, this situation has its ironies and its lessons. It is important to remember that it was from late nineteenth-century arguments about what cultural science might be, in relation to history and especially in relation to new categories of analysis of economic and political systems, that an important part of modern sociology emerged. The difficult term, *culture*, has a longer and even more significant history. Beginning as a noun of process, the culture of crops and of creatures and by extension the culture of the mind, it became in the late eighteenth century, especially in German and English, a term of configuration and generalisation for the whole way of life of a people. Herder[1] first used the significant plural, *cultures*, in distinction from a singular and as we would now say unilinear sense of *civilization*. This use has been exceptionally important in the development of anthropology and sociology, but the term has remained complex: not only retaining its older sense of process but developing a new sense to group the specific practices and institutions of meaning and value in a society: practices and institutions also grouped and specialized as religion, learning, education, the arts. A persistent interaction and occasional confusion between these alternative senses may at times be regretted, but the interaction is important because it again indicates the questions which were at issue in the attempt to define a science of culture. It is precisely the difficult relations between practices and institutions of meaning and value and the whole general nature of political and economic—in a word, social—institutions that were then, and are still, at issue. The attempt to develop a sociology of culture is then not only an attempt to develop social methods and disciplines, for the understanding of these distinguishable practices and institutions, but, necessarily, an attempt to contribute to a more general understanding of all social practices and institutions, from a standpoint in which the complex questions of the making of meanings and values are explicit.

2. Contributions of Mainline Sociology

Three areas of contribution from mainline sociology can be distinguished: studies of *effects*, of explicitly structured *institutions*, and of intellectual *formations*. These contributions have been scattered and uneven. In the predominantly empirical sociology of the English language tradition the study of *effects* was the area most accessible to developed methods of inquiry. It has been impossible, in the middle of the twentieth century, to overlook the question of the effects of extended communications systems of new kinds, notably the modern press and broadcasting. Work on the effects of television, for example (cf. Halloran, 1970) has been solid and useful; its kinds of controlled and systematic inquiry have been especially necessary in a social context of assertion and speculation about effects. Characteristically, however, this work has assumed certain limited sociological norms: there is normal political process—how, if at all, does television politics affect it?; there is a normal process of socialization, through family, community, education—how do 'mass communications' affect it? Some answers can be given, within this perspective. But there are some inevitable limitations on the questions. The displacement of explicit practices of meaning and value to an area from which they merely modify norms has had a double effect: it has limited investigation of the processes of meaning and value within the norms themselves; it has also (here following general tendencies in psychology, communications theory and literary criticism) separated reception and observable response from the social processes of the production of meaning and value. Each tendency is evident in the disastrous description of this field as the study of 'mass' communications, where *mass* functions, by external derivation, to indicate publics and audiences of large numbers, and specifically, within the terms of capitalist thought, to connect with conceptions of the *mass market*. In fact the sociology of television, at any level (and this would be true, in different ways, of press and radio; it is significantly different in cinema) requires structural categories of virtually an opposite kind. Any vocabulary would have to be difficult, but an adequate sociology can only begin when we find categories and procedures which bear on these real systems: when we can see the television audience as an abstract and phased identity, serial and multiple but significantly not massed, receiving not discrete messages but a specific and organized *flow*. I have recently tried to describe some of these necessary categories and procedures (Williams, 1974).

Study of the characteristic *institutions* of these new communications processes began, on the whole, outside sociology: usually as elements of radical critiques of capitalist and (in some cases) totalitarian social systems. The developed procedures of the analysis of institutions, especially in details of structure and in matters of formal interrelations, are very much needed in this continuing work. Through the mid-twentieth century many of these institutions, to speak only in terms of their size, complexity and level of investment, have become major elements of advanced industrial societies: institutions which, whatever confusions there may be about the character of their products, cannot reasonably be assigned to a specialized, marginal or superstructural status. In the United States especially, but also at an earlier stage in Britain, the necessary studies are beginning to be made, and it is here, most evidently, that many existing sociological procedures and categories can immediately contribute.

It is important to connect work of this kind, on formal institutions, with the third kind of study which has already been contributed from the main sociological tradition (though this contribution has been significantly less in cultures in which techniques of measurable classification have dominated social analysis). This is the study of intellectual *formations*: classically, groups and movements of cultural contributors, which have a significantly variable and often oblique relation to formal institutions. It is not accidental that we have better studies of the sociology of religion, and of the sociology of education—where the social structures of organization, training and practice are relatively easy to discern, and where at least in the case of religion the meanings and values are already to a large extent systematized—than of the sociology, say, of art, or of literature, or of social thought itself, where in modern societies new categories of social identification would be necessary. The work of Gramsci[2] on intellectuals remains, though unfinished, a model of its kind; the work of Mannheim[3] and of other, especially German, investigators has made at least a beginning in the area now called the sociology of knowledge (but which in being so called directs attention only to relatively static elements, the practices of enactment and performance, so crucial in any culture, being obviously harder to grasp). Clearly this work will go on being developed. It will interact, to some extent, with the study of effects, for no formation of this kind can in the end be isolated from other social groups with which it is in necessary relations. The sociology of the effects of television, for example, is beginning to be linked with the sociology of its production. There are descriptive and analytic studies of particular reading publics,[4] and descriptive and one or two analytic, often historical rather than strictly sociological, studies of the formation of creative groups. Benjamin's work, especially on the formation of a Parisian Bohemia,[5] is a notable landmark. Yet there is still most of the room in the world. The best sociology of reading, in English, is in the remarkable form of the operational survey of the Institute of Practitioners in Advertising. By contrast, where there is no immediate operational purpose to be served, nobody in Britain knows how many people go to the theatre, or any reliable social facts about them, or any facts about the relations between theatre publics and the production and writing of plays. Given the intricacy of relations between this minority form and the majority forms of televised and broadcast drama—itself a social phenomenon of a staggering kind, in which a majority of the population in advanced industrial societies spends more time watching various kinds of play than in, for example, eating—it is difficult to believe that even a relatively orthodox sociology of culture is in more than its early, indeed primitive, stage.

3. Contributions from Cultural Studies

For understandable reasons, related to the unfinished arguments of the period of formation of classical sociology, and since related to the concentration of sociology on the measurable effects of recognized and identifiable institutions, much active work in the sociology of culture has perforce been carried on in disciplines which not only lie outside mainstream sociology but which, offering to approach it, are often not recognized as systematic social inquiry: their procedures unfamiliar, ironically in the exact sense which, in Dilthey and Weber, provoked the definition of cultural science;

their definitions of cultural processes awkward, in the defensively professional world of a newly objective and quantifying discipline. But there have been, all the same, three kinds of contribution: on *traditions*, on *forms* and on the exceptionally complex *relations* between 'forms' in this intellectual, literary and artistic sense and 'forms' and 'formations' in more familiar social senses.

The work on traditions has been mainly empirical, within the disciplines of the histories of art, music, literature, philosophy and social thought. But it has sociological interest for two reasons: first, that *tradition* is an important and relatively undeveloped sociological concept; secondly, that work of this kind, as it is now usually done, involves active consideration of the relations between specific traditions and particular works and practices, and these are of great theoretical interest, in a wider field. If a tradition is seen as no more than a relatively inert segment of a particular social structure, it can be treated or even neglected as secondary. But the main contemporary emphases are, first, on a *selective* tradition, in which the specific formation of a tradition is a contemporary social act, indeed an aspect of contemporary social organization, though of course depending on elements of earlier social experience and on versions of effective continuity; secondly, on an *active* tradition, a working line through any contemporary social organization and therefore a constant reminder of the dangers of seeing a social organization in static and abstract ways. My own work on the sociology of contemporary culture is radically affected by these considerations, so that one tries to move beyond the questions that are usually put, about the relation of a given body of culture or cultural practice to a particular social structure, in ways that allow one to see both structural and historical dimensions. Any approach to unitary and generalizing relations must pass through this consciousness of tradition as both operative continuity and contemporary formation. The working terms I use to express this are *residual*, *dominant* and *emergent*, which may be separated as categories but which will often be found in specific combinations in particular cultural works; without some active conception of the *residual* and the *emergent*, especially, much cultural practice can not be understood, and cultural analysis is in danger of becoming merely reductive, or of being displaced to areas requiring categories which are absolutely resistant to sociological analysis: vision, imagination, fantasy, entertainment, the aesthetic. As real human practices, made possible by social achievements in language, in notations, in conventions, in traditions, in working skills, the works which actively embody and communicate these qualities (which are normally abstracted and distinguished because of our impoverished versions of what is social) push through as real elements of any social organization, and can be seen in their own terms as such.

The work on *forms*, which has been much more developed, is even more important. A particular form in art is evidently a social achievement, but it is characteristic of many of these forms that they are at once highly specific, in a sociological sense, and yet almost invariably have an important historical and traditional dimension: within the terms of any practice, most evidently, but often in wider ways. There was important nineteenth-century work on the *type* in fiction and drama, over a range from the stock character to the representative figure. This is of great sociological interest, and it connects with more recent work—at its simplest, content analysis; at its most sophisticated, analysis of recurrent themes, situations, actions, endings—where the connections between cultural analysis of works and more general social analysis of the culture are often especially clear. Analysis of the change in the conventional endings of novels, from the informing and continuing disposition and settlement of the whole group, in early Victorian fiction, to the emphasis on the individual breaking away, extricating himself, from his group, in twentieth-century fiction, is an obvious example of the kind of work which can be directly compared with the findings of direct sociological analysis; *compared*, rather than either projected as 'real inner history' or dismissed as mere 'literary' evidence. The terms of the comparison require work on the form, as well as work on the content. Meanwhile a whole gallery of social types—representative, mediating or ideological figures—is now daily spread before us: comparative work on the figuration of the detective or the policeman is for many reasons now urgent, but while this evident content is crucial, any full analysis must include analysis of the highly variable forms, including difficult technical matters such as narrative position, conventional relations between human figures and social and physical settings, levels of language and so on. The analysis can often be run in reverse. There is now an important body of work which starts from genres (Lukács, 1962), moments in a genre (Goldmann, 1956), specific mediations (Benjamin, 1973), forms of composition (Adorno, 1949), as points of entry into a sociological analysis. In my own work, certain analyses which were eventually seen as sociological began as quite formal inquiries: into such facts of drama as the stage as a room, mobility and transformation of scene, and the shift from group dialogue to the dialogue of a negative group (Williams, 1968). All such work overlaps, of course, with a quite distinct and often antagonistic tendency in the analysis of art, which can be traced through modern European culture in its stages of formalism, practical criticism, new criticism and synchronic structuralism. Work on form, in its widest sense, in these other tendencies, has been of the greatest importance, but at significant moments in each phase it has become explicitly antisociological, postulating separable or at least radically distinct areas of practice, and using work on tradition in the strictest and most formal ways. This is still, for us, a central area of controversy, and the current situation is exceptionally complicated. What has certainly happened, however, is that the work on forms, much more than the work on types, has radically complicated what in some earlier stages of the sociology of culture could be seen as satisfactory categories and procedures: reflection, representation, background, ideology, superstructure. In recent Marxist work there has been a significant conflict, which is indeed inevitable in just this phase, between those who, from their work on forms, have converted all social practices into forms (substituting epistemology for ontology: a position already reached within the later stages of the formalist tradition—Frye (1957), McLuhan (1964)), and those others who, retaining an insistence on direct social practice, have to restate, often radically, positions on ideology and on cultural hegemony, but also, and more crucially, positions on creativity and its sources and formations, to which the formalist tradition has delivered an inescapable challenge but to which, also, it has contributed important and indispensable evidence.

The result then is, in cultural sociology as a whole, that there is a proliferation of new theoretical positions. There is even a kind of preoccupation with this level of theory, which from some positions is indeed a natural development, most kinds of direct inquiry having been already written off as empiricist or positivist, or, even worse, as a contaminating humanism and moralism. But from other positions the preoccupation is also evident, and in strategic terms inevitable, since one main form of the contemporary social crisis is the rapid development of a kind of theory which in quite new ways, and with an appropriately unfamiliar technical vocabulary, represents the direct cultural practice of a now dominant kind of intellectual formation. That is to say, the older concern, in cultural analysis, with a very wide and general area of cultural contributions, has in part been shifted, because the culture has shifted, to a very important if very limited area, in which a new formation is evident: briefly, the institutional technology of higher education, in which several forms of cultural theory have become, within a privileged situation, privileged practices.

Lacking this dimension of cultural analysis, we would see only a bewildering variety of positions, with a consequent invitation not merely to eclecticism—which might in some cases be practice of a kind—but to that rapid conversion of knowledge into technology which is the real thrust of the social process.

Several new concepts of the relations between different kinds of social and cultural institutions and practices are now in active circulation. I can present them only briefly, before choosing a point of entry from which, in my view, certain resolutions are possible. One of the most powerful is the structuralist version of Marxism, well represented by Althusser (1969, 1970) and especially strongly established in anthropology and in linguistics. This tendency has achieved an important critique of earlier ideas of *superstructure*, and an equally important rethinking of the concepts of *structure* and of *practice*. But, more than any other, it is a theoretical displacement of real cultural practice, in the interest of what is, at the level of inquiry, a technology. Its preoccupation with formalized structures, and with systematic determinations, is in sharp contrast, at the level of local debate, with earlier concepts of reflected or reproduced content and of a centrally determined system (*base and superstructure*). But in just this preoccupation it recapitulates, in new technical forms, an objective idealism which has indeed always been, in cultural analysis, an attractive and persuasive position. The reductionism inherent in older kinds of Marxist analysis—a reduction of specific content to other content—has been superseded and then replaced by a new reductionism, in which the privileged observer reduces all practice to systematic configurations, which alone create and contend. The point becomes clearer when we set this beside one of its close cousins, the *genetic structuralism* of Goldmann (1970). Here the weakness of synchronic structuralism is effectively identified: even the deepest configurations and structures are seen, as they must be, as having a history: as forming and breaking down as well as achieving persistent and significant formation. But two of Goldmann's concepts illustrate how the argument can move either way. The idea of *homology of structures* is very important in cultural analysis; it avoids preoccupation with the cultural processes (which are nevertheless real) of simple reflection and reproduction; but at the same time it abstracts all cultural practice to its formal determinants, in ways that at once cast new light on many real works and projects and at the same time exclude, *a priori*, much of the specific experience and most of the actual historical cultural activity (cf. Goldmann's limitation of analysis to 'great works'). Again the very important idea of the *collective subject*, which is a way of going on from thinking about forms to thinking about formations (and is in that sense a radical corrective to orthodox structuralism), can in its turn be drawn to the kind of emphasis on formations which reduces all specific projects to a configuration, and in proposing an important new kind of historical subject can at times altogether disintegrate the specific continuities and the specific identities of historically material beings in an historically material world. What can replace men and women, in either version, is their own reified product: the formation, the structure, the category. There is the same kind of difficulty in Lukács' distinction between *actual consciousness* and *possible consciousness* (1923; the terms are especially difficult in English). As a way of thinking through problems of articulation and of hegemony—problems often empirically described as those *of levels* of culture—this is a suggestive idea. But it can be quickly converted into a restatement of *possible consciousness* as *ideal consciousness*—a kind of unification of theories of the political vanguard and theories of 'great works'—and as such needs to be traced to a misunderstanding of Weber and, more crucially, to the characteristic classicism of one kind of bourgeois Marxist. The failure of all these tendencies to engage with problems of popular culture is characteristic, but what has really to be seen is how their ideas protect them from this, and this protection is repeated in the privileged area of higher education which is their effective milieu and, at its worst, the natural base for the conversion of ideas into a technology.

The important work of the Frankfurt School has been especially significant in the sociology of culture. Its work on *mediation*, at its best in its studies of specific formations, ought to be central in this field. It can be usefully compared with Sartre's active idea of a *project* and its encounter with specific mediations. Meanwhile the revival of *semiotics* (which at one level needs to be studied in precise relation to economic developments and their political results, in the complex development of the theory and practice of data-processing) is in part a specific variant of structuralism, though characteristically more active; in part another way beyond it. The significant concept of *code* is often effective in cultural analysis, and this is again a useful way of rethinking the concept of ideology, in specific and active ways. Though subject to many of the same pressures, within the same limits of milieu, this kind of work, as in Barthes (1967), has engaged with a significantly wide cultural area, and in its work on film, for example,[6] is being forced beyond the closed categories of structuralist linguistics into analysis of a cultural system which it cannot fail (though the signs are that it will try) to recognize in the end as historical. This will probably be important, since in the area of popular cultural forms (where a rigorous sociological distinction of the variations and varieties *of the popular* is urgently necessary) the work of the Frankfurt School, theoretically so much better equipped, went into a curious and damaging symbiosis with American theories of *mass culture*, and in its radical underestimate of potentials for resilience, scepticism, and alternative creation, reached an ironic dead end (Marcuse, 1964).

Prospects

Work of all the kinds I have mentioned will undoubtedly continue. It will have its effect in other areas of sociology just because, at its best, it is engaging with some realities of social life—cultural *process* and cultural *formation*—which have been relatively neglected and which have wide general implications. But if I had to pick out one area in which significant development is likely, just because it brings to a head many of the underlying theoretical and practical problems, it would be the emphasis which I would describe as the *materiality of signs*. This is of great importance in a number of fields. The success of various kinds of formalism is due mainly to their correct emphasis on sign-systems, as the radical elements of all cultural process. It is not surprising that work of this kind is replacing *criticism*, which still residually dominates humanistic studies but which can now be seen more clearly as the theoretical and practical generalization of specifically bourgeois uses of culture; (the concepts *criticism, literature* and *art*, in their currently available forms, are all contemporaneous with bourgeois society, and are the theoretical forms of its cultural specialization and control). But formalism was only able to get through so far because the materialism it negated did not include the materialism of signs:

a materialism which we really cannot escape, in twentieth-century cultural systems, with their evident technology of media, but which is also there, fundamentally, in language itself. (The development of historical materialism in linguistics, against the dominant categories of the Saussurean and post-Saussurean tradition, is best represented, though in a tragically interrupted form, by Volosinov, 1973). In the sociology of our own culture, the decisive areas of investigation are those in which characteristic forms of social relationship (usually mystified as 'mass communications') and characteristic contributory formations (usually projected as 'media people', though the relations between what are called 'popular culture' and 'high culture' have changed dramatically, and the real formations are much wider) are specifically organized in relation, not only to institutions which are now of great social importance (the broadcasting organizations; the press and publishing conglomerates) but also to specific technologies; technologies, moreover, which are *not* media—neutral agencies of transmission—but are material organizations of specific systems of signs. Of course it is tempting, and often even necessary, to break down this extraordinary complex into separable fields: the sociology of audiences and publics, the sociology of contributors, the sociology of cultural institutions, and, trying to insert itself, the sociology of content. What is then not represented, however, is the sociology of systems of signs, and its absence is the reason for the successes of cultural structuralism, which speaks to such systems but at the price of excluding, as contingent, all other real practice. A genuine sociology of systems of signs would be necessarily concerned, in historical and materialist ways, with the specific technologies which are now their dominant forms, but with these technologies *as systems of signs* and not at an abstracted technical level. Moreover, since at this level the technologies are necessarily seen as new and advanced forms of social organization, there is a basis for reworking not only the analysis of content (which is always a content of relationships) but also the analysis of institutions and formations (which are never independent of, though they are equally not controlled by, the technologies around which they now characteristically form). It has taken a long time, and in adequate demonstration will still take a long time, to get through to this position, from which, developing several kinds of existing work but in a new theoretical perspective, a sociology of culture which will be a sociology of the culture of advanced industrial societies can be foreseen and proposed.

Notes

1. HERDER, J. G. *Reflections on the Philosophy of the History of Mankind*. (1784–91). Chicago: University Press, 1973. XIV.
2. GRAMSCI, A. *Gli intellettuali e l'organizzazione della cultura*. Torino: Einaudi, 1949.
3. MANNHEIM, K. *Ideology and Utopia*. London: Routledge & Kegan Paul, 1949.
4. ALTICK, R. D. *The English Common Reader*. Chicago: University Press, 1963. WEBB, R. H. *The British Working Class Reader*. London: Allen & Unwin, 1955. ESCARPI, R. *Sociologie de la littérature*. Paris: Presses Universitaires de France, 1958.
5. BENJAMIN, W. *Baudelaire: a lyric poet in the era of high capitalism*. London: New Left Books, 1973.
6. Cf. *Screen*, Vol. 14, No 1/2, Spring-Summer, 1973. London: SEFT.

References

ADORNO, T. *Philosophie der neuen Musik*. Tubingen, 1949.
ALTHUSSER, L. *For Marx*. London: NLB, 1969.
ALTHUSSER, L. et al. *Reading Capital*. London: NLB, 1970.
BARTHES, R. *Elements of Semiology*. London: Cape, 1967.
BENJAMIN, W. *Baudelaire: a lyric poet in the era of high capitalism*. London: New Left Books, 1973.
FRYE, N. *Anatomy of Criticism*. London: OUP., 1957.
GOLDMANN, L. *Le Dieu Caché*. Paris: Gallimard, 1956.
GOLDMANN, L. *Marxisme et sciences humaines*. Paris: Gallimard, 1970.
HALLORAN, J. D. (ed). *Effects of Mass Communications*. Leicester: University Press, 1964.
HALLORAN, J. D. *Effects of Television*. Leicester: University Press, 1970.
JAY, M. *The Dialectical Imagination*. London: Heinemann, 1973.
LUKÁCS, G. *Geschichte und Klassenbewusstsein*. Berlin, 1923.
LUKÁCS, G. *Aesthetik*. Neuwied am Rhein: Luchterhand, 1957.
LUKÁCS, G. *The Historical Novel*. Harmondsworth: Penguin, 1962.
MARCUSE, H. *One-Dimensional Man*. London: Routledge and Kegan Paul, 1964.
MCLUHAN, M. *Understanding Media*. London: Routledge and Kegan Paul, 1964.

VOLOSINOV, V. N. *Marxism and the Philosophy of Language*. New York: Seminar Press, 1973.
VYGOTSKY, L. S. *Thought and Language*. Cambridge, Mass.; Beacon Press, 1962.
WILLIAMS, R. *Drama from Ibsen to Brecht*. London: Chatto and Windus, 1968.
WILLIAMS, R. *Television: Technology and Cultural Form*. London: Fontana, 1974.

Biographical Note: Raymond Williams, born 1921 is Professor of Drama at the University of Cambridge and a Fellow of Jesus College. His published books include *Culture and Society, Communications, The Long Revolution, The Country and the City* and most recently *Keywords; a Vocabulary of Culture and Society.*

Reference

From *Sociology* 10, 1976, pp. 497–504. Copyright SAGE Publications, reprinted by kind permission.

13

REALISM AND NON-NATURALISM

In 1977, Williams addressed the Edinburgh International Television Festival, a gathering of mainly professionals within the television industry rather than academics. At the time, there was much debate on the politics of form within television that was also becoming of interest in academic cultural analysis. Many had argued for a Brechtian aesthetic of non-naturalism, which challenged the predominantly realistic aesthetic of television. Williams was keen to distinguish realism from naturalism, as György Lukács, the Marxist aesthetician had done before him. However, he was also concerned to defend modern experimentalism, exemplified for instance by Bertolt Brecht, against Lukács's exclusive promotion of nineteenth-century realism. The naturalistic representation of appearances and surface impressions did not define realism. Instead, realism sought to go beneath the surface to make sense of the underlying dynamics of reality. Therefore, realism was not reducible to naturalism and might, in practice, take various different forms.

Some very important questions about television drama are currently being discussed around the focal terms "realism" and "naturalism", In trying to follow the discussion what has most struck me is the extraordinary looseness and shallowness with which these terms are commonly used. They are both, in any case, very difficult and complicated terms and each has a long and complex history. The problems at which they are directed are also, obviously complicated and difficult. But the first intervention that I can usefully make is on the terms themselves. And before this is diagnosed as the pedantry of a professor who is also a writer, may I say that it is not only the confused and myopic terminology that has provoked me, but that through and past this some of the crucial creative and productive issues are being missed or displaced: the issues that interest me practically, as a writer who also happens to be a professor.

I will state some propositions about the terms "realism" and "naturalism" and refer those who wish to see them rather more fully argued to some things I have written previously, for which I have five references, in an appendix.

(i) The terms "realism" and "naturalism" did not originally refer to conventions and technical methods in art, literature and drama, but to changed attitudes towards "reality" itself, towards man and society, and towards the character of all relationships. Thus "naturalism" was a conscious alternative to "supernaturalism" and proposed the conscious presentation of human actions in exclusively human and secular terms, as distinct from earlier kinds of drama, fiction and art which had included, as a commanding or at least a referential dimension, a superhuman or extra-human power. "Realism" is more complicated but in its decisive modern development made the same emphasis, and at this level was often interchangeable with "naturalism" and with "materialism".

(ii) This is not a separable philosophical development, but was the basis for the making of new conventions and methods in art, fiction and drama. Thus naturalism, specifically associated with the new scientific natural history, proposed as a matter of principle that it was necessary to "describe" (present, embody, realise) an environment if we wish to understand a character, since character and environment are indissolubly linked. Thus naturalist dramatists did not include detailed physical and social settings because it was technically possible with new theatrical technology and resources, or because it was one kind of formal method as against others, but because they insisted that it was impossible to understand character and action unless the full physical and social environment which shaped character and action was directly presented, indeed as a kind of character and action in itself.

(iii) "Realism" in its nineteenth century artistic sense was similarly an emphasis on the "real world", as against the characteristic presentation of the world in "romance" and "myth"—seen as including extra-human, supernatural and in these terms irrational (non-comprehensible) forces. It was also an emphasis against "theatricality" and "fictionality": against the presentation of "substitute worlds", based on earlier writing and on the past, on the separation of "fancy" from "fact", and, crucially, on the interests and evasions of a bourgeoisie which wanted to avoid looking at the social and human world which it had created and now controlled.

(iv) Naturalism certainly, and realism to a lesser extent, became confined to certain particular conventions and methods, which in effect became separated from the original impulses which had provoked them. There is then a necessary distinction between "high naturalism" and the "naturalist habit". At the same time, new methods and conventions were developed *to take more account of reality, to include "psychological" as well as "external" reality, and to show the social and physical world as a dynamic rather than a merely passive and determining environment.* Between 1890 and 1920 these were often described as breaks "from naturalism" or "beyond realism", but the confusing irony is that most of them were attempts to realise more deeply and more adequately the original impulses of the realist and naturalist movements. They must for this reason be distinguished from those other methods and conventions which were based on attempts to restore the world-views which realism and naturalism had attacked: the deliberate reintroduction of supernatural or metaphysical forces and dimensions controlling or operating on human action and character, or the less easily recognisable introduction of forces above and beyond human history and "timeless" archetypes and myths. For these latter methods see the plays of Eliot, Yeats, some Beckett. For the former see the late plays of Strindberg, of the expressionists, of Brecht.

(v) In drama, realism is inextricable from new social forces and new versions of social relationships. The crucial moment is the development of "realism" as a whole form; this must be distinguished from earlier "realistic" scenes, episodes and insertions. The break to the new whole form is in eighteenth-century bourgeois drama, which made three innovations: that the actions of drama should be *contemporary* (almost all earlier drama, by convention, had been set in a historical or legendary past); that the actions and resolutions of drama should be *secular* (conceived and worked through in solely human terms, without reference to a supernatural or metaphysical dimension); and that the actions of drama should move beyond their conventional social exclusiveness (tragedy as confined to princes) and include the lives of all men ("let not your equals move your pity less"). This movement was not completed until the late nineteenth century; it is still predominant. Whatever immediate conventions and methods of presentation are employed, the great majority of plays have become, within the terms of this movement, contemporary, secular and socially extended (inclusive).

(vi) This movement was begun by the bourgeoisie, but in these critical respects—contemporaneity, secularity, social inclusiveness—was at once shared and taken further by the new opponents of the bourgeoisie in the working-class and socialist movements. At this level the diagnosis of "realism" as a bourgeois form is cant. It makes some sense backwards, as a diagnosis of bourgeois realism against feudal and aristocratic conventions. It makes no sense forwards, as a presumed radical or proletarian alternative to contemporaneity, secularity and the social extent of drama.

(vii) Central to these developments in world-view and form is the actual extension, and eventually qualitative change, in audiences. Drama moved out of dependence on court, church or state to commercial and post-commercial institutions which in their essential social composition were also contemporary, secular and socially extended. At the same time there were many contradictions between this general process and particular class affiliations and exclusions in certain institutions (cf. the split between "West End" and "popular" theatres in the nineteenth century; the social breaks involved in the new "free" and "Independent" theatres, all over Europe, in the 1890s, or in post-1930 "community" theatres and travelling companies). This process, with its contradictions, is very evident in theatre history. Broadcast, first in radio (but with internal specialisations; compare Sunday Night Theatre and the old Third Programme Drama) and then, decisively, in television, transformed even this general transforming change. Drama was for the first time ever regularly available to a total audience, and was in fact used at a much higher level of frequency than had ever previously been imagined.

Application to Problems of Television Drama

What then are the main issues in creation and production, in relation to this historical perspective, and to the actual complexity, as distinct from the short-term repetitions, of the terms we use to try to interpret it?

(a) The most important general fact about television drama is that it is in qualitatively new social relations with its audiences. It includes, potentially and actually, an incomparably wider social range than any earlier post-medieval drama, and by comparison with medieval and earlier drama it has moved the popular audience out of drama as structured occasion and into everyday access. As a social movement this is a culmination of processes historically associated with realism.

(b) This qualitative change has occurred within class societies, with contradictory results. Access has been negotiated as exposure; the new popular audience as a mass market. Yet compare literacy. It was propagated as a way of enabling working people to read the scriptures and simple instructions. But there was, fortunately, no way of teaching people to read the Bible and official notices which did not also enable them to read the radical press or anything else they chose. The problems shifted to questions of ownership of the means of production and of control at the point of production. Many contemporary arguments about form are displaced versions of these arguments (compare the last part of John McGrath's The Case Against Naturalism).

(c) Within the shifting complexities of the institutions the battle for "popular" drama has been and is still being unevenly and confusingly fought. As in the press, the "popular" tendency cannot be avoided; there is an imperative to produce "popular" work, including reproduction of wide areas of majority life, in one or other mode. This has included every kind of reproductive evasion or displacement. It has also, especially in Britain, included (usually with internal struggles) dramatisation, in several different ways, of areas of working-class life and history which had never before come into any comparably distributed production, and which also (quite apart from the size of audiences) had never in such numbers been previously produced in any cultural form. This phase can properly be seen in the historical perspective of the development of realism as a phase of developing class-consciousness (the demand to include hitherto excluded experience).

(d) The problems of immediate form have always to be considered in relation to content and to the nature of the audience. Form, theoretically, is always the fusion of specific methods of presentation, specifically selected experience, and specific relations between producer and audience. It is misleading to abstract "form" (methods of presentation) from these mutually determining relations. That, strictly, is formalism, which assumes that the choice of a method of presentation is purely technical. Formalism in this sense has been reinforced by a fetishism of the medium. The actual production process is a complex of material properties, the process of signification within them, social relations between producers, social relations between producers and audiences and the inherent and consequent selection of content. To reduce this complex to "the medium", with supposed objective, properties governing all these processes and relations, is strictly a fetishism.

(e) Form must not then be deduced from "the medium" but from the production process as a whole. In this difficult kind of analysis we must avoid the importation of terms which attempt to cover problems of the whole process but which are at best shorthand, at worst simple expletives. Moreover, since the production process is specific, we should avoid the unthinking repetition of terms from another specific process, which short-circuit the argument. (Cf. Troy Kennedy Martin, quoted by John McGrath: "The common denominator in all naturalist plays is that they tell a story by means of dialogue". To the extent that this is true of naturalist plays it is true of all written plays from Aeschylus onwards. To call all theatre drama naturalist is absurd. The recurrent and variably solved problem, in all drama, including television drama, is the relation between speech and other forms of signification. Naturalism actually used speech *less* than most other dramatic forms, because it relied, as a matter of principle, on including physical environments as signifying. If we are to get on with the argument, we have to drop this use of relatively meaningful historical descriptions as catchwords for all the varying things we are against. The other supposed specifying factor of naturalism—natural time—is in fact a well-known dogma of the *neoclassical* theatre).

(f) In the actual historical development, there was eventually a distinction between "naturalism" and "realism", which may still be relevant. Naturalism as a doctrine of character formed by environment could emerge—in part of the movement did emerge—as a passive form: people were stuck where they were; compare "the room as trap" within the late bourgeois version of "the stage as room". A counter-sense of realism, associated mainly with Marxism, insisted on the dynamic quality of all "environments", and on the possibility of intervention to change them, within the forms of this inherent movement. Thus much "post-naturalist" drama found conventions of mobility, discontinuity, alternation of viewpoint: not as new technical methods *per se*, but to signify and realise this sense of dynamic reality. Before the invention of the motion-picture camera (eg, in late

Strindberg) attempts were made to signify mobility, discontinuity and alternation on the stage. Obviously the technical possibilities of all these new kinds of signification were radically extended by the double (photographed and photographing) mobility of the camera and by processes of film and videotape cutting and editing. Thus television drama can move comparatively easily into this "post-naturalist" world.

(g) Yet mobility, discontinuity and alternation were, in the case of that new drama, tied, consciously, to the perspectives on reality which formed them. If they are abstracted as mere technicalities, they can be used, or apparently used, in quite different perspectives. Ironically they are now, within bourgeois culture, most frequently used to communicate unconnected and inconsequent impressions of a mind or a world that is mobile and dynamic as its surface only, the larger world-view which contains them being again and again the static properties of the "human condition" or the "symbolic" or "archetypal" permanences of a universalist psychology or a permanently alienated civilisation. Formalist analysis cannot distinguish between these radically different uses of the same apparent techniques.

(h) The opportunities for realism in television drama would then seem to be:

(i) altered, potentially altered and alterable relations between dramatic creators and audiences:

(ii) inclusion, within the contradictions of a necessarily "popular" medium, of historically excluded or subordinated areas of social experience, at many different leveis from the reproductive (because it has hitherto been excluded) to the disruptive and the reconstitutive;

(iii) access, within the production process, to actions of the most public kind, beyond the scale of the stage or set as room;

(iv) access, within the immediate signifying process, to procedures of mobility, discontinuity, alternation of viewpoint, *within the terms of the altered social relations and the deliberate recovery or innovation of content*. (Other work using these procedures in other terms can then be distinguished from realism, drawing on its older sense of opposition to "theatricality" and "fictionality"; its conscious adhesion to a contemporary, secular and socially extended world-view; its further political affiliation to majority experience and its accessible futures).

Within an expanding culture, all kinds of work tend to expand. I think the most interesting new work will be in the area of public actions and mobility and alternation of signification and viewpoint. But given the continuing and massive reproduction of a resigned, displaced and self-cancelling version of majority experience (the naturalist habit deprived of the most significant naturalist intentions, and miscalled realism) there is plenty of room also for the mobility and alternation of viewpoint which is simply the positive insertion, even by the most direct reproductive methods, of a hitherto excluded or subordinated experience. The battles which even this now so often provokes are part of the whole process of changing the culture, which is the only possible perspective for changing its forms.

Appendix

For the history of naturalism and realism as terms see *Keywords* (Fontana, 1976), pp. 181–4 and 216–20.

For versions of "realism" see *The Long Revolution* (Penguin, 1965), Part Two, 7.

For realism and naturalism in modern drama see *Drama from Ibsen to Brecht* (Pelican, 1973), 382–400.

For realism and a television play see *Screen*, Vol 18, Number 1, Spring 1977, 61–74.

From Edinburgh International Television Festival 1977 Official Programme, *Broadcast*, 1977, pp. 30–32. Reprinted with kind permission of the Edinburgh International Television Festival.

14

A LECTURE ON REALISM
(1977)

This lecture, given under the auspices of the Society for Education in Film and Television (SEFT) and published in SEFT's theoretical journal, Screen, *is something of a companion piece to 'Realism and Non-Naturalism'. It is quite unlike most of the other writing in* Screen *at the time, which was heavily influenced by French structuralism. Raymond Williams's writing here is grounded in the complex history of dramatic form even when analysing just one television film that was broadcast towards the end of the 1960s in the famous BBC* Play for Today *slot.* The Big Flame, *written by Jim Allen, directed by Ken Loach with Tony Garnett as producer, is an exemplary document of left-wing politics in Britain at the time. It imagines what might happen if a strike on the Liverpool Docks turned into a revolutionary occupation. In this sense,* The Big Flame *is a 'what if?' narrative.*

The Big Flame is a play written by Jim Allen, produced by Tony Garnett and directed by Ken Loach for BBC television. I want to discuss it in relation to our understanding of realism. It should be clear at the outset that except in the local vocabulary of particular schools, realism is a highly variable and inherently complex term. In fact, as a term, it only exists in critical vocabulary from the mid-nineteenth century, yet it is clear that methods to which the term refers are very much older. Let me make just one obvious general distinction between conceiving realism in terms of a particular artistic method and conceiving realism in terms of a particular attitude towards what is called 'reality'. Now if, taking the first definition, we concentrate on method, we put ourselves at once in a position in which the method can be seen as timeless: in which it is, so to say, a permanent possibility of choice for any particular artist. Certain things can be learned from this kind of emphasis, but once we become aware of the historical variations within this method, we find ourselves evidently dissatisfied with the abstraction of a method which overrides its relations with other methods within a work or with other aims and intentions.

Let me give one or two examples of this. Realism would be an obvious term for that well-known episode within the medieval play known as the Play of the Townley Shepherds, which is basically a play of the nativity and the annunciation of the birth of Christ to the shepherds, and in that sense a characteristic religious form of medieval drama indeed largely written in that way. The inserted episode to which I am referring is that in which, before the annunciation, the shepherds, recognisably shepherds of the district in which the play was written and played – that is to say, offering themselves for recognition in these terms – discuss the problems of their own life as shepherds and represent themselves in that very specific situation. Then comes the annunciation. Now, you can look at this either way: you can say that the scene is inserted because it is of interest to the people who know of that life or are sharing that life and who recognise this as the life of shepherds in their own district, in which case this definition can be assimilated to a common later definition of realism; or you can look at it in quite another way and say that the establishment of the locality, the local realism, of these Yorkshire shepherds is a condition of that work as a whole, in that the annunciation, presumed to have happened to shepherds in Palestine, is a universal annunciation, and the condition of the local realism is a condition for the universality of the religious event. In other words, you can only finally determine the function of that realism, and thence the critical significance of a description of it as that, when you have analysed not only the local method but the relation of that method to other methods and other intentions within the work.

Or, again, consider those scenes which are often inserted in English renaissance tragedies, usually with a conscious social movement from the major personages of the drama, personages of rank, to persons of a different social order who speak in different ways, and who again, interestingly, are often recognisably contemporary English characters, even within an action which can be that of an Italian court, or a Roman forum, or of some much earlier period. The intention at these points is not the same as that within the Townley shepherds play, where the locality-with-universality is a very specific convention. On the other hand, in terms of method, we have to describe certain scenes as realistic: the written speech moves much closer towards the imitation of everyday ordinary life: all these are later seen as conditions of realism. Yet the scene inserted within this very different kind of play can be described as realism with any accuracy only if the relation to the intentions of the larger work is made. Here we have not the local/universal specificity of the religious drama, but a problem of interrelation and extending action in which the contrast between the modes of action and the modes of speech of the principal characters and these subsidiary characters is itself a function of the definition of the dramatic action as a whole. The contrast between this version of realism as method and the alternative version of realism as fundamental attitude can, I think, only be appreciated historically when, looking through the development of dramatic forms, we come to the unmistakable qualitative difference which occurs when the realistic method, often very similar to that used in these earlier particular scenes, is extended to the construction of a whole form, and when the play as a whole is conceived as not only using these methods but as embodying entirely different intentions. If we are to discuss those later intentions, there is a certain obvious loss if we set intention aside and discuss only method, or think that we can reduce the question of intention to the question of method.

The crucial development of realism as a whole form occurs in the drama in the eighteenth century, although there are precedents. There is a very interesting case, for example, in restoration prose comedy, which happened to have an unusually integrated relationship between plays, actors and audience within the quite extraordinarily class-limited nature of the restoration patent theatres. The life of a small class around the court is written about by dramatists who belong to that life, and plays for audiences almost exclusively of that life, and as a whole form, these are perhaps the first realist plays – according to one definition – in English. There is a concentration on contemporary everyday reality within the terms of that class. The modes of speech have moved towards the imitation of conversation with a much greater consistency than in any earlier drama. Moreover, this is accompanied by certain changes, themselves not wholly determined by artistic intention: substitution of actresses for boy actors in the playing of female parts is only one obvious example. And yet it is significant how often the title of realism is refused to that kind of comedy of manners, as it is now usually classified, because, although the method and the intention is in these broad terms realist, the later definition of realism as a whole form was concerned with different and indeed consciously opposed, attitudes towards reality – it being assumed that the limited interests and the limited habits of this class, which found its embodiment in that particular dramatic form, are not in the full sense an engagement with contemporary reality.

It is indeed when we come on to this later drama, specifically the bourgeois drama of the eighteenth century, that we come to realism as a whole form, and that we need to identify certain defining characteristics. First there is a conscious movement towards social extension. There is a crucial argument in the early period of bourgeois tragedy about the need to extend the actions of tragedy from persons of rank, to whom by convention and precept tragedy had hitherto largely been confined, to – as it was put – 'your equals, our equals'. This movement of social extension – 'let not your equals move your pity less' – is a key factor in what we can now identify as a realist intention. Then, second, there is a movement towards the siting of actions in the present, to making action contemporary. It is remarkable that in most preceding drama it seemed almost a constituent of dramatic form that it was set either in the historical or in a legendary past, and the emphasis on the actions of the contemporary world is the second defining feature of this new bourgeois realism. And the third, which is perhaps in the end the most important, is that there is an emphasis on secular action, in the quite precise sense that elements of a metaphysical or a religious order directly or indirectly frame, or in the stronger cases determine, the human actions within the earlier plays. This dimension is dropped, and in its place a human action is played through in specifically human terms – exclusively human terms. This was seen as a loss of significance, as a narrowing of drama. It is often condemned as a sentimentalisation of the tragic action, and indeed in local terms this was often true. But it is impossible to overlook the connection between this conscious secularisation and the development of attitudes which we must associate with realism in a much wider sense than that of dramatic method, that is to say with the development of rationalism, of the scientific attitude, of historical attitudes towards society.

At the same time, within a specific situation, these general realistic intentions were limited by specific ideological features. Lello's play *The London Merchant* is an important example of this type. And yet, it is held within a particular local structure which has to do with the ideology of a particular class and not with these more general intentions; or rather these general intentions are mediated through the specific ideology. It is a story of the honest, hardworking, obedient apprentice who is contrasted with the apprentice who is seeking his own fortune and his own pleasure in his own way. This leads him into theft and murder, while the good apprentice marries his master's daughter and succeeds. The good apprentice and the daughter watch the execution of the bad apprentice and his mistress, and invite the audience consciously to mark their fate and learn how to avoid it. It is not surprising that this play was subsequently subsidised for annual performance to apprentices by a London guild of merchants, and that this went on for more than a century. And we can see that in a sense, just because of the ideological content, the realistic intention is obliquely confirmed. It is assumed that this picture of what happens is sufficiently clear and convincing in the terms of realism to be available as a lesson, a moral lesson, to people finding themselves in the same situation: they can directly apply the actions of the drama to their own lives.

The development of realism in the drama from these early bourgeois plays towards the important high naturalism of the late nineteenth century is slow and complex, and yet by the time, for example, that we come to Ibsen in the late nineteenth century, it is clear that what has developed from these three emphases is a new major form. The three emphases which are then often consciously described as realism are the secular, the contemporary and the socially extended. In a sense, those definitions have become so widespread, though never of course exclusive, that they have come to include within their overall definitions many local variations of method.

There is a complication here in that in the late nineteenth century there was an attempt to distinguish realism from naturalism, and it is worth considering this distinction for a moment. In fact, naturalism, even more clearly than realism, is not primarily defined as a dramatic or more general artistic method. Naturalism is originally the conscious opposition to supernaturalism and to metaphysical accounts of human actions, with an attempt to describe human actions in exclusively human terms with a more precise local emphasis. The relation to science, indeed consciously to natural history, the method of exhaustive analytic description of contemporary reality, and the terms naturalism and realism which have those philosophical connections, are for a time interchangeable, even complicated by the fact that in a famous definition Strindberg called naturalism the method which sought to go below the surface and discover essential movements and conflicts, while realism, he said, was that which reproduced everything, even the speck of dust on the lens of the camera. As I suppose we all now know, the eventual conventional distinction was the same but with the terms the other way round. Naturalism was seen as that which merely reproduced the flat external appearance of reality with a certain static quality, whereas realism – in the Marxist tradition, for example – was that method and that intention which went below this surface to the essential historical movements, to the dynamic reality. And within the terms of that distinction it is now a commonplace – it seems to be a picture that could be set up in type for every interview with a contemporary director or dramatist – that naturalism has been abandoned, naturalism in the sense of the reproduction of the appearance of everyday reality. It remains remarkable in view of all these declarations that the great majority of contemporary drama is of course the reproduction of everyday reality in precisely those terms, with really surprisingly small local variations. And realism, although permitted a wider extent because of the reference to dynamic movement, has tended to be swept up in this abstract and ultimately meaningless rejection – with various complications about psychological realism, neo-realism, and so on.

It is clear even from these few examples that we have to be especially careful about definitions which we have seen to be historically variable, and especially about definitions which abstract the method from an intention in ways that are finally insupportable in any substantial analysis. The best example I can give of this problem of the relation between a technical and a general definition is the case of the room on the stage in nineteenth-century drama. It is undoubtedly a quite specific historical development: the reproduction of the stage as *room*, or a room on the stage, which occurs during the nineteenth century in a wide area of the European theatre. Before that, even where rooms had been in question, the stage was still primarily a playing space. And of course given the nature of earlier actions, the room – the specifically domestic unit – was much less often used than the more public places of street, palace, forum, court. Now there is a familiar kind of technologically determinist history which relates the development of the room on the stage to developments in theatrical technology: the introduction of gas lighting, the improvement of stage carpentry, and so on. But it is in fact ludicrous to suppose that if people before the nineteenth century had wanted to create rooms on stages in the way that they were created in the late nineteenth-century and twentieth-century theatre they would have been technically unable to do so. The truth is that the production of the room on the stage was a particular reading both of the natural centre of dramatic action in terms of social extension and the emphasis on the contemporary; it was also as it happens in its later development a specific naturalist reading in the full sense of the indissoluble relation between character and environment, in which the room was a character because it was a specific environment created by and radically affecting, radically displaying, the nature of the characters who lived in it.

The true history is more complex than either a history in terms of increasing technical capacity, or a history in terms of this scientific version of a relation between character and environment. In fact, if you look at when the first 'box sets' with reproduced rooms were put on the stage in England (the English and French theatres moving at about the same rate in this respect), you will find that the rooms are there not to give any impression of recognition or demonstration of environment, but simply to display a certain kind of luxury. They are 'society' plays of a consciously displayed kind – of a fashionable kind, as we would now say – and most of the technology of the box set and the subsequent adaptation of theatres to the fully-framed box set, which was not complete until the 1870s, was more conditioned by this 'furnishing display' than by either of the other intentions. But there is a radical development, not so much in English drama as in Scandinavian, German, Russian, and then extending through Europe, of the room as the centre of the reality of human action: the private domestic room, which is of course entirely consonant with a particular reading of the place of human action – this *is* the life of the bourgeois family, where the important things occur in that kind of family room. All I mean is that if we are analysing a form of that kind it is not enough to note the method and relate it to some abstract concept of realism, or to assume that the reproduction of a room has some constant implication in overall dramatic intention.

This point is also relevant to the subsequent variable uses of film. It is clear that film could in certain ways more actively develop the reproduction of room, of mobility from room to room, of a variety of scenes conceived in those simple terms, that it could again move out of doors into the street, into the public places which on the whole the theatrical drama had left behind. At the same time, inherent in the fact of the camera was the possibility of the use of the image for quite different purposes. And since most uses of films were defined in terms of the received dramatic tradition, you find the same variation of message and intentions and variable combinations of methods and intentions, and the same variability – not to say confusion – of terms. It is in this sense that one can perhaps best approach the problem of definition of *The Big Flame* with a consciousness of inherent variation, and ask certain questions about it.

It might be worth asking first: how would the makers of *The Big Flame* themselves describe their work? Would they say that it was showing real life in the Liverpool Docks? They might. But I think that that is not all that they would say. One can see certain obvious continuities with the earlier history that I have described. In one sense, the movement to which this particular work belongs can be sited historically as a further phase of that social extension which defined the first period of bourgeois drama. When the bourgeois tragedians talked of moving out to a concern with 'your equals, their equals', they were moving towards their own class. Still there was very little extension towards a class beyond them. And there is a perfectly accurate way of reading the subsequent history of this kind of dramatic form in terms of its further social extension, one of the three key features of the definition of the bourgeois dramatic form. This is a conscious extension of dramatic material to areas of life which had been evidently excluded even from majority drama. And television was often conceived in this way as the site for a particular dramatic extension, since it had already a fully socially extended audience. It was seen as the proper site, in conscious opposition to the theatre with its persistent minority audience in social terms and its much more limited class audience, of the alternative which allowed a popular audience and the extension to themes of a much more fully extended drama, that of the drama of working-class life, bringing the working class to the centre of dramatic action.

There are still not enough examples of this to indicate that the movement is complete. In the theatre it is a very late movement: I don't know that it happens before, say, Hauptmann's *The Weavers* in 1892, which is a classic in the naturalist theatre, and which is accompanied by certain conscious political intentions. It is hardly possible to conceive of an extension of this kind without a certain conscious political viewpoint in the at first relatively open terms of taking a much wider social life to a much wider audience. And yet you only have to see *The Big Flame* once to realise that something more than simple extension is involved. It is not, as in some cases of the extension to working-class life, the realisation of something that is exotic to the audience. There is a sense in which what was earlier called the drama of 'low life' is a minor intention of bourgeois drama itself, where 'to see how the other half lives', as it was often put, was in itself a particular intention, even a particular form of entertainment. Indeed, one of the questions which has to be asked about *The Big Flame* is whether it is interpreting the particular action within the docks to a wider audience, or whether it is interpreting that class to itself. I think there is evidence of both intentions in the work, and to distinguish between them is important in any complete analysis. On balance I would say that *The Big Flame* belongs to a kind of realist drama for which a fourth term is necessary in addition to the defining characteristics of the socially extended, the contemporary and the secular; and that is the consciously interpretative in relation to a particular political viewpoint. It has an interesting cross-relation with, for example, the drama of Brecht. It is interesting that Brecht, although in many ways sharing the intentions and the philosophical positions which had underlain realism, had in much of his drama – although certainly retaining and increasing the secular emphasis – moved away from the contemporary. It remains a remarkable fact of his drama that so much of his work is set in the past, and the everyday is subject to that move. The intention of *interpreting* an event, which Brecht made so intrinsic a part of his dramatic form, distinguishing it from the form which offered an event for mere empathy, seems quite clearly evident in *The Big Flame*, and is probably even consciously derived from something of the influence of Brecht.

The Big Flame sets out to establish the level of existing working-class history and consciousness in a specific workplace. It is looking at the Liverpool Docks at the time of the Devlin report on the docks. It uses features of the developed realist film of this contemplative kind – that which had been developed in the Soviet cinema. for example, and indeed in the Soviet theatre in the early 1920's: the deliberate use of non-actors, of people 'playing themselves'. The locations are (or are in part) the locations of the historical action, the contemporary action, as well as being the locations of the dramatised action, and within these locally defining features a recognisable level of consciousness is established in the conversation of the dockers in the early part of the film. What then happens is perhaps inconsistent with the narrower definitions of realism in that, having taken the action to that point in this recognisable place, a certain dramatic, but also political, hypothesis is established. What would happen if we went beyond the terms of this particular struggle against existing conditions and existing attempts to define or alter them? What would happen if we moved towards taking power for ourselves? What would happen in specific terms if we moved beyond the strike to the occupation? Thus if we are establishing the character of realism in *The Big Flame*, we have to notice the interesting combination, fusion perhaps, and within this fusion a certain fracture, between the familiar methods of establishing recognition and the alternative method of a hypothesis within that recognition, a hypothesis which is played out in realistic terms, but within a politically imagined possibility. The thing is played through. It is not, incidentally, played through in a Utopian way. What happens in the move to occupation is of course a good deal of success, a good deal of exhilaration, the familiar idea of the release of energy when people take control of their own lives. But within it there are all the time movements towards betrayal, demonstrations of certain kinds of inadequacy of organisation, lack of preparation, the absence of any real warning against the eventual attack by the army; there is the insistence that against the demonstration of the workers' own power the forces of the State will act, and will act both by fraud and by violence, and in the end the particular hypothesis is shown as defeated, but defeated in terms of the local action, and not, while it is retained as a hypothesis, defeated as an idea. There is a very characteristic ending in which, although the particular action has been defeated, the organising committee replaces itself, and in the final scene boys come out from behind the men who are assembling to reconstitute the occupation committee: the boys of the next generation who will take over, and this within a teaching perspective that the working class must understand and learn from its defeats as well as its victories. It is interesting to look more closely at the specific techniques within this general movement. At first, the techniques are those of the realist film in the simplest sense: the camera is a single eye, there is no possibility of an alternative viewpoint, the viewer has to go along or detach him or herself, he or she has no complex seeing within the action. Indeed, a great deal is taken for granted in knowledge and recognition of the situation. The Devlin report is referred to, but whether it is known or not is in a sense taken for granted. Nothing is done specifically to establish it. What is established is a sense of militancy which is yet an incomplete militancy because it can only react negatively. The key transition from this limited militancy to the next phase of the conscious taking of power is introduced by an alteration of technique. The strong man with a clear view of what can next happen is introduced, again without much identification, and interestingly without much precise specification of political roots or relation to this action, but he comes in as the voice of a different consciousness, and there is a movement in that part of the film from the rather ragged discussion which is done within naturalist terms to the conscious voice-over presentation of an alternative point of view. The mode of the transition is the introduction of a convention which allows complex-seeing, variable viewpoints when the hypothesis is dramatised in terms of a recognisable action, again largely within naturalist terms. This convention is on the whole not used again, and at the end particularly this absence is significant because the learning from defeat is done by that final scene, insofar as it is done at all, by offering the implication that the class will renew itself in subsequent generations and in self-replacement, rather than by the use of conventions which would show the actual learning of lessons, the attainment of a new consciousness by analysis of what has happened – the convention which Brecht, unevenly but persistently, tried to establish in his kind of drama.

There is one local point here which is rather interesting to analyse. There is a quite effective short scene of a television interviewer who has come to discover what the occupation is about, but to discover this within the terms of his function as a reporter for a particular kind of television service. In fact, we are shown him falsifying in his summing-up what has been said to him, and this is an effective satiric presentation of what many working-class people feel about the function of television interviewers when they come to report events of this kind. As an isolated scene it is effective. Yet it is interesting also because of the general naturalist presentation. If we remember what we have heard outside that scene, we have in fact heard, though at a much more dispersed level than would give any warrant to the interviewer's summary, that kind of feeling: that the thing is too much effort, that people would like to get back to work. It is as if that scene was conceived as a satiric presentation in its own right. This use of yet another convention dependent on our awareness of the modes of television interviewing and its insertion into the dominant convention of the rest of the film creates a certain unresolved tension, even a contradiction.

Or take another problem of point of view, one which requires a more positive emphasis: one of the unnoticed elements of the production of meaning within what is apparently the reproduction of what is happening, the familiar media claim to be showing things as they occur. Here it is a question of the position of the camera when there is fighting between the police and others who are presented as engaged in some kind of social disturbance. It is quite remarkable, and of course the reasons are obvious, how regular and how naturalised the position of the camera *behind the police* is in either newsreel or in fictionalised reports of that kind of disturbance. The police are seen *with* the camera. The crowd, the disturbance, is object. It is significant that in *The Big Flame*, in contrast with the normality of this convention, the viewpoint is with the people being attacked. This is a useful reminder, both for an analysis of this film and for analysis of the many hundreds of examples which must be seen as working the other way round, of the way in which the convention of showing things as they actually happen is inherently determined by viewpoint in the precise technical sense of the position of the camera.

Another local point worth analysis is the scene in the court towards the end of the work, where there is a problem of undefined political viewpoint. I have already said that the work is a combination of the techniques of classical realism in its extended sense – of realism plus hypothesis – and of political intention in the broad sense, to understand the nature of the movement from one kind of militancy to another, the development of consciousness, which at this level is still, although a specific left viewpoint, the viewpoint of a rather broad left. What happens in the court scene is the development of something else which I think in fact is the result of a more specific, indeed sectarian, viewpoint within the film. The judge in his speech moves well beyond the conventions of the naturalist method which has sustained the rest of the work. He makes an extraordinary assertion about the relation between dockers and students: that it's all right for students to have ideas of this sort, but if working men get them it's very dangerous. The idea that it's all right for students is, I think, the product of a particular sectarian position which develops into an implication about intellectuals generally; and the judge is in effect made a straight man for this sort of sectarian point. It would not be so noticeable were it not inserted within a work which on the whole develops along more consistent conventions in which what is said is conceived as what is typical. The judge speaks more like a character in a Brecht presentation, and this inconsistency is significant not just as a problem about method and technique, but as an illustration of the way in which, as I think, inevitably, specific uses of method and technique are in the end inseparable from fundamental conscious or unconscious positions, viewpoints and intentions.

Towards the end of the film, there is the singing of the 'Ballad of Joe Hill', and this is worth a brief consideration. Obviously in one sense this is the classic ballad for the expression of a defeat from which new energy, new consciousness, can be derived: that Joe Hill was killed but never died, and the mood of the ballad moves straight into the mood of the final scene, in which out of defeat comes the slow new organisation, new consciousness, the possibility of the future. It is interesting because at one level the ballad and the mood are consonant, but it raises a very specific problem about the naturalist convention, because it is of course the introduction of a much wider history, a much wider consciousness of the working-class movement as a whole, a use of a song of another place, another time; and again it is a problem, as throughout in the film, of the matching (often the failure to match) of the most immediate kinds of naturalist reproduction and the attempted (and often successfully attempted) introduction of the consciousness, classically defined as realism in contrast with naturalism, of the movements of history which underlie the apparent reality that is occurring. This is so deep and permanent a problem of the methods of naturalism and realism that this local example has a very obvious general bearing.

Then, finally, the question of the use of the 'real people', the non-actors, indeed the dockers, among actors in this play about dock life and dock struggle. The use of non-actors was extensive in early Soviet film and theatre: indeed, the problem of crowds could perhaps within that kind of production only be handled in that way, not necessarily for more than logistical reasons. But again it raises a question about the method. It is interesting for example that in Hauptmann's *The Weavers* what emerges, which is most uncharacteristic of plays about the working class, is the shape of the class as a whole rather than the more familiar figures of the representative or, even more commonly, the leader. As this comes into the question of dramatic method, there are some very interesting differences to note. In the film, undoubtedly the overall intention is the presentation of the general life, and when the dockers speak as themselves it is possible for the trained ear to recognise that speech which is at once authentic and rehearsed. That is to say, it is authentic in that it is the accent and the mode of speech of men reproducing their real-life situations. It is also rehearsed in that it is predetermined what they will say at that point and in what relation to each other. This is of great interest, and Loach and Garnett have given us more valuable material for thinking about this than any others in their generation.

It is interesting to look into the detail of this at the point of production, because the relation between the producers and the people whom they are at once serving and reproducing and, it should not be forgotten, directing, is something we should explore and know more about, because there is a sense in which one can see the production of this kind of work developing into the gaining of consciousness by the producer rather than only, what the method implies, the reproduction of the development of consciousness according to an already finished script, which seems to be the dominant method. Indeed, we do need to explore, in detail and with many examples, the process of production on this precise point of the relation between the prepared script and the use of people who are, in the significant phrase, 'playing themselves' – but 'playing themselves' as roles within a script. There is also the problem in this reproduction of people in their own situations trying to understand their own conditions, developing their consciousness within the very act of production of the film, a problem of the relation between this and what is also evidently a kind of 'speaking to' both the real people finding themselves in their situation – presenting an argument to them about what they need to do next (because that, remember, is the hypothesis of *The Big Flame*; it is not what they have done but what they could do next), and the mode of speaking beyond them, to an audience, of what they could do next. There is a clear implication at the end of the film that the report of the occupation, although it is shown as defeated, is getting out to other people, and is shown as providing a model on which they could act. If we remember the period of the late 1960s in which the film was made – and indeed that period continuous to the present – then the movement towards occupation, the movement towards this new phase of working-class consciousness and action has been significant in British politics; it is perhaps the most significant contemporary action within it, and undoubtedly, I think, Garnett – who has spoken about this – would see the film as a whole (leave aside the dramatic hypothesis within the naturalist film) as a hypothesis within this larger relation of the work and the television audience. It is in that sense, feeling very much on the side of the makers of this film – that is to say sharing with them evident general political values, general dramatic intentions – that the problems, both the technical problems within the realist and naturalist modes and the problems of consistency within them, seem to me to deserve this kind of analysis.

What I have done is fairly preliminary, raising questions rather than answering them. But I wanted first to take the discussion of realism beyond what I think it has been in some danger of becoming – a description in terms of a negation of realism as single method, of realism as an evasion of the nature of drama, and the tendency towards a purely formalist analysis – to show how the methods and intentions are highly variable and have always to be taken to specific historical and social analyses, and then with that point established, to begin to approach this very difficult task of analysing what are at once the significant realist works and the quite unresolved problems of this kind of work. In our own immediate situation, if I have one final emphasis to make, it is that we live in a society which is in a sense rotten with criticism, in which the very frustrations of cultural production turn people from production to criticism, to the analysis of the work of others. It is precisely because these makers are contemporaries engaged in active production, that what we need is not criticism but analysis, and analysis which has to be more than analysis of what they have done: analysis of a historical method, analysis of a developing dramatic form and its variations, but then I hope in a spirit of learning, by the complex seeing of analysis rather than by the abstractions of critical classification, ways in which we can ourselves alter consciousness, including our own consciousness, ways in which we can ourselves produce, ways in which indeed if we share the general values which realism has intended and represented, we can ourselves clarify and develop it.

Reference

From Raymond Williams, A Lecture on Realism (1977) *Screen* 18.1: 61–74. Copyright © 1977 Raymond Williams. Reprinted by permission of Oxford University Press.

15

MEANS OF COMMUNICATION AS MEANS OF PRODUCTION (1978)

In this essay, originally delivered in a talk at a conference in Zagreb, Croatia, before the collapse of socialist Yugoslavia, we see the materialism of Williams's theoretical position manifested sharply, which he was to come to name as 'cultural materialism'. He insists that communications are part of the productive system of society and not just secondary and superstructural phenomena. Williams is also concerned to delineate specific forms of communication in relation to technical mediation. And, he resists yet again the kind of technological determinism that is so prevalent today with regard to digital media. Williams here, as elsewhere in his writing, stresses the materiality of signification and significatory practice, that is, culture.

As a matter of general theory it is useful to recognize that means of communication are themselves means of production. It is true that means of communication, from the simplest physical forms of language to the most advanced forms of communications technology, are themselves always socially and materially produced, and of course reproduced. Yet they are not only forms but means of production, since communication and its material means are intrinsic to all distinctively human forms of labour and social organization, thus constituting indispensable elements both of the productive forces and of the social relations of production.

Moreover the means of communication, both as produced and as means of production, are directly subject to historical development. This is so, first, because the means of communication have a specific productive history, which is always more or less directly related to general historical phases of productive and technical capacity. It is so, second, because the historically changing means of communication have historically variable relations to the general complex of productive forces and to the general social relationships which are produced by them and which the general productive forces both produce and reproduce. These historical variations include both relative homologies between the means of communication and more general social productive forces and relationships, and, most marked in certain periods, contradictions of both general and particular kinds.

Three Ideological Blocks

This theoretical view of the means of communication, within a perspective of historical materialism, is, in our own time, overlaid or blocked by three characteristic ideological positions.

First, the means of communication, having been reduced from their status as means of social production, are seen only as 'media': devices for the passing of 'information' and 'messages' between persons who either generally, or in terms of some specific act of production, are abstracted from the communication process as unproblematic 'senders' or 'receivers'. People are seen, that is to say, as abstract individuals, who are then either diagrammatically represented in terms of these abstract functions, or are at best broadly characterised (i) as bearers of a generalized ('human') sociality (communication as abstract 'socialization' or 'social process'); (ii) as bearers of a specified but still abstract sociality (communications between 'members' of a social group, usually national or cultural, without intrinsic reference to the differential social relations within any such group); or (iii), in an extreme form related to 'expressivist' theories of language, as unspecified 'individuals' (communication as transmission, but implying reception, by abstracted individuals, each with 'something of his own to say'). Much otherwise sophisticated work in information and communication theory rests on, and frequently conceals, this first, deeply bourgeois, ideological position.

Then, second, in a more plausible attempt to recognize *some* means of communication as means of production, there is the now commonplace distinction between 'natural' and 'technological' means of communication: the former characterized, and then usually neglected, as 'ordinary, everyday language', in 'face-to-face' situations; the latter grouped around developed mechanical and electronic communication devices and then generalized—with an especially noticeable ideological shift from technical means to abstracted social relationships—as 'mass communication'. This position has dominated a large area of modern bourgeois cultural science, but it has also, under the same title of 'mass communications', been uncritically imported into significant areas of socialist thinking, especially in its more applied forms.

It is theoretically inadmissible for two reasons. First, because the separation of 'mass communications' from 'ordinary, everyday language' practice conceals the fact that 'mass communication' processes include, in most cases necessarily, forms of 'ordinary, everyday language' use, to be sure in variably differential modes; and include also the simulation or conventional production of generally significant communication *situations*. Second, because the grouping of all or most mechanical and electronic means as 'mass communications' conceals (under the cover of a formula drawn from capitalist practice, in which an 'audience' or a 'public', itself always socially specific and differentiated, is seen as a 'mass market' of opinion and consumption) the radical variations between different kinds of mechanical and electronic means. In fact, in their differences, these necessarily carry both variable relations to 'ordinary, everyday language' in 'face-to-face situations' (the most obvious example is the radical difference of usage and communicative situation as between print and television) and the variable relations between the specific communicative relationships and other forms of social relationship (the variable extent and composition of audiences; variability of the social conditions of reception—the assembled cinema audience; the home-based television audience; group reading; isolated reading).

A variant of this second ideological position, associated especially with McLuhan, recognizes the specific differences between 'media' but then succumbs to a localized technological determinism, in which uses and relationships are technically determined by the properties of different media, irrespective of the whole complex of social productive forces and relationships within which they are developed and used. Thus the means of communication are recognized, but abstractly, as means of production, and are indeed, ideologically, projected as the only means of production, in which what will be produced is 're-tribalization', the supposed 'global village' of restored, 'unfallen' natural man. The superficial attraction of this position, beyond the essentially abstract materialism of its specification of media, rests on the characteristically rhetorical isolation of 'mass communications' from the complex historical development of the means of communication as intrinsic, related and determined parts of the whole historical social and material process.

There is then, third, an ideological position which has entered into some variants of Marxism, and which permits some accommodation with the bourgeois concept of 'mass communications'. This rests on an abstract and *a priori* separation of means of communication from means of production. It is related, first, to the specialized use of the term 'production' as if its only forms were either capitalist production—that is, the production of commodities, or more general 'market' production, in which all that is ever produced takes the form of isolable and disposable objects. Within Marxism it is further related to, and indeed dependent on, mechanical formulations of base and superstructure, in which the inherent role of means of communication in every form of production, including the production of objects, is ignored, and communication becomes a second-order or second-stage process, entered into only *after* the decisive productive and social-material relationships have been established.

This received position must be quite generally corrected, so that the variable, dynamic and contradictory forms of both 'base' and 'superstructure' can be seen historically, rather than subsumed, from a bourgeois habituation, as necessary universal forms and relations. But also in twentieth-century societies, it requires an especially sharp contemporary correction, since the means of communication as means of social production, and in relation to this the production of the means of communication themselves, have taken on a quite new significance, within the generally extended communicative character of modern societies and between modern societies. This can be seen, very strikingly, within the totality of modern 'economic' and 'industrial' production, where, in the transport, printing and electronic industries 'communicative production' has reached a qualitatively different place in its relation to—more strictly its proportion of—production in general. Moreover this outstanding development is still at a relatively early stage, and in electronics especially is certain to go very much further. Failure then to recognize this qualitative change not only postpones correction of the mechanical formulations of 'a base' and a 'superstructure', but prevents or displaces analysis of the significant relations of communicational means and processes to the crises and problems of advanced capitalist societies and – it would seem—to the different crises and problems of advanced industrial socialist societies.

Towards a History of 'Communicative Production'

A theoretical emphasis on the means of communication as means of production, within a complex of general social-productive forces, should allow and encourage new approaches to the history of the means of communication themselves. This history is, as yet, relatively little developed, although in some areas there is notable empirical work. Within the ideological positions outlined above, the most familiar kinds of history have been specialized technical studies of what are seen as new 'media'—from writing to alphabets through printing to motion pictures, radio and television. Much indispensable detail has been gathered in these specialist histories, but it is ordinarily relatively isolated from the history of the development of general productive forces and social orders and relationships. Another familiar kind of history is the social history of 'audiences' or 'publics': again containing indispensable detail but ordinarily undertaken within a perspective of 'consumption' which is unable to develop the always significant and sometimes decisive relations between these modes of consumption, which are commonly also forms of more general social organization, and the specific modes of production, which are at once technological and social.

The main result of a restated theoretical position should be sustained historical inquiry into the general history of the development of means of communication, including that especially active historical phase which includes current developments in our own societies. These remarkable developments have of course already directed attention to the crises and problems of modern communications systems. But in general, within the terms of one or other of the initial ideological positions, these tend to be treated statically or to be discussed as mere effects of other systems and other, as it were completed (or in general completely understood) historical developments. In few fields of contemporary social reality is there such a lack of solid historical understanding. The popularity of shallowly-rooted and ideological applications of other histories and other analytic methods and terms is a direct and damaging consequence of this lack. The necessary work, so immense in scope and variety, will be collaborative and relatively long-term. All that is possible now, in a theoretical intervention, is an indication of some of its possible lines.

Thus it is possible, in considering means of communication as means of production, to indicate, theoretically, those boundaries between different technical means which, as they are drawn, indicate basic differences in modes of communication itself. It should also then be possible to indicate the main questions about the relations of these modes to more general productive modes, to different kinds of social order, and (which in our own period is crucial) to the basic questions of skills, capitalization and controls.

It is useful, first, to distinguish between modes of communication which depend on immediate human physical resources and those other modes which depend on the transformation, by labour, of non-human material. The former, of course, can not be abstracted as 'natural'. Spoken languages and the rich area of physical communicative acts now commonly generalized as 'non-verbal communication' are themselves, inevitably, forms of social production: fundamental qualitative and dynamic developments of evolutionary human resources; developments moreover which are not only post-evolutionary but which were crucial processes in human evolution itself. All such forms are early in human history, but their centrality does not diminish during the remarkable subsequent stages in which, by conscious social labour, men developed means of communication which depended on the use or transformation of non-human material. In all modern and in all foreseeable societies, physical speech and physical non-verbal communication ('body language') remain as the central and decisive communicative means.

It is then possible to distinguish types of use or transformation of non-human material, for communicative purposes, in relation to this persistent direct centrality. This yields a different typology from that indicated by simple chronological succession. There are three main types of such use or transformation: (i) *amplificatory*; (ii) *durative* (storing); (iii) *alternative*. Some examples will make this preliminary classification clearer. Thus, in relation to the continuing centrality of direct physical communicative means, the *amplificatory* ranges from such simple devices as the megaphone to the advanced technologies of directly transmitted radio and television.

The *durative*, in relation to direct physical resources, is, in general, a comparatively late development; some kinds of non-verbal communication are made durable in painting and sculpture, but speech, apart from the important special case of repetitive (conventional) oral transmission, has been made durable only since the invention of sound recording. The type of the *alternative*, on the other hand, is comparatively early in human history: the conventional use or transformation of physical objects as signs; the rich and historically crucial development of writing, of graphics, and of means of their reproduction.

This typology, while still abstract, bears centrally on questions of social relationships and social order within the communicative process. Thus, at a first level of generality, both the amplificatory and the durative can be differentiated, socially, from the alternative. At least at each end of the amplificatory and most durative processes the skills involved—and thus the general potential for social access—are of a kind already developed in primary social communication: to speak, to hear, to gesture, to observe and to interpret. Many blocks supervene, even at a primary level, as in the different languages and gesture-systems of different societies, but within the communicative process itself there is no *a priori* social differentiation. Problems of social order and relationship in these processes centre in issues of control of and access to the developed means of amplification or duration. Characteristically these are of direct interest to a ruling class; all kinds of control and restriction of access have been repeatedly practised. But it is still a shorter route, for any excluded class, from such control and restriction to at least partial use of such means, than in the case of alternative means, in which not only access but a crucial primary skill—for example, writing or reading—has also to be mastered.

The problem of social order cannot be left as one of simple class differentiation. There is a reasonably direct and important relation between the relative powers of amplification and duration and the amounts of capital involved in their installation and use. It is much easier, obviously, to establish a capitalist or state-capitalist monopoly in radio-transmission than in megaphones. Such monopolies are still of crucial social and political importance. Yet within the amplificatory and durative means there are many historical contradictions. The very directness of access, at each end of the process, allows substantial flexibility. The short-wave radio receiver, and now especially the transistor radio, enable many of us to listen to voices beyond our own social system. The crucial phase of monopoly-capitalist development, including capitalist control of the advanced technologies of centralized amplification and recording, came also to include the intensive development of such machines as transistor radios and tape-recorders, which were intended for the ordinary channels of capitalist consumption, but as machines involving only primary communicative skills gave limited facilities also for alternative speaking, listening and recording, and for some direct autonomous production. This is still only a marginal area, by comparison with the huge centralized systems of amplification and recording, based on varying but always substantial degrees of control and selection in the interests of the central social order. Yet though marginal it is not insignificant, in contemporary political life.

Moreover there are many technical developments which, within the always contradictory social productive process, are extending this range: cheaper radio transmitters, for example. Within a socialist perspective these means of autonomous communication can be seen not only, as under capitalism or in the difficult early stages of socialism, as alternatives to the central dominant amplificatory and durative systems, but in a perspective of democratic communal use in which, for the first time in human history, there could be a full potential correspondence between the primary physical communicative resources and the labour-created forms of amplification and duration. Moreover this profound act of social liberation would itself be a qualitative development of the existing direct physical resources. It is in this perspective that we can reasonably and practically achieve Marx's sense of communism as 'the production of the very form of communication', in which, with the ending of the division of labour within the mode of production of communication itself, individuals would speak *'as* individuals', as integral human beings.

There are greater but not insuperable difficulties in those communicative processes which are technically *alternative* to the use of direct physical communicative resources. The most remarkable fact of electronic communications technology is that, coming very much later in human history than the technologies of writing and printing, it has nevertheless, in some of its main uses (with certain critical exceptions which we shall have to discuss), a much closer modal correspondence to direct physical communicative forms: speaking, listening, gesturing, observing. This means that there are in fact fewer obstacles, within this general mode, to abolition of the technical division of labour. The problems of the general social and economic—revolutionary—abolition of the division of labour are of course common to all modes, but there are here, as in other areas of production, significant technical differentiate which, even within a revolutionary society, will affect at least the timing of the practical ending of such divisions.

The first fact about the alternative communicative modes is that they require, for their very performance, skills beyond those which are developed in the most basic forms of social intercourse. Writing and reading are obvious examples, and the extent of illiteracy or imperfect literacy, even in advanced industrial societies, to say nothing of pre-industrial or industrializing societies, is evidently a major obstacle to abolition of the division of labour within this vital area of communication. Literacy programmes are thus basic within any socialist perspective. But their success, essential as it is, reaches only to the point already achieved within more direct physical communicative processes, in that there is then potential access at each end of the process. The problems encountered in the direct modes remain for solution: problems of effective access, of alternatives to class and state control and selection, and of the economics of general distribution. Theoretically these are of the same order as those encountered in democratization of the direct modes, but the costs of the transformation processes which are inherent in all alternative forms may significantly affect at least the timing of their solution.

Here also, however, technical developments are making some kinds of common access simpler. Mechanical and electronic forms of printing and reproduction are now available at relatively low capital costs. Beyond these there is a dynamic area of technical development which is socially and economically more ambiguous. From computer typesetting to the electronically direct composition of type—and beyond these, perhaps, though it is still some years away, direct electronic interchange, each way, between voice and print—there are now changes in the means of communicative production which at once affect class relations within the processes, and lead also to changes—indeed a rapid rise, at least in the first phase—in the necessary level of capitalization. Thus the relationship between writing and printing, developed in traditional technology, has been an outstanding instance of what is at once a technical and a social division of labour, in which writers do not print, but that is seen as only a technicality, and, crucially, printers do not write but are seen as merely instrumental in the transmission of the writing of others. The class relations within newspapers, for example—between editors and journalists who have things to say and who write them, and a range of craftsmen who then technically produce and reproduce the words of these others—are obvious and now acute. There is an ideological crisis within the capitalist press whenever, on important occasions, print craftsmen assert their presence as more than instrumentality, refusing to print what others have written, or, more rarely, offering themselves to write as well as print. This is denounced, within bourgeois ideology, as a threat to the 'freedom of the press', but the terms allow us to see how this bourgeois definition of freedom is founded, deeply, in a supposedly permanent division not only of labour but of human status (those who have something to say and those who do not).

Yet now, in the new technology, journalists, who 'write', may also, in a direct process, compose type. Traditional crafts are threatened, and there is a familiar kind of industrial dispute. Its terms are limited, but in any pre-revolutionary society the limits are an inevitable consequence of the basic social division of labour. Theoretically the solution is evident. Any gain in immediate access to print is a social gain comparable with the gains of direct transmission and reception of voices. But the capital costs are high, and the realities of access will be in direct relation to the forms of control over capital and the related general social order. Even where these forms have become democratic, there is still a range of questions about the real costs of universal-access communication, and obviously about the comparative costs of such access in different media. Much of the advanced technology is being developed within firmly capitalist social relations, and investment, though variably, is directed within a perspective of capitalist reproduction, in immediate and in more general terms. At present it seems more probable that self-managing communication systems, with forms of universal access that have genuinely transcended the received cultural divisions of labour, will come earlier in voice systems than in print systems, and will continue to have important economic advantages.

'Direct' and 'Indirect' Communication

Thus far we have made only a first-level comparison between amplificatory and durative systems, on the one hand, and alternative systems, on the other. This comparison takes us a long way into the problem, but there is an important second-level comparison to which we must now turn.

The technical forms which are primarily amplificatory and durative include, as we have seen, within any class-divided society, certain social conditions which qualify their abstract definitions of general availability. Amplification can be, and indeed almost everywhere is, highly selective; only some voices are amplified. Duration is radically affected by this and by further selective processes. But what has then to be distinguished, theoretically, is a qualitative difference, within the means of communication as means of production, between the amplificatory (and to a lesser extent the durative) and those alternative systems which now include not only such modes as writing and print but modes which in some of their uses seem to be only amplificatory or durative.

Thus in radio and television there can, technically (leaving aside, for the moment, the powerful processes of social control and selection), be direct transmission and reception of already generalized communicative means: speech and gestures. But most radio and television—and this tendency is necessarily strengthened when a durative function is in question—involve further labour of a transforming or partly transforming kind. The processes of editing, in the broadest sense—from shortening and rearranging to the composition of new deliberate sequences—are qualitatively similar, at least in effect, to fully alternative systems. Yet this is very difficult to realize just because what is then transmitted has the appearance of direct transmission and reception of the most generalized communicative means. We hear a man speaking with his own voice, or he 'appears as himself' on the screen. Yet what is actually being communicated, after the normal processes of editing, is a mode in which the primary physical resources have been—usually in what are by definition hidden ways; the edited-out words cannot be heard—transformed by further intermediate labour, in which the primary communicative means have become material with which and on which another communicator works.

It is not only a matter of excision and selection. New positive relations of a signifying kind can be made by the processes of arrangement and juxtaposition, and this can be true even in those unusual cases in which the original primary units are left in their original state. In film, in which by definition there is no direct transmission of primary physical communicative resources—since all are intermediately recorded—there is a variation of this general position, and the central communicative act is customarily taken as precisely this composition, in which the primary communicative processes of others, whether or not under specific direction, are in effect raw material for communicative transformation by others.

It is in this sense that radio and television, in all forms other than the simplest direct transmission, and then video and film, have to be seen finally as alternative modes, rather than as simply amplificatory or durative. Even in direct transmission in television, so apparently technical a matter as the positioning of the camera is a crucial signifying element. In a confrontation between police and demonstrators it matters absolutely, for example, whether the camera is placed (as so regularly) behind the police, or, as in a different social perspective it can be, behind the demonstrators, or again, which can sometimes happen, in impartial relations to both. What is 'being seen' in what appears to be a natural form is, evidently, then in part or large part what is 'being made to be seen'. The traditional alternative systems, in which speech is rendered or recorded in print, or in which, by habituation, there is direct communicative composition for print, are then often easier to *recognize* as alternative systems, with all their initial social difficulties of acquiring the necessary skills, than these effectively alternative systems in which the appearance of direct communication has in effect been produced, by specific processes of technical labour.

Thus Marx's revolutionary perspective, within which modern universal communication can be subordinated to individuals only by subordinating it to all of them, raises problems of a new kind in addition to those problems which are inherent in any such social transformation. We can foresee a stage of social development in which general appropriation of the means of communicative production can, by integrated movements of social revolution and the utilization of new technical capacities, be quite practically achieved. For example the creation of democratic, autonomous and self-managing systems of communal radio is already within our reach, to include not only 'broadcasting', in its traditional forms, but very flexible and complex multi-way interactive modes, which can take us beyond 'representative' and selective transmission into direct person-to-person and persons-to-persons communication. Similar though perhaps more expensive systems can be envisaged for teletext, where there is a broad area for the general appropriation of communicative and especially durative means of production. Yet at the same time, within other modern alternative systems, which include many of the most valuable communicative acts and processes, there are problems in the modalities of any such appropriation which are of a more intractable kind. It is true that modes of communal autonomy and self-management will go much of the way, within the intrinsically transforming processes, to alter the generally existing character of such production. But whereas in the simpler and more direct modes there are readily accessible forms of truly general (universal) appropriation—by direct access to a technology which utilizes only primary and already distributed communicative resources—it must for a long time be the case, in those processes which depend on transformations, that a relatively abstract appropriation is more practical, and therefore more likely, than that more substantial appropriation—general and universal—of the detailed means of production which such systems necessarily employ. Of critical importance, in this respect, and as the necessary ground for any effective transition, is sustained discussion and demonstration of the inherent transforming processes involved in, for example, television and film. The modes of 'naturalization' of these means of communicative production need to be repeatedly analyzed and emphasized, for they are indeed so powerful, and new generations are becoming so habituated to them that here as strongly as anywhere, in the modern socio-economic process, the real activities and relations of men are hidden behind a reified form, a reified mode, a 'modern medium'.

But critical demystification can take us only part of the way. Reification will have to be distinguished from the open, conscious composition of works, or the only results will be negative, as in some contemporary semiotic tendencies, which demystify the practice by calling all such practice into question, and then predictably fall back on ideas of universal (inherent and unsurpassable) alienation, within the terms of a pessimistic and universalist psychology. The critical demystification has indeed to continue, but always in association with practice: regular practice, as part of a normal education, in this transforming labour process itself: practice in the production of alternative 'images' of the 'same event'; practice in processes of basic editing and the making of sequences; practice, following this, in direct autonomous composition.

We shall already have entered a new social world when we have brought the means and systems of the most direct communication under our own direct and general control. We shall have transformed them from their normal contemporary functions as commodities or as elements of a power structure. We shall have recovered these central elements of our social production from the many kinds of expropriator. But socialism is not only about the theoretical and practical 'recovery' of those means of production, including the means of communicative production, which have been expropriated by capitalism. In the case of communications, especially, it is not only, though it may certainly include, the recovery of a 'primitive' directness and community. Even in the direct modes, it should be institution much more than recovery, for it will have to include the transforming elements of access and extension over an unprecedentedly wide social and inter-cultural range.

In this, but even more in the advanced indirect communicative modes, socialism is then not only the general 'recovery' of specifically alienated human capacities but is also, and much more decisively, the necessary institution of new and very complex communicative capacities and relationships. In this it is above all a production of new means (new forces and new relations) of production, in a central part of the social material process; and through these new means of production a more advanced and more complex realization of the decisive productive relationships between communication and community.

Reference

Prilozi – Društvenost Komunika, Zagreb, 1978. Originally published in Raymond Williams's *Problems in Materialism and Culture*, Verso, 1980, pp. 50–63. Reprinted with kind permission of Verso.

16

'INDUSTRIAL' AND 'POST-INDUSTRIAL' SOCIETY
(1983)

In this chapter from his most important later book, Towards 2000, *Raymond Williams insists that industrialism is not defined exclusively by technology but is much better understood in terms of the relations of production. He reviews historical changes in the labour process and classifications of work – manufacturing, skilled and so forth. He challenges the popular American notion of 'post-industrialism', which is supposedly defined by the decline of manufacturing work and the growth of 'service' work, an extremely vague category indeed, in the older industrial states. The world is in no sense 'post-industrial', though a great deal of manufacturing work has been transferred from what had become comparatively expensive labour markets in the old industrial states to cheap labour markets in the newer industrial states. Moreover, the new forms of informational work are in no sense 'post-industrial'. In fact, the new technologies and their associated labour processes are characteristic of an advanced stage of 'industrialism'.*

'The industrial revolution, in an important technical phase, is continuing.' We can say that again. In the last quarter-century, the speed and extent of technical change have been remarkable in themselves but even more remarkable, especially in recent years, in their effects on habits and kinds of work. In the further development of these changes, persistent mass unemployment, of a structural kind, based in the further industrialisation of many existing kinds of work, has been widely predicted. Yet at the same time it is common to talk of these changes as leading to a 'post-industrial' society.

All the terms of this discussion need some new analysis. It has become common, in orthodox accounts, to refer not only to 'the industrial revolution' but to second and third industrial revolutions. The first industrial revolution, from the 1780s to the 1840s, is seen as based on the application of steam power. The second, between 1860 and 1910, is seen as based on the application of new forms of power from oil and electricity. In this kind of classification, the third industrial revolution has been seen as based on the new power of nuclear energy, from the 1950s, but a more familiar scheme, shifting the point of reference, defines it as the application of electronic systems – computers, automation, microchips – to widening areas of production and control.

The material significance of each of these major shifts is beyond question. Yet it is obvious that each of the descriptions depends on a solely technical sense of 'industrial revolution'. In fact, if we were to take this full emphasis, and enter the real history of the many major technologies, we would find such a sequence too simple and too abbreviated. We would have to speak of one, two, three, many industrial revolutions.

What has really to be said is very different. The full significance of the industrial revolution is not to be found only in the introduction and development of new *forces* of production. What began to be changed, from the 1780s, was the whole set of *relations* of production, which eventually constituted a new social order. It is obvious that there has been a close relation, from the beginning, between the new forces and the new relations of production. But it is a very weak kind of thinking to abstract the technical and technological changes and to explain the widespread social, economic and cultural changes as determined by them. This error, now identified as 'technological determinism', bears with particular weight on interpretation of all the later stages of industrialisation. It is especially misleading in descriptions and predictions of a 'post-industrial' society. For in the end it is impossible to understand the industrial revolution, in any of its phases, including the most recent and most imminent, by reference to the changes in the forces of production alone.

Consider first another sequence that could be as reasonably proposed: the institution of a capital market; the transformation of land ownership, leading to the displacement of millions of small farmers and agricultural labourers; the beginning of joint-stock companies;

the institution of free trade; the organisation of corporations and cartels; the development of new international monetary systems; the growth of multinational companies. Each of these events and their combined sequence (which again, to be complete, would require many more entries) affected the development of modern society as fundamentally as any of the major changes in techniques of production. It is only in the weak intellectual form of technological determinism, or in the established ideological form in which industrialisation is presented without reference to its historically inextricable capitalism, that the familiar reduced and excluding senses of 'industrial revolution' are possible.

There is a major problem, to which we must return in detail, in diagnosing the relations between industrial production and capitalism. Historically they have been so closely linked that they can often be seen as dependent on each other. Yet most modern socialists have believed that it would be possible to have modern industrial production without capitalism. Indeed in Eastern Europe this has been widely attempted and, as some would say, achieved. The results, however, both there and in more limited kinds of what has been called socialism in Western Europe, are still matters of basic dispute. This is not an intellectual problem for those who isolate the development of the forces of industrial production. Moreover, those who support and advocate capitalism have their own version of the fundamental relationship; it is, they say, the institutions and incentives of capitalism which develop the productive forces, and there is no other practicable way. For socialists, however, who typically believe that the forces and the relations of production are integrally connected and indeed mutually dependent, the proposition of modern forms of industrial production without capitalism has far more difficulties than are usually or at all admitted. This point is of intense practical significance in the historical phase which we have recently entered, under the heavy pressures of the latest changes in both technology and capitalism.

2

The point of entry for an analysis, either of the fundamental nature of the industrial revolution or of the severe crisis of industrial society which we are now beginning to experience, is the idea of *employment*. This goes beyond the earlier analysis in terms of the 'consumer' and the 'market'. There is now a regular association of *employment* with *work*. For most people of working age, it is widely believed, to be not employed is to be not working. A woman doing long and often heavy or demanding work in a home and family is said to be not a working woman, but if she is employed, in any capacity, she becomes one. So prepotent is this idea that even those people who work on their own account, as independent craftsmen, consultant professionals, freelances, contractors, owner-occupier farmers and so on, are said to be *self-employed*. A legal fiction, of an employer who employs himself, is invented to conform to the predominant idea that all work is employment.

The industrial revolution did not invent the institution or the idea of work as employment, but it powerfully strengthened both, and in its full development made them overwhelmingly dominant. In previous social orders millions of men and women had been practically subject, for their means of livelihood, to the controls of power and property. Yet the emergence of employment, in its basic sense of a contract of labour for a wage, and especially for a regular wage, is a major qualitative change. It is evident, in its early forms, for several centuries before anything that can be called an industrial revolution. Yet it is clear that the full development of the factory system, steadily displacing earlier forms of domestic and small-workshop production, greatly generalised the regular wage relationship. At the same time, and indeed earlier, several forms of rural livelihood, in small areas of land or in access to commons, were made marginal or were extinguished. The development of new forms of government, of commerce, of larger companies and of the money market itself produced new major areas of employment. It is only as these changes develop that we begin to hear of *employment* in that special sense indicated by its converse, *unemployment*, which in the course of the nineteenth century became a condition seen as outside the now normal and expected social organisation of work. It is this normalisation, the inner core of modern industrial society, which is now in its turn threatened by further major developments in the forces of production, most obviously in the introduction of newly automated systems.

Yet employment in this sense, of the regular contract for wage labour, while dominant, has never been anything like total. In the 1980s most industrial societies are suffering from mass unemployment, but most are also still characterised by mass *employment*, at historically high levels. If employment is expressed as a percentage of people of working age, the current figure in Britain is just below 70 per cent, as compared with below 60 per cent at the beginning of the 1930s (source: H. Neuburger, *Guardian* 21.7.82). The employment of men, at 80 per cent at the beginning of the 1930s, has now dipped below 80 per cent; the general difference is accounted for by the increased employment of women, from 36 per cent to 61 per cent. However, within this general movement, there are periodic and perhaps unrepeatable high points, reaching over 90 per cent for men in the 1950s and 1960s, and over 65 per cent for women in the 1970s. In this as in several other respects, modern industrial society, in its assumed norms, seems to have peaked in the major period of growth between the 1950s and the 1970s. The processes of centralising and rationalising production, begun in systematic ways in the first decades of the industrial revolution, brought with them a dominant definition of work as employment within these productive forms. It is ironic that the logic of their own further development has come to disturb and to threaten the very norm of employment on which the social order has come to depend.

Again this is more than a series of technical changes: the coming of robots or microchips or whatever. The purpose of these processes of centralising and rationalising production was not then and is not now the general welfare of all the people in the society. The benefits of increased production and of regular and rising wages have been real. But whenever the choice has had to be made between the true primary purposes – increase of production, reduction of costs, thus success in the market and higher returns on invested capital – and the variable secondary effects – increased employment, rising living standards for wage-earners, even overall levels of common wealth – there has never been any real doubt which way it would go. It is in this fundamental sense that we have still to speak of 'the industrial revolution', and more specifically of the revolution of industrial capitalism, in and through all its important technical and institutional changes. 'Structural unemployment' – that key phenomenon of the late twentieth century – is never only a 'technological' development; it is always also a function of the general relations of production, both within and between specific capitalist economies. This then has special effect on the orthodox prediction of a coming 'post-industrial' society.

3

The marks of a 'post-industrial' society are usually specified in terms of changes in 'work'. Manufacturing employment is seen as in major decline, especially in the old industrial countries. Service employment is seen as in major growth, in the same countries. New forms of service employment, in relation to collecting, processing and distributing information, are seen as becoming dominant. Indeed the 'post-industrial' society is often also called the 'information society'.

Real and major changes are being registered in this analysis, but in intellectually confused ways. The very facts that are produced to inform and illustrate the analysis are themselves subject to ideological presumptions which belong to the social order which the analysis both partly illuminates and partly obscures. We can see this most clearly in the founding definitions of categories of work.

There has been since the 1930s an orthodox tripartite division of kinds of work. This begins with a primary sector, in agriculture and the gaining of raw materials. There is then a secondary sector, in which goods (commodities) are manufactured. This is followed by a tertiary sector, often headlined as 'service industries', in which, within the orthodox definition of employment, everything else is done. Given these categories, it can be shown that the primary sector has dramatically declined: in the whole period of the industrial revolution from well over 50 per cent to under 10 per cent. The secondary sector, manufacturing, rose in the same period to a peak of more than 35 per cent but is now falling towards 20 per cent. The miscellaneous tertiary sector, quoted as 'services', provides the residual figures, and is now evidently, in these terms, an actual majority. This is then taken to be the nature of a 'post-industrial' economy.

This confusion has to be tackled at several levels. First, it has been shown by several recent analysts (cf. B. Jones, *Sleepers, Wake!*, 1982) that the orthodox tertiary sector is absurd. It includes work as diverse as building, construction and transport on the one hand and professional, commercial and entertainment employment on the other. Evidently some of these 'services' are the necessary infrastructure of manufacturing distribution; others are agencies of the public order; others again are services provided for individuals. In all of these, in fact, the growth of 'information' employment is marked; it has been aggregated at more than 50 per cent of all employment, in the most developed industrial societies.

But this kind of aggregation, within the received overall categories, is misleading. The special problems of what has been called the 'information society', and its major new technologies, will be examined more closely in the chapter on 'Culture and Technology'. What must be noted at this stage is the extent to which this classification of work is confused by the ideology of work as employment, within market terms. The three-sector model in fact reproduces the stages of production for a market within industrial capitalism, though by some residual traces from the real world it then succeeds in confusing them.

At its simplest, the model presupposes the gaining of raw materials, their manufacture as commodities, and then their distribution. A scheme of production for the market has then substituted itself for a society, even a society conceived primarily in terms of work. All that work which is the nurture and care of human beings, on whom the entire system depends, is excluded unless it is paid employment. All social development and education is either excluded or is relegated to the tertiary sector, where it can be seen as dependent on what have been defined as primary and secondary, although in reality all are mutually interdependent. Again, the care of people, in all phases of life but especially in sickness and age, becomes, in the model, what is attended to after the primary raw material and secondary manufacturing processes have been completed. This set of relegations and exclusions, in the interest of a scheme of increased and profitable production, is the inner history of industrial capitalist society. It has never in practice been able to shift all human priorities and interests into its desired ordering, but it has established itself as systematically dominant. It has done this by its control of the means and resources of production, which prevents all but a small minority from gaining their livelihood with their own means and resources, and which forces them into available employment.

There is a further point about orthodox classifications of work, as conceived within the assumptions of industrial capitalism. One of the delusions of modern production is its definition of *skill*, which appears in the occupational categories as *skilled, semi-skilled* and *unskilled*. One of the first extraordinary effects of this is that, interacting as it does with the definition of work as employment, it relegates most of the fundamental forms of human work to the *unskilled*. All the ordinary nurture and care of people, and all ordinary homemaking and preparation of food, are in this lowest category or beneath it. Then, even within employment, the old skills of farming, gardening, fishing, lumbering are written down as unskilled. Harry Braverman, who initiated analysis of this fantastic distortion (in *Labor and Monopoly Capital*, 1974), goes on to show in clear detail how the category of the *semi-skilled*, defined by routine operations with machines, has been used to support a quite false assertion of the increase of skilled labour in industrial production. It is not only, for example, that the deep skills of tending land and growing food are categorically reduced by comparison with relatively quickly learned operations with machines (a typical training for these is from a few weeks to a few months). It is also that the general tendency of industrial production has been to displace or reduce the industrially skilled craftsmen, whose apprenticed trades, on which all early mechanical production absolutely depended, may often be cut out by centrally automated processes. The confusion about skills is especially marked in the supposed tertiary sector, which manages to include some of the longest periods of formal training, a large number of relatively quickly learned routines, and those traditional skills which, dependent primarily on experience, have been ideologically classed as unskilled.

It is of course true at the same time that the development and application of advanced technology, in an increasing number of kinds of work, requires a growing number of very highly skilled workers, typically with theoretical as well as practical knowledge. But it is an outcome of the same process that there is a steady polarisation between this important group and an increasing majority of workers whose means of livelihood depend on the maintenance and reproduction of existing working routines: routines, however, which it is one of the central purposes of increasingly rationalised production to reduce or abolish. This is the crisis of employment which will dominate the coming generations. It can be summed up in the word which is now the battlecry of the directors of industrial capitalist production: overmanning. As labour processes are rationalised, and costs in a competitive market pressed to be reduced, this social order of work is saying to the people of the society not only that in this or that industry the workforce must be reduced but that, taken as a whole, the society itself is overmanned. It is this disastrous and ultimately fatal conclusion which is the true crisis of industrial capitalism, which in its own terms can think and act in no other ways.

4

Or are there other ways? The hope that there might be, within the existing kind of social and economic order, underlies the proposition of a 'post-industrial' society. It is believed that as the workforce in agriculture and manufacturing continues its steep decline, the transfer to 'service' employment, already strongly under way, and especially to 'information employment', will simply redistribute jobs. This belief in 'transfer', historically based on the entry of the displaced farm labourers into the factories, is uncritically extended to what are in fact quite new social conditions.

For, first, in much service employment (as in the techniques of 'fast food') and especially in information employment (computers, teletext, word-processors as against bookkeeping, typing and filing) the same processes of capital intensity and labour reduction are now being very strongly developed. Professional work of all kinds is unlikely to be reduced for any technical reasons, but already its natural growth is being restrained by problems of funding (as in medicine and education) within the priorities of a capitalist economy. The one great area of work that will never be made redundant, though it may continue to gain useful technical supports, is in the nurture and lifelong care of people. The permanent need for such work, often now dramatised by its relative neglect under other pressures and priorities, makes it nonsense to say that in any future society there will not be enough work to go round. At different phases of life, but especially in infancy, sickness, disability and old age, the ratio of work is never less than one to one and can be as high as three to one, if it is to be properly carried out. But then it is precisely in this area of permanent need that the category of 'employment' exerts its worst distortions. Within the terms of a capitalist economy, the raising and care of healthy and capable human beings is emphatically not seen as 'the creation of wealth'.

Yet it has been widely hoped that the results of labour-saving could be used to create a new kind of society. It would be one in which the worst physical burdens were lifted, in which working years and hours could be dramatically shortened, and in which – in that highly significant phrase, expressing a permanent response to the social order of capitalist employment – people could have 'more time to themselves'. These are reasonable hopes. The technical conditions for them already exist. But then everything depends on which of the two meanings of 'labour-saving' we choose.

The humane choice is clear enough. Nobody who for any length of time has done heavy, dirty or dangerous labour, or for that matter endlessly repetitive routine impersonal tasks, could wish for anything but the further development of true labour-saving. Some critics of industrial production or electronic technology as such, usually writing at comfortable distances from the actual labour these replace, have lost human contact with most actual people. It is true that there are better kinds of work than either and that in very diverse ways most of us would like to have more time for them. But the only way in which enough or all of us can get such conditions of choice is through the further development of all real labour-saving, in all necessary burdensome, fatiguing or boring work.

On the other hand the dominant meaning of 'labour-saving' is now very different. It is not so much the labour that will be saved as the labourers: the 'employees', the 'labour costs', the payroll. This connects with an important retrospective argument about the industrial revolution itself. It has been widely argued recently that (all) critics of the industrial revolution have been hostile to progress and production. It has even been said that there is some element in English culture which makes it resistant to such progress, and which is now responsible for the British industrial decline. This is an intolerable confusion. The element in English culture which has been hostile to production and trade has a precise location in a *rentier* sector and in its supporting writers and thinkers. This sector, living on rents from land or on profits from internal and external production and trade, has kept its physical distance from both agricultural and industrial development. Yet for all its expansion of an almost wholly monetary world it has forged significant cultural continuities with the older culture of the landed gentry, in carefully preserved and imitated styles and titles and rituals. Essentially defined by privileged money, it has of course theoretically opposed production and trade. Its main demand has been that they should be profitably (to itself) carried on by others and as far away as possible – a condition which the export of productive capital is well on its way to realising.

But this sector is a world away from those others who are now loosely called Luddites. The actual Luddites were engaged in one of the first crises of the meaning of 'labour-saving'. Few working men and women have ever wanted to refuse machines or methods which would reduce their labour. Indeed their positive commitment to them is a major impulse which the industrial capitalist order has abused. What they have resisted, and continue to resist, is the introduction of machines and methods which will take away their employment and therefore, in conditions in which the means of independent production have been sharply reduced or altogether taken away, their income, their means of livelihood. It is an abuse of reason to confuse such men and women with the privileged distastes of the *rentiers*. Moreover it is now an ideological abuse, since it is used to block thought about the one necessary question. Are the new means of labour-saving to be used for the general wellbeing? If so, this absolutely includes the wellbeing of all those people whom the new machines and methods displace. Yet the common practice now is that they are from the beginning, in market terms, used to reduce costs, to dispense with large numbers of workers, and so to restore or maximise the profits of production. The basic choice is very clear, but it has been intolerably muddled by false ideas of work and of its possible and variable social ordering.

How does this bear on the idea of a 'post-industrial' society? To begin with, the society that is now emerging is in no sense 'post-industrial'. Indeed, in its increasingly advanced technologies, it is a specific and probably absolute climax of industrialism itself. What is often loosely meant is the declining relative importance of manufacturing, which is due to follow agriculture into being a small-minority sector of employment. The decline itself is real, in some societies, though even there its assessment is confused by tendencies in the export of manufacturing, within a world capitalist system, to countries with much lower labour costs and little or no working-class organisation. This aspect of the problem will be discussed further in the essay on 'Class, Politics, and Socialism'. Yet at this stage it is necessary to insist that a decline in manufacturing is not a decline in 'industrialism', and certainly not in industrial capitalism. The system of rationalised production by increasing applications of technology, within a system of regular wage-labour hired by the owners of the means of production, is not weakened but in its immediate terms strengthened when smaller and smaller numbers of workers are required to operate it. Moreover, service employment of a related kind, in distribution and checking, including the distribution and checking of information, is itself caught up in the same process, and is not, in its usual terms, the great residual to which the unwanted will transfer. The only available area for transfer, which is also the ground for great hope, is that of relatively direct human work and activity, for which, however, the market has no time except as a margin or an unavoidable residue.

It is by no means certain how fast a 'post-industrial' society, of this reduced market kind within the existing social order, will develop in practice. There are many centres of resistance to it, not only in trade unions but in habits of expectation of regular paid employment, which are still electorally powerful. There is also resistance of a deeper kind, from habits of work which have survived or developed within many of the most regulated systems. To the despair and anger of the great rationalisers of production, many people still spend a lot of their time at work talking to other people about other things, or in a host of marginal and unpaid activities. It is easy to say that these are compensatory activities; that people have to be there, for the money, but then make the best of it. It can be argued that it would be better to have much shorter hours and all go off home. But many people need a workplace just because it gives them these varied social relationships. In real terms these are choices for actual people to make. Much of the evidence so far, including the behaviour of those who are theoretically the great rationalisers, suggests a wealth of human ingenuity in finding something to do which appears to make a job indispensable. Of course, as most notably near the top of modern industry and services, this can become decadent. In some circumstances, under relatively tough conditions, it can even destroy the valued place. But taken together with what may be, for a time, the electorally enforceable demand for regular employment income or its direct substitutes, and with the stubborn though now in most conditions less enforceable resistance of the unions, concerned with simple job preservation, the introduction of this technically possible and (by its directors) theoretically desired economy may be slower in coming to completion than simple technical analysis suggests.

At some points, however, and in certain variable degrees, it is already making its mark. What then needs to be looked at is the major problem of the future of income and means of livelihood as the old employment system is steadily reduced. But before this, we should look at an important alternative account of what appears to be the same general process: not the coming of a 'post-industrial' society but, as in countries like Britain, a damaging and even frightening 'deindustralisation'.

5

Everyone seems to be saying that the British economy is being 'deindustrialised', but what this means is not clear. Should 'deindustrialisation' mean a decline in the total of industrial production, for example, or a decline in the total or the proportion of industrial workers? As it happens the British economy has recently experienced both, but it is still a key question to ask which is meant, and which matters more. In simple market terms, and within the habit of measuring production as an undiscriminated general total, it is obvious that the level of production matters more. The same or increased production, with fewer workers, is a sacred capitalist intention. At the same time falls in production, whether generally or in particular sectors, are usually bad news, since in conditions of stable or increasing demand they mean, as is now widely the case in Britain, that a greater share of production is being taken by competitors including crucially foreign competitors. In conditions of reduced demand, these competitive pressures are even heavier.

On the other hand, reduced industrial employment may be either an index of reduced production or a result of technical change. It is in practice very difficult, when both conditions are present, to analyse and assign figures to these distinguishable causes. Almost the whole of current politics circles around these questions, and in some cases is based on genuine concern. Those who choose the level of production as primary are determined, by a whole range of measures, including typically the reduction of 'overmanning', to make industry more competitive and in that way raise production again. Others, in a plausible option, choose both at once: more production *and* more jobs of an existing kind. Very few of us, faced with the urgency of these questions, can really see the argument through. Most of the choices involved are too radically disturbing, and even if they can be made in the head they become very different on the ground and with actual people.

What then most needs to be said is that the industrial revolution has not been a process of a single economy, and that at every stage it is insufficient or actually misleading to isolate an economy within national borders and propose policies within those unrealistic terms. It is true that there are periods of relative advantage and disadvantage between economies considered nationally. Diverse national policies and changing objective conditions have observable major effects. Yet what in its full development the industrial revolution created was not only a world market – some of the conditions for that had been created before general industrial production – but an interlocking, interdependent and (in national terms) interpenetrating world market. The current crises of both industrial production and industrial employment, on a world scale, show this underlying and persistent reality very clearly. Within it, all the time, there are ups and downs, shifts of advantage and disadvantage, but it is always the general process that is finally dominant. And what has then to be said, not as paradox, is that the various forms of local and national deindustrialisation have, as one of their principal causes, the general process of industrialisation itself.

It has always to some extent been so. By its inherent processes of centralising and rationalising production, the industrial capitalist system has been socially and economically uneven in its effects. When it was still only a matter of a single nation, disadvantaged and peripheral regions and smaller and more traditional types of production were steadily and at times ruthlessly marginalised or excluded. In a developing world trade, the same things were done to other societies and their native modes of production. As the whole process was generalised, and became ever more intense, a worldwide scramble for productive advantage and for markets was unleashed. Production was no longer defined by socially determined needs, but by the constant move outwards, leaving behind any worked-out areas or unprofitable communities. The deindustrialisation of certain sectors, regions, countries was thus a wholly predictable result of this ever more dominant mode of production.

It is hard when it happens to your own people: no harder, but more actual, than when it happens to others. Yet the only intelligent response is not then a further intensification of this at once necessarily productive and destructive process, but a search for the means of its rational control. This is not now what is generally happening. Within particular economics, most discussion is centred on the drive for competitive advantage, currently at the cost of mass unemployment and the impoverishment of all other parts of the society. It may seem for a time to make sense, until you realise that *everyone*, every economy, is doing this. I know that I have gone from reading the English newspapers on these familiar themes and then read for some weeks the French or the Italian or the German newspapers only to realise, beyond the differences of language, that the same analyses were being applied, the same remedies proposed, as if each were the only people in the world. This talk is described by its practitioners as tough and realistic, but even where it is benevolent it is a fantasy. It could only be by some almost inconceivable expansion of world trade, surpassing not only the probable limits of natural resources but also the hitherto intractable problems of the poverty and lack of buying-power of those most in need, that the aggregated export plans of the old industrial countries, the newly industrialising countries and those now planning industrialisation could possibly be realised, or come anywhere near their projections. However, instead of recognising this, the silly tough talk goes on. It is fully in the spirit of the history of industrial capitalism that its vocabulary is violent: 'aggressive marketing', 'market penetration', 'consumer impact'. Yet most of this talk is by smooth men in sleek offices taking no significant risks. The real toughness is all at the other end: where caring and efficient production can be turned by the arbitrary exploitation of temporary advantages; where the edge of the most currently competitive economies (at whatever costs to their own workers and citizens) can cut into other societies and depress or ruin them; or where, within a currently uncompetitive economy, millions are out of work while millions are in need.

There will be 'deindustrialisation', in certain sectors, just as there will be new industrialisation in others. But the only attainable general solution is some form of reconstruction of the basic mode of production itself. This can only be on the principle of combining necessary domestic production with planned foreign trade. The principle of a society sustained by its economy has to replace the practice of a society determined by a market.

There are then vast practical problems. The definition of the appropriate size of such a society is among the first. The obvious definition, in the nation-state, is inadequate in both directions. It includes, internally, depressed and marginalised regions, their production determined by the larger forces elsewhere. At the same time, in the actual diversity of resources and skills, it is often too small to sustain a stable and adequate economy from its own production. But then none of the economic problems is soluble, in any new ways, unless we begin from some realistic definition of a society and then directly determine its necessary production and trade, rather than as now, with increasing hopelessness, taking such society as is left after the operations of the international market.

5

Within any reconstruction of the mode of production, certain basic problems of work and income persist. Yet some already possible solutions come into view, and only come into view, when this major reconstruction has been begun. Within the terms of the capitalist market, and within the imposition of free trade by the temporarily strongest economies, necessary domestic production can not even be defined. The cheapest or most available or most recent products will be bought from anywhere, often financed by debt. Foreign trade, meanwhile, is not a matter of mutual and stable advantage, but an arbitrary interpenetrating process within an inherently unequal world economy. To draw back and begin to determine production and trade from the whole needs of the people of a society requires, evidently, first limiting and then breaking the arbitrary power of capital: increasingly, in practice, of international capital.

It is the detailed practicability of what could and would then happen that is now in question. The will to challenge and defeat the arbitrariness of capital is almost wholly dependent on a belief that the rest of us could in practice manage our own affairs, and that there is some other future than being its declining but inevitable employees.

At the most general level the reality of the hope can not be doubted. Freed from random external forces, a society could make its own patterns of production and use, its own scales and rhythms of work, within the material limits from which every society must in reality define itself. The possible arrangements are then very diverse. There is, to begin with, the choice within the range of effective societies: the range, for example, from Wales to Western Europe. There are major advantages in the larger societies, both in diversity of resources and in the capacity to sustain a stable economy in a world market which will not change all at once. At the same time, as my own land, Wales, has repeatedly experienced, a real society, deciding its own production and trade, can be lost along the way to some larger political unit. These problems and choices are discussed again in the essay on 'The Culture of Nations'.

More generally, and quite as hard to solve, there is the problem of the relation between work and income. It will be one of the main advantages of changing the mode of production that people, rather than only employers, will be able to decide, in specific cases, what amount and type of real labour-saving will be introduced, in relation both to its advantages and to its effects on available work. Nobody can predict how all these choices would come out, but it seems likely that the amount of necessary work, certainly in manufacturing and distribution, would decline. It is then obviously possible to share this, in each sector, by shorter working lives and hours, but of course what will also have to be shared is the income, the share of production. Moreover, given the probable and necessary increase in work directly concerned with people rather than with goods, there are quite new problems of determining value and therefore income, in work which by definition is not marketed. Again, beyond these different kinds of active workers, there is the problem of determining the level of transfer of the means of livelihood to those who are not working, by reason of age, sickness or disability, or who (as in proposals for a general minimum income unrelated to work) are for other reasons out of the work-income relationship. This problem will also materialise, at a very different level, in the changes already under way in both the idea and the practice of the family as a 'unit of household income'. The more diverse primary relationships which people seem likely to choose (and it is this diversity and relative freedom of choice which needs to be emphasised, rather than any new single pattern) will encounter some quite new conditions of material livelihood and relationship as the full-employment pattern weakens. Some new and renewed kinds of positive bonding, as distinct from the liberal 'independence' apparently offered by employment, are certain to be necessary.

If then the first problem of the coming economy is the recovery of control of our own production, the second problem is that of the politics and culture of income and transfer. It is true that the absolute link between employment and income has already been broken. Not only in the provision of public education and health services, but more directly in the extension of benefits to citizens rather than only to workers, the crude market principle has already been refined. Yet it would be stupid not to notice that this regulated distribution of benefits, in much the same way as the contested distribution of incomes, has produced many destructive confusions and resentments. In a society which did not yet fully control its own production, these might actually increase, in conditions of declining marketable employment. Certainly one common current projection, of skilled and highly skilled minorities very actively engaged at work, and of a majority not employed in profitable work but sustained from the energy and resources of the others, is wholly unrealistic and unstable. Its most likely product would be a more actively authoritarian and more criminal society.

It is only by a full recovery of control of production, and therefore of the fully social means of determining shares of work and of livelihood, that these problems can be solved, and even then only by very advanced forms of democratic discussion and decision. The current political market, like the economic market from which it in some respects derives, is altogether too crude for their complex resolution. What was argued in 1959, that the 'social services ... remain limited by assumptions and regulations belonging not to the new society but the old', is still true but incomplete. There was never any way in which the genuinely new ideas and provisions for a caring society could persist as an *exceptional* sector, contradicted by systematic inequality and competition everywhere else. In fact the models of relief and 'insurance', from the old order, provided a base from which, in a period of rising incomes, the idea of common social provision was steadily weakened and interpreted as selective 'entitlement' and burdensome 'cost'. It is not by bureaucratic regulation, however complex, but only by direct communal administration, that an idea of common welfare can become actual.

At the same time it is impossible that any of these problems can be solved by measures based on the kind of fantasy which has grown in the shadow of the capitalist ideal of ever-expanding, ever-competitive, ever-successful production. The kinder-sounding fantasy of giving everybody more and more, so that no choices need ever be made, is the death-cry of an old social democracy. The world is not only as tough as the capitalists keep telling us; it is very much tougher. There are hard material limits, wherever they may finally and unevenly fall, on the indefinite production and consumption of goods which the capitalist system and its political junior partners have assumed and promised. Real sharing will have to occur, in some cases within increased production and available time, in other cases within stable or actually reduced resources and availabilities. The profound political problems of sharing, which if it succeeds can take us beyond an industrial capitalist order, can be neither evaded nor postponed by the old fable of the cake. A sharing society, in any case, has to begin by really sharing what it has, or all its talk of sharing is false or at best marginal. Moreover, sharing is not only at the receiving end; it is also, from the beginning, a matter of shared effort and responsibility. These are the only conditions for anything but an imposed and arbitrary stability, or an unstable chaos.

6

What has finally to be said, though, is that the major changes in work and production which are now happening and which are only weakly interpreted by the received ideas of both industrial and post-industrial society, are evidence as much of opportunity as of danger. It is only within a false and unnecessary system that there can ever really be over-production, or unwanted work, or what are called, cruelly, 'redundancy' and 'overmanning'. In the reality of labour saving, and in the availability of new skills and activities, we could, quite practically, enter a new world of human work. Sharing the political effort to make it like that is then in practice our first task.

Reference

From Raymond Williams, *Towards 2000*, Chatto & Windus, 1983, Penguin, 1985, pp. 83–101. Reprinted with kind permission by The Random House Group Limited.

17

THE CULTURE OF NATIONS
(1983)

In a further chapter from Towards 2000, *Williams addresses the contradictions of nationalism and globalism, remarking upon how patriotic sentiment is typically contradicted by people's actions. However, such contradiction is not simply a matter of personal inconsistency but a salient feature of the social world today. He also points out that capitalism owes no necessary allegiance to any country in its endless search for labour, natural resources and markets. In addition, Williams returns to an earlier and extremely insightful concept of his,* mobile privatisation, *and explains why it is such a typical feature of everyday life at present.*

1

There was this Englishman who worked in the London office of a multinational corporation based in the United States. He drove home one evening in his Japanese car. His wife, who worked in a firm which imported German kitchen equipment, was already at home. Her small Italian car was often quicker through the traffic. After a meal which included New Zealand lamb, Californian carrots, Mexican honey, French cheese and Spanish wine, they settled down to watch a programme on their television set, which had been made in Finland. The programme was a retrospective celebration of the war to recapture the Falkland Islands. As they watched it they felt warmly patriotic, and very proud to be British.

2

The contradictions in what is meant by nationality, and even more by patriotism, are now very acute. If they are more noticed and thought about by some people than by others, they are still not of a kind to be projected only to those who are most evidently and practically confused. There is a strongly effective continuation of relatively old ideas of nationality, and beyond these of race, while at the same time there is an extraordinary and yet widely accepted penetration and coexistence of powerful international and paranational forms. These are to be found not only in the obvious cases of world markets in food and in manufactured commodities, but also in active membership of a political and military alliance and of a paranational economic community. Each of these has radically altered the nature of sovereignty, yet that idea is still quite centrally retained. Our couple may well not have noticed the American aircraft, armed with nuclear weapons, flying high above their house from an English base, or the new heavier lorries on the bypass, whose weight has been determined by an EEC regulation, yet regularly, systematically, these are there.

'Contradiction' is a curious analytic term. It can be applied quite easily to cases where people actually say contradictory things, or act on contradictory beliefs. If somebody says that his country means everything to him, but that as a consumer he must buy what he wants at the most suitable price and quality, whatever its national origin, the element of contradiction is obvious. But the term has been extended to much more difficult cases, when it is not so much what people say and believe that is contradictory but when actual forces in a society are pulling in opposite or at least different directions and thus creating tensions and instabilities. The former cases, of verbal or everyday practical contradiction, can be met by arguments. They are what most of us come to notice, at various points in our lives, when we have to decide what we really (most) believe. The other kinds of 'contradiction' are not so readily dealt with. Indeed it is already assuming a lot to say that they are simple contradictions. The mental model by which we test coherence or compatibility may be simply what we are putting into the situation, and what looks contradictory, in its selected terms, may in fact be no more than an unfamiliar system, which in its own terms is coherent enough. There is then still a problem of the things we say about it, which may be muddled or locally contradictory. But the system itself, not only creating but also containing and managing tensions and instabilities, is not something that can be refuted by argument alone.

This is now the case, I believe, in these central problems that are indicated by talk of 'nationality', 'patriotism' and – for it is part of the same complex –'internationalism'. There are innumerable muddles and stupidities, and there is some very powerful political and cultural exploitation both of these and of the genuine difficulties. But in general these are problems of the surface of politics and culture. They would be relatively easily solved if the underlying and obscured problems of contemporary societies, on which they feed, were not so great.

3

It is human nature to belong to a society, and to find value in-belonging to it. We are born into relationships, and we live and grow through relationships. There is a whole range of such forms, variable in different places and times, but any actual forms are close and specific to those who are living in and through them. Intellectual analysis, of an historical or comparative kind, can show very quickly how 'limited' or 'local' any such form may be. But while in times of pressure and change this wider perspective is encouraging, showing us that it is possible for people to find meaning and value in many different kinds of relationship and society, it can also be an effective evasion of the actual problems which, with such meanings and values as they have, people are trying to resolve.

Thus in several modern intellectual systems there has been rapid progress to forms of universality – what is believed to be true of all people everywhere – which are then used to define what most people are still trying to live by as mere local illusions and prejudices. Genuine progress towards establishing the universality of social situation by class is offered as a way of dissolving stubborn self-definitions by nationality or religion. A presumed universality of situation by primary relationships, as in psychoanalysis, is offered as a way of enlightening and questioning forms of relationship which are, nevertheless, being continually reproduced. Each of these systems, with other similar systems, clearly affects the ways in which many people have learned to think about their relationships, but, except in certain very specific groups, they have nowhere come near to realising their own apparent logic, by which the offered universalities would prevail over more local forms.

Yet this is only half the story. The real 'universalities' – large forms which do succeed in prevailing over more local forms – are not to be found in intellectual systems but in actual and organised relationships which achieve, over the relevant areas, effective power. This is the way to look at the urgent modern problem of the 'nation'. It is ineffective and even trivial to come back from a demonstration of the universality of the human species and expect people, from that fact alone, to reorganise their lives by treating all their immediate and actual groupings and relationships as secondary. For the species meaning, and the valuation of human life which it carries, is in practice only realised, indeed perhaps in theory only realisable, through significant relationships in which other human beings are present. No abstraction on its own will carry this most specific of all senses. To extend it and to generalise it, in sufficiently practical ways, involves the making of new relationships which are in significant continuity – and not in contradiction – with the more limited relationships through which people do and must live.

Thus there is little point in jumping from 'the nation' to a projected 'internationalism'. Instead we have to move first in the other direction, to see what in practice this widely accepted 'universality' now amounts to. 'All modern peoples have organised themselves as nations'. Have they? The artificialities of many forms of modern 'nationality' and 'patriotism' have often been noticed. Some relatively detached or mobile people see them as merely 'backward' or 'primitive', and have a good laugh about them, until some war makes them weep. But the real point of entry for analysis is that the artificialities are functional. That is to say, they are neither backward nor primitive but contemporarily effective and deliberate forms. That they are now increasingly artificial, with very serious effects on what is also residually quite real, is then the central point.

4

'Nation', as a term, is radically connected with 'native'. We are *born* into relationships, which are typically settled in a place. This form of primary and 'placeable' bonding is of quite fundamental human and natural importance. Yet the jump from that to anything like the modern nation-state is entirely artificial. What begins as a significant and necessary way of saying 'we' and 'our' (as so much more than 'I' and 'mine') slides by teaching or habit into bland or obscuring generalities of identity. The strongest forms of placeable bonding are always much more local: a village or town or city; particular valleys or mountains. Still today in societies as different as Wales and Italy people say where they come from, where they were formed or belong, in these insistently local ways. It is of course possible to extend these real feelings into wider areas: what are often spoken of now as 'regional' identities and loyalties. But that term, 'region', illuminates a very different process. A 'region' was once a realm, a distinct society. In its modern sense, by contrast, it is from the beginning a subordinate part of a larger unity, typically now a part of a 'nation'. What has then happened is that the real and powerful feelings of a native place and a native formation have been pressed and incorporated into an essentially political and administrative organisation, which has grown from quite different roots. 'Local' and 'regional' identities and loyalties are still allowed, even at a certain level encouraged, but they are presumed to exist within, and where necessary to be overridden by, the identities and the loyalties of this much larger society.

It is of course true that some of these wider identities and loyalties have been effectively achieved through real relationships. Even where, as in the great majority of cases, the larger society was originally formed by violent conquest, by repression, by economic domination or by arbitrary alliances between ruling families, there are usually generations of experience of living within these imposed forms, and then of becoming used or even attached to them. What is still in question, however, is the projection of those original 'native' and 'placeable' feelings to the forms of a modern state. Nothing is now more striking, for example, than the images of 'England' which are culturally predominant. Many urban children, when asked what is really 'England', reply with images of the monarchy, of the flag, of the Palace of Westminster and, most interestingly, of 'the countryside', the 'green and pleasant land'. It is here that the element of artifice is most obvious, when the terms of identity flow downwards from a political centre, and yet when the very different feelings of being 'native' and being 'loyal' are invoked and in this way combined.

In nations with long and complex histories the procedures of invocation and combination are deeply embedded in the whole social process. Yet it is an evident historical fact that the processes of political combination and definition are initiated by a ruling class: indeed to say so is virtually tautologous. The building of states, at whatever level, is intrinsically a ruling-class operation. The powerful processes that then ensue, in the complex transitions from conquest and subjection to more embedded formations, necessarily take place, however, over much wider social areas. War stands out as one of the fundamentally unifying and generalising experiences: the identification of an alien enemy, and with it of what is often real danger, powerfully promotes and often in effect completes a 'national' identity. It is not accidental that talk of patriotism so quickly involves, and can even be limited to, memories and symbols of war. Meanwhile the assembly of armies, from diverse actual communities into this single and overriding organisation, is one of the most notable processes of actual generalisation and unification.

In modern societies, engaged in the transition from a subject people to a civil society, education of every kind, in churches and then mainly in schools, exerts more regular pressures. When children start going to school they often learn for the first time that they are English or British or what may be. The pleasure of learning is attached to the song of a monarch or a flag. The sense of friends and neighbours is attached to a distant and commanding organisation: in Britain, now, that which ought to be spelled as it so barbarously sounds – the United Kingdom, the 'Yookay'. Selective versions of the history underlying this impressed identity are regularly presented, at every level from simple images and anecdotes to apparently serious textbook histories. The powerful feelings of wanting to belong to a society are then in a majority of cases bonded to these large definitions.

It is often the case that this bonding moves at once from the smallest social entity, within the family, to the available largest, in the nation-state. These are offered as non-contradictory. Indeed they are rationalised as levels, the personal and the social. Many other kinds of bonding may then occur: distinction by streets or by parts of a town or village; distinction by gender and age-group; distinction by city or region. Many kinds of active 'local' or 'regional' groups, and of more passive groups of fans or supporters, grow up around these and carry powerful feelings. But typically they are unproblematically contained within the initial bonding between 'family-individual' and nation', which in all important and central cases is felt either to be an extension from them (as in particularised army regiments) or to override them.

It is a matter of great political significance that in the old nation-states, and especially the imperial states, scepticism and criticism of such bonding has come almost exclusively from radicals. They have seen, correctly, that this form of bonding operates to mobilise people for wars or to embellish and disguise forms of social and political control and obedience. It is true that opposition comes also from incompletely assimilated or still actively hostile minority peoples who have been incorporated within the nation-state, but this characteristically takes the form of an alternative (Irish or Scots or Welsh or Breton or Basque) nationalism, relying on the same apparent bonding though within a political subordination. The complex interactions between such nationalisms and more general radicalisms have been evident and remarkable, though in general it is true that unique forms of national-radical bonding, unavailable by definition in the larger nation-state, come through and have powerful effects. It is sadly also true that not only the majority people, with 'their own' nation-state, but also many among the minority peoples, regard *this kind* of nationalism as disruptive or backward-looking, and are even confident enough to urge 'internationalism' against it, as a superior political ideal. It is as if a really secure nationalism, already in possession of its nation-state, can fail to see itself as 'nationalist' at all. Its own distinctive bonding is perceived as natural and obvious by contrast with the mere projections of any nationalism which is still in active progress and thus incomplete. At this point radicals and minority nationalists emphasise the artificialities of the settled 'commonsense' nation-state and to their own satisfaction shoot them to pieces from history and from social theory.

The political significance is then that radicalism becomes associated, even in principle, with opposition to 'the nation'. In the old nation-states this has been profoundly damaging, yet it can be understood only by reference to the history and formation of actual social orders. For what has been most remarkable in the twentieth century has been the successful fusion of nationalism and political revolution, including armed struggles, in many other parts of the world, from Cuba to Vietnam. The conditions of such fusion evidently derive from a pre-existing colonial or semi-colonial status, in which relatively direct and powerful bonds of identity and aspiration are formed as against both foreigners and exploiters. There are then usually major problems, at a later stage, in relations with other national-revolutionary states, and the elements fused in the struggle enter a new stage in which the bonding can no longer be taken for granted. Meanwhile the political problem, for radicals back in the old nation-states, who are quick to identify with the national-liberation struggles of the ex-colonial peoples, lies in their fundamental attitudes to their own nation. For again and again, hurling themselves at the mystification of social reality by the ruling definitions of the nation and patriotism, they have found themselves opposed not only by the existing rulers and guardians but by actual majorities of the people in whose more fundamental needs and interests they are offering to speak.

There are many false ways out of this basic problem. All of them depend on subjection to the existing terms of the definitions. Contemporary social democrats, in particular, do their calculations and emerge with an amazing and implausible mix of patriotism, internationalism and social justice, drawing on each principle as occasion serves, or rhetorically proclaiming their compatibility or even identity. All this shows is their profound subordination to the forms of existing interests. The increasing irrelevance of social-democratic politics, in the old nation-states – indeed the transformation of social democracy itself, under a merely confusing retention of an old name, which in different conditions had more significance and coherence – is a direct result of this basic subordination.

For what they will not challenge, except in selected marginal ways, is capitalism itself. Yet it is capitalism, especially in its most developed stages, which is the main source of all the contemporary confusions about peoples and nations and their necessary loyalties and bonds. Moreover it is, in the modern epoch, capitalism which has disrupted and overriden natural communities, and imposed artificial orders. It is then a savage irony that capitalist states have again and again succeeded in mobilising patriotic feelings in their own forms and interests. The artificialities of modern nationalism and patriotism, in states of this kind, have then to be referred not to some intellectually dissolving universality, but to the precise and powerful functions which, necessarily in the form of artifice, they are now required to perform.

5

Both in its initial creation of a domestic market, and in its later organisation of a global market, the capitalist mode of production has always moved in on resources and then, necessarily, on people, without respect for the forms and boundaries of existing social organisations. Whole communities with settled domestic forms of production, from farming to brewing and clothmaking, and from small manufacturing to local services, were simply overridden by more developed and more centralised and concentrated capitalist and capitalist-industrial forms. Communities which at simpler levels had relatively balanced forms of livelihood found themselves, often without notice, penetrated or made marginal, to the point where many of their own people became 'redundant' and were available for transfer to new centres of production. Capitalist textile-production, ironmaking, mining, grain production and a host of other industrial processes set in train immigrations and emigrations, aggregations and depopulations, on a vast scale. Typically, moreover, people were moved in and out on short-run calculations of profit and convenience, to be left stranded later, in worked-out mining valleys or abandoned textile towns, in old dockyard and shipbuilding areas, in the inner cities themselves, as trade and production moved on in their own interests.

Through these large and prolonged dislocations and relocations, which are still in progress in every part of the world, the older traditional forms of identity and community were dislocated and relocated, within enforced mobilities and necessary new settlements. It is significant that William Cobbett, observing just these processes in one of their most decisive stages, is in effect the last authentic English radical: a man in whom love of birthplace, love of country, and root-and-branch opposition to the whole social order could be authentically integrated. Even in him there were tensions, underlying his radical change of political direction as his idea of the old England encountered the reality of the new. In all later periods, the kind of continuity which Cobbett still saw as ideal, from home and birthplace to county to country – none in tension with or cancelling the other – was increasingly unavailable. What took its place was an artificial construction, which had increasingly to be defined in generalising and centralised images because the only effective political identity still apparently compatible with the dislocating and relocating processes of industry was now at that deliberately distanced level.

But this was still only an early stage. What was done within the first industrial societies was soon also being done, at an accelerating pace, in every accessible part of the world. Whole tracts of land, where people had been living in their own ways, were ripped for minerals, ores, gems, fertilisers. Whole forests, in which people and animals had been living, were felled and exported. Simple subsistence farming communities were dispossessed and reorganised for plantations of rubber and cotton and sugar and coffee and tea, or for any and every kind of export-oriented monoculture which the physical conditions of the land, irrespective of the needs and preferences of its inhabitants, indicated for profit. The long forced trade in human beings, moving them as slaves into new kinds of work, was succeeded by various kinds of economic forcing, in which whole communities and peoples, or by selection their young men and women, had to emigrate to the new centres of work and subsistence.

Some of these developments struck back into the old economies, depressing or ruining other traditional kinds of production, and forcing new internal emigrations from what had been made into 'marginal areas'. Flows of people following these externally induced flows of trade and wealth broke up, at either end, the older types of settlement and community in which identity had been directly engaged. Moreover, as in the first industrial societies, it was never a movement once for all, into some new adjustment. As production and trading advantages shifted, vast numbers had to move yet again, or be left stranded in the debris of a worked-out economy. Massive movements of this kind are still occurring, in thousands of authorised and unauthorised emigrations and immigrations, and in the desperate trails from land dispossessed by agribusiness to the shanty towns on the edges of the already densely populated cities.

What is really astonishing is that it is the inheritors and active promoters, the ideologists and the agents, of this continuing worldwide process who speak to the rest of us, at least from one side of their mouths, about the traditional values of settlement, community and loyalty. These, the great disrupters, not only of other people's settlements but of many of those of their own nominal people, have annexed and appropriated, often without challenge, many of the basic human feelings about a necessary and desirable society. They retain this appropriation even while their hands are endlessly busy with old and new schemes in which the priorities are wholly different: schemes through which actual people and communities are depressed or disappear, under the calculations of cost-benefit, profit and advantageous production.

It is an outrage that this has happened and been allowed to happen. Yet while we can protest and fight in these terms, we can only analyse and understand if we bring in another dimension, which is now probably decisive. Instead of looking only at the promoters and agents of this vast dislocation and relocation, we have to look also at the changes that have happened and are still happening in the minds of those to whom, in effect, all this has been done.

6

Most human beings adjust, because they must, to altered, even radically altered conditions. This is already marked in the first generations of such shifts. By the second and third generations the initially enforced conditions are likely to have become if not the new social norms – for at many levels of intensity the conditions may still be resented – at least the new social perspective, its everyday common sense. Moreover, because so many of the shifts are enforced by a willed exploitation of new means of production and new products, sometimes ending in failure but much more often increasing goods of every kind, there are major if always unequal material advantages in the new conditions. Capitalism as a system, just because of its inherent one-dimensional mobility, can move on very rapidly from its failures and worked-out areas, leaving only local peoples stuck with them. By its very single-mindedness it can direct new and advantageous production in at least the short-term interests of effective working majorities. In any of its periodic crises it can make from one in ten to one in three of a numbered people redundant, but while it still has the other nine or the other two it can usually gain sufficient support or tolerance to continue its operations. Moreover, identified almost inextricably with positive advantages in improved products and services, it not only claims but is acclaimed as progress.

Thus while on an historical or comparative scale its forced operations are bound to be seen as arbitrary and often brutal, on any local and temporarily settled scale it flies with the wings of the dove. It brings factories and supermarkets, employment and affluence, and everything else is a local and temporary difficulty – out of sight, out of time, out of mind – or is the evident fault, even the malign fault, of those who are suffering. In any general examination, the system is transparent, and ugly. But in many, and so far always enough, local perspectives it is not only the tolerated but the consciously preferred order of real majorities.

For now from the other side of its mouth it speaks of the consumer: the satisfied, even stuffed consumer; the sovereign consumer. Sovereign? That raises a problem, but while the production lines flow and the shopping trolleys are ready to carry the goods away, there is this new, powerful social identity, which is readily and even eagerly adopted. It is at best a radically reduced identity, at worst mean and greedy. But of course 'consumer' is only a general-purpose word, on the lines of 'citizen' or 'subject'. It is accepted only as describing that level of life: the bustling level of the supermarket. When the goods from the trolley have been stowed in the car, and the car is back home, a fuller and more human identity is ready at the turn of a key: a family, a marriage, children, relatives, friends. The economic behaviour of the consumer is something you move out to, so as to bring the good things back.

There is then a unique modern condition, which I defined in an earlier book (*Television: Technology and Cultural Form*, 1974) as 'mobile privatisation'. It is an ugly phrase for an unprecedented condition. What it means is that at most active social levels people are increasingly living as private small-family units, or, disrupting even that, as private and deliberately self-enclosed individuals, while at the same time there is a quite unprecedented mobility of such restricted privacies. In my novel *Second Generation* (1964) I developed the image of modern car traffic to describe this now dominant set of social relations in the old industrial societies. Looked at from right outside, the traffic flows and their regulation are clearly a social order of a determined kind, yet what is experienced inside them – in the conditioned atmosphere and internal music of this windowed shell – is movement, choice of direction, the pursuit of self-determined private purposes. All the other shells are moving, in comparable ways but for their own different private ends. They are not so much other people, in any full sense, but other units which signal and are signalled to, so that private mobilities can proceed safely and relatively unhindered. And if all this is seen from outside as in deep ways determined, or in some sweeping glance as dehumanised, that is not at all how it feels like inside the shell, with people you want to be with, going where you want to go.

Thus at a now dominant level of social relations, systems quite other than settlement, or in any of its older senses community, are both active and continually reproduced. The only disturbance is when movements from quite outside them – movements which are the real workings of the effective but taken-for-granted public system – slow the flow, change the prices, depreciate or disrupt the employee–consumer connection: forcing a truly public world back into a chosen and intensely valued privacy.

The international market in every kind of commodity receives its deep assent from this system of mobile-privatised social relations. From the shell, whether house or car or employment, the only relevant calculations are the terms of continuing or improving its own conditions. If buying what such calculations indicate, from another nominal 'nation', leads directly or indirectly to the breaking or weakening of other people's shells, 'too bad' do we say? But the connections are not often as direct as that. They work their way through an immensely complicated and often unreadable market system. The results emerge as statistics, or as general remarks in television. Mainly what is wrong, we usually conclude, is what all those other shells are doing.

The fiercest drives of the modern international capitalist market are to extend and speed up these flows across nominal frontiers, these mutual if uneven penetrations that are properly called (including by some of the most surprising people) 'aggressive marketing'. If there is a fen of tended strawberries or an orchard valley of apples, each coming to fruit, it is of positive advantage, we are told, that at the crucial moment an entrepreneur who might be your neighbour ships in foreign strawberries or apples at a lower price, leaving your produce to be ploughed in or to rot. What is visible and wretched (and an annual occurrence) in grown natural produce is as wretched but less visible when it happens to every other kind of production. Thus a planned penetration or disruption of other people's economies, by the strongest national economies and by the multinational companies which are already operating without respect to frontiers, is offered as unambiguously in the general good. If you or you suffer from it, many more others benefit. All you have to do or can do is cut your costs and improve your product. If you cannot sufficiently do either, you must become redundant; go bankrupt; get out of the way of the leaner and fitter; join the real world.

It is an evil system, by all fully human standards. But what has then to be asked is why 'it' still has need of nations, of loyalty and patriotism, of an exaltation of flags and frontiers when the frontiers are only there to be economically dismantled and the flags, if the calculations come out that way, are quickly exchanged for flags of convenience? Why, in sum, in a modern free-trade capitalist international economy, have 'nations' at all?

7

The most dedicated consumer can only ingest so much. For other human needs, beyond consumption, other relationships and conceptions of other people are necessary. Similarly the market, great god as it is, can only exchange so much. It can produce and sell weapons, but it cannot, in any generally effective way, protect people. It can move and regulate producers and consumers, but it cannot meet all the essentially non-profitable human needs of nurture and care, support and comfort, love and fidelity, membership and belonging.

Where then will these needs be met? The current orthodoxy rules off many of them as private, not public matters at all. Yet it is surely a public matter that there are now in materially rich societies so many neglected, deprived, emotionally dissatisfied and emotionally disabled people; so many problems of loneliness and of unbearable while undrugged depressions, tensions, despairs. Leave all that to the market? But the decision-makers know, even if some of them keep working to forget, that this would be unacceptable and dangerous. It is a matter then of where the lines are drawn. A welfare state, a health service, an education system: the mainstream political parties move through these with differences of degree. It is where something national – 'national assistance' – is still necessary but at levels to be negotiated, subject always to the needs of 'the economy'. Protection? Now that is another matter. Even the market itself, to say nothing of its luckiest beneficiaries, cannot stand unprotected among so many random and unpredictable individual wills. Thus 'law and order': armed forces called a 'defence force' even when some of their weapons are obviously aggressive: these, unambiguously, are the real functions of a state. And then the basis of a state is a nation, and the circle is squared.

It can be seen either way: as a cynical retention of just those nation-state powers which defend the existing social and economic order and head off, at minimum cost, movements of discontent which its enemies might exploit; or as a more generous if still limited recognition that there are social purposes which must still be sustained, if necessary by protection from the market. It matters very much which of these interpretations is at any particular time more true – for indeed, as purposes and methods, they vary and fluctuate. But it matters even more to see that on either interpretation there is a nation-state which does not even claim to be a full society. What it actually is, whether cynically or generously, is a deliberately partial system: not a whole lived order but a willed and selected superstructure.

This is the functional significance of its artifices. It is significant. that the aggressive radical Right who are now in power in so many countries combine a pro-State rhetoric and practice, in military forces and a heavily policed law-and-order, with an anti-State rhetoric and practice in social welfare and the domestic economy, and in international monetary and trading exchange. This can be said, in a comforting way, to be a 'contradiction', but it is better seen as an open and class-based division of powers which is a genuine adjustment to an intensely competitive and profoundly unstable late capitalist world.

The national statism is to preserve a coherent domestic social order, both for general purposes and as a way of meeting the consequences of its commitment to open 'international' competition. It permits the ruin of certain 'national' industries by exposure to full transnational competition, but it does this as a way of enforcing transnational efficiency in what remains: the efficiency, indeed, of 'the Yookay', no longer a society but a market sector. At the same time it permits and even encourages the outflow of socially gathered capital (in pension funds and insurance and in the more general money market) to investment in whatever area of the global economy brings the highest money returns. So far as it can, against the established interests of communities and workers who are still its political electorate, it withdraws what it sees as distorting or enervating support for its own 'national' enterprises.

Thus an ideal condition is relentlessly pursued. First, the economic efficiency of a global system of production and trade, to include a reorganised and efficient 'national' sector within an open and interpenetrating market flow. But at the same time a socially organised and socially disciplined population, one from which effort can be mobilised and taxes collected along the residual but still effective national lines; there are still no effective political competitors in that. It is to this model of 'a people' that the rhetoric of an increasingly superficial and frenetic nationalism is applied, as a way of overriding all the real and increasing divisions and conflicts of interest within what might be the true nation, the actual and diverse people.

I repeat that this is a genuine adjustment to late twentieth-century conditions. It is a conscious programme to regulate and contain what would otherwise be intolerable divisions and confusions. Moreover, there is no way back from it to some simple and coherent nationalism. Some alternative programmes are now being offered, combining a recovery of full political and military sovereignty with a national economic recovery plan, including heavy domestic investment and controls on the export of capital and on selected imports. It is at first sight very surprising that this fails to strike any resonant 'national' chord. But this is the real complication, that this kind of emphasis on the nation-state taking control of a national political and economic life contradicts very openly the practices and ideals of market mobility and free consumer choice. To substantiate 'nationality' at the necessary depth, for alternative policies, means drawing on resources in active social relations which both mobile privatisation and consumerism and the most superficial and alienated versions of nationalism and patriotism have seriously weakened.

Thus 'nationalisation' is not perceived as connected to 'nationalism'. It is widely seen as an alien intrusion, from the other side of the statist coin. Meanwhile 'patriotism' has been so displaced to its functional images – the monarchy, the heritage, the armed forces, the flag – that alternative policies not only do not connect with them but by talking about other emphases and priorities often literally contradict them. Thus a 'nationalising' programme can be perceived as 'unpatriotic' – 'unBritish', 'unAmerican' – while a transnational strategy, pursued even to the point where a national economy loses heavily within unrestricted competition, is by its structural retention of the most artificial national images perceived as the 'patriotic' course.

8

What headway can be made against such intolerable confusions? Little or none, I judge, by the familiar intellectual jump to this or that universality. It is not in the mere negation of existing social perceptions that different forces can be generated. It is in two positive and connected initiatives: first, the cultural struggle for actual social identities; and second, the political definition of effective self-governing societies. I will first consider these separately.

What is most intolerable and unreal in existing projections of 'England' or 'Britain' is their historical and cultural ignorance. 'The Yookay', of course, is neither historical nor cultural; it is a jargon term of commercial and military planning. I remember a leader of the Labour Party, opposing British entry to the European

Community, asserting that it would be the end of a 'thousand years of history'. Why a thousand, I wondered. The only meaningful date by that reckoning would be somewhere around 1066, when a Norman–French replaced a Norse–Saxon monarchy. What then of the English? That would be some fifteen hundred years. The British? Some two thousand five hundred. But the real history of the peoples of these islands goes back very much further than that: at least six thousand years to the remarkable societies of the Neolithic shepherds and farmers, and back beyond them to the hunting peoples who did not simply disappear but are also among our ancestors. Thus the leader of a nominally popular party could not in practice think about the realities of his own people. He could not think about their history except in the alienated forms of a centralised nation-state. And that he deployed these petty projections as a self-evident argument against attempts at a wider European identity would be incomprehensible, in all its actual and approved former-European reorganisations, if the cultural and historical realities had not been so systematically repressed by a functional and domineering selective 'patriotism'.

All the varied peoples who have lived on this island are in a substantial physical sense still here. What is from time to time projected as an 'island race' is in reality a long process of successive conquests and repressions but also of successive supersessions and relative integrations. All the real processes have been cultural and historical, and all the artificial processes have been political, in one after another dominative proclamation of a state and an identity. It is obvious that there can now be no simple return to any of what may be seen as layers of this long social and physical process. But it should be equally obvious that this long and unfinished process cannot reasonably be repressed by versions of a national history and a patriotic heritage which deliberately exclude its complexities and in doing so reject its many surviving and diverse identities. Thus the real inheritance of these hundreds of diverse and unevenly connecting generations cannot be reduced to a recent and originally alien monarchy or to a flag which in its very form records their enforced political unification. The consequences of the long attempts to suppress or override a surviving and remade Irish identity ought to show, clearly enough, the bloody stupidity of the prevailing versions of patriotism. Yet characteristically the consequences are functionally projected to the Irish themselves, butts of hatred or of complacent jokes. Again, it is a common ruling-class cultural habit, carefully extended by most schools, to identify with the Roman imperial invaders of Britain against what are called the mere 'native tribes'. Can such people monopolise 'patriotism'? In practice yes, since many of those whose actual ancestors were slaughtered and enslaved have reconstructed them in the images dispensed by their conquerors: savages in skins; even, in comic-strip culture, cavemen.

I do not know how far any real knowledge of the physical and cultural history of the peoples of this island might prevail against the stupidities of this narrow orthodox perspective. I cannot believe that it would make *no* difference, and I am encouraged by the growing positive interest in these misrepresented and obscured pasts. But at any time what has also to be faced is the effective stage of their current integration. It is here that there is now a major problem in the most recent immigrations of more visibly different peoples. When these interact with the most recent selective forms of identity – 'the true-born Englishman' who apart from an occasional afterthought is made to stand for the whole complex of settled native and earlier-immigrant peoples; or the imperial 'British', who in a new common identity used economic and military advantages to rule a hundred peoples across the world and to assume an inborn superiority to them – the angry confusions and prejudices are obvious.

At the same time many generations of formerly diverse peoples have experienced and adapted to a differently rooted though overlapping social identity, and as at all earlier stages of relative integration are at best deeply uncertain of, at worst openly hostile to, newcoming other peoples. This is the phenomenon now crudely interpreted as 'racism'. It is not that there is no actual racism: it flows without difficulty from the most recent selective forms, as it flowed also, in modern times, against the Irish and the Jews. But it is a profound misunderstanding to refer all the social and cultural tensions of the arrival of new peoples to these ideological forms. The real working of ideology, both ways, can be seen in that most significant of current exchanges, when an English working man (English in the terms of the sustained modern integration) protests at the arrival or presence of 'foreigners' or 'aliens', and now goes on to specify them as 'blacks', to be met by the standard liberal reply that 'they are as British as you are'. Many people notice the ideological components of the protest: the rapid movement, where no other terms are available, from resentment of unfamiliar neighbours to the ideological specifications of 'race' and 'superiority'.

But what of the ideology of the reply? It is employing, very plainly, a merely legal definition of what it is to be 'British'. At this strict level it is necessary and important, correctly asserting the need for equality and protection within the laws. Similarly, the most active legal (and communal) defence of dislocated and exposed groups and minorities is essential. But it is a serious misunderstanding, when full social relations are in question, to suppose that the problems of social identity are resolved by formal definitions. For unevenly and at times precariously, but always through long experience substantially, an effective awareness of social identity depends on actual and sustained social relationships. To reduce social identity to formal legal definitions, at the level of the state, is to collude with the alienated superficialities of 'the nation' which are the limited functional terms of the modern ruling class.

That even some socialists should reply in such terms – socialists who should entirely depend on deeply grounded and active social identities – is another sign of the prepotence of market and exchange relations. One reason is that many minority liberals and socialists, and especially those who by the nature of their work or formation are themselves nationally and internationally mobile, have little experience of those rooted settlements from which, though now under exceptionally severe complications and pressures, most people still derive their communal identities. Many socialists are influenced by universalist propositions of an ideal kind, such as the international proletariat overcoming its national divisions. Many liberals are influenced by North American thought, where for historical reasons a massively diverse mobility was primarily integrated at legal and functional levels. There can then be a rapid intellectual supersession of all the complex actualities of settled but then dislocated and relocated communities, to the point where some vanguard has a clear set of general 'social' positions only to find that the majority of its nominally connected people have declined to follow it. When this turns, as sometimes, to abusing them, there is a certain finality of defeat.

A socialist position on social identity certainly rejects, absolutely, the divisive ideologies of 'race' and 'nation', as a ruling class functionally employs them. But it rejects them in favour of lived and formed identities either of a settled kind, if available, or of a possible kind, where dislocation and relocation require new formation. It happens that I grew up in an old frontier area, the Welsh border country, where for centuries, there was bitter fighting and raiding and repression and discrimination, and where, within twenty miles of where I was born, there were in those turbulent centuries as many as four different everyday spoken languages. It is with this history in mind that I believe in the practical formation of social identity – it is now very marked there – and know that necessarily it has to be lived. Not far away there are the Welsh mining valleys, into which in the nineteenth century there was massive and diverse immigration, but in which, after two generations, there were some of the most remarkably solid and mutually loyal communities of which we have record. These are the real grounds of hope. It is by working and living together, with some real place and common interest to identify with, and as free as may be from external ideological definitions, whether divisive or universalist, that real social identities are formed. What would have seemed impossible, at the most difficult stages, either in that border country or in those mining valleys, has indeed been achieved, though this does not mean that it happens naturally; there are other cases, as in the north of Ireland, where history and external ideologies still divide people and tear them apart.

This connects with the second emphasis: on the redefinition of effective self-governing societies. It is now very apparent, in the development of modern industrial societies, that the nation-state, in its classical European forms, is at once too large and too small for the range of real social purposes. It is too large, even in the old nation-states such as Britain, to develop full social identities in their real diversity. This is not only a problem of the minority peoples – Scots or Welsh or Irish or West Indian – but of the still significantly different cultures which are arbitrarily relegated to 'regions'. In this situation, imposed artificial definitions of 'Britishness' of 'the United Kingdom' and 'The Yookay', of the 'national interest' and of 'nationwide' lines of communication, are in practice ways of ratifying or overriding unequal social and economic development, and of containing the protests and resentments of neglected and marginalised regions and minorities within an imposed general 'patriotism'. The major economic and political divergence of the North and the South-East of even the supposedly unified and clamorous 'England' is an obvious current example.

It is clear that if people are to defend and promote their real interests, on the basis of lived and worked and placeable social identities, a large part of the now alienated and centralised powers and resources must be actively regained, by new actual societies which in their own terms, and nobody else's, define themselves. All effective socialist policies, over the coming generations, must be directed towards this practice, for it is only in the re-emphasis or formation of these full active social identities that socialism itself – which depends absolutely on authentic ideas of a society – can develop. In particular, it is only in these ways, as identifiable communities and regions are broken by movements of the national or international market, that there is the possibility of overcoming those reductive identities as mobile consumers which positively depend on advantage and affluence.

At the same time it is obvious that for many purposes not only these more real societies but also the existing nation-states are too small. The trading, monetary and military problems which now show this to be true, and which have so heavily encroached on the supposed 'sovereignty' of the nation-states, would not disappear in any movement to placeable communal self-management. It is not necessarily true that they would become more difficult. Many of the toughest trading and monetary problems flow directly from the system of international capitalist competition, and quite new forms of planned external trade would be possible in societies which genuinely began from the interests of their own people rather than from the interests of a 'national' ruling class integrated in and serving the international economy. The military problems are also very difficult, but it can now be seen that it is the arbitrary formation of generalised hostile blocs, overriding the diversities of real popular interests, which increasingly endangers rather than assures our necessary defence and security.

We cannot say, at any level, that these placeable self-managing societies could be 'sovereign'. Even to say that they could be 'autonomous' is taking a very limited sense. What has really to be said is different: that we have to explore new forms of *variable* societies, in which over the whole range of social purposes different sizes of society are defined for different kinds of issue and decision. In practice some of this now happens, as in the supposed 'division of powers' between local, regional, national and international bodies. But this is a false kind of division. The local and regional are in practice, as their names indicate, essentially subordinate to and dependent on the national. What goes through to an international level is first centralised or simply substituted by this national system ('it is felt *in London*'; '*Britain* has refused to ratify the Law of the Sea'). Meanwhile many of the most effective international forms – not only the multinational corporations but also the World Bank and the International Monetary Fund – are in effect wholly irresponsible to any full actual societies; indeed it is often their specific business to override them.

A variable socialism – the making of many socialisms – could be very different. There would be an absolute refusal of overriding national and international bodies which do not derive their specified powers directly from the participation and negotiation of actual self-governing societies. At a different level, there would be a necessary openness to all the indispensable means of mutual support and encouragement, directly and often diversely (bilaterally as well as in variable multilateral groupings) negotiated from real bases. Moreover, much of this negotiation would be at least in part direct rather than through the necessarily alienating procedures of 'all-purpose representatives'. The true advantages of equal exchange, and of rooted contacts and mobilities, would be more fully realised in this variable socialism than in the current arbitrary mobilities, or in any merely defensive reversion to smaller societies and sovereignties.

To bring together these two emphases – on the cultural struggle for actual social identities, and on the political redefinition of effective self-governing societies – is, I believe, to indicate a new and substantial kind of socialism which is capable both of dealing with the complexities of modern societies and also of re-engaging effective and practical popular interests.

Very much remains to be done by way of detailed discussions and proposals, but we cannot in any case live much longer under the confusions of the existing 'international' economy and the existing 'nation-state'. If we cannot find and communicate social forms of more substance than these, we shall be condemned to endure the accelerating pace of false and frenetic nationalisms and of reckless and uncontrollable global transnationalism. Moreover, even endurance is then an optimistic estimate. These are political forms that now limit, subordinate and destroy people. We have to begin again with people and build new political forms.

Reference

From Raymond Williams, *Towards 2000*, Chatto & Windus, 1983, Penguin, 1985, pp. 177–199. Reprinted with kind permission by The Random House Group Limited.

18

RESOURCES FOR A JOURNEY OF HOPE (1983)

In this concluding chapter to Towards 2000, *Williams offers a sweeping conspectus of world politics at century's end. It is possibly his most enduringly significant piece of political writing. Williams remarks upon a ruling ideology that he names 'Plan X'. We might refer to it today as 'neoliberalism'. For him, it was exemplified by Reagan's stepping up of the arms race in the 1980s, which was to contribute to the defeat of communism, and is perhaps represented yet more profoundly by the political and economic response to the oil crisis of the 1970s that brought in the present era of capitalism. Williams describes Plan X as 'a new politics of strategic advantage' that has 'connections with much older forms of competitive scheming and fighting'. From the vantage point of the 2010s, in the wake of the economic crisis caused by hyper-financialisation and risky speculation, it is notable that Williams links Plan X here to a pervasive culture of gambling that has grown immensely in popularity since his own day. Williams, of course, was interested in political currents that are oppositional to Plan X: 'peace, ecology and feminism'. In fact, Williams's own affiliations and arguments point strongly towards green-socialist solutions in politics to economic and ecological crises.*

1

It is usually taken for granted that to think about the future, as a way of changing the present, is a generous activity, by people who are not only seriously concerned but also, in those familiar adjectives, forward-looking, reforming, progressive. All the good ideas are on this side; all the bad or disappointing practice on the other. There is a question of how far we can go on with this easy assumption. As things now are, all the good ideas, and especially the ways in which they connect or might connect with how people are actually living, have to be rigorously re-examined.

Yet there is also another check to the assumption. It used to be taken for granted that the opposing forces were not themselves forward-looking: that they were, in those equally familiar adjectives, conservative, regressive, reactionary. Many of them indeed still are, but we misread the current situation if we rely on this easy contrast. There is now a very important intellectual tendency, with some real bases in political power, which is as closely concerned with thinking and planning the future as any reforming or progressive group. Within this tendency the signals are not being jammed but are being carefully listened to. Yet there is then the deliberate choice of a very different path: not towards sharing the information and the problems, or towards the development of general capacities to resolve them. What is chosen instead, intellectually and politically, is a new hard line on the future: a new politics of strategic advantage.

I call this new politics 'Plan X'. It is indeed a plan, as distinct from the unthinking reproduction of distraction. But it is different from other kinds of planning, and from all other important ways of thinking about the future, in that its objective is indeed 'X': a willed and deliberate unknown, in which the only defining factor is advantage. It is obvious that this has connections with much older forms of competitive scheming and fighting, and with a more systematised power politics. There are all too many precedents for its crudeness and harshness. But what is new in 'Plan X' politics is that it has genuinely incorporated a reading of the future, and one which is quite as deeply pessimistic, in general terms, as the most extreme readings of those who are now campaigning against the nuclear arms race or the extending damage of the ecological crisis.

The difference of 'Plan X' people is that they do not believe that any of these dangerous developments can be halted or turned back. Even where there are technical ways they do not believe that there are possible political ways. Thus while as a matter of public relations they still talk of solutions or of possible stabilities, their real politics and planning are not centred on these, but on an acceptance of the indefinite continuation of extreme crisis and extreme danger. Within this harsh perspective, all their plans are for phased advantage, an effective even if temporary edge, which will always keep them at least one step ahead in what is called, accurately enough, the game plan.

The first obvious signs of Plan X politics were in the nuclear arms race, in its renewal from the mid-1970s. It was by then clear to everyone that neither staged mutual disarmament (the professed ultimate aim) nor any stable strategic parity (the more regular political ratification) could be achieved by the development of radically new weapons systems and new levels of overkill. Many sane people called these new developments insane, but within Plan X thinking they are wholly rational. For the real objective is neither disarmament nor parity, but temporary competitive advantage, within a permanent and inevitable danger.

There were further signs of Plan X in some of the dominant responses to the rise in oil prices. Other groups proposed a reduction in energy consumption, or a reduction in dependence on oil, or negotiations for some general stability in oil and other commodity prices. Plan X people think differently. Their chosen policy is to weaken, divide and reduce the power of the oil producers, whatever the long-run effects on supply, so that a competitive advantage can be retained. To argue that this cannot be a lasting solution is to miss the point. It is not meant to be a lasting solution, but the gaining of edge and advantage for what is accepted, in advance, as the inevitable next round.

Again, Plan X has appeared recently in British politics. As distinct from policies of incorporating the working class in a welfare state, or of negotiating some new and hopefully stable relationship between state, employers and unions (the two dominant policies of post-1945 governments), Plan X has read the future as the certainty of a decline in capitalist profitability unless the existing organisations and expectations of wage-earners are significantly reduced. Given this reading, Plan X operates not only by ordinary pressures but where necessary by the decimation of British industrial capital itself. This was a heavy and (in ordinary terms) unexpected price to pay, but one which had to be paid if the necessary edge of advantage was to be gained or regained. Again many sane people say that this policy is insane, but this is only an unfamiliarity with the nature of Plan X thinking. Its people have not only a familiar hard drive, but one which is genuinely combined with a rational analysis of the future of capitalism and of its unavoidable requirements.

In this kind of combination, Plan X people resemble the hardest kinds of revolutionary, who drive through at any cost to their perceived objectives. But the difference of Plan X from revolution is that no transformed society, no new order, no lasting liberation seriously enters these new calculations, though their rhetoric may be retained. A phase at a time, a decade at a time, a generation at a time, the people who play by Plan X are calculating relative advantage, in what is accepted from the beginning as an unending and unavoidable struggle. For this is percentage politics, and within its tough terms there is absolute contempt for those who believe that the present and the future can be managed in any other way, and especially for those who try to fudge or qualify the problems or who refuse the necessary costs. These wet old muddlers, like all old idealists, are simply irrelevant, unless they get in the way.

Does it need to be said that Plan X is dangerous? It is almost childish to say so, since it is, in its own terms, a rational mutation within an already existing and clearly foreseeable extremity of danger. There is often a surprising overlap between the clearest exponents of Plan X and their most determined political opponents. The need for constant attention to the same kinds of problem, and for urgent and where necessary disturbing action in response to them, is a common self-definition by both groups. The difference, and it ought to be fundamental, is that Plan X is determined solely by its players' advantage. Any more general condition is left deliberately undefined, while the alternative movements see solutions in terms of stable mutual advantage, which is then the principle of a definable and attainable general condition: the practical condition which replaces the unknown and undefined X.

If we put it in this way the general choice ought to be simple. Yet we are speaking about real choices, under pressures, and we have then to notice how many elements there are, in contemporary culture and society, which support or at least do not oppose Plan X. Thus the plan is often presented in terms of national competitive advantage: 'keeping our country a step ahead'. In these terms it naturally draws on simple kinds of patriotism or chauvinism. Any of its damaging consequences to others can be mediated by xenophobia, or by milder forms of resentment and distrust of foreigners. Very similar feelings can be recruited into the interests of a broader alliance, as now commonly in military policy. Again, at a substantial level, there is a deep natural concern with the welfare of our own families and our own people. That they at least should be all right, come what may, inspires extraordinary effort, and this, in certain conditions, can appear as Plan X. Moreover, from the long experience of capitalist society, there is a widespread common sense that we have always to look to our own advantage or we shall suffer and may go under. This daily reality produces and reproduces the conditions for seeing Plan X as inevitable. It has then made deep inroads into the labour movement, which was basically founded on the alternative ethic of common wellbeing. When a trade union argues for a particular wage level, not in terms of the social usefulness of the work but, for example, in terms of improving its position in the 'wages league table', it is in time with Plan X.

There are also deeper supporting cultural conditions. Plan X is sharp politics and high-risk politics. It is easily presented as a version of masculinity. Plan X is a mode of assessing odds and of determining a game plan. As such it fits, culturally, with the widespread habits of gambling and its calculations. At its highest levels, Plan X draws on certain kinds of high operative (including scientific and technical) intelligence, and on certain highly specialised game-plan skills. But then much education, and especially higher education (not only in the versions that are called business studies) already defines professionalism in terms of competitive advantage. It promotes a deliberately narrowed attention to the skill as such, to be enjoyed in its mere exercise rather than in any full sense of the human purposes it is serving or the social effects it may be having. The now gross mutual flattery of military professionalism, financial professionalism, media professionalism and advertising professionalism indicates very clearly how far this has gone. Thus both the social and cultural conditions for the adoption of Plan X, as the only possible strategy for the future, are very powerful indeed.

At the same time Plan X is more than any one of these tendencies; it is also more than their simple sum. To emerge as dominant it has to rid itself, in practice, whatever covering phrases may be retained, of still powerful feelings and habits of mutual concern and responsibility, and of the very varied institutions which support and encourage these. Moreover, to be Plan X, it has to be more than a congeries of habits of advantage, risk and professional play. This is most evident in the fact that its real practitioners, still a very small minority, have to lift themselves above the muddle of miscellaneous local tendencies, to determine and assign genuine major priorities. At the levels at which Plan X is already being played, in nuclear-arms strategy, in high-capital advanced technologies (and especially information technologies), in world-market investment policies, and in anti-union strategies, the mere habits of struggling and competing individuals and families, the mere entertainment of ordinary gambling, the simplicities of local and national loyalties (which Plan X, at some of its levels, is bound to override wherever rationally necessary) are in quite another world. Plan X, that is to say, is by its nature not for everybody. It is the emerging rationality of self-conscious elites, taking its origin from the urgent experiences of crisis-management but deliberately lifting its attention from what is often that mere hand-to-mouth behaviour. It is in seeing the crises coming, preparing positions for them, devising and testing alternative scenarios of response, moving resources and standbys into position, that it becomes the sophisticated Plan X.

To name this powerful tendency, and to examine it, is not to propose what is loosely called a conspiracy theory. There are many political conspiracies, as we eventually learn when at least some of them are exposed, usually after the event. Elements of Plan X are inherently conspiratorial. But we shall underestimate its dangers if we reduce it to mere conspiracy. On the contrary, it is its emergence as the open common sense of high-level politics which is really serious. As distinct from mere greedy muddle, and from shuffling day-to-day management, it is a way – a limited but powerful way – of grasping and attempting to control the future. In a deepening world crisis, it is certain to strengthen, as against an older, less rational, less informed and planned politics. But then the only serious alternative to it is a way of thinking about the future, and of planning, which is at least as rational and as informed in all its specific policies, and which is not only morally much stronger, in its concern for a common wellbeing, but at this most general level is *more* rational and *better* informed. For the highest rationality and the widest information should indicate a concern for common wellbeing, and for stable kinds of mutual general interest, as the most practical bases for particular wellbeing and indeed for survival.

2

This is where the real political problems start. We can begin by trying to assess the actual and immediately potential resources for any radical changes of direction. Two sectors are at once apparent. There is now a growing body of detailed professional research, most of it dependent on the still expanding scientific community, in the key areas of ecology, alternative technologies and disarmament. There is also a rapidly growing movement of specific campaigns, most visible in the peace movement and in ecological initiatives but also extending over a very wide social and cultural range. Here, certainly, are actual and immediately potential resources for radically new kinds of politics.

Yet it has to be recognised that in some ways these are two very different groups of people. In some of their forms of activity they are quite distinct and unconnecting. Thus much of the most useful scientific work is directed, as if it were still orthodox research, at existing political leaders or generalised public opinion. Because by current definitions much of it is 'not political', but rather an objective assessment of physical facts, there is a tendency to resist its involvement with the simplifications of politics or with the street cries and emotionalism of demonstrations. Again, by their own best values, many of the campaigns are concerned primarily with forms of public witness and protest, with direct personal involvement in opposition to some evil, or with the growth of immediate relationships of an alternative kind. They can then be generalised, by some of their representatives, as movements of conversion, analogous to early religious movements, and as such disdainful both of what is seen as mere intellectualism and of the whole system of organised politics.

These differences have to be recognised. Yet the most remarkable fact about both the peace and the ecology movements of recent years has been their relative success in combining scientific information, at quite new levels of practical development, with the direct action, in witness and exposure, of both small-group protests and huge public demonstrations. This is never either an easy or a stable combination, but in the degree it has practically reached, in many countries, it is already a new political factor.

A similar kind of combination has been evident in the most recent phases of feminism. There is now a remarkable and growing body of distinctively feminist scholarship and argument, shifting our intellectual perspectives in many fields, while at the same time there has been a major expansion of supportive groups and initiatives, as well as sharp public and private challenges to old dominative and subordinating habits. This degree of combination is relatively stable, resting as it does on more immediate identities and bondings than are available in the peace and ecology movements. At the same time, as is evident from the quality of the intellectual work, the specific directions of what is called 'the women's movement', but is more often an association of distinctive movements with different bases and intentions, are still being formed and are subject to crucial interactions with other forms of political organisation, many of these not yet resolved.

It would be possible to project, from these humane and growing movements – peace, ecology and feminism – an immediately potential and effective political majority. Yet the general situation is not really like that. The potential cannot reasonably be doubted. It is the immediacy that is the problem. There is now a major risk that there will be a jump from this sense of potential, centred in the reasonable belief that these movements represent the deepest interests of large human majorities, to an option of indifference towards all other organised and institutionalised political and social forms. The jump seems irresistible, time and again, as we look from these dimensions of concern and possibility to the mechanical thinking and manoeuvring practice of most of these forms for most of their time. Yet this is still not a jump that can be reasonably made, especially by some loose analogy with early religious movements or with heroic minorities whose objective time will come. That option should already have been rejected in the experiences of the sixties, even if there were not such clear intellectual arguments against it.

For it is not only in the movements of peace, ecology and feminism that the shift has begun. It is also in the vigorous movement of what is called an alternative culture but at its best is always an oppositional culture: new work in theatre, film, community writing and publishing, and in cultural analysis. But what has been learned very clearly in all this work, and in new kinds of political and ideological analysis, is that the relations between small-group initiatives and potentials and a dominant system are at the very centre of the problem. It is there that we have learned how new work can be incorporated, specialised, labelled: pushed into corners of the society where the very fact that it becomes known brings with it its own displacements. It is possible here also to persist as a minority, but in the cultural system as a whole it is soon clear that the central institutions are not residual – to be disregarded, for their often residual content, until the emergent minority's time has come – but are dominant and active, directing and controlling a whole connected process towards which it is impossible to be indifferent. And if this is true of the cultural system, it is even more strongly true of the general social and political system which the institutionalised forms control and direct.

At the practical centre of this problem are the existing political parties. For it is clear that at all effective levels it is towards such parties that the system now directs us. Yet it is equally clear that the central function of these parties is to reproduce the existing definitions of issues and interests. When they extend to new issues and interests, they usually lead them back into a system which will isolate, dilute and eventually compromise them. If there is one thing that should have been learned in the years since 1945, it is this. Indeed in Britain, where in the early 1960s the popular cause of nuclear disarmament was entrusted to an apparently welcoming Labour Party, only then to sink without trace, for some fifteen years, at either effective popular or institutional levels, the lesson has been very sharp and should be unmistakeable. Moreover, it is not of a kind that can be reversed by the now systematic apologias for such events, assigning merely local and proximate causes and assuring everyone that it is bound to be different next time. In their present forms the parties are practically constituted to be like this. They absorb and deflect new issues and interests in their more fundamental process of reproducing and maximising their shares of the existing and governing dispositions.

It need not stay like this. For comparable in importance to the growth of new issues and movements is a steady withdrawal of assent to orthodox politics by what is in all relevant societies a sizeable minority of a different kind, and in some societies an already practical majority. Thus except in conditions of unusual stability, which are not going to be there, the pressures on existing political forms and institutions will in any case become irresistible. It is because one likely outcome of these pressures is a harsh movement beyond the now familiar forms, into new and more open kinds of control and repression, that there can be no jump to any kind of indifference to the institutions. On the contrary, just because there will be so many pressures of a negative, cynical and apathetic kind, it is essential that the carriers of the new and positive issues and interests should move in on the institutions, but in their own still autonomous ways.

This point has special reference to the institutions of the labour movement. It is clear that these began, in all or most of their original impulses, beyond the terms of what were then the governing definitions. They were genuine popular responses, slowly built over generations, to changes in the social and economic order which were at least as fundamental as those which we are now beginning to experience. Yet any comparative measure of degrees of change has to be assessed also in two further scales. First, the relative speed of current transfers of employment beyond the societies in which the institutions were shaped, and the interaction of this with internally generated structural unemployment. Second, the basic orientation of the institutions to predominantly male, predominantly stable, and above all nationally-based and nationally-conceived economic processes.

In both these respects the existing institutions have become not only insufficient but at certain key points actually resistant to new kinds of issue. The new issues of peace and of feminism have been included in certain ways: the former as a commitment to nuclear disarmament, but characteristically of a 'unilateral', nationally-based kind; the latter as a limited responsibility to women workers as trade unionists, but largely omitting, in theory and especially practice, response to the wider critique of hierarchy and dominance. The relative indifference of the institutions to the new cultural movements is notorious. Their confidence in their sets of received ideas – keeping new kinds of thinking at a distance ratified by the disdain for 'intellectuals' and 'academics' which they share with their capitalist masters – has ensured that at the broadest public levels they have been losing the decisive intellectual arguments. In relation to the ex-colonial world, the political affiliations of an earlier epoch have been sustained but there has been a radical unwillingness to face the consequences of the contemporary domination of the international economic order by capitalist trading forms within which, from positions of advantage, their own 'labourist' economic policies and assumptions are still based.

It is possible and necessary to believe that substantial changes can be made, on each of these issues, in the general direction of the existing institutions. Yet by their nature this cannot be done by any form of intellectual affiliation to them. On the contrary, the only relevant approach is one of challenge. This is especially important in what is often the most urgent practical area, that of elections. There is an orthodox electoral rhythm in the society as a whole. But there is also a rhythm of radical thought, in which periods of intense activity on the decisive long-term issues are punctuated by silences, compromises, evasions, expressions of meaningless goodwill and artificial solidarity, which are thought appropriate because an election is imminent. It is not only that much of this is in any case vanity. What a radical minority does or does not do in these large spectacular events, dominated by the deployment of competitive leaderships, is not in practice very important. But what is much more serious is the practical surrender of the real agenda of issues to just that version of politics which the critique has shown to be deceptive and is offering to supersede.

There are some elections which are genuinely decisive: especially some which it is important not to lose, with all the evident consequences of some reactionary or repressive tendency being strengthened. Specific decisions to be electorally active in these terms are entirely reasonable. There are also some rarer occasions when an election can be much more positively worked for, because it contains the probability of some coherent advance. But even in these cases there can be no intellectual affiliation to the adequacy of the processes themselves, and no defensible temporary pretence that they are other than they are. The challenging move towards the existing institutions, which can be effectively made only if there are already alternative institutions and campaigns on a different issue-based orientation, is in no way reducible to elections, or even to party programmes and manifestos. The central approach is always to the actual people inside them, but then on the same terms as the much wider approach to the significant number of people who are at their edges or who are leaving or have left them.

This approach, by definition, has to be in good faith, candid, open to learn as well as to teach: in all those real senses comradely. But we should now have reached the end of a period in which campaigners and intellectuals acquired the habit of going as petitioners or suppliants, touched by guilt or by an assumed deference to so much accumulated wisdom. There is hardly anything of that kind to go to any longer, and any of it that is genuinely wise will not require deference or sidelong flattery. If it is indeed the case, as now seems likely, that the most the existing institutions can do, in their fixed terms, is conduct losing defensive battles, then much deeper loyalties are in question, in the survival and welfare of actual people.

3

The toughest element in all the changes that will need to be made is in the economy. It is significant that the new movements are active and substantial in almost every area of life except this. It is as if everything that was excluded by the economic dominance and specialisations of the capitalist order has been grasped and worked on: in the real issues of peace, of ecology, of relations between men and women, and of creative artistic and intellectual work. Movements of a new kind race ahead in these areas, with new bodies of argument and action. But meanwhile, back in the strongholds of the economic order itself, there are not only the dominant institutions and their shadow subordinates. There are, for most of the time, most of the people.

Thus it has been possible to move relatively large numbers of people on popular versions of the issues of disarmament, protection of the environment, the rights of women. There is then an apparent asymmetry between these real advances and persistent majorities of a different kind: conservative (in more than one party); nationalist; consumerist. Some people make desperate attempts to prove that this is not so, seizing on all the exceptions, all the local breaks, all the local resistances. But while these must of course be respected, there is no real point in pretending that the capitalist social order has not done its main job of implanting a deep assent to capitalism even in a period of its most evident economic failures. On the old assumptions it would have been impossible to have four million people unemployed in Britain, and most of our common services in crisis or breaking down, and yet for the social order itself to be so weakly challenged or political support for it so readily mobilised. Yet that is where we now are.

It is then no time for disappointment or recrimination. All that matters is to understand how this can happen, and this is not in fact difficult. All the decisive pressures of a capitalist social order are exerted at very short range and in the very short term. There is a job that has to be kept, a debt that has to be repaid, a family that has to be supported. Many will fail in these accepted obligations after all their best efforts. Some will default on them. But still an effective majority, whatever they may do in other parts of their minds or in other areas of their lives, will stick in these binding relations, because they have no practical alternative. The significance of predominantly middle-class leadership or membership of the new movements and campaigns is not to be found in some reductive analysis of the determined agencies of change, it is, first, in the fact of some available social distance, an area for affordable dissent. It is, second, in the fact that many of the most important elements of the new movements and campaigns are radically dependent on access to independent information, typically though not exclusively through higher education, and that some of the most decisive facts cannot be generated from immediate experience but only from conscious analysis.

What is then quite absurd is to dismiss or underplay these movements as 'middle-class issues'. It is a consequence of the social order itself that these issues are qualified and refracted in these ways. It is similarly absurd to push the issues away as not relevant to the central interests of the working-class. In all real senses they belong to these central interests. It is workers who are most exposed to dangerous industrial processes and environmental damage. It is working-class women who have most need of new women's rights. The need for peace in which to live and to bring up our families is entirely general. But then it is a consequence of the social order that, lacking the privileges of relative social distance and mobility, or of independent (often publicly funded) access to extended learning, the majority of employed people – a significantly wider population than the working-class in any of its definitions – have still primarily to relate to short-range and short-term determinations.

Even the issues that get a widening response are marginalised as they encounter this hard social core. Moreover what is repeatedly experienced within it, and has been put there to be experienced, is a prudence, a practical and limited set of interests, an unwillingness to be further disturbed, a cautious reckoning and settling of close-up accounts. Whatever movement there may be on issues at some distance from these local and decisive relations, there is no possibility of it becoming fully effective until there are serious and detailed alternatives at these everyday points where a central consciousness is generated. Yet it is at just these points, for historically understandable reasons, that all alternative policies are weakest.

4

The hard issues come together on two grounds: the ecological argument, and changes in the international economic order. There are times when all that seems to flow from these decisive issues is a series of evident and visible disadvantages, losses of position, to the employed majorities in the old industrial economies. Some campaigners still race ahead, on defensible grounds of universal need or justice.

But they can hardly then be surprised that they are not followed. Indeed what often happens is that their proposals soon become even more unrealistic. There is at times an indiscriminate rejection of all or most industrial production, supported by some option for local crafts or for subsistence agriculture. It is not that these are unavailable ways of life. It is that they are unavailable as whole ways of life for the existing populations of urban industrial societies. The association of such wholly unrealistic proposals with the central critique of industrial-capitalist society is then either an indulgence or a betrayal. It can still be either of these when it is accompanied by talk of an imminent moral conversion.

The means of livelihood of the old industrial societies will in any case change; are indeed already changing. But there is then need for more qualified, more rational and more informed accounts. The intellectual problem, however, is that while certain principles can be established, all actual policies have to depend on new and difficult audits of resources, which must by definition be specific. We can look first at the principles, but their full practical bearings cannot be set down except in this place and that, by this enquiry and that, in a sustained and necessarily negotiated process.

The principles that matter are as follows. First, we have to begin, wherever we can, the long and difficult movement beyond a market economy. Second, we have to begin to shift production towards new governing standards of durability, quality and economy in the use of non-renewable resources. Third, and as a condition of either of the former, we have to move towards new kinds of monetary institutions, placing capital at the service of these new ends.

These principles are very general, but some specific cases look different in their light. Thus, if we begin the movement beyond a market economy, it is by no means inevitable, as the capitalist order now threatens, that many or even most industrial assembly processes should be moved out of the old economies. Nor is it inevitable that transformation-manufacturing processes should be similarly moved out. On the contrary, the decisions about any of these would be subject to a different kind of accounting. The most obvious new reference point would be the relation of any of these processes to indigenous resources. It is only the capitalist accounting of cheap labour elsewhere that is exporting many kinds of assembly. On the other hand, processes which centrally depend on the import of major raw materials would be among the first to be transferred to those economies which could radically improve their own livelihoods by their own indigenous manufacturing and processing. There would doubtless be exceptions and anomalies, as these long shifts were negotiated, but if the principle of moving beyond the market economy is taken seriously such shifts have to be made. They can be accounted as losses in the old industrial economies, as many of them would necessarily be. But there can be corresponding gains, not only in some productive transfers to new advanced technologies, developed in relation to actual indigenous resources, but also in the retention of many kinds of assembly and manufacture which would otherwise, by the operations of the now dominant global market, be transferred elsewhere. They often become a false priority in those other societies, which could better determine alternative kinds of development from their own resources and needs. It follows, inevitably, that equitable kinds of mutual protection would then have to be negotiated, as alternatives to the destructive interventions which the market, following only its own criteria, would otherwise quickly impose.

Again, in the new emphases on durability, reclamation, maintenance and economy of resources, there are some immediate losses that would have to be negotiated. A significant part of current production is oriented by the market towards relatively early obsolescence and replacement, and many jobs depend on these cycles. Yet it is only the false accounting of the market system that makes reclamation now economically marginal, and it is probable that in many processes the result of the different emphases would be a broadly comparable area of work but with many quite basic real savings. The examples of badly-made and short-term houses, furniture, toys, cars and a whole range of everyday equipment are already clear, from our experience as users. There have been sharp declines in quality over a range even of genuine short-term goods, from bread to ironmongery. The market pressures for cheap standardised production based on minimal adequacy and early replacement have distorted the common sense of a whole economy. In certain sectors of the market, of a relatively privileged kind, this lesson has already been learned and there has been a movement towards greater quality and durability, avoiding the selling routines and devices of the 'mass' market. But to generalise this would mean gaining control over the central production processes, rather than the best that is now, within market terms, foreseen, of extending the 'quality' market. This is not, except in a very few areas, a return to 'crafts'. On the contrary, it is mainly a redirection of available and new advanced technologies to the priorities of production rather than the priorities of marketing. A wholly unreasonable proportion of technical development has been assigned to improvements in marketing – now the leading edge of the whole system – rather than to the improvements in production – durability, quality, economy – which will be centrally necessary in the material conditions which lie ahead of us.

There can be no changes of these kinds unless there is a successful challenge to the monetary institutions which, centred on a financial rather than a material world, and predominantly oriented to short-term profit, now sustain what should be seen as obsolescent economics. A large part of contemporary capital is now socially generated, through taxation, savings, insurance and pension funds, over and above the direct capitalist generation through surplus value. It should then be axiomatic that these are subject to direct social controls, for investment in a different kind of economy. But it is very doubtful if this can be achieved by any of the older socialist methods, and especially by procedures of state centralisation. The most promising way forward is through a combination of new kinds of auditing of resources, within self-determining political areas, with a related auditing of available monetary resources of these kinds. Instead of the existing and uninviting alternatives of state or corporate appropriation, there should be a linked process, democratically discussed and determined, of the actual planning of physical investment and the allocation of funds. Production and service decisions should be determined by locally agreed needs, and monetary investment similarly determined by local retention of its own self-generated funds. In the long and complex negotiations towards this radically alternative system there would undoubtedly have to be arrangements for transfers between relatively advantaged and disadvantaged areas. This process, structurally very similar to the complex negotiation of income transfers in quite new conditions of employment, will be the central political problem of the coming generations. But it has only to be compared with the predictable results of the existing alienations and appropriations of capital, and of the consequent dislocations and widening inequalities within and between societies, to stand out as necessary, and to generate the will to find new procedures.

All these changes would be occurring within the radical changes in working habits already discussed. The market economy, left to itself, will continue to produce massive redundancies, including of whole societies, which it has not the least chance of regulating and compensating by any orthodox political means. At the same time, in its current dominance, it is inducing fatalism by its ideological insistence that its processes, and its alone, are 'economic'. In fact, through the linked development of shorter working time and of new schemes of education and retraining, and through the new procedures of locally audited decisions on the kinds of work undertaken, there is every chance of making, even in very diverse and sometimes unfavourable circumstances, stable and equitable economies in which all necessary work is reasonably shared. Genuine labour-saving in certain kinds of production could be linked with a necessary expansion in all the caring services – themselves typically labour-intensive and relatively economical in resources and especially imported resources. But this can happen only if there are new kinds of linkage between production and expenditure, cutting out the institutions that now appropriate and distribute them by their own alienated priorities. What could be a major opportunity for easing the strains of work without discarding large numbers of people will be seized only if this kind of commitment to a directly determined social order, rather than to either corporate capitalism or a centralised socialist command economy, begins to grow from a popular base.

It is here that the assessment of political resources for so different a social order is at its most critical point. There is really only one sector in which these alternative kinds of thinking and planning can be effectively developed, and that is in the trade unions and professional associations. Many kinds of expert help – scientific, technical and economic – will be needed. But none of it can happen, in the necessary practical ways, unless trade-union organisation, now typically oriented to corporate-capitalist and national scales, becomes more flexible in two new directions: first in direct relations with effective smaller-scale political communities; and second, in extended relations with the international labour movement.

There are already some signs of such developments. But there is bound to be a long and difficult transition from the existing kinds of state-centred and industry-centred organisations and priorities. The signs of change, understandably, are occurring in crisis-hit enterprises – as in the alternative production plans of the Lucas Aerospace shop stewards – or in areas which already have some distinctive political identity and have been especially hard hit by the current depression – Scotland, Wales, London, the English

North-East. The political problem is to extend and generalise these early shifts of direction, beyond the emergencies which now govern them, until there is a labour movement of a new kind, determined to take direct responsibility for the organisation of work and resources, and capable of taking such responsibility, through new kinds of open and qualified research and planning.

In fact the extension of the trade-union movement to workers in some of the most complex areas of technology, management and finance offers a real possibility of this kind of cooperative transformation. At every level this would be very different from the reproductive and defensive strategies which are still dominant. These old strategies, excluding broader public considerations or merely projecting them to an incompetent all-purpose political party, now hold the movement back from the real work it has to do.

It is in what will happen in this central economic area that the future of the social order will be determined. Once there is significant movement here, the alternative movements and campaigns which can alone make general sense of the kind of society which an alternative economic order must serve will move into a radically different set of political relationships and possibilities.

5

What is now beginning to emerge, to support these changes, is at least the outline of a unified alternative social theory. This involves three changes of mind.

First, as I argued in my analysis of the industrial revolution, the connection between the forces and the relations of production has to be restated. It is evidently false to abstract the forces of production, as in technological determinism. But it is equally false to abstract the relations of production, as if they were an independent variable. It is no longer reasonable to believe, as in most modern forms of socialism, that these can be independently altered or transformed. On the contrary, what is at issue within both the forces and the relations of production is a set of alternatives at a more fundamental level of decision. The dominant version has been a basic orientation to the world as available raw material. What has been steadily learned and imposed is a way of seeing the world not as life forms and land forms, in an intricate interdependence, but as a range of opportunities for their profitable exploitation. It is then true that this has been most damaging within a capitalist economy, in its relentless drives for profit and for the accumulation of capital. But this cannot reduce the argument to one against the property and wage forms of capitalism. If that were true, we would have no way of explaining the continuing appropriation and exploitation of the world as raw material in the 'communist' or 'actually existing socialist' economies.

The necessary new position is that this orientation to the world as raw material necessarily includes an attitude to people as raw material. It is this use and direction of actual majorities of other people as a generalised input of 'labour' which alone makes possible the processes of generalised capital and technology. Thus the drive to use the earth as raw material has involved, from the beginning, the practical subordination of such majorities by a variety of means: military, political, economic, ideological. The system of capitalist property and wage relations is only one such form. Slavery and serfdom preceded it. Modern forms of the mobilisation and direction of labour can succeed it. In any of these cases, what is most at issue is the basic orientation itself, in which relations to other people and to the physical world have changed and developed in a connected process, within which the variations are important but neither absolute nor, in our present situation, decisive.

It is clear from our material history that what we can now see as a basic orientation was developed through several critical stages, each increasing its practical effects. Its first stage can be seen in the complex of changes which are summarised as the Neolithic and Bronze Age Revolutions, in which, with the development of farming, stockbreeding and metalwork, decisive interventions in a constituted nature were successfully made. Yet this stage, which was indeed the appropriation and transformation of certain life forms and land forms as raw material, was still highly selective and coexisted with other forms of social and natural orientation. We can see this very clearly if we compare it with the last stages of this orientation. through which we are now living. In the development of much more powerful technologies, and in their capture by a class which defined its whole relationship to the world as one of appropriation, what was once selective and guided by conscious affinities with natural processes has been replaced by a totalitarian and triumphalist practice in which, to the extent that it succeeds, there is nothing but raw material: in the earth, in other people, and finally in the self.

The early interventions in a constituted nature were, in the strict sense, new means of livelihood. It has taken a very long time to transform these reasonable intentions and practices to the stage at which we now find ourselves. There has been a remarkable increase in such means of livelihood but *as part of the same process* (which we are now in a position to observe) a remarkable increase also in forms of death and destruction. Each part of the process is beyond the terms of a constituted nature.

It is then tempting to try to revert, if only in principle, to a stage before these conscious interventions. But this is neither possible nor necessary. We are now in a position where we can monitor our interventions, and control them accordingly. We can select those many interventions which support and enhance life, in continuing ways, and reject those many other interventions which have been shown to be damaging or to involve the reasonable possibility of damage. This is the central ecological argument. But it can only prevail if we unite it with the political and economic argument, in ways that then change what we have become used to as politics and economics. For it is the ways in which human beings have been seen as raw material, for schemes of profit or power, that have most radically to be changed. Some of these changes are already inscribed in the deepest meanings and movements of democracy and socialism. But not all of them are, and the exclusions now limit and even threaten to destroy these two most hopeful forces of our world.

What is most totalitarian about the now dominant orientation is its extension beyond the basic system of an extraction of labour to a practical invasion of the whole human personality. The evidence of treating people as raw material is not to be gathered only in accounts of wages and conditions, or of real absolute poverty, serious and often grave as these are. It is present also in an area which has been conventionally excluded from both politics and economics. It is quite clear, for example, in those sexual attitudes and practices which have been correctly identified, principally by feminists, as treating people as 'sex objects'. There is now a major interpretation of sexual relationship as finding, in another person, the raw material for private sensations. This has been profitably institutionalised in pornography, but there are much more serious effects in the actual physical treatment of others, with women and children especially vulnerable.

Failure in such versions of relationship is wholly predictable since relationship is precisely an alternative to the use of others as raw material. But what is most totalitarian about this failure is that it extends not only to the cruel punishment of others, who indeed in these terms cannot yield the lasting satisfactions that are sought, but also to the cruel punishment of self: in alcoholism, in addiction to damaging drugs, in obesities and damaging asceticisms. For the very self is then only raw material in the production of sensations and identities. In this final reach of the orientation, human beings themselves are decentred.

Thus there are profound interconnections in the whole process of production – that version of relations with others and with the physical world – to which the now dominant social orders have committed themselves. The way forward is in the neglected, often repressed but still surviving alternative, which includes many conscious interventions in a constituted nature but which selects and directs these by a fundamental sense of the necessary connections with nature and of these connections as interactive and dynamic. This can emerge, in practice, only if it is grounded in a conception of other people in the same connected terms. But this is where the intellectual difficulties of uniting the ecological and economic arguments, in a new kind of politics, are most evident. This brings us to the second necessary change of mind.

The concept of a 'mode of production' has been a major explanatory element of the dominant social orders through which we have been living. It has enabled us to understand many stages of our social and material history, showing that the central ways in which production is organised have major and changing effects on the ways in which we relate to each other and learn to see the world. But what has now to be observed is that the concept itself is at some important points a prisoner of the social orders which it is offering to analyse. It has been most successful and enlightening in its analysis of capitalism, and this is not accidental, for its own conceptual form it seized the decisive element of capitalism: that this is a mode of production which comes to dominate both society as a whole and – which is less often stressed – the physical world. The eventual inadequacy of the concept is then that it has selected a particular historical and material orientation as essential and permanent. It can illuminate variations of this orientation, but it can never really look beyond it. This fact has emerged in the most practical way, in that the great explanatory power of Marxism, where this concept has been most active, has not been accompanied by any successful projective capacity. For all that follows from one mode of production is another, when the real problem is radical change, in hard social and material terms, in the idea of production itself.

Thus it is not surprising to find that Marx shared with his capitalist enemies an open triumphalism in the transformation of nature, from the basic orientation to it as raw material. He then radically dissented from the related and cruel uses of people as raw material, and looked for ways in which they could organise to transcend this condition and control production for themselves. This is his lasting and extraordinarily valuable contribution. Yet in basing his thought on an inherited concept of production – one which is in no way a necessary outcome of the most rigorous historical materialism – Marx was unable to outline any fully alternative society. It is not only the attempts and failures to find such alternatives, in the name of such thinking however diluted or distorted, which confirm this conclusion. The problem and the obstacle are in the concept itself.

For the abstraction of production is a specialised and eventually ideological version of what is really in question, which is the form of human social relationships within a physical world. In his justly influential idea of 'man making himself' Marx seized one specialised moment which connected with the developed processes he was observing in his own time: the intervention in nature to transform it as new means of livelihood: that is, to *produce*. Yet 'man' – actual men and women – had been 'making themselves', developing their social and material skills and capacities, long before this specialised and conscious intervention. Living within a constituted nature, in the hunting and gathering societies, they had already developed high social and technical skills. The long subsequent shift, through successive stages of intervention and production, altered both nature and people but was nevertheless in some major respects continuous with that earlier human phase. The sense of a connection with constituted nature was still the ground of the most successful innovations, in that selective breeding of plants and animals which positively depended on continuing interactive observation. It is in the major interventions we now class as technological – from metal working to modern chemistry and physics – that the sense of transforming intervention is strongest, but all these, in practice, at their most useful, have similarly depended on continuing interactive observation, within both a physical and a social world. It is then only at the point when these processes are abstracted and generalised as 'production', and when production in this sense is made the central priority over all other human and natural processes and conditions, that the mode of intervention – at once material and social – becomes questionable. The decisive question is not only about intervention – 'production' – itself, but about its diverse practical effects on nature and on people.

It is this which social analysis based only on a 'mode of production' prevents us from seeing or from taking seriously. For, just as capitalist production, in practice, attempted to substitute itself for the broader and more necessary principle of human societies in a natural world, so this concept, in theory, attempted to substitute itself for the broader bases of human social and material activities. It was common to see human history before such specialist interventionist production as a mere prehistory; almost in effect pre-human. What has now to be seen, at this most intense stage of the isolation and dominance of interventionist production, spreading rapidly over the entire planet and beyond it, is another stage of prehistory, or, better, a second but now concluding stage of history, as active but also as limited as that which preceded it.

For the consciousness of the possibilities of intervention, which inaugurated that phase of history which connects to our own time, is now, at a point of great danger, being succeeded by a new consciousness of its full effects. They are at once its real and sustainable advantages and its at first inextricable recklessness and damage to people and to the earth. It is in this new consciousness that we again have the opportunity to make and remake ourselves, by a different kind of intervention. This is no longer the specialised intervention to produce. The very success of the best and most sustainable interventions has made that specialised and overriding drive containable. Where the new intervention comes from is a broader sense of human need and a closer sense of the physical world. The old orientation of raw material for production is rejected, and in its place there is the new orientation of livelihood: of practical, self-managing, self-renewing societies, in which people care first for each other, in a living world.

A third change of mind follows, when we have replaced the concept of 'society as production' with the broader concept of a form of human relationships within a physical world: in the full sense, a way of *life*. This change appears in one special way, in the current movement beyond the specialisation and contrast of 'emotion' and 'intelligence'. It is understandable that people still trapped in the old consciousness really do see the new movements of our time – peace, ecology, feminism – as primarily 'emotional'. Those who have most to lose exaggerate this to 'hysterical', but even 'emotional' is intended to make its point. The implied or stated contrast is with the rational intelligence of the prevailing systems. In reaction to this there is often a great business of showing how rational and intelligent, in comparable ways, the campaigns themselves are. Moreover, and increasingly, this is true. But a crucial position may then be conceded. For it is in what it dismisses as 'emotional' – a direct and intransigent concern with actual people – that the old consciousness most clearly shows its bankruptcy. Emotions, it is true, do not produce commodities. Emotions don't make the accounts add up differently. Emotions don't alter the hard relations of power. But where people actually live, what is specialised as 'emotional' has an absolute and primary significance.

This is where the new broad concept most matters. If our central attention is on whole ways of life, there can be no reasonable contrast between emotions and rational intelligence. The concern with forms of whole relationship excludes these specialised and separated projections. There are still good and bad emotions, just as there are good and bad forms of rational intelligence. But the habit of separating the different kinds of good from each other is entirely a consequence of a deformed social order, in which rational intelligence has so often to try to justify emotionally unacceptable or repulsive actions.

The deformed order itself is not particularly rational or intelligent. It can be sharp enough in its specialised and separated areas, but in its aggregates it is usually stupid and muddled. It is also, in some of its central drives, an active generator of bad emotions, especially aggressiveness and greed. In its worst forms it has magnified these to extraordinary scales of war and crime. It has succeeded in the hitherto improbable combination of affluent consumption and widespread emotional distress.

Informed reason and inquiry can explore these complex forms, but it is not surprising that the strongest response to them has appeared at the most general 'emotional' levels. Before any secondary reasons or informed intelligence can be brought to bear, there is an initial and wholly reasonable reaction, carrying great emotional force, against being used, in all the ways that are now possible, as mere raw material. This response can develop in several different directions, but where it is rooted in new concepts, now being steadily shaped, and in many kinds of relationship – forms of genuine bonding which are now being steadily renewed and explored – it is already generating the energies and the practical means of an alternative social order.

It can then make a difference that this alternative is being clarified theoretically. The central element is the shift from 'production' to 'livelihood': from an alienated generality to direct and practical ways of life. These are the real bases from which cooperative relationships can grow, and the rooted forms which are wholly compatible with, rather than contradictory to, other major energies and interests. They are also, at just this historical stage, in the very development of the means of production, the shifts that most people will in any case have to make.

6

It is reasonable to see many dangers in the years towards 2000, but it is also reasonable to see many grounds for hope. There is more eager and constructive work, more active caring and responsibility, than the official forms of the culture permit us to recognise. It is true that these are shadowed by the most general and active dangers. They are shadowed also by the suspicion – which the official culture propagates but which also comes on its own – that as the demonstration disperses, as the talk fades, as the book is put down, there is an old hard centre – the reproduction of a restricted everyday reality – which we have temporarily bypassed or ideally superseded but which is there and settled and is what we have really to believe.

Two things have then to be said. First, that the objective changes which are now so rapidly developing are not only confusing and bewildering; they are also profoundly unsettling. The ways now being offered to live with these unprecedented dangers and these increasingly harsh dislocations are having many short-term successes and effects, but they are also, in the long term, forms of further danger and dislocation. For this, if we allow it, will be a period in which, after a quarter of a century of both real and manufactured expectations, there will be a long series of harshly administered checks; of deliberately organised reductions of conditions and chances; of intensively prepared emergencies of war and disorder, offering only crude programmes of rearmament, surveillance and mutually hostile controls. It is a sequence which Plan X can live with, and for which it was designed, but which no active and resilient people should be content to live with for long.

Secondly, there are very strong reasons why we should challenge what now most controls and constrains us: the idea of such a world as an inevitable future. It is not some unavoidable real world, with its laws of economy and laws of war that is now blocking us. It is a set of identifiable processes of *realpolitik* and *force majeure*, of nameable agencies of power and capital, distraction and disinformation, and all these interlocking with the embedded short-term pressures and the interwoven subordinations of an adaptive commonsense. It is not in staring at these blocks that there is any chance of movement past them. They have been named so often that they are not even, for most people, news. The dynamic moment is elsewhere, in the difficult business of gaining confidence in *our own* energies and capacities.

I mean that supposing the real chances of making a different kind of future are fifty-fifty, they are still usually fifty-fifty after the most detailed restatement of the problems. Indeed, sometimes, in one kind of detailed restatement, there is even an adverse tilt. It is only in a shared belief and insistence that there are practical alternatives that the balance of forces and chances begins to alter. Once the inevitabilities are challenged, we begin gathering our resources for a journey of hope. If there are no easy answers there are still available and discoverable hard answers, and it is these that we can now learn to make and share. This has been, from the beginning, the sense and the impulse of the long revolution.

Reference

From Raymond Williams, *Towards 2000*, Chatto & Windus, 1983, Penguin, 1985, pp. 241–269. Reprinted with kind permission by The Random House Group Limited.

19

STATE CULTURE AND BEYOND
(1984)

Raymond Williams's keen interest in issues of cultural policy is illustrated here in a talk that he gave at London's Institute of Contemporary Arts. He makes a crucial distinction between what can be called cultural policy as display, *exemplified by policies of national aggrandisement and economic reductionism; and* cultural policy proper, *that is, public patronage of the arts, media regulation and negotiated constructions of cultural identity, in effect, what have more recently been referred to as 'cultural rights' (see McGuigan,* Rethinking Cultural Policy, *(2004), for further explication).*

We can perhaps distinguish five senses of the State in relation to this argument. It may be important to do so because we are often reduced to a rather simple polar contrast between a monopoly State and a market with the State as a friend. In reality the situation is more complex. There is one aspect of the State in relation to culture which is almost always forgotten because we absorb it so very early that we can hardly recognize it as cultural policy at all. It is worth remembering that the State has always had this double sense: it is not only the central organ of power, but of *display* – indeed often specifically the public pomp of a particular social order. You don't have to look far in any particular society to see a culture which is not recognized as a cultural policy or an arts policy specifically, but which is culturally concerned with display.

There are some interesting overlaps here with what Bagehot called the theatrical element of the constitution. It is genuinely difficult watching the state opening of Parliament not to realize that one is in the presence of performance. The fact of an overlap between performance, which in a sense is quite analogous to theatre, and the actual display of certain aspects of state power, is there. Now, one may be very conscious of some of the eccentricities of the British constitution in this respect but in fact most States have this kind of public panoply – their changing of the guards. There is usually a public performance of power, often in form residual from much earlier periods; a great occasion for producing costumes, for presenting a version of the national heritage. Quite quickly (and one should not forget this historically) elements of the arts are consciously involved in this, over and above the actual state rituals. Thus there is a *stately* sense of cultural policy. Indeed at times, in its more reproductive forms, it is a kind of lying-in-state of the national heritage, in which the version of the culture that is intended to be offered to the public has, so to say, been officially consecrated.

I think it would be quite wrong to overlook this as a cultural policy because you can then make a move toward a second sense of the State, in which, although you're now moving into a much more modern and active and practical world, the attitude towards the arts as embellishing either the public power or the preferred orthodox idea of the nation is extended to areas of genuine artistic practice. I'm surprised how often in arguments about public funding of the arts people mention tourism rather early. Now it is not an irrelevant consideration; it is a wholly relevant one, for example, to the survival of the London theatre. But it's a very curious thing to introduce it first. Because it does mean that one is thinking in terms of the shape of a contemporary public power which is that of a nation-state, which has business and tourism, which has commercial interests, which has international interests in exchanges of visits with other nation-states and their representatives. And elements in the arts, particularly within the great metropolitan institutions, are quite quickly involved in that kind of version of the State. Indeed not only in the extension to the arts as tourism, but very specifically now, the arts as business entertainment; this is a very conscious policy in the greater metropolitan institutions. And it's a significant overlap, with some versions of sponsorship of the arts by the larger private companies. Indeed, in this sense an arts policy of a certain kind turns out when examined to be not a policy for the arts but a policy for embellishing, representing, making more effective a particular social order or certain preferred features in it.

That distinction has to be insisted upon because a policy for the arts should be (I'm going to argue) primarily a policy *for the arts*, in relation to a whole and very diverse life, rather than the representation (which has happened through many different social orders) of the arts as purveyors of the most evident delights as attachments to these quite other purposes. And this happens especially in arguments about the representation of a particular national culture to other national cultures, in which quite clearly a cultural policy can be an aspect of foreign policy, and determined by such. Alternatively a cultural exchange policy can be that more equal sharing of cultural experiences which all peoples need and benefit from.

Now I mention those two senses of the State because they are often overlooked before real argument of a professional kind starts. That real argument now is between a version of the State as patron and a version of the State as the promoter of an active cultural policy.

The State as Patron

Of the State as patron there is much to say. When the first approaches were made to the British State, early in the war, for the immense sum of £35,000 to encourage the arts, they got an enthusiastic response from the then President of the Board of Education. I can't resist quoting it; he had 'Venetian visions of a post-war Lord Mayor's show on the Thames in which the Board of Education led the arts in triumph from Whitehall to Greenwich in magnificent barges and gorgeous gondolas, orchestras, madrigal singers, Shakespeare from the Old Vic, ballet from Sadler's Wells, shining canvasses from the Royal Academy, folk dances from village greens, in fact a Merrie England.' Now that first approach eventually led to what Keynes called a half-baked state patronage. But it was almost immediately assimilated to my first sense of State: the Lord Mayor's show. One has only to imagine the Royal Ballet on those barges, or the canvasses in those gondolas, to realize that what was thought of as happening was a vision, however retrospective

The patronage version, as Keynes put it forward, was an idea of encouraging people who were already operating. That is to say, he did not, in his first thinking about the matter, foresee an active policy of *promotion* of the arts. People would engage as individuals and as companies in artistic events and the State would then move out and sensibly encourage them. But then, and this is where it begins to move into the fourth sense of the State in cultural policy, there should be attempts to improve public access to things which were already happening.

But the great difficulty was – and one could spend a great deal of time on this – that there is a major problem of defining the arts if one has simply this version of patronage. Indeed the first constitution of the Arts Council was very strict; it said 'the fine arts exclusively'. That's a very difficult definition because music and the visual arts (visual arts in the old sense: painting, sculpture) are included. Theatre is rather curiously included, curiously because there is a sense in which theatre has always both been and not been a fine art. Literature however, is typically excluded, partly on the grounds that it is already covered by public libraries. But beyond all these there were the new arts, already with a half a century of achievement behind them: cinema; new work in broadcasting including work which was not just transmission of earlier forms; photography; television. And it's still an intense argument within any arts body whether these, which are undoubtedly by this stage of the twentieth century major arts, should be regarded as parts of an arts policy or fine arts policy. What this exclusive definition can very quickly become is an abstraction of certain traditional arts from what is otherwise seen, and contentedly seen, as a cultural market. It is assumed that the contemporary arts will make their way in the cultural market but that the traditional arts must be in some sense preserved from it. In that sense only the State acts as patron.

Now there are substantial theoretical objections to that, but there are also I think very severe practical objections. It can set up relationships between the public body and practising artists which skew actual practice towards received and traditional things. Moreover very quickly it meshes with the notion that the metropolitan institutions of the traditional arts are where excellence occurs, so that within this form of thinking one can assume in advance that a play at the National Theatre is a more significant and excellent event than a new play by an unknown company in a road show somewhere in the North. Under the influence of this traditional notion of art, the arguments about photography, for example, that I heard when I was on the Arts Council had to be heard to be believed. A quite unproblematic acceptance of a certain kind of theatre as art was very suddenly withdrawn when it came to contemporary arts which were often as or more creative and significant.

So the problem of patronage has always been the identification of that special area which is to be the object of patronage, and the most significant element has been a degree of preservation from the cultural market. But what I think has made that position, even in the attractive form in which Keynes first put it forward, impossible to hold is that overwhelmingly in the second half of the twentieth century, whatever else has happened, the prime distributors of all kinds of artistic activity have been the new media. And in those new media there have to be public policies of a different kind from patronage. Yet the way in which they too relate to the market creates its problems. It is there, in the most significant sense, that there can be a shift to a positive cultural policy as distinct from patronage and limited intervention.

That is where the experience of many different countries in Western Europe has been interesting because you can have this policy in a hard state version which is most evident in Eastern Europe, in which there is a very conscious and heavily funded cultural policy, admirable in many ways in its degree of extension of access, but carrying quite unmistakeable and unacceptably negative features in which the policy includes a preliminary definition – often from outside the arts – of what kinds and styles of art are to be promoted. Often we recognize this sense of the State only in the hard version. In the soft versions, especially since the rise of broadcasting, the creation of any cultural policy must, if we are serious about it, involve some public body and within state terms typically some central body. This body makes choices which are all too often disguised behind counters of argument which are very difficult to specify. I mean vague terms like 'standards' and 'excellence' which much more often than not function as ways of deflecting the argument rather than having it, especially when you think of the hangover from distinctions between traditional and new kinds of art.

Towards a Future Policy

My own view is that we have to move beyond all these notions of state cultural policy, just as we have to move beyond the notions of patronage and market protection. It happens now that in Britain we have a fight on our hands even to preserve the minimum definitions. But the best way to preserve them may be to outline a policy which can move beyond state cultural policy and its evident dangers whether in the hard or the soft versions. Now while I can't go into detail on this I would just like to put two emphases on it.

First, that now in some ways the nation-state, for all sorts of purposes, is both too large and too small. It is too small, particularly in the world of the media as they are now developing, to be able to sustain genuine national cultural policies. It may do so in certain protected areas but at the effective level, where the big public is participating, the nation-state is beginning to lose the powers of direction and policy, however enlightened, that it has previously tried to exercise. At the same time it is too big to be able to promote the diversity of cultural policy which ought to occur even within a relatively homogeneous culture like the British.

I think there are two things of a hopeful kind that one can now see emerging. The first undoubtedly is the European dimension. There is a possible European cultural dimension which would take us beyond certain of the limitations of a nation-state policy. But there is also the *civic* tradition, which in terms of European history has a much finer record in cultural policy than that of any State. It is in fact the great cities of Europe which have been the most successful promoters of cultural policy. This again is a contemporary fight to preserve the necessary powers of cities, but it is one in which there is the possibility of relating a cultural policy to an actual community rather than to a relatively abstract and centralized state.

What emphases then follow? First, that the management of arts enterprises is best left to self-managing companies of artists where they are in any sense collective art, or to co-operative arrangements where there is the practice of individual artists. The relation of that to a civic-level policy seems to me very much easier to devise. Second, there is still a role for the kind of public power, whether it's at civic or national level, which has the prime responsibility of keeping the means of production in art publicly available, not allowing them to be available for auction and yet not tempted either to appropriate them to its own kind of organization and to its own definition of interests. I believe there is a possibility of defining a principle of holding the artistic means of production in public trust, but then of leasing them by a variety of possible arrangements to self-managing groups of artists of all kinds, who will get the use of those means of production in relation to a stated policy, under lease, and subject to review and renewal. It is in that direction that – with the civic emphasis and with a broadening European emphasis – we should begin to move. We shall then be moving, as we would, farthest away from the two kinds of state policy that I, at least, most oppose. Not only the hard version of state cultural policy which we have to oppose in view of its controlling record, but also from the often unnoticed state policy with which I began, the State as a public power which merely enhances itself with the arts, which engages in its own reproduction using the arts and culture for its decoration and imagery, and not really for the development of the arts themselves.

Reference

From Lisa Appignanesi, ed., *Culture and the State*, Institute of Contemporary Arts, 1984, pp. 3–5. Reprinted with kind permission of the Institute of Contemporary Arts (ICA).

20

THE FUTURE OF CULTURAL STUDIES (1989)*

Towards the end of his life, Raymond Williams reflected on the trajectory that the new interdisciplinary field of Cultural Studies had taken in his lifetime. Unlike other such accounts, Williams told the story of a popular educational project that had germinated in the efforts made by adult educators to address questions raised by students themselves. In Britain, university extension classes and Workers Educational Association (WEA) courses had sought to compensate people who had missed out on higher education. However, following a similar trajectory to the study of literature itself, the enfants terribles of Cultural Studies and related fields such as Media Studies were eventually incorporated into mainstream university curricula. Something was gained and something was lost. While the university of the air, the Open University, carried on the work of adult education in the Humanities and Social Sciences, there was also an inevitable process of academic codification and institutionalisation taking place. At the same time, vocational education was back on the agenda without the broader cultural learning that Williams and others had sought to deliver in the past. And, in the universities, idealist theories were turning the newly ensconced field of Cultural Studies into the kind of detached academicism that had hitherto been resisted by the popular-educational project and, thereby, rendered what had been gained less and less relevant.

---

*Originally delivered as a talk at the Association of Cultural Studies Conference, Polytechnic of East London, 1986.

> *Most significantly, crude instrumentalism in education has become yet more pronounced since Williams's death. The progress of critical knowledge in the Humanities and Social Sciences has been assaulted, frustrated and endangered by a simplistic 'impact' agenda for university education and research, especially in Britain. The kind of values that Raymond Williams stood for are now seriously beleaguered in a commodified and inegalitarian higher educational system. However, a reading of his work, which in itself is a resource of hope, might contribute to reviving the critical project and eventually turning the tide away from 'Plan X' and towards more humane purposes.*

I wish here to address the issue of the *future* of Cultural Studies, though not as a way of underestimating its very real current strengths and development – a development which would have been quite impossible, I think, to predict thirty or so years ago when the term was first beginning to get around. Indeed, we should remind ourselves of that unpredictability, as a condition likely to apply also to any projections we might ourselves make, some of which will certainly be as blind. Yet we need to be robust rather than hesitant about this question of the future because our own input into it, our own sense of the directions in which it should go, will constitute a significant part of whatever is made. And moreover the clearing of our minds which might lead to some definition of the considerations that would apply in deciding a direction is both hard and necessary to achieve, precisely because of that uncertainty.

I want to begin with a quite central theoretical point which to me is at the heart of Cultural Studies but which has not always been remembered in it. And this is – to use contemporary terms instead of the rather more informal terms in which it was originally defined – that you cannot understand an intellectual or artistic project without also understanding its formation; that the relation between a project and a formation is always decisive; and that the emphasis of Cultural Studies is precisely that it engages with *both*, rather than specializing itself to one or the other. Indeed it is not concerned with a formation of which some project is an illustrative example, nor with a project which could be related to a formation understood as its context or its background. Project and formation in this sense are different ways of materializing – different ways, then, of describing – what is in fact a *common* disposition of energy and direction. This was, I think, the crucial theoretical invention that was made: the refusal to give priority to either the project or the formation – or, in older terms, the art or the society. The novelty was seeing precisely that there were more basic relations between these otherwise separated areas. There had been plenty of precedents for kinds of study which, having looked at a particular body of intellectual or artistic work related it to what was called its society; just as there was a whole body of work – for example, in history – which described societies and then illustrated them from their characteristic forms of thought and art. What we were then trying to say, and it remains a difficult but, I do believe, central thing to say, is that these concepts – what we would now define as 'project' and 'formation' – are addressing not the relations between two separate entities, 'art' and 'society', but processes which take these different material forms in social formations of a creative or a critical kind, or on the other hand the actual forms of artistic and intellectual work. The importance of this is that if we are serious, we have to apply it to *our own* project, including the project of Cultural Studies. We have to look at what kind of formation it was from which the project of Cultural Studies developed, and then at the changes of formation that produced different definitions of that project. We may then be in a position to understand existing and possible formations which would in themselves be a way of defining certain projects towards the future.

Now that is, in a summary way, a theoretical point; and I'd like to give one or two examples of it. First, not in Cultural Studies but in one of the contributors to it; namely English or Literary Studies. It is very remarkable that in every case the innovations in literary studies occurred outside the formal educational institutions. In the late nineteenth century, when there was in fact no organized teaching of English literature at all, the demand came in two neglected and in a sense repressed areas of the culture of this society. First, in adult education, where people who had been deprived of any continuing educational opportunity were nevertheless readers, and wanted to discuss what they were reading; and, even more specifically, among women who, blocked from the process of higher education, educated themselves repeatedly through reading, and especially through the reading of 'imaginative literature' as the phrase usually has it. Both groups wanted to discuss what they'd read, and to discuss it in a context to which they brought their own situation, their own experience – a demand which was not to be satisfied, it was very soon clear, by what the universities (if they had been doing anything, and some informally were) were prepared to offer, which would have been a certain kind of history or a set of dates, a certain description of periods and forms. The demand, then, was for a discussion of this literature in relation to these life-situations which people were stressing outside the established educational systems, in adult education and in the frustrated further education of women. Hence some of the most remarkable early definitions of what a modern English course might be arose from Oxford Extension lecturers who'd gone out and formed their ideas in relation to this quite new demand. And when this new kind of study of literature – outside traditional philology and mere cataloguing history – finally got into the university, its syllabus was written, for example at Cambridge, almost precisely on the lines which that early phase in the late nineteenth century and early twentieth century had defined. It was said by one of the founders of Cambridge English that the textbook of that period was virtually a definition of their syllabus.

But then look what happened: having got into the university, English studies had within twenty years converted itself into a fairly normal academic course, marginalizing those members of itself who were sustaining the original project. Because by this time what it was doing within the institution was largely reproducing itself, which all academic institutions tend to do: it was reproducing the instructors and the examiners who were reproducing people like themselves. Given the absence of that pressure and that demand from groups who were outside the established educational system, this new discipline turned very much in on itself. It became, with some notable advantages, as always happens, a professional discipline; it moved to higher standards of critical rigour and scholarship; but at the same time the people who understood the original project, like Leavis for example, were marginalized. The curious fact is that they then tried to move outside the university, to set going again this more general project. But because of the formation they were largely, if one wants to be strict in the usual terms, a group of people from petty-bourgeois families, almost equally resentful of the established polite upper middle class which thought it possessed literature, and of the majority who they felt were not only indifferent to it but hostile and even threatening – they chose a very precise route. They went out, and sent their students out, to the grammar schools to find the exceptional individuals who could then come back to the university and forward this process. What had been taken as their project into the university was not any longer the same project, so they went outside. But because they conceived themselves as this minority institution, seeking to educate a critical minority, it was now a different project and not the general project of the first definition. And so all the people who first read what you could now quite fairly call 'Cultural Studies' from that tendency – from Richards, from Leavis, from *Scrutiny* – who were studying popular culture, popular fiction, advertising, newspapers, and making fruitful analyses of it, found in time that the affiliation of this study to the reproduction of a specific minority within deliberately minority institutions created a problem of belief for them, and also a problem for defining what the project was.

If you then look at the site in which there was a further process of change and in which a different project was defined, it was again in adult education. Indeed, it can hardly be stressed too strongly that Cultural Studies in the sense we now understand it, for all its debts to its Cambridge predecessors, occurred in adult education: in the WEA, in the extramural Extension classes. I've sometimes read accounts of the development of Cultural Studies which characteristically date its various developments from *texts*. We all know the accounts which will line up and date *The Uses of Literacy, The Making of the English Working Class, Culture and Society*, and so on. But, as a matter of fact, already in the late forties, and with notable precedents in army education during the war, and with some precedents – though they were mainly in economics and foreign affairs – even in the thirties, Cultural Studies was extremely active in adult education. It only got into print and gained some kind of general intellectual recognition with these later books. I often feel sad about the many people who were active in that field at that time who didn't publish, but who did as much as any of us did to establish this work. In the late forties people were doing courses in the visual arts, in music, in town planning and the nature of community, the nature of settlement, in film, in press, in advertising, in radio; courses which if they had not taken place in that notably unprivileged sector of education would have been acknowledged much earlier. Only when it reached either the national publishing level or was adopted – with some recoil – in the university, was this work, in the typical ways of this culture, perceived as existing at all. There were people I could tell you about who did as much as any of us in my generation, whose names the people now teaching Cultural Studies would simply not know, and they were doing it in a site which was precisely a chosen alternative to the Leavis group. And it should be stressed that it was a *choice*: it was distinctly as a vocation rather than a profession that people went into adult education – Edward Thompson, Hoggart, myself and many others whose names are not known. It was a renewal of that attempt at a majority democratic education which had been there all through the project, but which kept being sidetracked as elements of it got into institutions which then changed it. Thus there was an initial continuity from the Leavis position of certain analytic procedures which eventually were thoroughly changed, because these people wanted precisely a democratic culture, and did not believe that it could be achieved by the constitution of a Leavisite 'minority' alone. They were nevertheless aware, because this was a very practical and pressed kind of work, that the simplicities of renouncing mass-popular education and democratic culture, when you have to go out and negotiate them on the ground, would not be easily resolved.

I give this example because so often the history of each phase of Cultural Studies has been tracked through *texts*. Such accounts talk about this individual having done this work; this tendency; this school; this movement labelled in this or that way; which looks very tidy as this type of idealist history – a very academicized kind of literary or intellectual history – always is. Yet that is in a sense only the surface of the real development, and is moreover misleading because what is happening each time is that a formation in a given general relationship to its society is taking what you could otherwise trace as a project with certain continuities, and in fact *altering* it, not necessarily for the better. There have been as many reversions as there have been advances; and one of the reversions comes, I think, in the next phase. Because as some of this work began to be recognized intellectually, as it was both in discussion and in periodicals and to some extent in the universities, it was thought to be a much newer thing than it was. If you take my book *Communications* which was commissioned because the National Union of Teachers called a conference on 'Popular Culture and Personal Responsibility' which in fact came out of the 1950s concern about horror comics – the root is as odd as that – I actually made the book, which didn't take long to write, out of the material I had been using in adult classes for fifteen years. Thus the sense of novelty which is easily conveyed by tracing the texts is in fact misleading, since the real formation of the project was already there. But when this began to happen it made a certain significant intellectual difference in the university, though never one which could shift its most central institutions and assumptions.

But then a period of expansion in education occurred which created new sites for precisely this kind of work, and a new kind of formation – one perhaps continuous until today – came into existence. I can still remember my own students getting their first jobs and coming back and saying 'I went to meet the principal as the newly appointed lecturer in Liberal Studies, and I asked him what Liberal Studies was and he said, "I don't know; I only know I've got to have it".' They were, then, in that unprecedented situation, for most people starting their first job, of being able to write a syllabus, which otherwise you labour and drag yourself for a lifetime to climb towards, and then probably fail to do. They had the option to put down certain ideas, and what they put down, in the majority, in new universities, in polytechnics, in colleges of further education, in some schools even, as this new phase got around, was precisely this area of work which the university was rather warily looking at but keeping well outside its really central and decisive areas. And they were able to do this because the option for Liberal Studies had been so vague; it had been based on nothing much more than the sense – itself based, perhaps, in the lingering cultural distrust of science and technology as too worldly – that people should discover certain of the finer things of life.

In this way, and without any well-established body of work to base itself on, a new formation in these new institutions began to develop, but with certain consequences. First, that precisely as you move into the institutions – as you pass that magic moment when you are writing the syllabus and have to operate it, to examine it; as you are joined by colleagues; as you become a department and as the relations between departments have to be negotiated, as the relative time and resources are given to them – what then takes place is precisely the process which emasculated English at Cambridge. At the very moment when that adventurous syllabus became a syllabus that had to be examined, it ceased to be exciting. And just at the moment when this new work flooded into what were, for all the welcome elements of expansion, still minority institutions – still, moreover, formed with certain academic precedents around departments, about the names of disciplines and so on – then certain key shifts in the project occurred.

Yet there is one other kind of institution which I'd first like to mention which also occurred in just this period – I'm talking of the sixties – and that's the Open University. On this, two crucial points need to be made, as it were, simultaneously. First, that this was an extraordinary attempt in the tradition of that movement towards an open-access democratic culture of an educational kind – not the bureaucratically centralized imposition of a cultural programme which would enlighten the masses but one of a genuinely open and educational kind. At the same time, however, it was a deliberate break with the traditions of its own society in adult education and the Co-operative Guild, in all the local self-educating organizations of working people and others, which had been based precisely on a principle which it could not realize: that intellectual questions arose when you drew up intellectual disciplines that form bodies of knowledge in contact with people's life-situations and life-experiences. Because of course that is exactly what had happened in adult education. Academics took out from their institutions university economics, or university English or university philosophy, and the people wanted to know what it was. This exchange didn't collapse into some simple populism: that these were all silly intellectual questions. Yet these new students insisted (1) that the relation of this to their own situation and experience had to be discussed, and (2) that there were areas in which the discipline itself might be unsatisfactory, and therefore they retained as a crucial principle the right to decide their own syllabus. This process of constant interchange between the discipline and the students, which was there institutionalized, was *deliberately* interrupted by the Open University, a very Wilsonian project in two senses. It was on the one hand this popular access; on the other hand it was inserting a technology over and above the movement of the culture. This project would bring enormous advantage but it lacks to this day that crucial process of interchange and encounter between the people offering the intellectual disciplines and those using them, who have far more than a right to be tested to see if they are following them or if they are being put in a form which is convenient – when in fact they have this more basic right to define the questions. These people were, after all, in a practical position to say 'well, if you tell me that question goes outside your discipline, then bring me someone whose discipline *will* cover it, or bloody well get outside of the discipline and answer it yourself.' It was from this entirely rebellious and untidy situation that the extraordinarily complicated and often muddled convergences of what became Cultural Studies occurred; precisely because people wouldn't accept those boundaries. Yet the Open University, as a major example of a breakthrough beyond a minority institution, had this element in it of a technology inserted over and above the social process of education: it had this characteristic double dimension.

I now come to my controversial point. At just this moment, a body of theory came through which rationalized the situation of this formation on its way to becoming bureaucratized and the home of specialist intellectuals. That is to say, the theories which came – the revival of formalism, the simpler kinds (including Marxist kinds) of structuralism tended to regard the practical encounters of people in society as having relatively little effect on its general progress, since the main inherent forces of that society were deep in its structures, and – in the simplest forms – the people who operated them were mere 'agents'. This was precisely the encouragement for people not to look at their own formation, not to look at this new and at once encouraging and problematic situation they were in; at the fact that this kind of education was getting through to new kinds of people, and yet that it was still inside minority institutions, or that the institutions exercised the confining bureaucratic pressures of syllabus and examination, which continually pulled these raw questions back to something manageable within their terms. At just that moment – which I hope is still a moment of fruitful tension – there was for a time a quite uncritical acceptance of a set of theories which in a sense rationalized that situation, which said that this was the way the cultural order worked, this was the way in which the ideology distributed its roles and functions. The whole project was then radically diverted by these new forms of idealist theory. Even the quite different work of Gramsci and Benjamin was subsumed within them; and of the powerful early challenge to such Modernist idealisms launched by Bakhtin, Voloshinov and Medvedev, little or nothing was heard. Even (and it was not often) when formations *were* theorized, the main lesson of formational analysis, concerning one's own and other *contemporary* formations, was less emphasized than more safely distanced academic studies.

In its most general bearings, this work remained a kind of intellectual analysis which wanted to change the actual developments of society, but then locally, within the institution, there were all the time those pressures that had changed so much in earlier phases: from other disciplines, from other competitive departments, the need to define your discipline, justify its importance, demonstrate its rigour; and these pressures were precisely the opposite of those of the original project. Now there was indeed a very great gain in this period, as anybody who compares the earlier and later work will see. When I wrote *Communications* we were analysing newspapers and television programmes, with material strewn over the kitchen floor and ourselves adding up on backs of envelopes, and when I look now at Media Studies departments and see the equipment they have to do the job properly I of course recognize the advances as being marked. Similarly with film studies, we never knew whether the film would (a) arrive, (b) work with that projector, (c) whether in an adult class people wouldn't be so dazed after watching the film that when you asked for discussion you never got a word; now film courses operate in a proper institution, and I've never doubted the advantages of this; just as nobody in the centre of the English Faculty at Cambridge now could believe for a moment that what they do isn't infinitely superior to Leavis's work. I mean, in certain new ways it *is* always more professional, more organized, and properly resourced. On the other hand, there remains the problem of forgetting the real project. As you separate these disciplines out, and say 'Well, it's a vague and baggy monster, Cultural Studies, but we can define it more closely as media studies, community sociology, popular fiction or popular music', so you create defensible disciplines, and there are people in other departments who can *see* that these are defensible disciplines, that here is properly referenced and presented work. But the question of what is then happening to the project remains. And in a sense the crisis of these last years should remind us of the continuing relation between the project and the formation: the assumption that we were witnessing the unfolding of some structure which was, so to say, inherent – a continuation of some simple line, as in those accounts of the history of Cultural Studies which had shown people gradually, although always with difficulty, overcoming their residual errors and moving on a bit – has been brutally interrupted by the very conscious counter-revolution of these last years.

This is where I come to the question of the future. For what we now have is a situation in which the popular cultural institutions have changed so profoundly through the period in which Cultural Studies has been developed, with relative alterations of importance – for example between broadcasting and print – of a kind that no one would have believed possible in the fifties. We've got new sets of problems both inside the different kinds of study we do, as to which of them really bear on the project, and also the question of considering our own formation in this now very changed situation. I'll take a couple of examples first from the internal process of the subjects themselves, illustrating the contradictory effects of this welcome development but simultaneous institutionalization of Cultural Studies. If you take the question of popular culture, or popular fiction, it has been clearly quite transformed in the eighties from its situation in the fifties, not only because people have been more prepared, because of general social and formational changes, to relate directly to popular culture, putting themselves at a very conscious distance from Richards and Leavis in the twenties and thirties who saw it only as a menace to literacy – an element which survives, perhaps, although always as uncertainly and ambiguously as ever, in Richard Hoggart's book. But at the same time that earlier tension between two very different traditions and kinds of work can as easily be collapsed as explored. It is necessary and wholly intellectually defensible to analyse serials and soap operas. Yet I do wonder about the courses where at least the teachers – and I would say also the students – have not themselves encountered the problems of the whole development of naturalist and realist drama, of social-problem drama, or of certain kinds of serial form in the nineteenth century; which are elements in the constitution of these precise contemporary forms, so that the tension between that social history of forms and these forms in a contemporary situation, with their partly new and partly old content, partly new and partly old techniques, can be explored with weight on both sides. This can very easily not happen if one is defining the simpler kind of syllabus because the teacher can say 'well, for that you'd have to go to drama', or literature or fiction, 'we're doing popular fiction'. Yet how could you carry through the very important work now being done on detective stories, for instance, without being able to track back to the crime stories of the nineteenth century and grasp the precise social and cultural milieu out of which that form came, so that you are then able to add an extra dimension of analysis to what we now say about the form of the detective story? Or, in the sociological dimension of Cultural Studies, there is the whole problem of the relation between very close up contemporary work which is crucially necessary to history, and the very complicated interpretations of history which are not to be diminished, in my view, simply to labour history or popular history, because otherwise one isolates a class precisely from the relations which, in a sense, constitute that class. I give these cases as examples of how in the very effort to define a clearer subject, to establish a discipline, to bring order into the work – all of which are laudable ambitions – the real problem of the project as a whole, which is that people's questions are not answered by the existing distribution of the educational curriculum, can be forgotten. And people, when they are free to choose – though they are often not, because of quite natural pressures and determinations and a reasonable ambition to qualify – again and again refuse to limit their questions to the boundaries of the set course. So that the interrelations between disciplines, which are the whole point of the project, have this inherent problem in what is otherwise a valuable process of defining and modelling the subject.

But the more crucial question now is this: that even after the expansion we've had, which was first halted and then turned back by a succession from Callaghan to Thatcher and Joseph, we are facing a situation which is quite different in kind but just as challenging as that which faced any of those people who developed the project in particular circumstances in earlier periods. What we have got now, and what was not available when the studies were getting into the new institutions, is the effective disappearance of those kinds of teenage work which were profound anti-educational pressures at just the time that some of these developments were happening. There were then understandable pressures of money and work against the problems of staying on with that kind of school, that kind of education. We've now got the extraordinary institution of courses which in a sense are deliberately placed beyond the reach of education. We have the effective education of the majority in the age-group of sixteen to eighteen being removed as far as possible from what are conceived as the old damaging educators. We now encounter a definition of industrial training which would have sounded crude in the 1860s when something very like it was proposed – and we might be glad if it *had* then happened: at least it would have solved one set of problems. It is again being said that people must gain work experience within the forms of the economy to which they must adapt, and as *that* syllabus is written, as that programme of work experience is written, no place at all is envisaged for people like us. I don't mean that individual initiatives don't happen, but rather that a whole substitute educational provision is being made with certain very powerful material incentives, including the possibility of employment. And while the labour movements say of such work experience that it's merely 'cheap labour' or whatever, I say what educators must say – and this is, as a matter of fact, where I see the future of Cultural Studies. Here is a group which – if it is given only what is called 'work experience', but which is actually its introduction to the routines of the foreseen formations of this new industrial capitalism – will be without that dimension of human and social knowledge and critical possibility which again and again has been one of the elements of our project. And if it seems hopeless that people in their own hard-pressed institutions, which of course we have to defend, should be asked to look towards this area which has very consciously, as a matter of political policy, been removed as far as possible from professional educators, I would say this: that there is the prospect, after all, within two, three, four years, of another kind of government; there is the possibility of the renewal of the existing institutions or at least the easing of some of their resource and staffing problems. When that comes, shall we simply cheer that the budgetary crisis is over, the establishment crisis relieved a bit? If we do, then those cheers should only be uttered out of one side of the mouth because if we allow an absolutely crucial area of formative human development to remain deliberately isolated from educators – moreover an area in which what Cultural Studies has to contribute is particularly relevant – then we shall have missed a historic opportunity; just as related opportunities were nearly missed or only partly realized, or to a large extent incorporated and neutralized, in earlier phases. We shall have missed that historic opportunity because we had become, in our very success, institutionalized.

I have deliberately not summarized the whole development of Cultural Studies in terms of the convergence of intellectual disciplines, which is another way of writing this history; an internal and illuminating way, but nevertheless insufficient unless you relate it all the time to the very precise formations and social institutions in which these convergences happened and *had* to happen. For that approach in terms of intellectual history may obscure from us what is, as we enter the coming period, a historic opportunity for a new Cultural Studies formation. And the time to prepare this new initiative, which would indeed be much resisted by many vested and political interests, is precisely *now*. Because it is only when a persuasive, reasoned and practical proposal is put forward to a favourable local authority or government, which would then have you sort through the ways in which you would teach it, that this new work will become more than a resented interruption from what is otherwise taught. If this is thought through now, if we fight for it, even if we fail we shall have done something to justify ourselves before the future. But I don't think we need fail at all; I think that the results will be uneven and scattered, but this is where the challenge now is. If you accept my definition that this is really what Cultural Studies has been about, of taking the best we can in intellectual work and going with it in this very open way to confront people for whom it is not a way of life, for whom it is not in any probability a job, but for whom it is a matter of their own intellectual interest, their own understanding of the pressures on them, pressures of every kind, from the most personal to the most broadly political – if we are prepared to take that kind of work and to revise the syllabus and discipline as best we can, on this site which allows that kind of interchange, then Cultural Studies has a very remarkable future indeed.

Reference

From Raymond Williams, *The Politics of Modernism*, Verso, 1989, pp. 151–162. Reprinted with kind permission of Verso.

INDEX

academic/educational institutions 6, 127
  and cultural studies 317, 318, 319, 321, 325
  and literary studies 316
  and the selective tradition 37–8
active tradition 190
Adorno, Theodor 191
adult education xviii, 15
  and cultural studies 313, 317–8
  democratic culture in 320
  and literary studies 315–6
Advertisement Tax, reduction and abolition 61
advertising,
  actors and 166–7
  aggression and hostility in 78, 117
  annual spend 15
  as art 73
  'classified' 58, 59, 61, 150
  and communications 79–81
  criticism of 69–70
  development of 60–5
  expenditure (1935) 70
  history 57–60
  by 'independent' reporters 71
  new cheapjacks 5
  in power 70–2
  as a profession 67
  'psychological' 67, 68
  and 'public relations' 71–2
  as source of finance 11, 16–17, 72–3, 158
  as subject of study 317
  as system of magic 72–9
  transformation 65–70
Advertising Acts (1939, 1941) 69
advertising agencies, development of 66–7
Advertising Association 69
Advertising Code of Ethics (1924) 69
Advertising Code of Standards (1950) 69
aesthetic analysis 179, 181
Allen, Jim 207
alternative cultural practice 119, 128–9, 130, 132
alternative movements and campaigns 285–6, 288, 296
  middle class leadership 290–1
  unrealistic proposals 291–2
Althusser, Louis 193

Alton Locke (Kingsley) 45, 51
Anglo-Saxon race 108
angry young men 4
Answers 67
anthropology 177, 186
  Marxist structuralism 193
Antigone (Sophocles) 30–1
architecture
  1840s 54
  and society 169–70
aristocrats, 1840s
  fictional portrayal 48
  social character 47
  see also ruling class
Arnold, Matthew 41, 44, 53
Arnold, Thomas 41, 44, 49
art(s)
  advertising as 73
  advertising compared 79
  analysis of form 192
  and commercial communication systems 88
  financial loss defended 16
  and 'fine arts' 308
  and future cultural policy 310–11
  as national inheritance 6–7
  plea for public provision 15–16
  as a practice 135–7
  relations with society 31–33, 44–5, 52–4, 132–4, 314–5
  state patronage 307–9
  and structure of feeling 34
  as tourism/business entertainment 306
art works, as objects of consumption 134–5
Arts Council 15, 308
Association of British Advertising Agents 67
audiences
  as abstract, phased identity 188
  expansion 23–4
  inclusion in communication studies 183
  as 'mass' 10, 25, 179, 187, 203, 225
  qualitative change 162, 202–3
  and realist drama 209, 211, 214, 215, 221
  relationship with writers 94
  social relations with producers 204, 205
  social history 227

Audit Bureau of Circulations 67
Austen, Jane 40
authoritarian communication systems 85, 86–7, 91–2

Back to Methuselah (Shaw) 115
Bagehot, Walter 104–5, 167, 305
Bain, Alexander 146
Baird, John Logie 153
Bakewell, F. C. 146
Bakhtin, Mikhail 321
'Ballad of Joe Hill' 219
Barrett Brown, Michael xix
Barthes, Roland 195
base/superstructure model xix, 119, 128–32, 125, 128, 131, 135, 136–7, 193, 226, 227
Beckett, Samuel 201
Bell, Timothy 41
Bell System 147
Bell's Penny Dispatch 39
Benedict, Ruth 33
benefits, resentment over 254
Benjamin, Walter 189, 191, 321
Berzelius, Jöns Jacob 146
Big Flame, The (Allen, BBC drama) 207, 214–22
bill posting 58
black cultural projects 27–8
book publishing
  and advertising 58, 62
  effects of social change, 1840s 44
bourgeoisie
  cultural incorporation 130
  English culture beyond 6–7
  ideology 224, 225, 226, 232
  realism and realist drama 201, 202, 204, 205, 214, 215
'box sets' 213
Braun, Karl 146
Braverman, Harry 244
Brecht, Bertolt 199, 201, 215, 217
'British' identity 272–5, 276
British industrial decline 246, 249, 281
British Broadcasting Corporation (BBC) 158, 207
  paternalism 85
  revenue 82
British/English Constitution, theatricality 105, 305–6
British Dental Association 59
British Sociological Association (BSA) xv, 185
broadcasting 133, 149, 151–59
  and arts policy 308
  capitalist development 153

broadcasting *cont.*
  development, 1920s 153–4
  effects studies 187
  importance relative to print 322
  and mass-communication 22–3, 152, 179
  as means of social integration and control 152
  'predestined' 151–2
  privatised reception 152, 158
  production control and financing crisis 158
  as solution to mobile privatisation 154–5
  state intervention 153
  state protection 80
  transmission preceding content 153, 156, 157
broadcasting institutions 158–9, 182, 196
Brontë, Anne 51
Brontë, Charlotte 40, 43–4, 51
Brontë, Emily xx, 40, 44
Browning, Robert 41, 44
'Bubbles' poster 64

Cambridge teashop
  anti-democratic feelings 17
  notion of culture 3–4
Cambridge English xvii–xviii 316
Cambridge University xv, 2, 3, 5–6, 161
  English Department xxi, 176, 316, 319, 322
Campbell Swinton, Alan 146
capitalism
  and adverting 65–6, 67, 70, 72–3, 74, 79, 81
  'aggressive marketing' 251, 269
  American 101
  anti-democratic power 17
  care of people disregarded 243, 245
  and the classification of work 243–4
  conflict with socialism 74–5
  control of the means of communicative production 229–30, 236
  corporate 65–6, 83, 295
  cultural incorporation 130
  and development of broadcasting technology 152, 153
  and 'improved' local conditions 267
  increased production/fewer workers goal 249
  indifference to alternative literature 132
  industrial 104, 154–5, 241, 243–4, 247–8, 250–1, 325
  international/global 247, 252, 269
  maintained by Empire 50
  majority assent 290
  and mass culture 16–17

capitalism *cont.*
   and mobile privatisation xxiii, 154–5
   'mode of production' in analysis of 299
   New Left critique xix
   and Plan X xxii, 279, 281, 283, 288
   and population dislocation and relocation 264–7
   and postmodernism xx
   post-war Labour Party management xvii
   radical critiques 188
   relations with industrial production 239
   and Social Darwinism 101, 104
   and transformation of culture 96
   uneven socio-economic effects 250
   and the uses of nation states 270–2
   violence of vocabulary 251
Carey, George R. 146
Carlyle, Thomas 41, 44, 53, 54, 63
Caselli, Giovanni 146
catch-phrases 64
censorship 86, 87, 92
Chadwick, Edwin 42
Chartism 42, 43, 45, 47, 54
Chekhov, Anton 170
Christian Socialism 43
church 42, 45
cinema xv, 11, 22–3, 179, 181, 187
   and arts policy 308
   and the availability of drama 162
   broadcasting compared 156–7, 158
   Soviet 216, 220
Civil War, and press development 150
Civilisation (Bell) 4
civilization
   and cultures 186
   as survival of the fittest 105–6
class
   and culture 6–7, 94, 95, 96
   and human practice 131–2
   industrialism and new structure 10
class-consciousness 152, 203
class relations
   newspapers 231–2
   and the 'pecking order' 117
class society 76, 98, 233
   1840s 42, 44, 45, 48
   access to drama, literacy compared 203
   attempt to preserve 95–6
   and social intention 125
class struggle, Darwinian analogy 109–10
Clough, Arthur Hugh 41
Cobbett, William 265
codes 195
Coleridge, Samuel Taylor 53
collective subject 194

commercial communications systems 85, 87–8, 92
commercial culture *see* popular culture
common culture 9, 14, 93–100
Commonwealth, and press development 150
communication as practice 175–7
communication, means of as means of production xx–xxi. 223–36
   alternative modes 229, 230–2, 234–5
   amplificatory modes 228, 229, 232, 233
   'direct' and 'indirect' modes 232–6
   durative modes 228, 229–30, 233, 235
   ideological blocks 224–7
   'natural'/'technological' split 225–6
   productive history 224, 227–32
   untransformed human modes 228
communication institutions 174
   and cultural exclusion/inclusion 97, 98, 100
   development of the press as 150–1
   modern significance 173, 188, 196
   need for comprehensive study 181, 188
communication systems 85–92
   authoritarian 85, 86–7, 91–2
   commercial 85, 87–8, 92
   control vs. freedom 86, 92
   democratic 85, 88–91, 92
   paternal 85, 87, 92
communication technologies xxi, xxiii, 173–4, 175, 182
   and audience/transmitter divisions 10
   social history of 144–59
   as systems of signs 196
Communications (Williams) 85, 318, 322
communications, and advertising 79–83
communications studies xv, 19, 85, 173–83
   cultural studies/cultural science approach 175–83
   exclusion of intention 181
   inter-disciplinary hostility 174, 175, 178–9
   and 'mass-communications' 179–80
   television discussion example 181–3
communism xvii, 230, 279
Communist Party xvii, 7
competition 103–4, 106
   and extension of education 111
   and financial inheritance 107
   between notions of society 105
Coningsby (Disraeli) 45, 51
consciousness 31
   actual vs. possible 194
   and dramatic analysis 222
   dramatization of 168
   as guiding element in cultural process 177

consciousness *cont.*
　old new and 301, 302
　possible as ideal 194
　and the process of production 220–1
　social determination 128, 124
　working-class 216, 217, 218, 219, 221
Conservative government xviii
conspiracy theories 284
'consumer credit' 68–9
consumers
　as identity 268, 277
　users as 75–7
consumption, critical theory as 134–5
'consumption' perspective 187, 227
Corn Laws repeal 47
corporations 153, 239
　and advertising 79, 80, 81–2, 83
　multinational 269, 278
Corpus Christi day 162
crisis-management 284
critical dissent 169
critical theory as consumption 134–5
criticism
　analysis preferred 221–2
　and 'documentary' cultural
　　analysis 28–9
　'English' tradition xvii
　New 134–5
　replacement by formalism 195
　text and genre 137
cultural analysis xvii, xviii, xxi, xxii, 27–55, 199, 286
　1840s example 39–55
　and code 195
　connections with social analysis 191–2
　holistic 27, 30–33, 35, 54–5
　Marxist 128, 121, 126–7
　multidimensional xxi
　new intellectual formation 192–3
　rebuked as 'sociology' 179
　see also selective tradition; structure of feeling
cultural artefacts 174, 175–6, 178
cultural evolution 112
cultural expansion 13
cultural formations
　'media people' 196
　relationship with cultural forms 193–4
　study of 185, 188–9
cultural forms
　and the production process as a whole 203–4
　relationship with cultural formations 193–4
　study of 91–2

cultural institutions 33, 179
　battle for 'popular' drama 203
　changes, recent 322–3
　changes, 1840s 41–2, 44–5
　class affiliations and exclusions 202
　for democratic communication 89–90
　dominant and active nature 286–7
　mass 16
　metropolitan 306, 308
　and money from advertising 16
　relation with cultural practices 193–4
cultural materialism xvi–xvii, xxii–xix, 223
　as a sociological methodology xxi
　Williams' definition xxi
cultural polarization 14–15
cultural policy 305–11
　civic tradition 310
　proper and as display xxiii, 305–7
　State patronage 307–9
　towards a future 309–11
cultural practice(s)
　and cultural objects/artefacts 135–7, 175–6
　relations between 176–7
　relationship with cultural institutions 193–4
　and 'superstructure' 123
　and traditions 190–1
　see also alternative cultural practice; oppositional cultural practice
cultural prescription 7
cultural rights 305
cultural science 173, 175, 177–8, 186, 189, 225
cultural studies xix, xxiii, 19, 173, 313–26
　absorption into academic mainstream 313, 319, 321–2
　as approach to communications studies 173, 175–83
　contributions to the sociology of culture 189–96
　future of 314, 322–6
　institutionalisation 313, 319, 323, 325
　origins and development xviii, 313, 315, 318–23
　suspicion of 181
　William's contribution xv–xvii
cultural theory, Marxist 119–38
culture
　commercial exploitation 41, 42, 76
　debate about the nature of 94–5
　documentary definition 27, 28, 29, 30, 31, 32, 35, 39
　and 'do-gooding' 4–5
　history of term 176–7, 186

culture *cont.*
   ideal definition 27, 28, 29–30, 30–1
   idealist vs. materialist views 177
   and inequality 93–4
   mass 'threat' to 20
   as ordinary xviii, 1–18, 96
   social definition 27, 28–7, 30, 31, 39
   as specific national development 177
   supporting Plan X 283
   'teashop' sense 3–4
   traditional and creative aspects 2–3
   and writer/audience relationship 94
   see also common culture; democratic culture; dominant culture; emergent culture; minority ('high') culture; popular culture; residual culture
Culture (Williams) xxii, 185
Culture and Society 1780–1950 (Williams) xv, xvii, xviii, 19, 93
cultures, first use of term 186

Daguerre, Louis 146
Daily Mail 64
Dalziel, Edward 48
Darwin, Charles 101, 102, 104, 108, 109
Darwin, Erasmus 102–3
Davy, Humphrey 145
De Vries, Hugo 110
deindustrialisation xxii, 249–51, 281
democracy 75, 298
   denied by 'mass-communication' concept 25
   educated and participatory 93, 98–9
   fear of cultural dilution by 95
   and free communication 85–6
   and the growth of education 24
   mass- and class- 20–1
   popular belief in 17–18
democratic communication systems 85, 88–91, 92
democratic culture 89–90, 318, 320
department stores, beginnings 64
detective stories 323
determinism
   in base/superstructure model 128–9
   determination preferred xxi–xxii, 128–9, 123
   materialist 177
   see also technological determinism
Devlin report 216, 217
Dickens, Charles 40, 43–4, 51–2
Dilthey, Wilhelm 177, 189–90
Disraeli, Benjamin 40, 42, 43, 51
division of labour 80, 230–1, 231–2

Dombey and Son (Dickens) 45
dominant culture 127–9, 137, 190
   contribution of the arts 133–4
   human practice outside or against 131–2
   incorporation of emergent culture 129, 130
   incorporation of residual cultures 129, 130
   modes of incorporation 127–8
drama 161–71
   analysis of types 191
   battle for 'popular' 203
   and dissent 169
   distance from myth and ritual 165–6
   and the isolated figure 168–9
   medieval 162, 208
   new convention of deliberate overlap 166–7
   new investigative function 164
   pervasiveness in modern media 162–3, 189, 202
   pervasiveness in modern society 161, 167–9
   and presentation of power 165
   realism 201–2, 202–4, 208–15
   relationship with modern society 169–71
   shift from group dialogue to the dialogue of a negative group 170–1, 192
   stage as a room 155, 164–5, 170, 192, 204, 212–13
Drama from Ibsen to Brecht (Williams) xv
Drama from Ibsen to Eliot (Williams) xv
Drama in Performance (Williams) xv

Eagleton, Terry xix
Eastbourne Gazette, The 61
Eastern Europe 239, 309
ecological argument for change 291, 298, 299
ecology movement xxii, 279, 280, 285, 286, 290, 302
economic crisis, recent 279
Economist 104
economic reductionism xix, 119, 123, 305
economic concentration 83
economic history 43
economy(ies) xvii, 9
   cultural 15
   capitalist 70, 74, 124, 241, 245, 269, 297
   centralised command 295
   communist 297
   consumer 75, 76–7, 142
   'deindustrialisation' 249–51
   and the development of advertising 16–17, 58, 65–7, 70, 74, 79, 81

economy(ies) *cont.*
   educational needs 14
   industrial 44, 291, 293
   international/global 252, 258, 269, 271, 278, 288
   market 103, 292, 293, 294–5
   Marxist view of relationship with culture 6, 96, 121
   'mixed' 80
   national recovery plan 272
   needs paramount 270
   possibilities of change 252–5, 292–6, 298, 299
   neo-liberal political xxii
   'post-industrial' 242
   resistance to change 248, 289–91
   socialist 17, 297
   traditional ruined by population dislocation 266
Edinburgh International Television Festival 199
Edison, Thomas 146
Education Act (1870) 11
education
   centrality of grammar and rhetoric 173
   for a common culture 99
   content 14–15
   and cultural exclusion 97, 98
   and expansion of audiences 24
   extension, and fear of cultural dilution 95
   fictional portrayal, 1840s 48–9
   and the market 76
   and national identity 262
   as ordinary 3, 13–15
   popular equated with commercial culture 10–11
   and promotion of competition 111
   and protection of 'high' culture 8, 93
   relegation to the tertiary sector 243
   restriction of access 6, 13–14
   and the selective tradition 27–8, 37–8
   and transmission of dominant culture 127, 128
   see also higher education
effects studies 134–5, 140, 181, 185, 187–8, 189
elections 288–9
elective affinities 177
electricity, inventions and developments 144–5
Eliot, George 53
Eliot, T. S. 93, 95–6, 201
Elizabethan commercial theatres 162
Elster, Julius 146

emergent culture 119, 129–30, 131, 134, 137, 190
   incorporated/not incorporated 130
   literature and 133
   sources 131–4
emotion/intelligence dichotomy 301–3
Empire, in 1840s fiction 50
employment *see* work
Engels, Friedrich 109–10, 121
English renaissance tragedies 208–9
ethics, and modification of natural law 112
Ethics of Advertising, The 69

1840s, England 39–55
eugenics 107–8
European cultural dimension 310
evolution
   human communication crucial 228
   vs. revolution 110–11
evolutionary theory
   pre-Darwinian 102–3
   social component 102
   see also Social Darwinism

Fabians 111
factory legislation, 1840s 42, 45, 47
factory system 20, 60, 65, 70, 74, 240
Fascism 112, 153
feminism 27–8, 279, 285–6, 288, 290, 302
Festival of Dionysus 162
fiction, analysis of types 191 *see also* literature; popular fiction
film 22–3, 114, 133, 161, 286
   inherent transforming processes 233–4, 235
   relationship between method and intentions 214
   semiotic analysis 195
   Soviet 216, 220
film studies 317, 322
First World War 108, 151
   advertising 68
fly-posting 63
forces of production
   and base 123–4
   connection with relations of production 239, 296–9
   development 238, 240
   and means of communication 223, 224, 225–6, 227
foreign trade 252
formalism 186, 192, 195, 203–4, 205, 321
formations
   neglect of contemporary 321
   relation with projects 314–5, 322
   see also cultural formations

Frankfurt School 194, 195
Fraser, Robert 86
free trade 42, 45, 63, 239, 252
Friese-Greene, William 146
Fromm, Erich 33
Frye, Northrop 192
functionalist social theory 181

gambling 279, 283, 284
Garnett, Tony 207, 220, 221
Gaskell, Elizabeth 40, 43, 51
Geitel, Hans 146
General Strike (1926) 43
genes 191
globalisation xxii *see also* internationalism
Gobineau, Arthur de 108
Godwin, William 52
Goebbels, Joseph 152
Goldmann, Lucien 191, 193–4
Gramsci, Antonio xix, 119, 126, 127, 131, 188, 321
Great Depression (1875–1890s) 65
Greek tragedy 161
Guinness advertisements 69

Hall, Stuart xvii, xix
handbills 63
Hardy, Thomas 115
hegemony xix, 126–7, 131, 192, 194
Helena Fleetwood (Tonna) 48
Herder, Johann 186
'high' culture *see* 'minority' culture
higher education
    commodification 313–4
    expansion, 1960s 319
    inertia 174–5
    insertion of technology 320, 321
    and movement between classes 94
    new movements dependent on access 291
    and professional advantage 283
history 177, 315, 323
    of advertising 57–60
    of communicative production 227–32
    cultural 32–3
    of cultural studies 317–22
    of literary studies 315–17
    Marx's sense 96, 122
    material 297, 299, 301
    of the people of Britain 272–4
    of 'realism' and 'naturalism' terms 199–200
    of realist drama 208–15
    Social Darwinist interpretation 103, 109, 110, 117

history *cont.*
    working-class 215, 219
    see also economic history; political history; social history
Hobbes, Thomas 103–4, 109
Hofstadter, Richard 101–2
Hoggart, Richard xvi, 317, 323
holistic approach xix, 27, 119
homology of structures 193–4
human practice 131–4
human work (care of people) 243, 245, 248, 253, 255, 295
Huxley, Aldous 69
Huxley, Julian 112
Huxley, Thomas 112, 113

Ibsen, Henrik 115, 164, 212
idealist philosophy xx, 119, 128, 177, 193, 313, 321
ideology xix, 192, 211, 321
    blocks to means of communication as means of production 224–7
    bourgeois 224, 225, 226, 232
    and code 195
    of extra-human determination 128
    hegemony compared 126, 128
    and identity of immigrants 274–5
    of 'the masses' 179
    transmission of 150
    of work as employment 243
    see also Plan X; Social Darwinism
immigration
    and community integration 276
    'racist' tensions 274–5
    see also population dislocation
Imperial Tobacco Company 66
imperialism 6, 50, 101, 108
    economic 66
Incorporated Society of British Advertisers 67
Independent Television Authority 86
industrial development/industrialization
    1840s 42
    and competitive individualism 104
    and the creation of local and national deindustrialisation 250
    Empire as lever 50
    and new social needs 145
    rentier resistance 246
    resistance to loss of employment 246–7
industrial monopoly, rationalization 106
industrial production
    advantages of electric power 145
    and 'consumer durables' 154

industrial production *cont.*
  and labour-saving 246
  man as consumer/man as user 75
  new needs and new possibilities 148
  and problems of social organization 74
  and reduction of skilled craftsmen 244
  rejection by new movements 292
  relation to communicative production 226–7
  relations with capitalism 239
  see also deindustrialisation; factory system
industrial revolution(s) 95, 242
  benefits 9
  and changes in advertising 60
  continuing 237–8, 241
  critics called hostile to progress 246
  and interpenetrating world markets 249–50
  miraculous advances 54
  and new class structure 10
  and physical 'massing' 10, 152
  and press development 150
  and work as employment 240, 241
industrial society(ies) 22, 113, 188, 189, 196, 227, 292
  'post-industrial' notion critiqued xxii, 237–55
  and replacement of traditional with commercial culture 8
  ugliness not inevitable 10
  value 9
inequality 95, 254, 276
  of culture 94
  global xxii
information work 237, 242, 245
inheritance 106–7
Institute of Contemporary Arts 305
Institute of Practitioners in Advertising 181, 189
intelligence 13–14
intention
  exclusion in communication studies 181
  in realism 209, 210, 211, 215
  and social totality 125
  in technological innovation xxii, 139, 144, 147–8
  of transmission 24–5
interdisciplinary study xxii, 173, 323–4
international bodies 277–8
International Monetary Foundation 278
internationalism 258, 259, 263, 264
Ireland 276
Irish identity 273
Iron Heel , The (London) 113

Jameson, Frederick xx
Jenkins, Charles Francis 153
Johnson, Samuel 60
Jones, B. 242

Keats, John 53
Kellner, Douglas xxi
Keynes, John Maynard 307, 309
Keywords (annual publication) xvi
Keywords (Williams) 19
Kidd, Benjamin 111
Kingsley, Charles 40, 43, 51
Kitchener, Herbert 68
Kropotkin, Peter 112

labour movements 324
  influence of Plan X 283
  institutional resistance to change 287–8
  international 295
  as resource for change 295–6
Labour Party xvii, xix, 2, 15, 272
  anti-democratic planners 17
  and the failure of nuclear disarmament 287
  submission to the market 82
labour-saving 245–7, 253, 255, 295
Lamarck, Jean-Baptiste 106
Latin studies conference 174
Lawrence, D. H. 115–16
Leavis, F. R. xvi–xviii, 8, 13, 69, 93, 95, 316, 317, 318, 322, 323
'Left Leavisism' xviii
liberal studies 13, 319
liberalism, classical 79–80
libraries, public 42, 308
license system, broadcasting 82, 158
linguistics
  and communications studies 174, 182
  historical materialism 196
  Marxist structuralism 193
Listener, The xvi, 57
literacy
  effects of propagation 203
  gap between high and common 14–15
  menaced by popular culture 323
  as obstacle to abolition of division of labour 231
  pre-1870 11
literary scholarship xv–xvi
  academic time-stops 176
  and communications study 175
  progressive specialization of 'literature' 178–9
literary studies 313
  development 315–17
  institutionalisation 316–7

literature 94
  emergent 133
  exclusion from Art Council funding 308
  narrowing-down process 178–9
  notations 136
  'popular' 179
  primacy 96
  relationship with society 132–4
  residual 133
  selective tradition, 1840s 40–1, 43–4
  and Social Darwinism 112–16
  Soviet sensitivity to 132
  structure of feeling, 1840s xxi, 50–2
Liverpool Docks 216
Lloyd, Edward 41
Loach, Ken 207, 220
local identity 261
London, Jack 113
London Journal 41
London Merchant, The (Lello) 211
Long Revolution, The (Williams) xvi, xviii, xx, 27
Lord Mayor's show 307
Lucas Aerospace 295
Luddites 246–7
Lukács, György 124, 191, 194, 199

Macaulay, Thomas 41, 43, 44
magic
  in 1840s fiction 49–50, 51
  and advertising 73–9
magic lanterns 146
Mallock, W. H. 111–12
Malthus, Robert 102, 108, 109
'man the hunter' 117
Mannheim, Karl 188
manufacturing
  decline 237, 242, 247
  transfer to cheap labour markets xxii, 237, 247
Marey, Étienne-Jules 146
market
  control 66, 70, 153
  cultural 88, 305, 308, 309
  effects on free communication 88
  international/global 250, 252, 258, 264–5, 269, 271, 277, 284–5, 293
  Labour submission to 82
  organization 68, 74, 79, 80, 153
  political 76, 254
  and 'post-industrial' society 238, 240, 241, 243, 247, 248, 249, 252
  ubiquity and domination xix, 75, 76
  unable to meet human needs 270
  as zeitgeist xx
  see also mass market

'market' production 226
marketing vs. production 294
Marx, Karl 95, 96, 109, 128, 121, 122, 123, 125, 177, 230, 234, 300
Marxism xvii, xix, 6–7, 13, 95, 226–7
  bourgeois 194
  conflict over formalism 192
  cultural theory 119–38
  lack of projective capacity 299
  and realism 204, 212
  transition from Marx to 128
  Western-Marxist revival xix
  see also base/superstructure model
Marxism and Literature (Williams) xx
Mary Barton (Gaskell) 45, 51
mass and masses 10–11, 19–22, 76
  concept of 21–2
  as mob 10, 19, 20, 21, 25, 152
  'othering' 10–11
  'mass communication' 19, 22–6, 152, 179, 225, 226
  and communications studies 179, 187–8, 196
  intention of transmission 24–5
  multiple transmission 23–4
  sources vs. agents of transmission 25–6
mass culture *see* popular culture
mass markets 187, 203, 225, 293
'mass media' 179
'mass meetings' 20, 152
'mass organisations' 152
'mass production' 20, 152
'mass society' xviii, 179–80
materialism xx, 226
  historical 224, 300
  insufficient in the face of advertising 73–4
  of signs 195–6
  see also cultural materialism
materialist determinism 177
materialist philosophy xix–xx
May Day Manifesto xviii–xix
May, Joseph 146
McGrath, John 203, 204
McLuhan, Marshall 192, 225
means of production 203, 247, 267, 303
  in art, public availability 310
  English socialization 7
  minority ownership 74, 81, 109–10
  means of communication as xx–xxi, 223–36
media
  deterministic view xxi, 223, 225–6
  new, and new cultural policy 309
  ubiquity of drama 161

media studies xv, 19, 173, 313, 322
mediation 121–2
　Frankfurt School approach 194
Medvedev, Pavel 321
middle class
　attitudes to dissident working-class, 1840s 44
　(dominant) social character, 1840s 47
　reformers, 1840s 54
military policy 282
military requirements, and new technology 148, 149, 153–4
Mill, John Stuart 41, 44
minority ('high') culture 93, 95, 96, 97–8, 179, 196
Miss Julie (Strindberg) 113
Mitchell, Julia xviii
mobile privatisation xvii, xxiii, 154–5, 157, 257, 268–9
mode of production 123, 131, 230, 250
　and 'base' 122
　concept as obstacle 299–300
　international destruction wrought by capitalist 264–5
　reconstruction 251, 252, 253
monetary institutions, need for alternative 292, 294
Morning Post 61
motion pictures 175, 227
　development 144, 146, 147, 151, 153, 170
motion-picture theatres 147
multinational companies 269, 278
museums 4, 15, 42
music 133, 136
music-halls 41, 46, 54, 162
mutual aid, in nature 112

Napoleonic wars 145
nations and nation states xxii, 257–78
　bonding to 262–3
　capitalist uses 270–2
　cultural policy xxiii, 305–11
　and 'native' feelings 260–1
　processes of formation 261–2
　radical opposition to 263–4
　and social identity 272–6
　too big and too small xxiii, 251, 266–8, 310
　and universality 260
National Union of Teachers 318
nationalism
　alternative radical 263
　contradictions and artificialities 257, 264, 271, 278

nationalism *cont.*
　'nationalisation' unconnected 272
　and political evolution 263–4
nationality, contradictions in 258–9, 260, 272
natural selection, social application 102, 103, 111
nature/natural world
　connected intervention 297, 299, 300
　as a source a raw material 296–7, 300
naturalism 212–13
　as alternative to supernaturalism 200, 211
　character/environment link 200, 204, 213
　as degraded 'realism' 206
　distinction from realism 204, 211–12
　'high naturalism'/'naturalist habit' distinction 201
　history of term 199–200, 201
　as a passive form 204
　and the use of dialogue 204
Nazi Germany 152
neighbourliness 8
neo-liberalism xix, xxi, xxii *see also* Plan X
Neolithic and Bronze Age Revolutions 297
New Criticism 134–5, 192
New Left xvii, xviii–xix
New Left Review 57
News From Nowhere xv–xvi
News of the World, The 60
newspapers
　advertising 58, 59–60, 60–3, 63–4, 80
　advertising funding 11, 16, 67, 70, 73
　advertising managers 66–7
　class relations between journalists and printers 231–2
　economic concentration 83
　entry of speculators 41
　free press ideal 79
　increasing circulation, post-1855 63
　paid 'personality' items 72
　reduction in number and variety 80
　selective tradition of 1840s 39
　as subject of study 317, 322
Niepce, Nicéphore 146
Nipkow, Paul Gottlieb 146
non-actors, use in drama 216, 220
'non-verbal communication' 228
Northcliffe, Alfred Harmsworth 11, 64, 67
Northcliffe Revolution 11
novels
　analysis of change in endings 191
　detective 323
　popularity of historical, 1840s 53–4
　reflection of social change, 1840s 45
　and the selective tradition 36–7
　structure of feeling, 1840s 50–2

nuclear arms race 279, 280, 281
nuclear arms strategy 283
nuclear disarmament 287, 288

oil crisis (1970s) 279, 281
Open University 313, 319–21
oppositional cultural practice 119, 128–9, 130, 290
overmanning 244, 249, 255
Owen, Robert 104
Oxford University literature study 176

parks, beginnings of public 42
parliamentary politics 128
Parlour Library 40, 41
Past and Present (Carlyle) 45
patent foods, advertising 64, 65
patent medicines
  advertising 58–9, 62–3, 64, 67
  advertising banned 69
paternal communication systems 85, 87, 92
patriotism 269, 273, 274, 276
  contradictions and artificialities 257, 258–9, 260, 264, 272, 276
  and Plan X 282
  and war 68, 262
pattern, as key-word in cultural analysis 33
'pattern of culture' 33
peace movement 279, 280, 285, 286, 288, 290, 301
'penny dreadfuls' 41
Penny Magazine 41
people
  abstracted from communication process 224
  as 'agents' 321
  as raw material 297, 298, 300
periodicals, 1840s
  and control of working-class opinion 41–2
  entry of speculators 41
  growth of new kinds 41
  structure of feeling 48–50
photography
  and arts policy 308
  development of 145–6, 151
Physics and Politics (Bagehot) 104–5
Pinkney, Tony xvi
Plague, London 59
Plan X xxii, 279, 280–4, 303, 314
  challenges to 284–304
Play for Today 207
Play of the Townley Shepherds 208

point of view
  alternative consciousness 217
  and camera position 218, 234
  undefined political 218–9
political advertising 71, 73, 82
political history, 1840s 42–3
  reflection in literature 45
  selective interpretation 43
political institutions 7, 186
  necessity of challenge 287–9
  resistance to change 287–8
political parties 76, 270, 287, 296
political theory, and Social Darwinism 104–12
political viewpoint 215, 218–9
politics 2, 187, 221, 249, 259
  centralisation of power 150
  inadequate for a caring society 254
  incorporation of oppositions 128
  and the market 76, 82
  Plan X 280–4
  resources for new 284–9, 395–6, 298
  Williams' formation xvi–xxii
  see also democracy; radicalism; socialism
Politics of Modernism, The xvi
Poor Law 42, 45, 46
popular (commercial, 'mass') culture 8, 9–13, 42, 91, 117
  association with badness 11
  and capitalist society 16–17
  equated with popular education 10–11
  equated with quality of living of consumers 11–12
  Gresham's Law analogy 12–13
  as subject of study of 195, 196, 317, 323–4
popular fiction 48–9, 179, 317, 322, 323
population dislocation 264–5
postmodernism xix, xx
post-structuralism xix
practical criticism 72, 192
Pre-Raphaelite Brotherhood 54
press
  bad popular, pre-1870 11
  creation of modern structure 67
  development 150–1
  effects of modern 187
  effects of social change, 1840s 44
  independent 152–3
  Northcliffe Revolution 11, 67
  status divisions 232
  as subject of study 317

print
  as alternative communication mode 233, 234
  costs of access 232
  importance compared to broadcasting 322
printing
  impersonality 23
  relationship with writing 231–2
  specialist histories 227
  technical changes 22, 41
private property 98
production
  link with expenditure 295
  overlooked in emphasis on 'effects' 135, 181, 187
  of realist drama 220–1
  recovery of control 252–3, 254, 293
  relationship with culture 6–7
  shift to 'livelihood' 301, 303
  shift towards quality and sustainability 292, 293–4
  specialized Marxist use 226
  see also forces of production; industrial production; means of production; mode of production; relations of production
professional associations, as resources for hope 295
projects
  relation with formations 314–5, 322
  Sartre's notion 194
protests, 1968 xix
psychology
  and advertising 67, 68
  and communications studies 174, 182–3
  'components' view of art 135
  'effects' studies 185, 187
Public Health Act (1848) 42
public relations 71–2
public service 47, 67, 83, 89
public stage 167
Pugin, Augustus 41, 44

race theories 108–9
racism 274
radicalism 41
  and opposition to 'the nation' 263–4
radio (wireless) xxiii, 23
  accessibility of short-wave receivers and transistor 229–30
  as alternative communication mode 233, 234
  as amplificatory communication mode 228
  and expansion of drama 162, 202

radio *cont.*
  commercial 70–1, 83
  communal 234
  development 147, 151, 154, 155–6
  specialist histories 227
  as subject for study 317
Radio 1 82
Railway Library 40, 41
railway 2, 41, 42, 45, 145, 154
rationalism 210
Raymond Williams (Inglis) xvi
Raymond Williams (Smith) xvi
Raymond Williams Society xvi
Reade, Charles 40
reading
  Institute of Practitioners of Advertising survey 181, 189
  as skill 99, 229, 231
Reagan, Ronald xxii, 279
realism 199–206, 207–22
  in *The Big Flame* 214–22
  combined with imagined hypotheses 216
  contemporary action 201, 210, 211, 213
  distinction from naturalism 204, 211–12
  history of term 199–202
  and intention 209, 210, 211, 215
  as a method 207–9
  and political viewpoint 215
  'post-naturalist' 204–5
  relations between technical and general definition 212–14
  secular action 201, 210, 211
  and social extension and inclusivity 201–2, 210, 211, 213, 22
  as a whole form 201, 209–11
reductionism, new 193
regional identity 261
'regions' 261, 276
relations of production xx, 236
  as 'base' 122
  connection with forces of production 239, 296–9
  and 'industrial revolution' 237, 238, 241
  and means of communication 223, 224, 225–6
rentier sector 246, 247
Repeal of the Corn Laws (1846) 42
residual culture 119, 128, 137, 190
  incorporated/not incorporated 130
  and literature 133
  persistence 131, 133–4
  sources 131
restoration prose comedy 209–10
Reynolds, G. W. M. 40, 41
Richards. I. A. 134, 317, 323

Richardson, Samuel 52
Right, pro- and anti-state rhetoric 271
Road to Damascus (Strindberg) 168
Rockefeller, John D. 106
Romantic movement 53–4
Rosing, Boris 146, 153
Rossetti, Dante Gabriel 41
ruling class
  control of means of communication 229
  definitions of social identity 275
  monopoly of patriotism 274
  'national' interests 277
  and state-building 262
Ruskin, John 41, 44, 169–70
Russell, Bertrand 69

sandwich-men 63, 65
Sartre, Jean-Paul 194
Sayers, Dorothy 69
science fiction 114
scientific research, as resource 285
Screen 207
Scrutiny 317
Second Generation (Williams) 268
Second World War xvii, 71, 151, 157
selective tradition xviii, xx, 27–8, 35–9, 127–8, 190
  operation on the 1840s 39–45
self, as raw material 297, 299
semiotics 194–5
sensibility 134
'service' work
  absurdity of category 242–3
  seen as growth sector 237, 242
  'transfer' to unlikely 245, 247–8
sexualisation 77, 298
Shakespeare, William 57, 161
sharing society 255
Shaw, George Bernard 115
signification, and alternative communication modes 229, 233–4
signs
  materiality of xx–xxi, 185, 186, 195–6, 223
  technologies and systems of 196
slave trade 266
social character 33, 35, 130 1840s 45–8, 49, 50, 52
  structure of feeling compared 47–8, 49, 50, 52
social communications, pre-technological 149–50
Social Darwinism 101–18
  described 101–4
  in literature 112–16
  new wave 117–8

Social Darwinism *cont.*
  responses to applications 111–12
  variations and applications 104–11
social democracy xvii, 111, 254
  increasing irrelevance 264
social disintegration 4, 10
social identity 272–6
  legal definition 274–5
social history 1840s 41–3, 45
  and literature 45
  and the selective tradition 42, 43
  of television 144–59
social institutions 2, 6, 8, 47, 54, 140, 141, 283
  broadcasting as 151–2
  economic determination xix
  indifference to new movements 288
  and pre-technological communication 149–50
  and 'social' definition of culture 28, 29
  and the sociology of culture 186–7
  superstructural elements 125
  working-class 6, 7
social types 191
social totality 124–5
socialism xvi, 298
  and common culture 98
  conflict with capitalism 74–5
  and exploitation of natural resources 296–7
  and industrial production without capitalism 239
  and new communicative capacities 230, 236
  and 'natural/technological' communications split 225
  opposed by Social Darwinism 105–6
  and social identity 275–6, 276
  and realist drama 202
  variable 278
society(ies)
  bourgeois 127, 130, 195
  capitalist xix, 16–17, 73, 74, 75, 130, 152, 154–5, 227, 243, 283, 292
  and common meanings and values 2–3, 13, 14, 96–7, 99–100
  contemporary interests, and the selective tradition xx, 37–8
  culture as way of thinking about 94–5
  democratic 20–1, 75, 89, 90, 98–9
  dramatized 161–71
  effective self-governing 75, 276–8
  English/British 7, 8, 58, 97–8
  and the 'magic system' of advertising 72–9
  primary production of 124

society(ies) *cont.*
  relationship with art 31–3, 44–5, 52–4, 314–5
  relationship with literature 132–4
  technology and 139–59
  wanting to belong 259, 262
  see also class society; industrial society(ies); mass society; sharing society
Society for Checking the Abuses of Public Advertising (SCAPA) 64–5
Society for Education in Film and Television (SEFT) 207
sociology
  and communications study 174, 175
  contribution to sociology of culture 186, 187–8
  and cultural analysis 179
  emergence of new part in response to cultural science 177, 186
  prevalence of impact-studies 181
  Williams' contribution to xv–xvi
  Williams' 'turn' to xv, 169–70
sociology of culture 185–98
  attempts to relate forms to formations 185–6, 193–5
  effects studies 185, 187–8, 189
  materiality of signs 195–6
  study of forms 185, 191–2
  study of formations 185, 188–9
  study of institutions 185, 186–7, 188
  study of traditions 185, 190–1
sociology of knowledge 188–9
sound recording 229
Soviet Union/USSR 14, 132
  film and theatre 216, 220
Spencer, Herbert 101, 103, 104, 105, 106, 115
St Paul's, London 58
Stalinism xvii
Stamp Duty, reduction and abolition 61, 63
Star, The 66
states *see* nations and nation states
Strindberg, August 113, 168, 170, 201, 204–5, 212
structuralism 186, 207, 321
  cultural 196
  French 207
  genetic 193–4
  Marxist 193, 321
  and semiotics 194–5
  synchronic 192
structure of feeling xvii, xviii, xx, 27, 33–5
  1840s 47–54
  and advertising 78
  transience 171
  Zeitgeist compared xx

Sumner, William 105–6, 111
Sunday press, 1840s 39, 41
supernaturalism 200, 201
Surbiton 8
'survival of the fittest' 101, 103, 105–6
  'fittest' as best adapted 112
  and nineteenth-century everyday experience 107
Swansea University xvi
Sybil (Disraeli) 45, 51
symptomatic technology 139, 141–2, 143–4

taste 134
Tawney, R. H. 93
tea advertising 58, 62
technological determinism xx–xxii, 139–40, 143–4, 213, 223, 225–6, 238, 239, 296
technology(ies)
  conversion of ideas into 193, 194
  developments, 1840s 41, 44
  insertion into higher education 320, 321
  and intention in innovation xxii, 139, 144, 147–8
  and Plan X 284
  and society 139–59
  as systems of signs 196
  as a transforming intervention 300
  and the vision of 'raw material' 297
  see also communication technologies; symptomatic technology
telegraphy, development of 144, 145, 151, 153–4
telephony, development of 145, 151
teletext 234–5
television xvi, xxiii, 22, 23, 139–59
  advertising funding 73
  as alternative communication mode 233, 234, 235
  as amplificatory communication mode 228
  and arts policy 308
  cause and effect 139–40, 141–4
  commercial 71, 80, 86
  creative possibilities frustrated 158
  effects studies 181, 187
  need for new categories and procedures 187–8
  public service/commercial co-existence 80
  social history, as technology 144–8
  social history of the uses of technology 148–59
  specialist histories 227
  as subject of study 322
Television: Technology and Cultural Form (Williams) xvi, xxiii

television discussion, example of communications study 181–91
television drama
    extension to the working class 214
    realism and non-naturalism 202–6
    speech by a 'negative' group 171
    ubiquity of 161, 162–3, 164–5
    see also Big Flame, The
television interviews, satiric presentation 217–8
Ten Hours Bill (1847) 42, 47
Tennyson, Alfred, Lord 41, 44, 53
territoriality, 'natural' basis 117
Thackeray, William Makepeace 40, 43–4
theatre 1840s 41, 44, 54
    and class 202, 214
    dramatic verity 161
    expansion and contraction 162
    as 'fine art' 308
    lack of sociological study 189
    naturalist 215
Thompson, Denys 69, 71
Thompson, Edward xix, 317
Time Machine, The (Wells) 113–14
Times, The 13, 39, 40, 60, 64
tobacco advertising 66, 67
Tom Brown's Schooldays (Hughes) 49
toothpaste advertising 59
Tory Party 42, 46
totality 124–5
    and intention 125
tourism 306
Towards 2000 (Williams) xviii, xxii, 237, 257, 279
trade 50, 61, 150, 246, 265
    international/ global 145, 250, 251, 252, 271, 277
    see also free trade
trade unions 2, 248, 281
    influence of Plan X 283
    as resources for hope 295–6
traditions, study of 185, 190–1
types, in fiction and drama 191

unemployment 240
    Britain 290
    mass 237–8, 240, 250
    structural 241, 288
United Kingdom Billposters Association 63, 64–5
universality 167, 208, 259–60, 272, 275
university extension classes xviii, 313, 317
United States/America xxii, 14, 66, 146
    legal integration of mobile populations 275
    mass culture theories 195

United States/America cont.
    public television 157
    race theory 108
    Social Darwinism 101
    study of institutions 188
utopias, in fiction 114–15

Veblen, Thorstein 111
Victoria, Queen 63
vocational training, without broader cultural leaning 313, 324–5
Voloshinov, Valentin 196, 321
Von Moltke, Helmuth 109

Waiting for Godot (Beckett) 169
Wales 252–3, 261, 276, 295
Wallace, Alfred Russel 102
War of the Worlds, The (Wells) 114
war
    and patriotism 64, 262
    rationalization 109
Weavers, The (Hauptmann) 215, 220
Weber, Max 177, 189–90, 194
Wedgwood, Thomas 145
welfare state xvii, 281
    dismantling xxii
Wells, H. G. 113–15
Whigs 46
White Fang (London) 113
Williams, Raymond xv–xxiii
    adult education teaching xviii
    background and family xv, 1–2, 3, 4, 6, 8–9, 11–12, 275–6
    biographies xvi
    Communist Party membership 7
    contribution to cultural studies and sociology xv–iii
    education and academic career xv, xvii–xviii, 2
    fiction writing xvi
    intellectual and political formation xvii–xxii
    literary scholarship xv–xvi
    social scientific turn xv, 169–70
    twenty-first century xxii–xxiii
    wartime career xvii
Wilson, Harold xviii
women
    emancipation xviii
    employment 241
    and literary studies 315–6
Women in Love (Lawrence) 116
women's rights 290, 291
words, historicity and accumulated meanings 19
Wordsworth, William 165

work
　association with employment 239–41, 243
　effects of technical change 237–8
　possibility of change 252–3, 294–5
　in 'post-industrial' society 242–9
　relation with income 253–4
　skilled/semi-skilled and unskilled 243–4
　tripartite division 242–3
Workers Education Association (WEA) xviii, 313, 317
working class
　control of opinion through periodicals, 1840s 41–2
　development of political consciousness 42
　development of social character, 1840s 46–7
　emigration, 1840s 50
　ethos 13
　fictional emergence 113
　inclusion in drama 203, 214
　mass-action 20
　and mass-democracy 21
　middle class attitudes to dissident, 1840s 44

working class *cont.*
　portrayal in *The Big Flame* 215–21
　quality of living 6–7, 11–12
　relevance of new movements 291
　social and political movements 43, 54, 202, 219
World Bank 278
writer/audience relationship 94
writing
　as alternative mode of communication 229, 233
　centrality in cultural materialism xxi
　relationship with printing 231–2
　as a skill 99, 229, 231
　specialized histories 227
Wuthering Heights (Brontë) xx, 44, 52

Yeats, William Butler 201
'Yookay' 262, 271, 272, 276
Young England 42, 45, 46
Young, Robert 102

Zeitgeist xx, 27
Zworkin, Vladimir 153